THE EUROPEAN COMMISSION

The European Commission

edited by
GEOFFREY EDWARDS and DAVID SPENCE

STOCKTON

THE EUROPEAN COMMISSION

Published by Longman Group Limited, Longman Information & Reference,
Westgate House, The High, Harlow, Essex, CM20 1YR, United Kingdom.
Telephone 0279 442601
Telex 81491 Padlog
Facsimile (0279) 444501

ISBN 0–582–21019–4

**A catalogue record for this publication is available from the British
Library.**

Co-published in the United States and Canada by Stockton Press,
49 West 24th Street, New York, NY 10010-3206, USA
Telephone: 212-627 5757
Facsimile: 212-627 9256

ISBN 1-56159-078-9.

Printed and bound in Great Britain by Bookcraft (Bath) Ltd.

To Victoria and Arnhild

CONTENTS

CONTRIBUTORS

Christopher Docksey* Legal Service, European Commission

Martin Donnelly* HM Treasury, formerly in the *Cabinet* of Sir Leon Brittan, European Commission

Geoffrey Edwards Alderson Director of Studies, Centre of International Studies, University of Cambridge, Fellow of Pembroke College, Cambridge

Sonia Mazey University Lecturer in Social & Political Sciences, University of Cambridge, Fellow of Churchill College, Cambridge

Simon Nuttall* Director, DG 1, European Commission

Jeremy J. Richardson Professor of European Integration and Director, European Public Policy Institute, University of Warwick

Ella Ritchie Lecturer in Politics, University of Newcastle

Dietrich Rometsch Research Fellow, Institut für Europäische Politik, Bonn

Michael Smith Professor of European Studies, University of Loughborough

David Spence* Head of Training, DG 1A, European Commission

John A. Usher Professor of European Law, University of Exeter

Wolfgang Wessels Professor of Political Science, University of Cologne, formerly Director, Institut für Europäische Politik, Bonn

Martin Westlake* Secretariat General, European Commission

Karen Williams* Merger Task Force, European Commission

*Those marked with an asterisk write in their personal capacities and in no way commit the institutions to which they are attached.

PREFACE

This collection of papers has been some time in the making — enough time, indeed, for perspectives on the European Commission to change fairly significantly and for editors and authors to become aware of the prospect of further changes as the Maastricht Treaty finally came into force and the third Delors Commission moved into its final year. And in the summer of 1994, not only was there the débâcle over the appointment of Mr Dehaene to replace Mr Delors, which revealed divergent views among the Member States over the role of the Commission and its President, but the final close vote in the European Parliament on the appointment of Mr Santer to the Commission Presidency points to a potentially new relationship between the Parliament and the Commission.

Despite the importance of the European Commission — whether as a force for integration or as a scapegoat for lost national sovereignty — there has been a surprising dearth of studies on it. The last full-length book — at least in English — was that of David Coombes in 1970, and while it remains of immense value in pointing to the essential roles and functions of the Commission, it is inevitably out-dated. The renewed dynamism of the Commission during the second half of the 1980s and into the 1990s, which at least coincided with if it was not brought about by Jacques Delors, brought about a revival of interest. Hence this book.

We have sought to fulfil two objectives: first, to provide an up-to-date guide to the Commission as an institution, describing its functions, how it works and who works in it; and, secondly, to explain why it works in the way that it does, analysing the pressures to which it is subject, its relationship with the Member States through the Council machinery and with the European Parliament and lobby groups, the opportunities its role provides and the implications of its execution of that role. We see these two aims as complementary rather than competitive; there is too often an inverse proportion of anecdote to hard information on which to base any authoritative assessment of the Commission and its work. It was, for example, a surprise to discover how difficult it was to lay hands on a comprehensive list of Commissioners, let alone a breakdown of staffing ratios within the Commission. The layman or even an academic may well discourse on the bureaucratic nightmare that is Brussels but there are too few texts that both explain and guide one through the comitological maze and, we hope, look at the implications of it all so that one can better understand how the policy-making process is likely to develop. We might not be able to provide enough *piston* to any potential *sousmarin* or *parachutiste* actually to get a job in the Commission. However, we would hope that, armed with this volume, the reader will be able to blast his or her own path through the barriers that protect any bureaucracy (not least that of jargon) to an understanding of its role and functions — though, it must said in its defence that the Commission is a good deal more open than most civil services.

This dualism of purpose reflects both the interests and positions of the editors and contributors, who are a mix of practitioners and academics. Editors are always indebted to their contributors; we are particularly conscious of their patience and forebearance and offer them our thanks. We are similarly indebted to John Harper at Longman Information & Reference without whose pressure (but also long-suffering good nature) we should probably have been still writing, and to Nicola Greenwood for her sub-editing. Finally, we owe an immense debt to Ann Tuite, without whose industry and help in chasing up statistics as well as authors (and editors), and general administrative support, there would certainly not have been a final volume.

Geoffrey Edwards   *David Spence*
Cambridge   Brussels

August 1994

ABBREVIATIONS AND ACRONYMS

ACP	African, Caribbean & Pacific countries signatory to the Lomé Conventions
ASEAN	Association of South East Asian Nations
CAP	Common Agricultural Policy
CCP	Common Commercial Policy
CFSP	Common Foreign & Security Policy
CMEA	Council for Mutual Economic Assistance
COPA	Committee of Professional Agricultural Organizations
COREPER	Committee of Permanent Representatives
CSCE	Conference on Security & Cooperation in Europe
DG	Directorate General
EAGGF/FEOGA	European Agricultural Guidance & Guarantee Fund
EBRD	European Bank for Reconstruction & Development
EC	European Communities
ECJ	European Court of Justice
ECOSOC	Economic and Social Committee
ECSC	European Coal & Steel Community
ECU	European Currency Unit
EDC	European Defence Community
EEA	European Economic Area
EEC	European Economic Community
EFTA	European Free Trade Area
EIB	European Investment Bank
EMS	European Monetary System
EMU	Economic & Monetary Union
ENA	*Ecole Nationale d'Administration*
END	*Expert national détaché* (seconded national expert)
EP	European Parliament
EPC	European Political Cooperation
ERDF	European Regional Development Fund
ERT	European Round Table
ESPRIT	European Strategic Programme for Research & Development in Information Technology
EU	European Union
Euratom	European Atomic Energy Community
G-7	Group of Seven (Western industrial states)
GAP	*Groupe des affaires parlementaires* (of the European Commission)
GATT	General Agreement on Tariffs and Trade
IGC	Intergovernmental Conference
IIA	Inter-Institutional Agreement
LA	Linguistic Administration grade
MEP	Member of the European Parliament
NATO	North Atlantic Treaty Organization
OECD	Organization for Economic Cooperation & Development
OJ	Official Journal

PDB	Preliminary Draft Budget
PHARE	Poland & Hungary: Aid for the Restructuring of Economies
QMV	Qualified majority voting
QUANGOs	Quasi non-Governmental organisations
RACE	Research in Advanced Communications for Europe
SCA	Special Committee on Agriculture
SEA	Single European Act
SEM	Single European Market
SG	Secretariat General
SGCI	*Secrétariat Général de la Comité Interministérielle pour les questions de cooperation économique européenne*
SMEs	Small- and medium-sized enterprises
TA	Temporary Agent
TAC	Total allowable catch
TACIS	Technical Assistance to the Commonwealth of Independent States
TEU	Treaty of European Union (Maastricht Treaty)
UNICE	Union of Industries of the European Community
VAT	Value-added tax
WEU	Western European Union

1. The Commission in perspective

Geoffrey Edwards and David Spence

Introduction

Given its importance in the integration process and the controversy that has often surrounded its role, there has been a surprising dearth of academic or other study of the European Commission. This has been despite claims that it was the most original and unprecedented of institutions (Hallstein 1972) and that the Community would not have been constructed without it (Committee of Three 1979). To Jean Monnet, the first President of the High Authority, the Commission, like the High Authority, was to be an independent arbiter of the European interest (Monnet 1978). To Walter Hallstein, the first President of the EEC Commission, it was a body committed to economic and political integration (Hallstein 1972). But opinions have varied: to General de Gaulle, the Commission comprised a group of pretentious technicians (de Gaulle 1971); to Helmut Schmidt, when Federal German Chancellor, the Commission at times appeared inadequate and incompetent (Feld 1981); to other Eurosceptics, especially in the UK, the Commission has been portrayed as a group of faceless bureaucrats (or worse, failed politicians) intent upon centralisation and involvement in every nook and cranny of national society (Hurd 1993). Yet from whichever perspective it has been held up for political inspection, it has received only limited serious coverage in recent years (Louis and Waelbroeck 1989; Ludlow 1991).

The lack of academic attention is also curious in view of the interest shown in other European institutions. Academics have looked at the Council of Ministers, the European Council and the processes of inter-state bargaining, yet the one permanent factor in an otherwise changing constellation of people and coalitions has been the Commission. Intergovernmentalism and the interactions among Member States seemed to fit broader interpretations of the international system and the role of the nation state within it, especially for American theorists (see, for example, Keohane 1984). But lack of interest in the supranational Commission as an innovative feature of this diplomatic process obscures the reality of European political life.

There was, of course, disappointment and disillusionment during the 1970s and early 1980s on the part of practitioners and academics alike. Federalism

as a political movement may have retained its adherents (even in the UK —
see Burrows *et al.* 1978) and certainly much of the debate was conducted in
terms of federalist rhetoric, but as a political theory it appeared somewhat
passé (not least, of course, in the United Kingdom — Pentland 1973; Harrison
1974). Moreover, neofunctionalism, which to many provided a much needed
theoretical explanation of European integration of the 1960s, and which laid
such stress upon the central institutions — and especially the Commission —
seemed to be wholly inadequate and misguided in a Europe dominated by
General de Gaulle and his legacy (Hoffmann 1966).

The Luxembourg Compromise of 1966 appeared to set limits both to the
integration process and to the independence and initiative of the
Commission. It introduced a period of disenchantment with
supranationalism in practice, even if the rhetoric was retained. The more
negative approach of national politicians was reinforced by the seeming
stagnation of the 1970s when, in the face of recession, inflation, and monetary
instability, the Commission appeared able only to propose meaningless and
unacceptable measures of harmonisation. The most dynamic elements within
Western Europe seemed to be associated with the coordination of foreign
policy through European Political Cooperation (EPC) — even if dismissed as
"procedure as a substitute for policy" (Wallace and Allen 1977). As Nuttall
points out in Chapter 11, EPC had been set up deliberately outside the
Community framework on an intergovernmental basis in order to exclude the
Commission and keep supranationalism off the agenda. It was perhaps not
surprising that in the absence of anything but a return to theoretical 'realism'
(often with a neo- prefix), interest in the role of the Commission waned. David
Coombes' *Politics and Bureaucracy in the European Community* of 1970 was the
last of any full-length studies for nearly two decades.

There were occasional attempts to revive interest, not least on the occasion
of enlargement in 1973, when, for example, Altiero Spinelli sought to
reinvigorate the Commission's role both through his writings (*The European
Adventure* 1972) and through actual participation in the Commission itself as
Commissioner responsible for Industrial Policy. Again from within the
Commission, Roy Jenkins when President, sought to re-establish the
Commission, and its Presidency, as the primary motor of integration through
the setting of new goals and proposals such as that on monetary union, and
as representative of the European interest — or at least as representative of the
European Community (Jenkins 1989).

But the position of the Commission was well summed up in the Report of
the Committee of Three (otherwise known as Three Wise Men — Barend
Biesheuvel, the former Dutch Prime Minister, Edmund Dell, a former British
Trade Minister, and Robert Marjolin, the French former Commissioner). At
President Giscard D'Estaing's initiative, the three were given a mandate by
the European Council to report on the institutions of the Community and
possible adjustments to machinery and procedures that might be desirable.
They robustly declared that concern over "the failures, omissions and
inadequacies in Community performance" lay not in the mechanisms or
procedures, they were merely secondary, but in "the political and economic
strains that discouraged initiative and limited resources, and the lack of clear
guidelines for advance such as existed at an earlier stage" (Committee of
Three 1979, pp. 1–2). But there had, they found, been a clear shift in the

institutional balance towards the intergovernmental institutions of the Council of Ministers and especially the European Council. The latter had been established on a formal basis in 1974 and appeared in legal texts only with the Single European Act of 1986. The Commission's task in the years that followed was to try to regain the initiative.

A great part of the problem was that the economic and political conditions facing the Community had changed so that the Commission could no longer rely for legislative initiatives on the detailed guidance of the Treaties. Policy initiatives came to derive much more from the Member governments, with the Commission acting sometimes as little more than yet another pressure group attempting to push Member States towards particular goals. Even within the remit of the Treaties, the Three Wise Men found that the Commission's role had been circumscribed by the move away from qualified majority voting (QMV). The Luxembourg Compromise had led to a lack of coherence within the Commission itself, reinforcing the increased bureaucratisation of its operations, with a resultant adverse impact on efficiency as well as morale.

These last issues were taken up by the Commission's own 'Wise Men's' report (typically, according to sceptics, requiring five rather than three people, even though focusing only on the Commission), led by the Dutch former ECSC Commissioner, Dirk Spierenburg. The Report (Spierenburg 1979) was presented in September 1979. Neither of the Reports had any great impact; Roy Jenkins, however, opining: "Neither transformed Europe, but I think mine produced more practical results than did his [Giscard's]" (Jenkins 1989, p. 310).

It was not until the 1980s, with the veritable relaunching of the Community, that attention focused once again on the role of the central institutions. At issue was the European Parliament, directly elected for the first time in 1979 and intent (again very largely under Spinelli's inspiration) on achieving political legitimacy for itself by proposing considerably increased powers in its Draft Treaty on European Union of 1985. The role of the European Court of Justice, with landmark decisions such as the *Cassis de Dijon* case of 1979 and others was also a crucial point of reference. In addition, a new dynamism came to characterise the Commission, much of it becoming associated with the Presidency of the French former Finance Minister, Jacques Delors. Whatever his personal role in enhancing the Commission's status, the conjunction of political factors (*pace* Margaret Thatcher, though ironically, it was she, reportedly, who insisted on Delors when the French proposed the former Commissioner and French Foreign Minister, Claude Cheysson) provided the support for a high Commission profile.

The incoming Commission of January 1985 was able to exploit the alarm over Europe's increasingly adverse position *vis-à-vis* US and Japanese competition, the tentative steps towards a research and development programme already taken in conjunction with the leading European information technology industries (Sandholtz and Zysman 1989; Peterson 1991) and the readiness even of the most reluctant of European governments to back a change in the institutional procedures to attain the goal of a single market. There was, too, the new situation created by the resolution of Britain's budgetary problem, with the Commission finding a novel ally on proposals making for deregulation and liberalisation. The White Paper on the

Completion of the Internal Market was formally presented to the European Council in June 1985 (Commission 1985) and the need to expedite decision-making to bring about that completion was perhaps the most critical element leading to the SEA of 1986. The reforms embodied in the SEA drew attention to interaction of the central institutions, especially the Commission, different interest groups and the Member States. It led also to a revival of academic interest in integration theory (see, for example, Moravcsik 1991 and 1993). All this accompanied the 'Euphoria' that marked the later 1980s and at least the first year of the 1990s; before, that is, the problems of ratifying and implementing the Maastricht Treaty began to assert themselves.

The functions of the Commission

One of the questions explored in the Chapters that follow is how or whether the basic role and functions of the European Commission have changed over the decades. Coombes (1970) grouped the Commission's roles within five broad headings which have been used in many texts ever since. These roles are:

- the initiative role, since with few exceptions the Commission has the responsibility for initiating legislation;
- the administrative role, in areas such as agriculture, which have been delegated to the Commission by the Member States;
- the normative role — both as guardian of the Treaties and the *acquis communautaire* (i.e., all the Community's legislation) and as the conscience of the Community in proposing ideas and recommendations whether or not covered by the Treaties;
- the mediative role, i.e., mediating among the Member States and between the institutions in order to reach agreement and a decision;
- the representative role, the diplomatic representation of the Community in third countries and in many international organisations.

All but the first of these are dealt with in the following Chapters. Here the focus is on the first role of initiator, since in several important respects, it provides a weather-vane of the fortunes of the Commission itself in the inter-institutional and intergovernmental structure of the European Community/Union. It also raises the question of who sets the EU agenda and where the focus on legitimacy and decision-making now resides.

As Coombes pointed out, such diverse roles have demanded different types of organisation. In a very real sense, the history of the Commission is one in which it has sought the means of reconciling the different demands laid upon it, with the Member States and their representatives rarely looking on with indifference. Indeed, few if any of the roles assigned to the Commission under the Treaties have not raised controversy at some stage or other with one or more of the Member States, perhaps inevitably. As Rometsch and Wessels point out in Chapter 8, there have been significantly different models of relationship between the Commission and the Member States, with the Commission as putative government of a United States of Europe at one extreme and as a traditional international secretariat at the other. Too often perhaps the resultant relationship between the Commission and the Member States has been regarded as a zero-sum game: the acquisition of responsibilities by the Community equalling the loss of the same by the Member States, which is then popularised as the diktat of Brussels. The difficulties encountered in ratifying the Maastricht Treaty suggest that such attitudes are not restricted to the British public.

What, however, is clearly central to Community decision-making is the interaction between the Commission and the Council — with the growing involvement of the European Parliament since the SEA. The independence of the Commission may rarely have been directly challenged since the departure of General de Gaulle, who, for example, brought about the effective dismissal of Hirsch as President of Euratom and refused to allow the reappointment of Hallstein for a third Presidency of the Commission (Federal Trust 1974), though its freedom of manoeuvre has sometimes been severely curtailed, even during the Delors years. Significantly, even during the period of 'Eurosclerosis' in the 1970s, lipservice at least was still paid to the Commission's independence; Community politics has always been conducted within a pro-Community rhetoric. And indeed, it would be a misreading of the Commission's role to see it as wholly dependent on the Member States. But clearly, Commission Presidents, even when they have sought to provide leadership, have not always been given the opportunity to do so.

But it is clear, too, that the relationship between the Commission and the Member States was a good deal more complicated than some more recent Community myths might allow; even during the halcyon days before de Gaulle turned his full attention on the Community. Both Marjolin and Spinelli, for example, pointed to the close interaction of Commission and Member States, especially via the Committee of Permanent Representatives (COREPER), though from radically different vantage points. Marjolin did so from the perspective of being highly critical of Hallstein in 1965 for not continuing the practice of informing, consulting and entering into pre-negotiations with the Member States before a proposal was formally launched. He thought it mistaken, that is, that Hallstein should have sent the proposals for the introduction of agricultural levies, the introduction of the principle of 'own resources' and a greater role for the European Parliament directly to the Parliament rather than to the Member governments, a mistake which led the French to pursue an 'empty chair' policy and ultimately to the Luxembourg Compromise. Hallstein's ambition, coupled with a misreading of his immediate political environment, especially the likely reaction of de Gaulle, led him to go too far, as perhaps did Delors, though in radically different circumstances in 1992. Marjolin saw the period 1958–65 as a sort of honeymoon and one particularly productive "in that the proposals made and put before the Council of Ministers were certain to get a favourable reception or, in any case not to encounter an outright veto which would have left no room for negotiation" (Marjolin 1989, p. 314). But the key, according to Marjolin, was in Commission–Member State interaction:

"The truth of the matter is that, inevitably, the members of the Commission, however dedicated to the European idea, had to take the positions of national governments into account or else risk losing all effectiveness. An essential part of their action . . . consisted in reconciling what they considered to be the common interest with what they knew of the concerns of the different governments, including the government of the country to which they belonged." (*ibid.*)

Looked on positively therefore, such a constant interaction between the Commission and COREPER was necessary in order that the Commission could be productive; as Hallstein, himself, later put it: "these constant contacts at different levels help to create an intellectual and psychological climate in which cooperation comes easily and naturally. People become involved and work together to find solutions to the Community's problems in accordance with the Treaty" (Hallstein 1972, p. 71). *'Engrenage'*, this meshing together of a specialised 'European' coterie of national officials, was regarded by neofunctionalists such as Lindberg as an important factor in the integration process (Lindberg 1963, pp. 53–54). The French, indeed, tended to argue that the Community itself would benefit if the Commission was made up of seconded national officials who then returned 'Europeanised' to their capitals (Coombes 1968). Not everyone was convinced. The tensions between the push for a multi-nation European civil service and the issue of national secondments are taken up in Chapter 3.

But the more negative aspect of the interaction was highlighted by Spinelli, who tended to see it as reinforcing a "Europe of offices":

"The very manner of the functionalist thinking, which is at the foundation of this undertaking and which is shared almost completely by members of the Commission, counselled against expressing its work in open political terms and urged concentration upon the quiet construction of a Europe of offices which would move forward in agreement with the offices of the member states." (Spinelli 1966, p. 71)

His opposition to the bureaucratisation of the Commission, at all levels, including the college of Commissioners, was based on his perception of its growing habit of reacting "suspiciously and fastidiously to intrusions of the political world upon well-ordered administrative activity" (*ibid.*, p. 72), with all the dangers that that entailed for the Commission's role as the political motor for integration.

This tension between the bureaucratic and the political responsibilities of the Commission, while easily over-simplified, has been present since the establishment of the High Authority. Only in the early years of the ECSC did it seem possible to reconcile them. As Mazey and others have shown (Mazey 1992; Conrad 1989), Monnet had been concerned to establish a small, non-hierarchical, flexible organisation, well able to establish close contacts with national officials and technicians but in order to tap their expertise in the 'European interest'. But even Monnet feared that, despite its crucial role in the construction of Europe, a 'European civil service' ran the risk of bureaucratisation and, as he put it in 1953, "faire dominer dans des administrations en plein développement les droits dûs à la présence au détriment des droits résultants de la compétence" (Conrad 1989). However, as responsibilities increased, so the limits of the Monnet approach began to appear and a more traditionally hierarchically-structured body took over. Coombes suggests that up to the merger of the Communities in 1967, "the

Commission was still regarded by some close observers as a relatively intimate and cohesive body" (Coombes 1970, p. 253), but thereafter collegiality and cohesiveness declined and bureaucratic pressures exerted themselves.

The impact of the Luxembourg Compromise was clear (and will be referred to again below). The nature of the Treaty of Rome as a framework for action rather than a detailed programme for legislation lent support to the Three Wise Men's view that the exhaustion of terms of the Treaty dealing with negative integration, that is, the removal of barriers and distortions of trade, was one of the reasons why the collegiality of the Commission declined. The establishment of European Political Cooperation (EPC), which may have been justified or rationalised as a step towards Political Union, clearly challenged the Community method, as Nuttall points out in Chapter 11. And this was further reinforced (though only after de Gaulle's resignation) by the consequences of enlargement, and, indeed, successive rounds of enlargement.

The accession of Britain, Denmark and Ireland, and later Greece, Portugal and Spain, inevitably challenged the cohesion and solidarity of the Community itself. For the Commission, the problems of what was politically possible in a very much more heterogeneous Community were compounded by the ever greater complexity of managing a multinational bureaucracy. Spinelli noted the problem even among the original Six when he wrote:

"an elementary human solidarity is always present in greater measure among functionaries of the same nation, with their common habits and language, and subtle currents of xenophobia among functionaries of one country toward those of other countries appear rather easily. This combination of circumstances accounts for the inevitable presence in the bosom of the administration of considerable national loyalty and sometimes even national *omertà* [code of silence]." (Spinelli 1966, p. 73)

With enlargement the situation was compounded, especially given the strong bureaucratic tradition of the British. As Spence suggests in Chapter 3, a mixture of nationalities brings obvious differences in attitude and behaviour which clearly affect management methods. Colleagues of different nationalities do not always share a collective approach to questions of authority, discipline and basic managerial tradition. The problem pinpointed by Spinelli continues. Language groups if not nationalities tend to come together as they do in leisure activities (Anthropology 1994). But language and nationality are not the whole story. There are further cultural affinities whether expressed in terms of wine or beer drinkers, Southerners or Northerners, the political Left or Right and so on. Such affinities, perhaps inevitably, spill over into the wider policy framework. A shared cultural or national background may produce a certain harmony of interests between officials and those needing information or attempting to influence policy.

Given such differences and tensions within the Commission it is not surprising that there are very different perceptions of what the Commission's role could and should be. Most may have been convinced of the Commission's role as motor of integration, the initiator of legislation in the European interest, but they may not always have same attitude as to what the art of the possible allowed.

Whatever the current views of those within the Commission, its authority and effectiveness — whether as an administration, motor of integration, or mediator among national and sectoral interests — rests still in its independence and its ability to project a European interest that represents more than simply the aggregation of Member State interests. Independence is assured under Article 157 (EEC) (Annex A) and is underwritten by the non-dismissability of the Commission by Member governments, at least during the four (with the Maastricht Treaty, five) years of its life. The Commission is formally accountable (even if *en bloc* rather than individually) to a separate power base, the European Parliament. That is not to say, of course, that Member governments have not sought to exercise considerable influence over individual Commissioners short of calling for their dismissal, thereby undermining the Commission's collegiality, and have refused to re-appoint their own nationals if they have too obviously 'gone native' (a fate suffered by at least one British Commissioner). Coombes quotes the case of the then French Foreign Minister, Michel Debré, who had been incensed by the outspoken attacks of Commissioner Mansholt on French foreign policy. Such were the pressures on Commission solidarity that the Commission President, Jean Rey, was led to reply:

> "J'aurais peut-être pu ajouter que M. Mansholt est une personalité politique, dynamique et batailleuse, et que si nous avons bénéficié, dans la construction européenne, de ce dynamisme, il faut peut-être en supporter avec patience quelques inconvénients." (Agenor 1968)

But of critical importance to the Commission's independence is the Commission's right of initiative (Federal Trust 1974). This was set out in Article 155 (EEC) (see Annex A). There are references in almost all areas of Community legislation to the need for the Council to act "on a proposal from the Commission". Indeed, the right is extended under Article 235 to include even proposals on issues lying outside the scope of the Treaties, providing such action is justifiably intended to realise the objectives of the Community.

However, although the Commission retains the sole right to initiate legislation, in a number of respects it has become a more formal responsibility rather than the source of power and authority in setting the Community agenda as originally conceived. The Council, for example, has had frequent recourse to Article 152 (EEC) which allows it to request the Commission to "undertake any studies the Council considers desirable for the attainment of the common objectives and submit to it any appropriate proposals". A 'trigger mechanism' is, in other words, embedded in the Treaty itself enabling the Council in broad terms to set the agenda and undermine or usurp the intended role assigned to the Commission. More importantly, if one distinguishes the formal right of initiative from the power of initiative, the latter has moved perceptibly towards the Council, notably after 1966, and to the European Council, specifically established by Giscard d'Estaing in 1974 to provide political leadership.

The Luxembourg Compromise of 1966 had no legal validity but a massive political consequence. It removed the obligation to accept qualified majority voting (QMV) where a Member State declared that 'a vital national interest' was at stake. It meant that the predisposition to accept compromise inherent in QMV which enhanced the Commission's ability to pursue a European interest was lost. The Commission had to take account in its proposals of the minimalist position of each Member State; it was no longer a question of unanimity in the Council to amend a Commission proposal (under Article 149) but unanimity to achieve acceptance. Moreover, it was not only a case of the Commission being increasingly obliged to discover the lowest common denominator determined by a unanimous decision, rather than the highest common factor. In addition, the French in their document known as the 'Heptalogue' — it had originally been a decalogue but was pruned in order to win acceptance by the rest of the Six (Newhouse 1968) — included seven points which sought further to reduce the role of the Commission. Under points one and two, the Commission was not to adopt a proposal without prior consultation of COREPER (the normal if informal practice before 1965) and could not make public its proposal before the debate in the Council, thereby allowing the Member States a supervisory power over the Commission's information activities. The Commission was, in other words, to be deprived of much of the 'oxygen' of publicity and its ability to outflank Member governments by seeking support from interest groups and other non-governmental organisations. As Emanuel Gazzo, the long-time federalist and editor of the daily *Agence Europe,* despairing argued "The Commission [was]. . . no longer a place where policies were conceived, but an executive secretariat for policies conceived and elaborated elsewhere" (Gazzo 1972).

Even if the Commission rarely kept to all the restrictions of the Heptalogue, it was not surprising that the 'Europessimism' of the 1970s played down its effective role. Yet the Commission continuously sought to formulate and propose new policies, by which the Community's, and thus the Commission's, competence might be extended. But its ability to set the Community's agenda gave way, especially after 1966, to a more complicated and more dependent relationship with the Council of Ministers and this was emphasised still further with the establishment of the European Council when strategic and long-term goal-articulation was deliberately taken on by heads of state and of government.

When established on a formal footing, the European Council was regarded as Bonvicini and Regelsberger (1988) put it:

"as a further grave blow to the prestige and power of the Commission. Orientation towards the process of integration that leaned more towards intergovernmental philosophy did not objectively leave much hope for the political future of the Commission." (1988, p. 191)

But to Giscard d'Estaing, especially, though with the support of Schmidt, the German Chancellor, and others, it was clear that the formal Community decision-making process had become one more example of uninspired decision-taking. That to deal with the growing problems caused by structural economic change compounded by global monetary instability, oil crises and the soon-to-be-realised threat of recession, Europe had to fall back on its 'ultimate resource', the leaders of Europe themselves (Bulmer and Wessels 1987).

Initially, consistency with Community activities was to be ensured by Foreign Ministers acting as initiators and coordinators, but a more formal agreement was reached in June 1977 in the London Declaration on the European Council (*ibid.*, p. 148). Here the three functions of the Council were set out: the "cosy fireside chats", i.e. informal exchanges not designed to lead to formal decisions; discussions "designed to produce decisions, setting guidelines for future action or lead to the issue of public statements"; and the settlement of issues "outstanding from discussions at a lower level", on which if Community competence was involved, the Council would conform to the appropriate procedures. From the beginning, however, the President of the Commission has been present with one of the vice-presidents, a situation that may have enhanced the President's status and provided him with a certain additional area of manoeuvre (see also below). However, on Community-related decisions, while many of the normal procedures might have been followed on the basis of "some Commission proposals submitted to the Council", the Presidency and other Heads of State or of Government", also submit ideas and compromises and the Commission "clearly plays a less prominent role than in the Council [of Ministers]". More than that:

> "given the lack of clear Treaty obligations in many new areas of Community activities, and given the lack of basic consensus among member countries on major Community activities, it has not been the European Council as such but the whole environment which has caused a different set of functions for the Commission from what was hoped for in Community orthodoxy." (Hoscheit and Wessels 1988, pp. 22–23)

Thus, the result during much of the 1970s and early 1980s was an often more passive and more bureaucratic responsiveness on the part of the Commission. There was a much greater sense of initiating measures arising from commitments already agreed, which even if it was not unexpected given the size of the Commission and the growing scope of Community responsibilities, had an adverse psychological impact. In fact, relatively few policy initiatives have ever derived directly from the fervid imaginations of faceless Commission bureaucrats. Some have had their source in the need to introduce Community legislation to implement international agreements as well as in the need to carry out policy decisions agreed by the Member States.

With the shift in the institutional balance towards the Council, the Commission also faced the need to coordinate its programme and activity with the Member State holding the Presidency. The opportunities available to any individual Presidency to push ahead in particularly favoured areas of policy may be constrained by the existing agenda within any six-month period, but there has been a clearly perceived need for the Commission and the Presidency to liaise closely even if only in the interests of efficiency (O'Nuallain 1985; de Bassompierre 1988). Not all Member States take a highly positive view but all see coordination with the Commission at the beginning of each Presidency and throughout as unavoidable; there are too many time and other pressures. As de Bassompierre put it, it is essential "because of the Commission's special powers and its unique role in introducing legislation, but, more to the point, because it is able to modify its proposals as the discussion goes on in the Council" (ibid., p. 25).

Yet other initiatives derive from a Community response to the demands of particular industries. Whether this interest intermediation rescued the Commission for the European 'motor' might be a moot point: on the one hand, Bulmer and others have seen the rise of the European Council as a response to the increased activity of such domestic interests (Bulmer and Wessels 1987); others have regarded the move to the single market and the

SEA as determined by different but not dissimilar interests (Peterson 1991). The Commission and the lobby are discussed more fully in Chapter 7. Here the point is that, whether as a vehicle or originator of initiatives, the Commission established a close dialogue with interest groups, especially industry, as well as national officials, which was to prove of great significance in re-establishing the Commission's own sense of purpose and importance during the 1980s and the Delors' Presidencies.

The relaunching of European integration in the mid-1980s and the signature of the SEA in 1986 revitalised the principle of QMV and widened the extent of its application. Indeed, such was the sense of *relance* that majority voting was firmly in place well before the final ratification of the SEA in 1987, including during the period of the British Presidency of 1986. That was not to suggest that the Luxembourg Compromise was dead; the Greeks used it successfully in 1988 and Douglas Hurd, the British Foreign Secretary, believed that the veto "does sometimes hover over the discussion", though he also pointed out that a Member State did not always have to use it, strictly speaking, because "we would support Member States who did use it. Even if we were passionate for the proposal that was being vetoed we would support a Member State who felt they must invoke it" (Foreign Affairs Committee 1990, p. 89).

Nonetheless, a major (if not the major) point in the adoption of the SEA was the need to expedite Internal Market business especially through the greater use of QMV. To use the example cited by Keohane and Hoffmann (1991, p. 17), when Margaret Thatcher was asked why she had agreed to sign the SEA, she replied that "we wished to have many of the directives under majority voting because things which we wanted were being stopped by others using a single vote. For instance, we have not yet got insurance freely in Germany as we wished". Indeed, even despite Douglas Hurd's commitment above, the British, along with other Member States, including the Greeks and other Mediterranean states who were regarded as more concerned with issues relating to cohesion and solidarity rather than the internal market, vied with each other to achieve agreement on as many directives as possible during their Presidencies of the Council.

But the SEA also moved the EC into new areas of competence, some presaged in the Summits of 1972 and 1974, but which had remained based on the 'catch-all' Article 235. The creation of a string of new Community policy areas, such as environment, research and development and social policy, with their legal base in the SEA, extended and developed the role of the Commission. It had to initiate proposals in sectors where not only were national administrations the source of expertise but they were often active lobbyists (Spence 1992). A new range of interest groups were also involved, often with the Commission's encouragement. The policy focus therefore shifted to Brussels and to the Commission as part usually of a two-pronged lobbying exercise — or even sometimes three-pronged if the regional level was significant as well as the national and European. It was against this background that Delors could pursue his plans to increase and reorganise the Community's finances, double the structural funds and reform the CAP. The enhanced profile of the Commission President was such that Delors became the first President since Hallstein to be re-appointed beyond a four-year term of office, and was indeed reappointed for a further period as head of the 1993–1995 Commission.

At the same time, QMV revealed (*pace* Hurd) a more general disposition to accept compromise. For the Commission, the key lay in finding the necessary majority in support and in preventing a blocking minority being established, if possible only through some fine-tuning of its proposals. In that process the Commission was often helped by the Council Presidency whose mediatory role had increased significantly during the 1970s (Edwards and Wallace 1977). On the other hand, the Commission (whether Commissioner or official) had one particular advantage over the Presidency: it was the one institution always present in negotiations. Presidents of the Council came and went, troikas shifted in their membership, and even Permanent Representatives and Political Directors sometimes moved on. But the Commission was the constant element in all inter-institutional interaction, including, after the 1981 London Report, EPC as well as EC activity. It was also, despite the various alliances and coalitions and bilateral talks and negotiations among the Member States and between them and the Presidency, the body charged with mediating and seeking compromise — however strongly it believed in the validity and appropriateness of its own proposals.

In addition, the SEA introduced the cooperation procedure with the European Parliament which brought it more closely into the policy-making process and changed further the nature of the relationship with the Council. As Westlake points out in Chapter 9, the Commission became a more powerful mediator between the Council and the Parliament. The enhanced role of the Commission that resulted was further reinforced through external recognition, most notably perhaps when the Community and therefore the Commission was given responsibility for coordinating the technical assistance programmes to Central and Eastern Europe by the Group of 24 in 1989.

The Delors factor

This new authority based on the SEA was in many respects reinforced by a new sense of purpose on the part of the Commission Presidency. Since the change in the Commission's fortunes largely coincided with the Presidency of Jacques Delors, it is not surprising that the 'Delors factor' has been seen as of critical importance (Ludlow 1991; Dinan 1994). Delors, after all, held office longer than any of his predecessors. He was also in the enviable position, at least until 1991, of having a vision of a Community that appeared to fit with what was politically possible, or which was at least shared with those of crucial importance at precisely the right moment, whether this was in terms of the completion of the internal market, a more cohesive social space or, with the end of the Cold War, a strong sense of Europe's destiny. He also had the political authority and determination to pursue his own vision, well able to exploit his relationship with President Mitterrand and, especially in view of his early, positive role over unification, with Chancellor Kohl (Spence 1992).

There was perhaps little even at the outset of his Presidency that indicated the role Delors was to play in the relaunching of the integration process. His appointment followed the usual round of bargaining and negotiation. He fitted the profile of previous incumbents (see Annexes B and C). All were male, late middle-aged, and thoroughly immersed in their own countries' political processes. The Luxembourger, Gaston Thorn, Delors' immediate predecessor, had led a lack-lustre Commission and there was no question of his remaining in office. It seemed to be Germany's turn to provide a candidate since no German had held the office since Walter Hallstein in the 1960s. But Chancellor Kohl was unsuccessful in securing a candidate of any stature, largely as result of domestic political disagreements. The Belgians then sought to promote Etienne Davignon, who had been a particularly dynamic Vice-President in Jenkins' Commission (and who, in 1980, had been considered by Jenkins as likely to make "a very good President" in succession to him — Jenkins 1989, p. 611). However, Davignon's high profile had created opposition (as well as reluctance that Thorn's successor should come from another small state) with Germany unenthusiastic because of his efforts to restructure the Community's steel industry in the early 1980s, and France unsupportive (Dinan 1994, p. 203). Nonetheless, a Frenchman would not normally have been expected to take the office, since Ortoli had held the Presidency between 1973 and 1977. But President Mitterrand used the opportunity of the absence of a German candidate to offer an alternative from one of the larger Member States, nominating his Finance Minister, Delors, rather than, as had been expected, his Foreign Minister, the former Commissioner Claude Cheysson. Despite a relative lack of Brussels experience (although he had briefly been an MEP), Delors' reputation, as an experienced and able administrator, with shrewd political judgement and (especially important for the UK and Germany) a firm grasp of economics, was such that he easily won acceptance.

The Community's achievements in the 1980s owed much to Delors' personal and the Commission's political leadership. Above all, Delors was able to capitalise on both a Community and a national reputation. As the architect of the single market programme, as well as the broker of the budgetary agreements and author of the report on EMU, he was able to assert a much stronger Commission identity both within the EC and on the broader international stage. With the end of the Cold War, he was able to take advantage of the reticence of other European leaders to contribute positively to a European solution to the problems arising from German unification. It was the Commission that was given responsibility for coordinating the G24 assistance to Central and Eastern Europe, and so on. But what enhanced his stature even further and distinguished him from other Commission Presidents was the perception of Delors as a potential President of France, and not merely as President of the European Commission. Malfatti may have resigned from the Commission in order to contest Italian parliamentary elections, and Jenkins may have returned to Britain to help establish the Social Democrat Party, but few other Presidents were regarded as having political futures. That had invariably weakened their leverage when dealing with political leaders in the Member States. Delors, on the other hand, was often spoken of as a successor to President Mitterrand — at least until the changes in the Left's fortunes in France and the set back of Maastricht, to which the French electorate agreed only by the narrowest of margins.

His political position was especially significant in the relationship he was able to establish in the European Council. Gaston Thorn, his predecessor, had rarely made any great impact at Council meetings. Delors, by contrast, "revelled in the limelight" (Dinan 1994, p. 204). As one French observer has commented:

"Avec ses humeurs de diva, son inaptitude naturelle à la langue de bois, son activisme incéssant, sa compétence, dont il a hautement conscience, M. Delors a hissé la Commission à un niveau inégalé avant lui". (de la Guérivière 1992)

But as Ludlow has pointed out, it was not only a question of strengthening the long-term capacity of the Commission for leadership, it was also in providing leadership for the Community through the European Council (Ludlow 1991, p. 117).

Within the Commission itself, Delors' personal style, and that of his *cabinet*, inevitably had an impact on the Commission's sense of collegiality that had to be set against its new-found status and sense of purpose. In establishing a presidential system and a position beyond that of *primus inter pares*, a degree of tension was inescapable. By the time his second Commission took office in January 1989, Delors had unrivalled control of such policy areas as monetary affairs, and had even divided Lord Cockfield's internal market portfolio among three new Commissioners. He was in addition able to rely on a powerful *cabinet*, the *cabinet* being led by Pascal Lamy, described as "arguably the single most powerful individual in the Commission after Delors himself" (Ross 1993, p. 26). The power of the Delors network, run by his *cabinet*, turned the upper reaches of the Commission into an *'administration de mission'* as opposed to an *'administration de gestion'*. As such, it was able to ride above the concerns of the Commission services and, sometimes, of their Commissioners, adding a further layer to the separation between the politics of the College and the bureaucracy of the services (see Chapter 2).

It would seem, however, that the higher the profile, the easier it is to become the scapegoat when things begin to go wrong. So it was with the Commission and its President in the difficult period during which the Maastricht Treaty was ratified — which raises particular problems in relation to the Commission's legitimacy (see below). Ironically, the Commission had had a much reduced role in the IGC when compared to the SEA (Laursen and Vanhoonacker 1992), Delors having committed himself to the need for a drastic revision of the Community's institutions, including a much strengthened Commission. During the IGC, Delors, preoccupied with so many other issues — with progress on the single market, its development towards EMU and its extension into the EEA, as well as preparing Opinions on the new applicants and negotiating mandates for the Uruguay Round — possibly understandably, overplayed his hand. Certainly, he bore a good deal of the criticism for what much of the public and some in government saw as further 'centralising' tendencies on the part of the Union's institutions — not least in Denmark after the publicity given to his views on a strengthened Commission and a reduced role for smaller Member States in an enlarged Community. As he later put it: "the Maastricht Treaty . . . text is based on compromises, often at the expense of clarity and effectiveness". What national governments had appeared to do, however, was effectively to curb the Commission's involvement in important aspects of the putative EPU and then set about to denigrate it, making the Commission, again in Delors' words, "the ideal scapegoat" (Delors 1993).

The rhetoric surrounding Maastricht was thus in marked contrast to the 1970s and was clearly intergovernmental. As the former French Prime

Minister and leader of the Gaullists, Jacques Chirac, put it in a radio interview in March 1993, the Commission had to be "brought back to what it should be . . . an executive body and not one with parity with the other institutions" (Chirac 1993). In view of the growth in hostility to Delors and the Commission, both Ludlow (1993) and Dinan (1994) have suggested that the basic structure of the Commission is not strong enough to sustain the achievements of a dynamic President. Dinan, for example, having pointed to the factors which Delors was able to exploit when compared to the situations that had confronted Hallstein and Jenkins during their Presidencies, goes on to suggest that the challenges to the Commission's authority derive at least in part to controversies aroused by the President himself (over the Commission's role in the IGC, over his role in the ratification process, especially in the Danish referendum, and his undermining of the Commission's collegiality). Certainly Delors' own dynamism led Member States to appoint more politically significant Commissioners, such as Sir Leon Brittan, Martin Bangemann and, in the 1993–94 Commission, two former Foreign Ministers, Hans van den Broek and João de Deus Pinheiro. Such political figures only rarely eschew political controversy whether within the college or in relations between the Commission and the Council, and certainly, as in the Uruguay Round of the GATT, there were controversies enough.

But however dynamic the Presidency, its role can still be constrained by the institutional system that exists. As Ludlow (1991, p. 117) has suggested, the Delors regime was "aided and abetted" by the Secretariat General and the Council Secretariat. Delors' pursuit of a new role for the Commission coincided with the arrival in 1987 of a new Secretary General, David Williamson. In place of the personal dominance exercised by Emile Noël, there was a greater emphasis on systematic coordination and information sharing, targeting and monitoring. Nonetheless, as Ludlow went on to point out (Ludlow 1993), such changes met only some of the criticisms levelled by Spierenburg and more structural reform continued to be long overdue, that intra-Commission rivalry, a ramshackle structure and the simple inappropriateness of a body designed for the demands of the 1950s required serious attention.

The Commission as the motor for integration

The independence of the Commission and its right of initiative, both formal and informal, continue to be of the greatest significance. As Delors himself suggested during the celebrations in Rome to mark the thirtieth anniversary of the Community, the Commission was a "strategic authority" established by the founding fathers to "guarantee the continuity of the [integration] project despite the political or geopolitical hazards". Acting as the "custodian of European interests . . . [and] as a repository of past achievements", the Commission had a unique obligation to point "the way to the goal ahead" (EC Bulletin 1987). However that obligation could not be carried out in isolation; as Delors also put it, this time when speaking to the European Parliament in January 1988, "the Commission itself cannot achieve much but it can generate ideas. Its main weapon is its conviction" (Commission of the European Communities 1988). The Commission therefore needs an independent base to ensure such a generation of ideas, but its independence is not necessarily undermined by close cooperation with other institutions or even by the fact that policy initiatives come from the European Council or other bodies. Rarely over the past two decades has the Commission actually been absent from the European Council's deliberations and many of its Reports, whether called for by the Council or by itself, have proved critical. The linkage between the completion of the internal market and EMU was made in a number of Commission and other reports — as in, for example, the report of the Padoa Schioppa group (1987). In addition, of course, the Commission has often worked closely with the Presidency or one of the Member States to win acceptance for its position or report; Delors, for example, worked closely with Mitterrand to persuade Kohl and the others to give him responsibility for the report on EMU. As a result, as Hoffmann has suggested, "while the Community's progress has depended on a series of bargains among its main members, Delors has skilfully prodded them and enlarged the opportunities for further integration" (Hoffmann 1991).

The significance or rather the balance in the interaction between the Commission and the Council suggests that Europe's construction has not followed quite the pattern envisaged by the founding fathers, or at least how that pattern has often been interpreted. A linear growth in the competencies of the European Commission and a concomitant reduction in the areas of exclusive national competence inevitably oversimplifies the complexity of the Community–Member State relationship. As suggested earlier, it makes more sense to see the interplay between supranationalism and intergovernmentalism as a positive sum game (Lindberg and Scheingold 1970), even if national governments and their supporters (perhaps especially their supporters) continue to regard it as zero-sum, particularly when their preferred policies do not wholly conform to the compromise policies agreed at the European level. The extension of Community competence may shift decision-making to the European level, can impose new obligations on Member States and involve additional or different expenditures, and can determine the final arbiter of new laws to be the European Court of Justice in Luxembourg rather than national courts. It is also the case that the Commission construes the 'European interest' and its own part in its formulation and execution in an expansive fashion; it is after all given the responsibility for doing so. But not all extensions of Community/Union competence automatically imply an increase in the Commission's competence — the three-pillar structure of the Treaty of European Union is an effort by the Member States precisely to avoid this. Moreover it is rare, even in the areas of agriculture and commercial policy, for the Community/Union to have exclusive competence (see Chapter 10).

Nonetheless, Community competence is the legitimate sphere of action of the EC/Union based on the Treaties and the *acquis communautaire* (and though based only on a political commitment so far, on the *acquis politique*). Even the most cursory comparison of the list of areas in which the Union has responsibility to that under the Treaty of Rome, shows that the locus of decision-making, if not always the accepted centre of legitimacy, has changed over the decades. At the outset of the EEC in 1958, it would have been unthinkable for 'high' political areas such as foreign policy, security and defence and the control of monetary policy and exchange rates to have their formal locus of decision-making outside the state. Indeed, an observer of the Community in 1970 would have been on strong ground arguing that even environment, health, education and social affairs were virtually the sole preserve of national decision-making. Indeed, by the mid-1970s many of the leading neo-functionalists, such as Haas, had given up hope for the integration process and had moved on to other issue areas (Haas 1976).

By 1994 things had changed considerably. No area of concern of the traditional nation-state now escapes some kind of involvement at a European level. Competence may not have moved exclusively from the national to the European levels in any sphere, but the extension of the Community's involvement into so many areas, as well as the commitments entered into under the second and third pillars, inevitably create profoundly important constraints on the Member States.

The manner in which the Commission has achieved this greater involvement raises important issues both in terms of policy-making in Europe and theoretical explanation. The latter, as was suggested earlier, has aroused lively academic debate, especially over the assumptions that can now be made about the role of the state, inter-state bargains, and transnational and supranational actors (see for example, Moravcsik 1991; 1993). What the Commission has achieved, with Member State support, of course, has been a sometimes rapid change in the formal, legal basis of Community action. Several steps can be discerned, such as an initial use of Article 235 which allows the Commission to propose Community action not foreseen in the Treaties. Once Article 235 has been used, the Commission has sought to bring about a change in the legal base and a shift from unanimity to majority voting.

The case of environmental legislation is significant and not untypical. In the 1970s, legislation was based on Article 235, there being no specific Treaty provision. The SEA changed this by introducing a specific legal basis for environmental legislation, albeit requiring unanimity (and with a first reference to subsidiarity). The next stage was inclusion in the TEU of new provisions switching the voting base from unanimity to qualified majority. The question of whether the Commission is successful in its attempts to expand competence is thus far from rhetorical. Of course, it may be that Member States would have moved down this path without the role played by the Commission. However, given the issue's lack of political salience in some Member States, it is not unreasonable to suggest that the Commission has been a powerful catalyst in creating environmental standards as a European issue.

Another area of primary importance where the Community's competence has been gradually expanding is that of social policy. New Commission initiatives began with the 1985 White Paper on the completion of the internal market, which touched briefly on the free movement of people as well as of goods, and addressed questions arising for border formalities and employment. This was developed more significantly once the European Council in Hanover in 1988 had indicated the need for the internal market to benefit everyone, by improving working conditions, living standards, health and safety standards, vocational training and so on. At the same time, similar ideas were being canvassed in other institutions including the European

Parliament and the Economic and Social Committee. Even more importantly, the social dimension was ranked as a high priority during the French Presidency of 1989. What emerged from the Commission was the European Social Charter, which 11 of the Member States, but not the UK, accepted at the European Council of 1989. While it was not a specific proposal for legislation, it set the parameters for later legislative proposals and, indeed, the inclusion of several relevant areas in the Treaty of European Union.

In 1985, the European Council also called for a report on 'the People's Europe'. A committee was set up under the chairmanship of a former Italian MEP, Pietro Adonnino. Both the committee and its report were overshadowed by the Dooge Committee, the intergovernmental committee set up at the same time under the chairmanship of the Irish Senator, James Dooge, to report on the institutions of the Community. Indeed, the Report on the People's Europe was largely ignored in the short term, yet it, too, is suggestive of how initiatives are taken up and developed. The Report covered such topics as culture, youth, education, and sport; that is, issues believed to touch on the daily lives of the average European citizen. The Treaty of Rome had made no provision in relation to culture. The Solemn Declaration on European Union, agreed by Heads of State and of Government in Stuttgart in 1983, provided a few outlines. Adonnino extended and developed these and gave rise to several projects in the cultural field supported by the European Parliament and funded by *"actions ponctuelles"* (special budget lines with no specific legal base). The inclusion of specific treaty articles on culture in the Treaty on European Union were the culmination of a gradual process of expanding competence.

Moreover, there are many other fields where a similar process has applied. In Chapter 10, Smith demonstrates how important the questions of exclusive and mixed competence have proved in the external relations field and how there is a constant tussle between the Commission and the Member States on where competence really lies. The Treaty on European Union is a classic example of legislative legitimacy being granted *a posteriori*. Many of the new areas of competence in the Maastricht Treaty simply provided a legal base for what had already occurred in practice.

The existence of pressure outside the Commission, and sometimes well beyond the Council (as in the case of the G24 and the coordination of aid to Central and Eastern Europe), has led to an acceptance, at least in principle, that in such areas there ought to be a European policy. This has frequently provided the Commission with the justification for action. At a technical level, the Commission has managed to put this into practice by delineating the content in so-called 'whereas' clauses or 'recitals' in Community legislation, which set out the legal and political basis for the proposal. But there are three other ways by which the Commission has sought to extend its competence. It has legitimately initiated research into an issue, for under Article 118, for example, "the Commission shall have the task of promoting close cooperation between Member States in the social field" and that "to this end the Commission shall act in close contact with the Member States by making studies, delivering opinions, arranging consultation both on problems arising at national level and those of concern to international organisations". As pointed out above, this has been one of the prime means by which legislative proposals have come about.

The Commission has also used the scope of existing Treaty bases where the original drafting may have been imprecise. Thus, Article 128 on vocational training has been used to make other proposals on education, youth policy and the disabled, Article 119 on equal pay and equal opportunities and directives under Article 235 have been used to make proposals in the field of child-care. Likewise Article 8a (the establishment of the internal market) has been used, together with the Community's principles and the Council declarations of principle on reducing frontiers, to stray into immigration, drugs and weapons.

The difficulty for governments, such as the British, which might not wish for legislation in a given area, is that the cumulative effect of such pressures from the Commission, the Parliament, the Economic and Social Committee, as well as various lobby groups, and extensive (often hostile) press coverage makes resistance a highly sensitive issue. Whether a government seeks to reject a proposed policy on procedural grounds (does the Community have competence?) or substantive grounds (is the policy desirable in itself?), it can become politically divisive, both in domestic political terms or among the Community institutions, with, frequently, the Commission as scapegoat.

The issue of legitimacy

The extension of the Community/Union's competence and the involvement of the Commission in decision-making in so many issues of hitherto domestic concern poses a challenge to the traditional concept of the nation state and raises, sometimes sharply, the issue of legitimacy. The Commission may have been effective in shifting political activity and decision-making to the European level, but it has not yet won for itself, or for the Union, that sense of legitimacy that has been the traditional claim of the nation state and its executive. The problems of ratifying Maastricht revealed only too clearly the doubts about the Commission's ability to create a sense of popular legitimacy to match its legal position under the Treaties. Certainly the Commission's poor press increased dramatically during the ratification process, despite its relative lack of impact in the negotiations and the fact that it did not benefit greatly from the TEU's provisions. Indeed, the Commission found itself in the uncomfortable position during the ratification process of advocating a Treaty it privately disliked, knowing that such advocacy was likely only to deepen the public's suspicion of it. In the autumn of 1992, *Eurobarometer* may have found that 56 per cent of the public saw the Commission as necessary but there was little else that commanded any great support. Despite the 'Delors factor', for example, only 30 per cent saw the Commission as being dynamic, 31 per cent regarding it rather as static, and some 46 per cent saw it as bureaucratic rather than innovative (see Figure 1).

Nonetheless, the role of the Commission has been critical to the integration process. Whether or not the Maastricht Treaty has 'stalled' the process remains open; expectations of the intergovernmental review conference in 1996 inevitably vary. Efforts to make decision-making more transparent are but one example of a wider malaise brought about by a lack of popular enthusiasm for integration now that the process touches them at so many

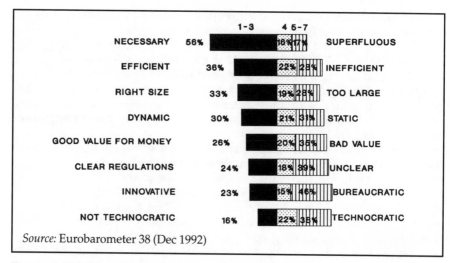

Figure 1: *How the EC public sees the European Commission*

different points. Hitherto, in part at least because of the nature of the issues under discussion, decision-making in the Community has always tended to be the preserve of the political and economic élites. In broadening the process out, including giving substance to the principle of subsidiarity, the Commission's relationship to the other central institutions, especially perhaps the Parliament to which it is accountable, may well change. But Delors' successor, Jacques Santer, faces also a more immediate problem, that of the efficiency and effectiveness of the Commission itself. With the unexpected rise in its responsibilities in 1989 and 1990 if not in the TEU, and no commensurate increase in size or efficiency, many officials felt that the institution was in a state of crisis.

References and Bibliography

Agenor (1968) No. 8. Quoted in Coombes (1970), *q.v.*

Anthropology (1994) *Approche Anthropologique de la Commission Européenne,* unpublished report prepared for the European Commission by three social anthropologists.

Bonvicini, Gianni and Regelsberger, Elfrieda (1988) 'The Organizational and Political Implications of the European Council' in Hoscheit and Wessels, *q.v.*

Bulmer, Simon and Wessels, Wolfgang (1987) *The European Council,* London: Macmillan.

Burrows, Bernard *et al.* (1978) *Federal Solutions to European Issues,* London: Macmillan.

Chirac, Jacques (1993) Radio Interview, Europe 1, 19 March.

Commission of the European Communities (1985) *Completing the Internal Market,* White Paper from the Commission to the European Council, Luxembourg.

Commission of the European Communities (1988) *Bulletin of the European Communities,* Supplement 1/88 p. 9.

Committee of Three (1979) *Report on European Institutions* (Three Wise Men's Report).

Conrad, Yves (1989) *Jean Monnet et les Débuts de la Fonction Publique Européenne: La Haute Autorité de la CECA 1952–53,* Louvain: CIACO.

Coombes, David (1968) *Towards a European Civil Service*, London: Chatham House/PEP.

Coombes, David (1970) *Politics and Bureaucracy in the European Community*, London: George Allen & Unwin.

Cosgrove, Carol Ann and Twitchett, Kenneth J. (1970) *The New International Actors: the UN and the EEC*, London: Macmillan.

de Bassompierre, Guy (1988) *Changing the Guard in Brussels: An Insider's View of the EC Presidency*, New York: Praeger.

de Gaulle, Charles (1971) *Memoirs of Hope: renewal and endeavour*, London: Weidenfeld & Nicolson.

de la Guérivière, J. (1992) *Voyage à l'Intérieur de l'Eurocratie*, Paris, Le Monde.

Dinan, Desmond (1994) *Ever Closer Union?* London: Macmillan.

Edwards, Geoffrey and Wallace, Helen (1977) *The Council of Ministers of the EC and the President in Office*, London: Federal Trust.

European Communities (1993) *Bulletin* Supplement 1/93, Jacques Delors, *Address to the European Parliament on the Occasion of the Investiture Debate of the New Commission*, Strasbourg, 10 February 1993.

Federal Trust (1974) 'The Institutional Structure of the European Communities' Report of a Federal Trust Study Group (Rapporteur — Stanley Henig), *Journal of Common Market Studies* XII(4), pp. 373–409.

Feld, W. (1981) *West Germany and the European Community*, New York: Praeger.

Foreign Affairs Committee (1990) *The Operation of the Single European Act Volume II*, House of Commons Session 1989–90, London: HMSO.

Gazzo, E. (1972) 'Le pouvoir d'initiative de la Commission', in *La Commission des Communautés Européennes et l'Elargissement de l'Europe*, Brussels: IEP.

Haas, Ernst (1976) 'Turbulent fields and the theory of regional integration', *International Organisation* 30 2, pp. 172–212.

Hallstein, Walter (1972) *Europe in the Making*, London: George Allen & Unwin.

Harrison, R. J. (1974) *Europe in Question*, London: George Allen & Unwin.

Hoffmann, Stanley 'Obstinate and obsolete? The fate of the nation-state and the case of Western Europe', Daedelus 95, Summer 1966.

Hoffmann, Stanley (1991) 'The case for leadership', *Foreign Policy* 81, Winter 1990–91.

Hoscheit, Jean-Marc and Wessels, Wolfgang (1988) *The European Council 1974–1986: Evaluation and Prospects*, Maastricht: IEAP/EIPA.

Hurd, Douglas (1993) *Financial Times*, 10 January.

Jenkins, Roy (1989) *European Diary 1977–1981*, London: Collins.

Keohane, Robert O. (1984) *After Hegemony: Cooperation and Discord in the World Political Economy*, New Jersey: Princeton University Press.

Keohane, Robert O. and Hoffmann, Stanley (eds.) (1991) *The New European Community: Decision-making and Institutional Change*, Oxford: Westview.

Laursen, Finn and Vanhoonacker, Sophie (1992) *The Intergovernmental Conference on Political Union*, Maastricht: IEAP/EIPA.

Lindberg, Leon N. (1963) *The Political Dynamics of European Economic Integration*, Stanford: Stanford University Press

Lindberg, Leon N. and Scheingold, Stuart A. (1970) *Europe's Would-Be Polity*, New Jersey: Prentice Hall.

Louis, Jean-Victor and Waelbroeck, Denis (1989) *La Commission au coeur du système institutionnel des Communautés Européennes*, Brussels: Editions de l'Université de Bruxelles.

Ludlow, Peter (1991) 'The European Commission', in Keohane, Robert and Hoffmann, Stanley (eds.) *The New European Community; Decision-Making and Institutional Change, q.v.*

Ludlow, Peter (1993) *Beyond Maastricht*, Brussels: CEPS.

Marjolin, Robert (1989) *Memoirs 1911–86: Architect of European Unity*, London: Weidenfeld & Nicolson.

Mazey, S. (1992) 'Conception and Evolution of the High Authority's Administrative Services (1952–1956): from Supranational Principles to Multinational Practices', in Erik Volkmar Heyen (ed.) *Yearbook of European Administrative History 4: Early European Community Administration*, Baden Baden: Nomos.

Milward, Alan S. (1992) *The European Rescue of the Nation State*, London: Routledge.

Monnet, Jean (1978) *Memoirs*, London: Collins.

Moravcsik, Andrew (1991) 'Negotiating the Single European Act', in Keohane, Robert O. and Hoffmann, Stanley, *q.v.*

Moravcsik, Andrew (1993) 'Preferences and Power in the EC: A liberal intergovernmentalist approach', *Journal of Common Market Studies*, 31 4, pp. 473–524.

Newhouse, John (1968) *Collision in Brussels*, London: Faber & Faber.

Noël, Emile and Etienne, Henri (1971) 'The Permanent Representatives Committee and the "Deepening" of the Communities', *Government and Opposition* 6 (4), pp. 422–47.

O'Nuallain, Colm (ed.) (1985) *The President of the European Council of Ministers*, London: Croom Helm.

Pentland, Charles (1973) *International Theory and the European Community*, London: Faber.

Peterson, John (1991) 'Technology policy in Europe: explaining the framework programme and Eureka in theory and practice', *Journal of Common Market Studies* XXIX 3, pp. 269–90.

Rosenthal, Glenda Goldstone (1975) *The Men Behind the Decisions*, Farnborough: D. C. Heath.

Ross, George (1993) 'Sliding into industrial policy: inside the European Commission', *French Politics and Society* 11 No. 1 (Winter), pp. 20–44.

Sandholtz, Wayne and Zysman, John (1989) '1992: Recasting the European bargain', *World Politics* 42, pp. 95–128.

Spence, David (1992) *Enlargement without Accession: the EC's Response to German Unification*, RIIA Discussion Papers 36, London: RIIA.

Spierenburg, Dirk (Chairman) (1979) *Proposals for Reform of the Commission of the European Communities and its Services*, Brussels: European Commission.

Spinelli, Altiero (1966) *The Eurocrats; Conflict and Crisis in the European Community*, Baltimore: Johns Hopkins Press.

Spinelli, Altiero (1972) *The European Adventure*, London: Charles Knight.

Wallace, William and Allen, David (1977) 'Political cooperation, procedure as substitute for policy', in Wallace, Helen, Wallace, William and Webb, Carole (eds.) (1977) *Policy-making in the European Communities*, London: John Wiley & Sons.

ANNEX A

Treaty establishing the European Economic Community	Treaty on European Union

The Commission | ## The Commission

Article 155 | ### Article 155

In order to ensure proper functioning and development of the common market, the Commission shall:

- ensure that the provisions of this Treaty and the measures taken by the institutions pursuant thereto are applied;

- formulate recommendations or deliver opinions on matters dealt with in this Treaty, if it expressly so provides or if the Commission considers it necessary;

- have its own power of decision and participate in the shaping of measures taken by the Council and by the European Parliament in the manner provided for in this Treaty;

- exercise the powers conferred on it by the Council for the implementation of the rules laid down by the latter.

In order to ensure proper functioning and development of the common market, the Commission shall:

- ensure that the provisions of this Treaty and the measures taken by the institutions pursuant are applied;

- formulate recommendations or deliver opinions on matters dealt with in this Treaty, if it expressly so provides or if the Commission considers it necessary;

- have its own power of decision and participate in the shaping of measures taken by the Council and by the European Parliament in the manner provided for in this Treaty;

- exercise the powers conferred on it by the Council for the implementation of the rules laid down by the latter.

Article 156 | ### Article 156

(*Article repealed by Article 19 of the Merger Treaty*)

[*See Article 18 of the Merger Treaty, which reads as follows:*

The Commission shall publish annually, not later than one month before the opening of the session of the European Parliament, a general report on the activities of the Communities.]

The Commission shall publish annually, not later than one month before the opening of the session of the European Parliament, a general report on the activities of the Community.

Article 157 | ### Article 157

(*Article repealed by Article 19 of the Merger Treaty*)

[*See Article 10 of the Merger Treaty, which reads as follows:*

1. The Commission shall consist of seventeen members, who shall be chosen on the grounds of their general competence and whose independence is beyond doubt.*

   The number of members of the Commission may be altered by the Council, acting unanimously.

   Only nationals of Member States may be members of the Commission.

   The Commission must include at least one national of each of the Member States, but may not include more than two members having the nationality of the same State.

2. The members of the Commission shall, in the general interest of the Communities, be completely independent in the performance of their duties.

   In the performance of these duties, they shall neither seek nor take instructions from any Government or from any other body.

   They shall refrain from any action incompatible with their duties.

   Each Member State undertakes to respect this principle and not to seek to influence the members of the Commission in the performance of their tasks.

The members of the Commission may not, during their term of office, engage in any occupation, whether gainful or not. When entering upon their duties they shall give a solemn undertaking that, both during and after their term of office, they will respect the obligations arising therefrom and in particular their duty to behave with integrity and discretion as regards the acceptance, after they have ceased to hold office, of certain appointments or benefits. In the event of any breach of these obligations, the Court of Justice may, on application by the Council or the Commission, rule that the member concerned be, according to the circumstances, either

1. The Commission shall consist of 17 members, who shall be chosen on the grounds of their general competence and whose independence is beyond doubt.*

   The number of Members of the Commission may be altered by the Council, acting unanimously.

   Only nationals of Member States may be Members of the Commission.

   The Commission must include at least one national of each of the Member States, but may not include more than two Members having the nationality of the same State.

2. The Members of the Commission shall, in the general interest of the Community, be completely independent in the performance of their duties.

   In the performance of these duties, they shall neither seek nor take instructions from any Government or from any other body. They shall refrain from any action incompatible with their duties. Each Member State undertakes to respect this principle and not to seek to influence the Members of the Commission in the performance of their tasks.

The Members of the Commission may not, during their term of office, engage in any other occupation, whether gainful or not. When entering upon their duties they shall give a solemn undertaking that, both during and after their term of office, they will respect the obligations arising therefrom and in particular their duty to behave with integrity and discretion as regards the acceptance, after they have ceased to hold office, of certain appointments or benefits. In the event of any breach of these obligations, the Court of Justice may, on application by the Council or the Commission, rule that the Member concerned be, according to the circumstances, either compulsorily retired in accordance with the provisions of Article 13 * or deprived of his right to a pension or other benefits in its stead.]

compulsorily retired in accordance with Article 160 or deprived of his right to a pension or other benefits in its stead.

First subparagraph of paragraph 1, as amended by Article 15 of the Act of Accession ESP/PORT.

Article 158

(Article repealed by Article 19 of the Merger Treaty)

[See Article 11 of the Merger Treaty, which reads as follows:

The members of the Commission shall be appointed by common accord of the Governments of the Members States. Their term of office shall be four years. It shall be renewable.]

*Article 13 of the Merger Treaty. See Article 160 below

Article 158

As amended by Article G(48) TEU

1. The Members of the Commission shall be appointed, in accordance with the procedure referred to in paragraph 2, for a period of five years, subject, if need to be, to Article 144.

    Their term of Office shall be renewable.

2. The governments of the Member States shall nominate by common accord, after consulting the European Parliament, the person they intend to appoint as President of the Commission.

    The governments of the Member States shall, in consultation with the nominee for President, nominate the other persons whom they intend to appoint as Members of the Commission.

    The President and the other Members of the Commission thus nominated shall be subject as a body to a vote of approval by the European Parliament. After approval by the European Parliament, the President and the other Members of the Commission shall be appointed by common accord of the governments of the Member States.

3. Paragraphs 1 and 2 shall be applied for the first time to the President and the other Members of the Commission whose term of office begins on 7 January 1995.

The President and the other
Members of the Commission whose
term of office begins on 7 January
1993 shall be appointed by common
accord of the governments of the
Member States. Their term of office
shall expire on 6 January 1995.

Article 159

(Article repealed by Article 19 of the Merger
Treaty)

[See Article 12 of the Merger Treaty which
reads as follows:

Apart from normal replacement, or
death, the duties of a member of the
Commission shall end when he
resigns or is compulsorily retired.

The vacancy thus caused shall be
filled for the remainder of the
member's term of office. The Council
may, acting unanimously, decide that
such a vacancy need not be filled.

Save in the case of compulsory
retirement under the provisions of
Article 13*, members of the
Commission shall remain in office
until they have been replaced.]

*Article 13 of the Merger Treaty. See Article
160 below

Article 159

As amended by Article G(48) TEU

Apart from normal replacement, or
death, the duties of a Member of the
Commission shall end when he resigns
or is compulsorily retired.

The vacancy thus caused shall be filled
for the remainder of the Member's term
of office by a new Member appointed by
common accord of the governments of
the Member States. The Council may,
acting unanimously, decide that such a
vacancy need not be filled.

In the event of resignation, compulsory
retirement or death, the President shall
be replaced for the remainder of his term
of office. The procedure laid down in
Article 158 (2) shall be applicable for the
replacement of the President.

Save in the case of compulsory
retirement under Article 160, Members
of the Commision shall remain in office
until they have been replaced.

Article 160

(Article repealed by Article 19 of the Merger
Treaty)

[See Article 13 of the Merger Treaty which
reads as follows:

If any member of the Commission no
longer fulfils the conditions required for
the performance of his duties or if he has
been guilty of serious misconduct, the
Court of Justice may, on application by
the Council or the Commission,
compulsorily retire him.]

Article 160

If any member of the Commission no
longer fulfils the conditions required for
the performance of his duties or if he has
been guilty of serious misconduct, the
Court of Justice may, on application by
the Council or the Commission,
compulsorily retire him.

Article 161

(Article repealed by Article 19 of the Merger Treaty)

[See Article 14 of the Merger Treaty which reads as follows:

The President and the six Vice-Presidents of the Commission shall be appointed from among its members for a term of two years in accordance with the same procedure as that laid down for the appointment of members of the Commission. Their appointments may be renewed.**

The Council, acting unanimously, may amend the provisions concerning Vice-Presidents.***

Save where the entire Commission is replaced, such appointments shall be made after the Commission has been consulted.

In the event of retirement or death, the President and the Vice-President shall be replaced for the remainder of their term of office in accordance with the preceding provision.]

** *First paragraph as amended by Article 16 of the Act of Accecssion ESP/PORT*
*** *Second paragraph added by Article 16 of that Act*

The Commission may appoint a Vice-President or two Vice-Presidents from among its Members.

Article 162

(Article repealed by Article 19 of the Merger Treaty)

[See Articles 15 and 16 of the Merger Treaty which read as follows:

Article 15:

The Council and the Commission shall consult each other and shall settle by common accord their methods of cooperation.

Article 16:

The Commission shall adopt its rules of procedure so as to ensure that both it and its departments operate in

Article 162

1. The Council and the Commission shall consult each other and shall settle by common accord their methods of cooperation.

2. The Commission shall adopt its Rules of Procedure so as to ensure that both it and its departments

accordance with the provisions of the Treaties establishing the European Coal and Steel Community, the European Economic Community and the European Atomic Energy Community, and of this Treaty. It shall ensure that these rules are published.]

operate in accordance with the provisions of this Treaty. It shall ensure that these rules are published.

Article 163

(Article repealed by Article 19 of the Merger Treaty)

[See Article 17 of the Merger Treaty which reads as follows:

The Commission shall act by a majority of the number of members provided for in Article 10.*

A meeting of the Commission shall be valid only if the number of members laid down in its rules of procedure is present.]

*Article 10 of the Merger Treaty. See Article 157 above

Article 163

The Commission shall act by a majority of the number of Members provided for in Article 157.

A Meeting of the Commission shall be valid only if the number of Members laid down in its Rules of Procedure is present.

ANNEX B

Presidents of the High Authority and the Commissions
(before the merger of the Institutions in 1967)

High Authority of the European Coal and Steel Community

August 1952 – June 1955	Jean Monnet (F)
June 1955 – January 1958	René Mayer (F)
January 1958 – September 1959	Paul Finet (F)
September 1959 – October 1963	Piero Malvestiti (I) Resigned May 1963
June 1963 – July 1963	Albert Coppe (B)
October 1963 – July 1967	Rinaldo Del Bo (I) Resigned March 1967
March 1967 – June 1967	Albert Coppe (B)

Commission of the European Atomic Energy Community (EURATOM)

January 1958 – January 1959	Louis Armand (F) Enrico Medi (I) Acting President from September 1958
February 1959 – January 1962	Etienne Hirsch (F)
January 1962 – July 1967	Pierre Chatenet (F)

Commission of the European Economic Community

January 1958 – January 1962	Walter Hallstein (D)
January 1962 – July 1967	Walter Hallstein (D)

B=Belgium   D=Germany (Federal Republic)   F=France   I=Italy

ANNEX C

Presidents of the Commission of the European Communities

July 1967 – July 70	Jean Rey (B)*	14 Members
July 1970 – March 1972	Franco Maria Malfatti (I) (Resigned)	9 Members
March 1972 – January 1973	Sicco Mansholt (NL)	9 Members
January 1973 – January 1977	François-Xavier Ortoli (F)	13 Members
January 1977 – January 1981	Roy Jenkins (UK)	13 Members
January 1981 – January 1985	Gaston Thorn (L)	14 Members
January 1985 – January 1986 – January 1989	Jacques Delors (F)	14 Members 17 Members
January 1989 – January 1993	Jacques Delors (F)	17 Members
January 1993 – January 1995	Jacques Delors (F)	17 Members
January 1995 – January 2000	Jacques Santer (L)	21 Members**

*   First Commission following Merger of the Institutions
** Assuming Enlargement to include Austria, Finland, Norway, Sweden

B=Belgium   F=France   I=Italy   L=Luxembourg   NL=Netherlands   UK=United Kingdom

2. The College of Commissioners and their *Cabinets*

Martin Donnelly and Ella Ritchie

Introduction

The European Commission is one of the important arenas in which exchanges and administrative bargains are negotiated within the European Union. It mediates among sectoral, national and European interests and performs an increasingly significant role in policy initiation and strategic leadership. It plays a critical role in the politics of what have been characterised as three simultaneous and linked games: the national game, in which individual nations attempt to extract as much as possible from the European Union; the institutional game, where institutions each seek to gain more power relative to the others; and third, the bureaucratic game, which involves the formation of separate and competing policy communities (Peters 1992).

This Chapter outlines the legal framework governing the tasks of Commissioners and then discusses the informal and formal factors which shape the day-to-day work of the members of the Commission. After analysing the background to the Commissioners' work, it then assesses the role of the *Cabinets*, stressing their increasing strength and importance and arguing that this reflects both the growing number and complexity of policy demands placed on the Commission and the inevitable tendency of advisory bodies to be drawn into the detail of formation, monitoring and implementation of policy.

Nomination of Commission members

The rights and duties of a Member of the European Commission are set out in articles 155–163 of the Treaty of Rome (see Annex A, Chapter 1). The post of Commissioner is a specific one given to individuals from the Member States. Collectively they make up the College of Commissioners, consisting (at least until the end of 1994) of 17 members, with the larger states, France, Germany, Italy, Spain and the United Kingdom, having two Commissioners and each of the other Member States one Commissioner. The custom in the larger states has been for both government and opposition to be represented. Thus, having two votes has not only allowed the larger states a greater weight in the policy-making process but has also enabled parties out of government in their home country to retain representation in the Commission.

The Treaty lays down that the number of Commissioners may be increased or reduced by unanimous agreement in the Council and the number of Commissioners has increased with each enlargement of the Community. The 1991 Intergovernmental Conference on Political Union discussed reducing the number of Commissioners from the larger Member States from two to one. This formed part of an ongoing debate about the efficiency of the Commission as a policy-making body in which critics argue that it is difficult for 17 people to be effective in collective decision-taking. In the event the efficiency arguments in favour of a smaller College were outweighed by the desire of four of the five larger Member States (the United Kingdom reputedly being the exception) to retain two Commissioners in the College's deliberations. It was agreed at Maastricht in December 1991 that the question of allowing every Member State only one nominee on the Commission would be discussed again in the event of an enlargement of the Community's membership.

Commission members are appointed by 'common accord' of the Member States' governments for a fixed term. From the signature of the Treaty of Rome until agreement at the Maastricht Intergovernmental Conference this term was four years for each Commission member. The President and Vice-Presidents are appointed for two years. In the case of the Vice-Presidents their renomination is a formality. Indeed, apart from the title, and a slightly larger salary, the post of Vice-President has no substantive advantages within the College, except the right to replace the President in the chair of Commission meetings during his absence. One of the current suggestions for improving the Commission as a policy-making body is to strengthen the powers of the Vice-Presidents. In recent years the re-appointment of the President has also been a straightforward matter, if not quite a formality. Nevertheless, Member States have been obliged to go through the formal renomination procedure half-way through the term of a Commission for the President to continue in office. The projected European Parliament approval of the Commission President from 1995, a new power for the European Parliament laid down in the Treaty on European Union (TEU) will, however, considerably strengthen the President's independent standing *vis-à-vis* Member States, while making the post more vulnerable to pressure from the European Parliament.

The choice of Commissioners is for each Member State to make and a firm convention has evolved that Member States do not interfere in each other's choices. A decision is then made by the Council of Ministers, normally the General Affairs Council, on the nomination of all the new Commission members just before the expiry of the term of office of the outgoing Commission. The December meeting of the Foreign Affairs Council is the normal vehicle for formal nomination. In the run-up to the formal nomination there are two principal sources of external lobbying on the Member States. One is from existing members of the Commission who wish to persuade their own national governments to renominate them. There is no time limit on the period which an individual may spend as a member of the Commission. Frans

Andriessen, the Dutch Commissioner, served for three consecutive terms from 1981 to 1992. (Annex A lists all Commissioners to date.) Presidents of the Commission also seek to influence Member States' choice of Commissioners, since they naturally want some say in the appointment of colleagues with whom they will work in the following years. On the whole, their efforts have met with mixed success. This is hardly surprising. For Member States, nomination of Commissioners is a useful piece of political patronage. It can be used to reward loyal service or to remove from the domestic scene individuals whose services are no longer required for a variety of reasons, but who cannot be safely dismissed altogether. The smaller Member States have always viewed a post in the Commission as an important political job in its own right. However, until recently, many governments from the larger states tended to view a post in the Commission as carrying relatively little kudos. With the growing powers of the Union and its increasing relevance to domestic politics, it has become the norm for Commission nominees to have held ministerial posts of cabinet rank in their national administrations. Of the 17 members of the 1993 Commission, 13 had previously held a ministerial post (especially in foreign affairs or finance). Of the remainder, one Commissioner had been a *Länder* politician and member of the German *Bundesrat*, one an MEP, one a Parliamentary Deputy and one a career diplomat and former ambassador (Annex B).

Commissioners are chosen by the heads of government, but appointments are subject to a high level of political bargaining. This is particularly the case in those Member States in which coalition government is the norm, but even in systems where the executive is typically formed by one or two parties, such as France and the United Kingdom, the head of government may not be able to exercise a free hand. President Mitterrand, for example, was reportedly obliged to reappoint Christiane Scrivener in 1992 when his own first choice decided to opt for a national position and, according to press reports, Conservative backbench pressure on Prime Minister John Major was one of the reasons why Neil Kinnock, the former Labour Party leader, was not nominated for the post of 'second' British Commissioner. Although they cannot control the composition of the Commission, Commission Presidents do have a significant, if not predominant, influence on the initial distribution of portfolios. This has to be agreed by consensus amongst the Commissioners, but once the initial allocation has been made it is very difficult for it to be changed. In allocating posts among the team, the President is faced with balancing national and personal preferences and trying to give some political shape and direction to the Commission. There is competition for the portfolios, with the "big" dossiers of Foreign Affairs, Economic Affairs, Agriculture, Competition and the Internal Market being particularly sought after. Governments are obviously keen for their nominees to have politically advantageous portfolios in the belief that this will open up a channel of influence for them on key issues. There is considerable evidence of governments lobbying the President on behalf of their Commissioners during the intense period of activity preceding the allocation of portfolios in the new Commission. The national Permanent Representations to the Community play a major role in this process.

In line with Monnet's vision of a supranational policy-making body, the Treaty lays down that members of the Commission "shall be completely independent in the performance of their duties". To underline the point, Article 157 also states "each Member State undertakes to respect this principle and not to seek to influence the members of the Commission in the performance of their tasks". Commission members must accept not to engage in any other occupation during their term of office and to refrain from any action incompatible with their duties. They give a solemn undertaking to this effect before the European Court of Justice at the start of their term of office.

In contrast to national politicians, Commissioners enjoy a remarkable security of tenure in office. Article 157 of the Treaty makes provision for compulsory retirement of a Commissioner on decision of the Court of Justice if he or she "no longer fulfils the conditions required for the performance of his duties or if he has been guilty of any serious misconduct". This procedure has never been activated in the history of the European Economic Community, nor of its predecessor, the European Coal and Steel Community. It might be compared to the impeachment of the President of the United States in its severity, and in the exceptional circumstances likely to be required for its use. It is in no sense a sanction for use against inefficient or difficult Commissioners. Outside this long stop legal constraint, neither the other members of the Commission, nor the Council of Ministers, nor the European Parliament can remove an individual member of the Commission.

The European Parliament does have the right to censure the Commission as a whole, but this cannot be used to enforce the removal of individual Commissioners. This restriction considerably weakens the effectiveness of the censure power. Concern that censure power might be misused on political grounds to attack members of a particular party has prevented its extension. Commissioners can be asked to account for their policies before committees of the EP or the full Parliament. The relationship between the Commission and the EP is not, however, adversarial. Parliament's scrutiny is part of the consensus-building which has operated between the Commission and the EP since the Single European Act and, in practice, Commissioners and their policies are rarely subject to detailed critical scrutiny. In short, Commissioners are not held to account in anything like the same way as national politicians (Jacobs, Corbett and Shackleton 1992). There is, moreover, nothing to prevent the Council of Ministers from reappointing the same individuals to the Commission.

A further element of stability derives from the distribution of portfolios which may be expected to remain in the same hands for the length of the Commission. So not only membership of the Commission but individual executive responsibilities within it remain relatively fixed (Annex C lists the portfolios of the Delors II and Delors III Commissions). The only exception to this is when enlargement of EC membership has required new members to be added to the Commission, which necessitates some redistribution of portfolios. Unlike a Minister in a national government, a Commissioner does not need to retain the political support of the President or even of his colleagues in order to retain his post. Nor can he hope to take over the portfolio of one of his colleagues through the strength of his performance or his lobbying abilities.

Such a high degree of political independence and security of tenure has several consequences for the policy approach taken by each Commissioner. Most directly, they underline and accentuate his or her freedom to take policy positions without influence from their home governments. This was, of course, one of the central objectives of the founding fathers of the Community. Even more importantly, the influence of Member States' governments on the Commission is thereby weakened. Although a newly-appointed Commissioner owes his post to his national government, there is no certainty that the same government will still be in office four years later when decisions on reappointment are made and consequently there are no further political advantages necessarily to be gained in the meantime by the maintenance of excessively close links. It is rare, though not unprecedented, for a Commissioner to resign before the end of his mandate in order to return to a post in national government. The relatively generous salary paid to a Commissioner may also help to maintain a stable membership of the College by discouraging its members from being lured into the private sector by the prospect of higher pay.

During its term of office the Commission can expect to see national elections in almost all of the 12 Member States. Between 1989 and 1992, the term of the second Delors Commission, there were elections in all the Member States except France and Denmark. Of the European Council members, only three, Mitterrand, Gonzalez and Kohl, were still in post in December 1992. The continuity of the Commission over this period, with only Commissioner Ripa di Meana resigning a few months early, both underpins its effective independence and enhances its potential political influence with the Member States.

Relationship with Member States

In order to be effective the Commission must function in a political as well as a legal and administrative context. Commissioners are not ambassadors for their Member States but they do articulate policy concerns which reflect their domestic political backgrounds or specific points of national concern. In this way the Commission takes account of differing national sensitivities in formulating a European policy. It is important, however, that the Commissioner is not seen as the captive of national interests. A Commissioner suspected of too close a relationship with one Member State is likely to face a more critical audience in the Commission for his policy proposals. The Commissioners' own links with their national political parties and national governments play an important role by offering a channel of communication and influence in both directions. Member States, for example, tend to explain their particular concerns to their nominated Commissioners, thereby hoping to influence Commission policy in their preferred direction. Likewise, a Commissioner will often wish to persuade his national government of the need to support Commission policy or at least to search for an acceptable compromise, particularly in his own area of responsibility. Good domestic political contacts allow a Commissioner to influence the policy debate in his home Member State. As Leon Brittan explained: "I am frequently consulted by Jacques Delors about what is going on in Britain. It would be bizarre if I could not answer. . . . I think that it is important that whoever holds my job should play a part in British public life since the EC itself is part of British public life . . . ."(*Financial Times*, 9.7.90)

Powers of Commissioners

Article 155 of the Treaty of Rome lays down four specific tasks for the Commission "in order to ensure the proper functioning of the internal market". These are, first, to ensure that the Treaty is properly applied — the so-called 'guardian of the Treaty' role. The Commission can and does take Member States to the European Court of Justice. Second, the Commission has a right to "formulate recommendations or deliver opinions" on Treaty issues at its own discretion. Together these clauses provide a justification of the Commission's role as an initiator of policy with responsibilities going beyond those of a secretariat to the Council of Ministers. Third, the Commission is explicitly recognised as having "its own power of decision" as an organisation, with the right to participate in the "shaping of measures taken by the Council and by the European Parliament". The Commission's role therefore extends throughout the legislative process, including negotiating with other institutions to achieve the degree of consensus needed for adoption of legal texts. Finally, the Treaty sets out the Commission's role as the 'executive' of the Community, in implementing rules laid down by the Council, in legislative or other form. The extent of the Commission's legitimate discretion in implementing legislation has proved to be a consistent source of dispute, however, with particular difficulties surrounding the choice of committee procedures for amending legislation — known as 'comitology' (see Chapter 6).

In addition to its formal roles, the Commission has come to play a greater part in informal mediation with Member States. This is most evident in the legislative process which requires constant informal bargaining with Member States to build the necessary majorities needed to approve legislation in the Council of Ministers. The Commission can, either with, or, on occasion, in place of the Member State currently holding the Presidency, take on this role of consensus-building. The Commission's bargaining with Member States has also become increasingly important in the enforcement of EC law. Potential infraction cases are often resolved by agreement between the Commission and Member States before they come to the European Court of Justice. In these cases, the Commission uses its own executive power to negotiate an acceptable settlement and then withdraws its formal legal action.

The Commission's role as an international negotiator has developed markedly since the Community's inception. It has become increasingly important as the EC's formal negotiator in external trade issues, a role enhanced by the progressive completion of the internal market. The break-up of the Communist bloc in central and Eastern Europe and the EC's increasing trade and economic links with the region further expanded the Commission's function in the external arena (see Chapter 10).

Policy making within the College

The principle of collegiality, which was advocated by the founding fathers of the Community and by its first President, Walter Hallstein, remains an important one in the operation of the Commission. As far as possible the Commission tries to reach a consensus on issues. In principle all voices carry the same weight in discussions. Inevitably, Commissioners from the larger countries are able to comment more authoritatively on likely national political reactions to certain sensitive proposals and their views on the general political situation within which the Commission works also tend to command more attention. Nevertheless, the requirement that an absolute majority of Commissioners (nine) must provide positive support, and, if necessary, vote in favour of a proposal means that individual influence is inevitably limited by members' ability to persuade others to vote for their proposals. Even the President has only one vote in Commission meetings. As voting does take place, it is therefore possible for the President to be outvoted on specific issues. Apart from threatening to resign, he has no means of preventing this; and once a decision is taken, the President is then as bound by collegiality as any of his colleagues. Voting is considered less satisfactory than achieving a consensus in Commission but it is regularly used to resolve contentious issues. Any member of the Commission may request a vote on a subject under discussion in the College. Voting is confidential, but the total votes in favour, against and abstentions are recorded formally in the Commission minutes and do, on occasion, become more widely known.

The requirement to find nine votes in support of a measure is rendered more difficult by the likelihood that, out of the 17 Commissioners, two or three are likely to be absent on business from any of the weekly Commission meetings. Voting is by a show of hands and votes cannot be cast by proxy. So the presence of the Commission member at the time that the vote is taken is necessary for it to be registered. Thus, in practice, it is usually safer to have more than nine votes in favour of any motion. Commissioners who are not present may be represented by a member of their *Cabinet* so that they have a record of the debate, but *Cabinet* members may not formally speak in debate or vote. The Commission may, however, choose to meet in restricted session to discuss personnel questions or particularly sensitive issues, and then only the Commissioners themselves may be present.

Non-contentious issues can be agreed through what is known as the written procedure. Here, all *Cabinets* receive copies of a draft proposal which must be available in all Community languages. A deadline is provided for objections and if none are made, the decision is agreed formally without further discussion. If one or more *Cabinets* object, the procedure is suspended while bilateral discussions take place to see whether the difficulty can be resolved. If it cannot, then the written procedure is abandoned and discussion of the proposal is shifted back to the normal *Cabinet* procedure involving oral discussion either to settle the issue or, if not, to prepare for Commissioners to do so. Written procedures are normally used for minor issues, such as amendments to customs' procedures and agricultural regulations. In cases of urgency and with the agreement of the President's *Cabinet*, the 'accelerated written procedure' may be used, allowing for the Commission to take a decision within 48 hours. This is useful for urgent but non-contentious issues such as the authorisation of emergency food relief or medical aid.

Each Commissioner is aware that at some point he or she may need the support of a majority of colleagues, and there is continuous lobbying among Commissioners. Ideological outlook or national experience may predispose agreement between certain Commissioners, but discussion is ultimately on an issue-by-issue basis. No member of the Commission can afford to take another's support for granted, nor allow unnecessary ill-feeling to develop even when disagreements take place. The requirements of continuing collegiality mean that no single issue can be made into a make or break question of confidence. Commissioners know that they must go on working with one another.

Despite the elaborate structure of *Cabinet* meetings to prepare the Commission agenda, debate within the College itself is frequently critical to the policy outcome. The effectiveness of each member's contribution is determined by a number of factors: their own portfolio responsibilities, their reputation amongst other Commissioners, wider political factors and personal interest in the subject. The portfolio which a Commissioner holds is of considerable importance in determining his or her weight in general policy-making. The way the Commission is organised has come increasingly to resemble that of a national government with only justice, home affairs and defence not explicitly covered by a Commissioner. As a result, a striking feature of the European Commission is the great variety of workload and policy responsibilities among the College. Some Commissioners, such as the Agriculture Commissioner, have important executive responsibilities and are involved in constant negotiation with the 12 Member States. The Agriculture Commissioner is probably the closest to a national Minister in his well-defined authority. DG V1, the agricultural directorate with 5,000 staff, functions like a national ministry, with a large number of executive as well as policy staff. At the other end of the spectrum, Commissioners with responsibility for areas whose direct policy competence is limited or disputed, such as energy, audio-visual or social affairs, are likely to have a less direct role with no executive responsibility and a relatively small policy staff. In general, areas such as foreign affairs or competition policy provide greater scope for a high public profile and mean that the Commissioner carries more weight among his colleagues. Some policy areas, such as the budget and financial control, provide the Commissioner with detailed insight into the range of the Commission's activities, which means that he will be equipped to intervene in areas outside his own competence.

Each Commissioner has a considerable degree of freedom of action in his own policy area, although the extent of this varies according to his precise responsibilities and the degree to which these have Treaty recognition. The Commissioner's own officials provide briefing on issues of direct portfolio concern. Thus, the Commissioner responsible for Environmental Affairs will be aware of his own Directorate General's position on, for example, a proposed industrial policy with environmental implications. The issues will have been made familiar to the other Commissioners through the preparatory meetings of *Cabinets*. The extent to which other Commissioners enter into a policy debate beyond their specific remit depends on their own strength of feeling on the issue, and on the amount of briefing which they have received from their *Cabinets*, which in turn may reflect pressure from a national administration to support a particular policy line. Some Commissioners are capable of mastering the detail of subjects outside their direct portfolio area and gain a reputation for doing this. It is not unusual for a Commissioner not directly involved in a policy disagreement to propose a compromise solution which finally attracts a consensus in the College.

Powers of the President

Under the Presidency of Jacques Delors, the President of the European Commission has emerged as a powerful figure on the European and international stage. However, he holds a position which is, to a significant degree, subordinated to the Commission's collegial structure. Although the President has considerable powers over the allocation of portfolios, he does not have the power to shift responsibilities nor to reshuffle his team. He does not therefore benefit from the powers of political patronage familiar to every national and most local political leaders. The Commission President does not even control the agenda of Commission meetings, either in substance or even in timing.

There is, however, considerable prestige attached to the office of the President. Until 1993, the Commission appointed six Vice-Presidents, so there was no clear deputy. Failure to agree on the nomination of Vice-Presidents at the start of the Delors III Commission in January 1993 meant that there were no deputies at all. It took, in fact, till June 30 to decide the six Vice-Presidents of the new Commission, a decision valid only until November 1, 1993 when the Treaty on European Union entered into force. Thereafter, the Commission was entitled to appoint one or two Vice-Presidents. The External Affairs Commissioner has always been seen as a major figure in the college, attending the General Affairs Council with the 12 foreign ministers of the Member States. However, as in national governments, the nature of the job means that the External Affairs Commissioner has to spend a lot of time away from Brussels, and is unable to attend all Commission meetings, thus diminishing his influence. The agreement in spring 1993 to split the external affairs portfolio between external trade and foreign relations further reduced the prospects of a clear deputy President emerging from among the 17 Commissioners.

The President has policy responsibility for the horizontal coordinating services in the Commission, particularly the Secretariat General and the Legal Service. This means that he is particularly well placed to know what is going on inside the Commission's organisation. Every proposal to be sent to the Commission for approval requires a prior opinion from the legal service as to its compatibility with the Treaty. In the Commission's law-based policy structure the opinion or *avis* of the Legal Service plays a key part in policy discussions and frequently goes beyond purely legal issues into the wider policy context. The Secretariat General provides the administrative structure for the processing of proposals and also acts as the Secretariat for policy meetings called to discuss them.

During Commission meetings, the President has to preserve a balance between effective chairmanship of the Commission and the maintenance of a collegiate consensus, while at the same time attempting to imprint a policy direction on the Commission. This tension between conflicting objectives is, of course, present in the role of every head of government. Indeed, the Presidency of the Council is in a similarly difficult position. But it is fair to say that, in the Commission, the requirements of collegiality mean that the President must spend more effort in seeking to build consensus, simply because the option of imposing a position on his fellow Commissioners is not normally open to him. There are many examples of the President finding it difficult to persuade Commissioners to adopt his preferred policy position. In September 1993, for example, press reports suggested that Delors' proposals for controls on foreign exchange markets, designed to stabilise exchange rates, did not have the backing of key members of the Commission. While the President may call for a vote at an appropriate moment in the discussion or seek to adjourn a final decision, he has no monopoly on these procedural weapons and they are not widely used.

The *Cabinets* — historical development

The role of the Commissioner is intimately bound up with that of his *Cabinet* or personal team of advisers, who support the Commissioner in his or her wide-ranging tasks. The *Cabinets* are central to the policy-making and political processes of the Community; they operate within a complex web of Community institutions and are a focus for lobbying from sectoral and national interests. They help to coordinate policy and mediate among competing interests both from within the Commission and from competing sources. Thus, they provide a useful lens through which to view the intricate and informal processes of Commission policy-making (Ross 1993).

A system of personal advisers or ministerial *Cabinets* giving political support and advice to Ministers was a familiar part of the politico-administrative systems in most of the founding Member States. While the system was not so developed in Germany, it was well established in Italy, Belgium and France. The practice was most developed in France, where *Cabinets* had four main functions (Searls 1978). First, *Cabinet* members were able to act as the political antennae for the Minister by keeping him alerted to politically sensitive or difficult issues and acting as a filter for parties and pressure groups. Secondly, the *Cabinet* typically provided policy advice to the Minister which counterbalanced policy advice coming from the specialist civil servants. Thirdly, over time *Cabinets* became the mechanism for intra- and inter-ministerial coordination, since it was often easier for policy disputes to be sorted out at the level of *Cabinets* than amongst permanent administrators, who were often preoccupied with defending the interests of their own departments or administrative *corps*. Finally, the *Cabinets* became increasingly interventionist in supervising and controlling the work of the permanent administration. While there are obvious advantages to the French *Cabinet* system — such as increasing the weight of the Minister in the department by providing him with a pool of reliable and politically loyal advisers — there are several drawbacks which are apparent, in different ways, in all systems of policy advice (Seymour-Ure 1987). There is, for example, the inevitable tendency of *Cabinets* to become bureaucratised over time as they institutionalise and formalise relationships with the civil service. These institutionalised patterns lead to functional specialisation which in turn tends to inhibit the ability of *Cabinets* to be innovative. The *Cabinet* system can also distance the Minister from his administration, as it is often easier for him to make decisions with hand-picked advisers than with permanent civil servants. This may have the effect of lowering the morale of the civil service. *Cabinet* members in France have a high level of technical expertise, which means that they can offer the Minister a well-informed choice of policy options and help to prevent the risk of policy being determined by officials with their own priorities, departmental interests and sectoral commitments. Nevertheless, the fact that advisers usually have no security of tenure and are reliant on Ministers for their jobs limits their willingness to give critical advice. On occasion, this has the effect of cocooning the Minister from the complex realities of policy formation and implementation. Finally, as in all systems of advice, it was difficult for the *Cabinets* to strike a successful balance between developing a long-term strategy and responding to current and pressing issues (Plowden 1987). Similar problems are becoming evident in the Commission's system of personal *Cabinets.*

Cabinets, based on the French model, had been used in the High Authority of the ECSC. However, Monnet had encouraged a dynamic and fluid system of policy advice during the early years of the ECSC and the *Cabinets* competed with other bodies in providing advice. Nevertheless, they were perceived as a natural support mechanism for members of the High Authority and key *Cabinet* members were highly influential in both policy advice and political negotiations. The new EEC Commission, appointed in 1958, inherited this practice and set up private offices largely on the pattern of French ministerial *Cabinets.* Hallstein, the President of the new Commission, was very keen to keep the *Cabinets* small because he realised that large interventionist *Cabinets* would be likely to jeopardise good working relations between Commissioners and civil servants. Hallstein also anticipated that the *Cabinets,* chosen by the Commissioners largely from their own nationals, might become poles of attraction for national interests within the Commission and this would inhibit the development of the Europeanism which he was trying to create (Mazey 1992).

It was agreed that Commissioners' *Cabinets* should consist of two members, plus a secretary and typist, and the President's *Cabinet* should consist of four advisers plus two secretaries. Commissioners soon began the practice of detaching high-flying civil servants from the DGs to serve in their *Cabinet.* This established a precedent for closer involvement between the *Cabinet* and the administration. The work of the early *Cabinets,* like that of the Commission itself, was very flexible and rapidly changing as new policies became established and the powers of the institutions began to be more clearly delineated. As personal aides to the Commissioners, the functions of *Cabinet* members were wide-ranging and varied; dealing with lobbyists, liaising with national governments, developing policy initiatives, writing speeches and generally organising the work of the Commission.

Hallstein tried to use the Commission to foster a European identity within the Member States and consequently Commissioners were expected to have a high public profile and to make regular visits around the Community. Often they were accompanied by members of their *Cabinets* or, on occasion, sent their *Cabinet* members as delegates. Hallstein also viewed the Commission as a collective body. All members were under pressure to be well briefed on general Community policy and, in addition to their own portfolio concerns, they were given ancillary responsibilities for two other policy areas. In effect, this meant that each policy area was discussed by a triumvirate of Commissioners. This placed an enormous strain on Commissioners who came to rely heavily on *Cabinet* members to give them advice, especially on issues outside their main sphere of responsibility. In practice, the system soon proved unworkable and became defunct, although the expectation that Commissioners should be well briefed over a range of policy areas has persisted.

It became apparent in the early years of the Community that for a policy to be successful it had to be vigorously negotiated with politicians, civil servants and interested parties in the Member States. Without this political backing, policies would have been untenable. Framing the CAP, for example, involved intense negotiations over several years between the Commission and Member States (Lindberg 1963). The *Cabinets* became a vital link in this process by identifying key interests within the Member States and by building package deals with Commission officials. Until the Permanent Representations of the Member States became established in the mid-1960s as a clearing house for national interests, the Commission was in frequent and direct contact with national élites. In most cases this contact was coordinated and supervised by the *Cabinets.* This meant national politicians and pressure groups put considerable pressure on the *Cabinets* to advance their claims. The *Cabinets* thereby became both a pressure point for national, and to a limited extent, sectoral interests and a focus for the accommodation of national and Community interests (Ritchie 1992).

As the policy competences of the EC grew in the 1960s, the patterns of decision-making became increasingly institutionalised and bureaucratised. This process led to problems endemic in bureaucracies such as internal conflicts, problems of coordination and a lack of strategic direction. Such problems were particularly acute in a system where the lines of political responsibility and accountability were not very clearly drawn. The *Cabinets* became an important mechanism for coordinating policy within the Commission, so contact between them was constant at formal and informal levels. High-level contact was facilitated by the institution of the Meeting of the Heads of *Cabinets,* a weekly meeting which anticipated the Wednesday meeting of the Commission. Over time the *Cabinets* also began to be used increasingly by Commissioners to liaise with their officials in the DGs. The problems of working with a multinational bureaucracy, with officials from various administrative backgrounds, were particularly difficult for newly-appointed Commissioners (Donnelly 1993). These problems were attenuated by the *Cabinets* which acted as interlocutors between the Commissioner and the administration. The work of the *Cabinets* was shaped by the functions, standing, prestige, experience and calibre of the Commissioners themselves. While the *Cabinets* could to some extent counterbalance a Commissioner's shortcomings and were used by Commissioners to strengthen areas where they were weak, in practice it was very difficult for advisers to compensate fully for the failings of policy-makers (Dror 1987).

Contemporary *Cabinets*

Cabinets have thus acquired a major influence over the day-to-day running of the Commission and this is reflected in the growth in the number of members and in their seniority and calibre. The Commission currently finances a *Cabinet* of six members for each Commissioner, at least one of whom must be a national of another Community Member State. In practice, *Cabinets* have had as many as eight members, with the additional posts being funded by the Commissioner's home administration through secondment or occasionally through a system of temporary attachments. The Spierenburg Report, commissioned by President Roy Jenkins in 1979, drew attention to the dangers inherent in the proliferation of *Cabinet* members, such as lowering the morale of the civil service and creating a barrier between the Commissioner and the DGs. *Cabinets* are usually a mixture of internal Commission staff, seconded to the *Cabinet* for the Commission's four-year term, and outsiders on leave of absence from the Commissioner's national administration or the private sector. The latter group tends to spend an average of two to three years in a *Cabinet*.

Cabinet members are directly responsible to the Commissioner and retain their posts at his personal discretion. They have, therefore, no security of tenure. National governments and political parties take considerable interest in the composition of their Commissioners' *Cabinets* because they are a vital point of contact for the Member States within the Community system. In the United Kingdom, the Cabinet Office draws up a list of civil service candidates for *Cabinet* posts. This is offered to both prospective Commissioners. In France, new Commissioners who have previously been national ministers often take members of their former ministerial *Cabinets* with them to Brussels. As in the United Kingdom, the French political system is quite centralised. In France, the SGCI (the Interministerial Committee for European Affairs) plays an influential role in proposing *Cabinet* members. The Permanent Representations of the Member States in Brussels are also a valuable source of candidates both for *Cabinets* and for senior posts in the Commission's administration. The Commissioner's own political party may wish to have a liaison member in the *Cabinet*, a job which is frequently combined with work on European Parliament issues. The Commission meets in Strasbourg during the European Parliament's plenary sessions and, since the introduction of the cooperation procedure in the Single European Act, liaison with MEPs is an increasingly important issue for Commissioners (see Chapter 9).

The internal workings of a *Cabinet* reflect the personality and working style of both the Commissioner and of the *Chef de Cabinet*. Some *Cabinets* meet their Commissioner on most working days and enjoy regular and direct access to discussions on all policy issues. Others tend to filter papers through the *Chef* who handles many issues with full delegated authority from the Commissioner. But the effectiveness of the *Cabinet* ultimately depends on the effectiveness of their Commissioner; as Dror (1987) astutely observes, advice is only good if leaders are prepared to use it. The other side of the coin is that the civil servants have to accept that *Cabinet* members are acting on the authority of the Commissioner. Increasingly, though, civil servants in the Commission are not accepting the authority of the *Cabinet* to supervise, monitor or override their views. It is a problem that tends to increase the larger the number of *Cabinet* members.

The *Cabinets* function as an extension of their own Commissioner. Their day-to-day activity inevitably reflects each Commissioner's own political as well as administrative objectives and priorities. All *Cabinets* are involved to different degrees with four basic functions: assisting the Commissioner with his policy responsibilities, enabling the presentation of the Commissioner's public image and political philosophy, administrative coordination and liaising with Member States. In British government terms, they provide a combination of private office secretariat, political advice and additional policy input.

Policy responsibilities

Since the Commission operates as a collegial body and Commissioners have to contribute to wide-ranging policy discussions, they need policy advice across the range of Community activities. *Cabinets* are expected to ensure effective coordination within the Commission's administrative structure in order to brief the Commissioners. Each *Cabinet*'s coordinating role is governed by the timetable of the Commission's weekly meetings, normally held on Wednesday. Issues requiring a Commission decision must be signalled at least 10 days in advance of the relevant Commission meeting. This is usually done at the *Chef de Cabinet* meeting held at the beginning of the previous week. An updated outline agenda is circulated each week by the Secretariat General. Indicative longer-term timetables of the Commission are also circulated. These are designed to help prevent excessive bunching of major issues at particular meetings. However, under the rules of procedure any Commission member has the right to insist that an item of business be placed on the agenda of a particular meeting. The management of business is therefore difficult to plan. In practice, July and December tend to be particularly busy months and September and January relatively quiet.

Substantive policy proposals are discussed at a meeting of representatives of all the Commissioners' *Cabinets,* known as a 'Special Chefs' meeting, which is chaired by a member of the President's *Cabinet*. These meetings can last for between one and 12 hours, or occasionally even longer, depending on the complexity and political sensitivity of the issue under discussion. During a normal week there are likely to be six or seven such *Cabinet* meetings, made up of *Cabinet* members specialising in the subject under discussion. Papers for these meetings have to be circulated 48 hours in advance, in three languages — French, English and German. The circulated papers provide an initial summary of the positions of those Directorates General which have been consulted. This allows other *Cabinets* to be aware of how much opposition remains to a proposal, where it comes from and why, and to alert their Commissioner accordingly. It is not, however, unknown for a *Cabinet* to disavow the objections of its own Commissioner's DG in a meeting of its *Chefs de Cabinet*. The conclusions of these meetings are drawn up by the President's *Cabinet*, which chairs all such meetings. The summing up of these meetings provides a first indication of the likely outcome in the Commission. It is open to individual *Cabinets* to place formal reserves on all or some of the conclusions, but not to have the conclusions rewritten. The 'Special Chefs' meeting therefore provides considerable scope for the President's *Cabinet* to construct a consensus around its own desired outcome.

The conclusions of these meetings then go as an input into the Monday meeting of the heads of the 17 *Cabinets*, the *Chefs de Cabinet* meeting. This meeting differs from the 'Special Chefs' in that it is chaired by the Commission's Secretary General. At this level, the permanent civil service input from the Directorates General becomes more important. But the parameters for debate have previously been set by the 'Special Chefs' meeting, and the President's *Chef de Cabinet* also plays a major role. A delicate balance is thus struck between collegiality and Presidential authority. The meeting of Heads of *Cabinets* follows the same agenda as the full Commission and seeks to achieve consensus on as many points as possible in advance of the Commission's meeting on the following Wednesday. Those points on which unanimous agreement are reached at the 'Chefs' meeting nonetheless remain on the Commission agenda as so-called 'A' points for agreement without discussion. This is to reflect the principle that the College of Commissioners itself takes all formal decisions, except where a specific delegation of powers, known as an *'habilitation'* (see Chapter 4), is given to one or more members. It is indeed open to any Commissioner to seek to reopen an item marked down as an 'A' point at the beginning of the weekly Commission meeting. However, as 'A' points reflect a consensus among Commission members it is rare for any such step to be taken, except as a political gesture, perhaps accompanied by a dissenting statement for the minutes. Coordination between the Commissioners' *Cabinets* therefore takes place within a tight time-scale and with firmly fixed procedures.

Presentation of policy

One of the key roles of the *Cabinet* is to ensure that the Commissioner's policy is effectively presented. *Cabinet* members assist the Commissioner in writing speeches and articles and they also ensure that the Commissioner has effective communication with his or her own government. This role is one of the most delicate and controversial of the *Cabinets'* functions. *Cabinets* are frequently suspected, not always unjustly, of leaking internal Commission documents to their national administrations in order to receive detailed briefing on their own government's concerns about a particular proposal before a Commission debate takes place. They are in constant contact with the national Permanent Representation in Brussels and, on occasion, with ministries in the Commissioner's home state in order to exchange information and points of view. But it would be misleading to see this process as instructions being given to the Commission by a government. More often it is a process of negotiation between *Cabinets* and their Commissioner's national government on the parameters of their respective positions.

Broker of interests

Cabinet members are constantly lobbied by pressure groups of their own nationality to raise points of particular concern at inter-*Cabinet* meetings. Although key interest groups obviously have close contact with the *Cabinet* of the DG which has policy responsibility for their areas of concern, they naturally also tend to exploit national contacts in other *Cabinets* and DGs. Europe-wide lobbyists focus on *Cabinets* before the Commission makes a decision. This lobbying tends to duplicate, albeit at a higher level, the pressure which will already have been directed at the Commission officials who have prepared the issues for discussion. The Permanent Representations of the Member States and of non-EC countries represented in Brussels tend to make lobbying at *Cabinet* level a priority (see also Chapter 8).

Administrative liaison

Cabinets perform an increasingly significant role in monitoring the work of Commission officials and in liaising between the Commissioner and his or her staff. This aspect of the *Cabinets'* work is particularly contentious. Commission officials feel that *Cabinet* members interfere too much in the detail of their work and take over too much of the substantive policy-making. On the other hand, many *Cabinet* members feel that it is essential for them to become familiar with dossiers in order to advise the Commissioner. This tension between policy advisers and administrative officials forms part of the dynamics of most systems of policy-making. Over time, advisers find that their pattern of relationships with permanent staff becomes institutionalised, and there is a tendency to become involved in detailed policy-making. There is certainly an increasing degree of functional specialisation in most *Cabinets*, with members 'overseeing' distinct parts of the DGs. Be that as it may, *Cabinets* do provide a direct link between the Commissioner and his permanent civil service in the Directorates General working in the policy areas for which their Commissioner is responsible.

Policy submissions are channelled from the *services* through the relevant *Cabinet* member to the Commissioner. The *Cabinet* seeks to ensure that the Commissioner's policy choices are understood and acted on by the permanent civil service. This sometimes leads to differences as senior civil servants object to being told what to do by *Cabinet* members; they also object to the practice, often used by *Cabinets*, of circumventing senior staff in the Commission and dealing directly with middle-ranking staff — *sous directeurs* or *Chefs de Service* — who are often at the centre of policy-making.

The administrative effectiveness of a *Cabinet* in working with its own Directorate General depends to a considerable extent on close liaison with the Director General's Assistant. This post, akin to that of a private secretary in a British ministry, involves supervision of the Directorate General's internal structures and procedures. Briefing requests, organisation of meetings and day-to-day contact with the Directorate General take place through the Assistant who is chosen by the Director General himself. The Commission tradition that the Assistant should be of a different nationality from the Director General generally holds and helps to prevent senior management being dominated by a single nationality in any given policy area.

Conclusions

The *Cabinet* system has become more central to the process of Community policy formation in recent years. This centrality has been evident in the Delors' Commissions in which several Commissioners have augmented their official quota of *Cabinet* posts with additional members financed from national governments or political sources. The recent growth in the policy competences of the European Union, following the Single European Act and the Treaty on European Union, has led to an increasingly pivotal role played by the Commission in the policy-making process. This has served to increase the power of the *Cabinets*. They operate at the centre of a complex web of European, national and functional interests which have to be balanced against each other. *Cabinets* filter policy demands up to the Commissioner and pass strategic policy decisions down to the Commission bureaucracy and to the Member States. In addition, *Cabinets* are increasingly instrumental in building policy majorities and package deals across Community institutions and with the Member States.

The *Cabinet* system clearly has many benefits for Commissioners who need personal support in order to carry out the onerous tasks of policy initiation and execution. Commissioners find it easier to share ideas with supportive *Cabinet* members than with officials whose administrative practices may be unfamiliar. The high calibre of *Cabinet* members means they are well qualified to assist the Commissioner in policy evaluation. They also provide the Commissioner with an invaluable source of policy advice across the whole range of Commission issues.

But the advantages of *Cabinets* need to be set against the inherent drawbacks of the system. First, with the growing number of *Cabinet* members and their increasing role in policy-making there is the danger of a parallel bureaucracy emerging within the Commission. Relations between the *Cabinet* and the permanent Commission officials is inevitably a delicate one. Ideally, a *Cabinet* should enhance the effectiveness of its Directorate General by ensuring that policy decisions are made rapidly and effectively, by providing informal guidance on the Commissioner's wishes and by supporting its own Directorate General's concerns in debate on policy priorities with other *services*. However, the distinction between policy guidance and interference is not always clear-cut. Commission staff tend to hold firm views on the correct policy line, and the risk of conflict between the *Cabinet* and permanent officials is a real one. In order to offer the Commissioner a genuine choice of policy options and to prevent the risk of policy being determined in a fragmented manner by individual policy units within the Commission bureaucracy, *Cabinets* are drawn to take over dossiers and intervene quite closely in the work of officials. This has the effect of damaging morale in the Commission bureaucracy and there is an increasing problem of civil servants not accepting the authority of the *Cabinet* to supervise or monitor them. A further source of sensitivity concerns the extent to which a *Cabinet* may be perceived as using its policy role to inject national preferences into a draft proposal prepared by the officials before it is discussed more widely. This can be interpreted as a demonstration of the *Cabinet*'s wider political approach, or as revealing undue sympathy for a particular Member State's position. The growth of lobbying at the Community level intensifies this problem. A final problem is the tendency of *Cabinets* themselves to become bureaucratised. This is a matter of pressing concern given the growing numbers of *Cabinet* personnel, the increasing functional specialisation within *Cabinets* and the increasingly institutionalised patterns of relationships between the permanent bureaucracy and the *Cabinets* and amongst *Cabinets* themselves.

Clearly, many of the advantages of a flexible and dynamic think-tank begin to be lost once the body becomes institutionalised. Nevertheless, given the nature of the Commission as a collegiate body and the need to provide personal support to Commission members often unused to the Brussels working environment, it is likely that the *Cabinets* will continue to grow in size and importance.

References

Donnelly, Martin (1993) 'The Structure of the European Commission and the Policy Formation Process', in Mazey, Sonia and Richardson Jeremy, J.(eds.) *Lobbying in the European Community*, Oxford: Oxford University Press, pp. 74–81.
Dror, Yehezkel (1987) 'Conclusions' in Plowden, William (ed.) *Advising the Rulers*, Oxford: Basil Blackwell, pp. 185–216.
Jacobs, Francis, Corbett, Richard and Shackleton, Michael (1992) *The European Parliament*, Harlow: Longman.
Lindberg, Leon N. (1963) *The Political Dynamics of European Integration*, Stanford, California: Stanford University Press.
Mazey, Sonia (1992) 'Conception and Evolution of the High Authority's Administrative Services 1952–1956: from Supranational Principles to Multinational Practices' in Morgan, R. and Wright, V. (eds.) *The Administrative Origins of the European Community*, Baden-Baden: Nomos.
Peters, Guy (1992) 'Bureaucratic Politics and the institutions of the European Community', in Sbragia, A.M. (ed.) *Europolitics: Institutions and Policy-Making in the 'New' European Community*, Washington DC: The Brookings Institute, pp. 75–122.
Plowden, William (ed.) (1987) *Advising the Rulers*, Oxford: Basil Blackwell.
Ritchie, Ella (1992) 'The model of the French ministerial *cabinet* in the early European Commission', in Morgan, R. and Wright, V. (eds.) *op. cit.*, pp. 95–106.
Ross, G. (1993) 'Sidling Into Industrial Policy', *French Politics and Society*, Vol. 11, No. 1, Winter, pp. 20–44.
Searls, Ella (1978) 'The Fragmented French Executive: Ministerial *Cabinets* in the Fifth French Republic', *West European Politics*, pp. 161–76.
Seymour-Ure, Colin (1987) 'Institutionalization and Informality in Advisory Systems', in Plowden, William (ed.) *op. cit.*, pp. 165–75.

ANNEX A

Commission of the European Economic Community

10 January 1958 to 9 January 1962

President: Walter Hallstein (D)
Vice-Presidents: Giuseppe Caron (I) (from 9 December 1959)
Piero Malvestiti (I) (resigned 15 September 1959)
Sicco Mansholt (NL)
Robert Marjolin (F)
Members: Hans von der Groeben (D)
Robert Lemaignen (F) (until 9 January 1962)
Lionello Levi Santri (I) (from 22 February 1961)
Giuseppe Petrilli (I) (until 8 February 1961 — resigned)
Jean Rey (B)
Lambert Schaus (L)

10 January 1962 to 5 July 1967

President: Walter Hallstein (D)
Vice-Presidents: Giuseppe Caron (I) (until 16 May 1963)
Lionello Levi Sandri (I) (VP from 30 July 1964)
Sicco Mansholt (NL)
Robert Marjolin (F)
Members: Guido Colonna Di Paliano (I) (from 9 September 1964)
Hans Von der Groeben (D)
Lionello Levi Sandri (I) (until 30 July when he became VP)
Jean Rey (B)
Henri Rochereau (F)
Lambert Schaus (L)

Commission of the European Communities
(following the Merger Treaty of 1967)

6 July 1967 to 30 June 1970

President: Jean Rey (B)
Vice-Presidents: Raymond Barre (F)
Fritz Hellwig (D)
Lionello Levi Sandri (I)
Sicco Mansholt (NL)
Members: Victor Bodson (L)
Guido Colonna Di Paliano (I) (until 8 May 1970 — resigned)
Albert Coppé (B)
Jean-François Deniau (F)
Hans von der Groeben (D)
Wilhelm Haferkamp (D)
Edoardo Martino (I)

Emmanuel Sassen (NL)
Henri Rochereau (F)

1 July 1970 to 5 January 1973

President(s):   Franco Maria Malfatti (I) (until 21 March 1972 — resigned)
                  Sicco Mansholt (NL) (from 21 March 1972)
Vice-Presidents: Raymond Barre (F)
                  Wilhelm Haferkamp (D)
                  Sicco Mansholt (NL) (until 21 March when he
                      became President)
                  Carlo Scarascia-Mugnozza (I) (from 22 March 1972)
Members: Albert Borschette (L)
                  Albert Coppé (B)
                  Ralf Dahrendorf (D)
                  Jean-François Deniau (F)
                  Altiero Spinelli (I)

6 January 1973 to 5 January 1977

President: François-Xavier Ortoli (F)
Vice-Presidents: Wilhelm Haferkamp (D)
                  Patrick Hillery (IRL)
                  Carlo Scarascia-Mugnozza (I)
                  Henri Simonet (B)
                  Sir Christopher Soames (UK)
Members: Raymond Vouel (L) (nominated 20 July 1976)
                  Albert Borschette (L) (until 8 December 1976 — deceased)
                  Jean-François Deniau (F) (until 11 April 1973 — resigned)
                  Claude Cheysson (F) (from 19 April 1973)
                  Ralf Dahrendorf (D) (until 31 October 1974 — resigned)
                  Guido Brunner (D) (from 11 November 1974)
                  Altiero Spinelli (I) (until 1 July 1976 — resigned)
                  Cesidio Guazzaroni (I) (from 13 July 1976)
                  Finn Olav Gundelach (DK)
                  Petrus Josephus Lardinois (NL)
                  George Thomson (UK)

6 January 1977 to 5 January 1981

President: Roy Jenkins (UK)
Vice-Presidents: Finn Olav Gundelach (DK)
                  Wilhelm Haferkamp (D)
                  Lorenzo Natali (I)
                  François-Xavier Ortoli (F)
                  Henk Vredeling (NL)
Members: Guido Brunner (D) (until 4 November 1980 — resigned)
                  Richard Burke (IRL)
                  Claude Cheysson (F)
                  Etienne Davignon (B)
                  Antonio Giolitti (I)

Christopher Samuel Tugendhat (UK)
Raymond Vouel (L)

6 January 1981 to 5 January 1985

President: Gaston Thorn (L)
Vice-Presidents: Etienne Davignon (B)
                     Wilhelm Haferkamp (D)
                     Lorenzo Natali (I)
                     François -Xavier Ortoli (F) (until 26 October 1984 — resigned)
                     Christopher Samuel Tugendhat (UK)
Members: Frans Andriessen (NL)
                     Michael O'Kennedy (IRL) (until 3 March 1982 — resigned)
                     Richard Burke (IRL) (from 1 April 1982)
                     Claude Cheysson (F) (until 23 May 1981 — resigned)
                     Edgard Pisani (F) (from 26 May 1981 until
                         3 Dec 1984 — resigned)
                     Giorgios Contogeorgis (EL)
                     Finn Olaf Gundelach (DK) (decd. 13 January 1981)
                     Poul C. Dalsager (DK) (from 20 January 1981)
                     Antonio Giolitti (I)
                     Karl-Heinz Narjes (D)
                     Ivor (Seward) Richard (UK)

6 January 1985 to 5 January 1989

President: Jacques Delors (F)
Vice-Presidents: Frans Andriessen (NL)
                     Henning Christophersen (DK)
                     Lord Cockfield (UK)
                     Karl-Heinz Narjes (D)
                     Lorenzo Natali (I)
Members: Claude Cheysson (F)
                     Stanley Clinton Davis (UK)
                     Willy de Clercq (B)
                     Nicolas Mosar (L)
                     Alois Pfeiffer (D) (decd. 1 August 1987)
                     Peter Schmidhuber (D) (from 22 September 1987)
                     Carlo Ripa Di Meana (I)
                     Peter D. Sutherland (IRL)
                     Grigorios Varfis (EL)

1986 — Following Enlargement to include Spain and Portugal, the following Commissioners were appointed:

Manuel Marin (ES)
Abel Matutes (ES)
Antonio Cardoso E. Cunha (P)

6 January 1989 to 6 January 1993

President: Jacques Delors (F)
Vice-Presidents: Frans Andriessen (NL)
                      Henning Christophersen (DK)
                      Manuel Marin (ES)
                      Filippo Maria Pandolfi (I)
                      Martin Bangemann (D)
                      Leon Brittan (UK)
Members: Carlo Ripa Di Meana (I) (resigned June 1992)
                      Antonio Cardoso E Cunha (P)
                      Abel Matutes (ES)
                      Peter Schmidhuber (D)
                      Christiane Scrivener (F)
                      Bruce Millan (UK)
                      Jean Dondelinger (L)
                      Ray McSharry (IRL)
                      Karel Van Miert (B)
                      Vasso Papandreou (EL)

6 January 1993 to 6 January 1995

President: Jacques Delors (F)
Vice-Presidents: Henning Christophersen (DK)
                      Manuel Marin (ES)
Members: Martin Bangemann (D)
                      Sir Leon Brittan (UK)
                      Raniero Vanni d'Archirafi (I)
                      Hans Van den Broek (NL)
                      Abel Matutes (ES) (resigned 27 April 1994)
                      Peter Schmidhuber (D)
                      Christiane Scrivener (F)
                      Bruce Millan (UK)
                      René Steichen (L)
                      Padraig Flynn (IRL)
                      Yannis Paleokrassas (EL)
                      João de Deus Pinheiro (P)
                      Antonio Ruberti (I)
                      Karel Van Miert (B)
                      Marcelino Oreja (ES) (from 27 April 1994)

B	=	België	Belgium
D	=	Deutschland	Germany
DK	=	Danmark	Denmark
EL	=	Ellas	Greece
ES	=	España	Spain
F	=	France	
IRL	=	Ireland	
I	=	Italia	Italy
L	=	Luxembourg	Luxembourg
NL	=	Nederland	The Netherlands

P   =   Portugal
UK   =   United Kingdom

Initials as used for rotation of Council Presidency, i.e. absolute alphabetical order using the name of the country in its own language

ANNEX B

Biographies of the 17 members of the 1993–95 Commission of the European Communities and the distribution of portfolios

Martin Bangemann (Germany): responsible for industrial affairs, information technologies and telecommunications.

Born in 1934, he is married with three sons and two daughters. *Education:* studied law at the Universities of Tubingen and Munich (doctorate 1962). *Professional Career:* barrister (1964–84). *Political Career:* joined the FDP (Free Democratic Party) in 1963 and was a member of the *Bundestag* (1972–80 and 1987–89). MEP (1973–84) and Vice Chairman of the Liberal Democratic Group in the European Parliament (1975–79) becoming Chairman (1979–84). Federal Minister for Economic Affairs (1984–88) and Federal Chairman of the FDP (1985–89). Became a Commissioner and vice-president in 1989 taking over the Internal Market, Industry and relations with the European Parliament portfolios.

Sir Leon Brittan (UK): responsible for external economic affairs (North America; Japan; China; CIS; Europe, including Central and Eastern Europe) and trade policy.

Born in 1939, he is married with two stepdaughters. *Education:* studied law at Cambridge and Yale. *Professional Career:* called to the Bar, Inner Temple (1962); Chairman of Bow Group (1964–65); editor of Crossbow (1966–67); Vice-Chairman of the National Association of School Governors and Managers (1970–78); Queens Counsel (1978); bencher of the Inner Chamber (1983). *Political Career:* Chairman of the Cambridge University Conservative Association (1960); member on the committee of the British Atlantic Group of Young Politicians (1970–78); MP for Cleveland and Whitby (1974–83) and for Richmond North Yorkshire (1983–88); Vice-Chairman of the Employment Committee of the Parliamentary Conservative Party; Opposition Spokesman on devolution and House of Commons affairs (1976–78) and on devolution and Employment (1978–79). Minister of State, Home Office (1979–81); appointed member of the Privy Council (1981); Chief Secretary to the Treasury with a seat in the Cabinet (1981–83); Home Secretary (1983–85). Became Secretary of State for Trade and Industry (1985) but resigned in 1986 amidst controversy over the future of the Westland Helicopter Company. Became an EC Commissioner and vice-president in 1989 with responsibilities for Competition and Financial Institutions.

Henning Christopherson (Denmark): responsible for Economic and Financial affairs; Monetary Matters (in agreement with Jacques Delors); Credit and Investments; Statistical Office.

Born 1939, married with one son and two daughters. *Education:* Degree in Economics, University of Copenhagen (1965). *Professional Career:* headed the economics division of the Danish Federation of Crafts and Smaller Industries (1965–70). An economics reporter for the periodical *NB* (1970–71) and for the weekly newspaper *Weekendevisen* (1971–78). *Political Career:* Elected to the *Folketing* (the Danish Parliament) in 1971; Deputy Chairman of the National Liberal Party (1971); member of the Finance Committee (1972–76); political spokesman for Liberal MPs (1973–78); National Auditor (1976–78). Chairman of the Liberal Party (1978); Minister for Foreign Affairs (1978–79); Leader of the Parliamentary Liberal Party (1979–82); Minister for Finance and Deputy Prime Minister (1982–84). Became Vice-President of the Commission (1985) in charge of Coordination of Structural Policies (1985–89); Budget, Financial Control, Personnel and Administration (1985–89); Economic and Financial Affairs (1985–); the Statistical Office (1985–); Monetary Matters (in agreement with Jacques Delors, 1993–) and Credit and Investments (1993–).

João de Deus Rogado Salvador Pinheiro (Portugal): responsible for relations with the European Parliament, relations with Member States on transparency, communication and information, culture and audio-visual policy and the office for official publications.

Born in 1945 and is married with four children. *Education:* University of Birmingham. *Professional Career:* university academic and scientist. Consultant for UNESCO on scientific policy; national delegate on the OECD. *Political Career:* junior minister in the 8th government; minister for education in the 9th and 10th governments; minister for foreign affairs (1987–92). Joined the Commission in 1993.

Jacques Delors (France): President of the EC Commission since January 1985.

Born in 1925, he is the oldest member of the present Commission and is married with one son (deceased) and one daughter. *Education:* University of Paris. *Professional Career:* Executive Officer and subsequently Head of Department at the Banque de France (1945–52); member of the bank's General Council (1973–79). Member of the Planning and Investment Section, Economic and Social Council (1959–62) and Head of the Social Affairs Department, *Commissariat général du plan* (1962–69). Lecturer, *Ecole nationale d'administration* (1963–65); Secretary-general, Inter-departmental Committee on Vocational Training and Social Advancement (1969–71). Became an Associate Professor of Company Management at the University of Paris-Dauphine (1973). Founder and Chairman of the "Echange et projets" association (1974–79); director of the "Travail et Société" research centre (1975–81); member of the national committee on scientific research (1976). *Political Career:* Adviser on social and cultural affairs to Jacques Chaban-Delmas, French PM (1969–71); *Chargé de mission* to the PM (1971–72). Joined the Socialist Party (1974); national coordinator for international economic affairs of the party (1976–79); became member of the central committee of the Socialist party (1979). Elected to the European Parliament (1979); Chairman of the European Parliament's Committee on Economic and Monetary Affairs (1979); Minister for Economic and Financial Affairs(1981–83); Minister for Economic and Financial Affairs and the Budget (1983–84); town councillor then mayor of Clichy (1983–84); President of the Commission of the European Communities since 1985; responsible for General Administration and Coordination of Structural Funds (1985–89); responsible for Monetary Affairs since 1985.

Padraig Flynn (Ireland): responsible for social affairs and employment, relations with the economic and social committee, immigration, home affairs and justice.

Born in 1939, he is married with four children. *Education:* St Patrick's College, Dublin. *Political Career:* councillor for Mayo (1967–87); vice-president of Mayo County Council (1975–77); elected as a *Fianna Fáil* deputy (1977).

Junior minister for transport and energy (1980–81); minister for Gaelic regions (1982); spokesman for commerce and tourism (1982–87); Minister of the Environment (1987–91); Minister of Justice (1992).

Manuel Marin Gonzalez (Spain): responsible for Cooperation and Development.

Born in 1949 and is married with two daughters. *Education:* Doctor of Law, University of Madrid: Diploma in Community Law, University of Nancy; Certificate in Advanced European Studies, College of Europe, Bruges. *Professional Career:* lecturer at the College of Europe, Bruges. *Political Career:* Member of the PSOE, Spanish Socialist Workers' Party (1974); Member of Parliament for Ciudad Real (Southern Spain); member and the PSOE spokesman on the Foreign Affairs Committee, Congress of Deputies; deputy chairman of the Confederation of Socialist Parties in the European Community and a member of the Consultative Assembly of the Council of Europe (1977–85). As State Secretary for relations with the European Communities (1983–85) was responsible for negotiating Spain's membership of the European Communities. Joined the Commission in 1986 with responsibilities for social affairs and employment, education and training. He became a vice-president of the Commission in 1986.

Abel Matutes (Spain): responsible for energy and the Euratom Supply Agency and transport.

Born in 1941 and is married with one son and three daughters. *Education:* graduated from Barcelona University in 1961 with a degree in law and economics. *Professional Career:* entrepreneur in tourism, finance and applied biotechnology; Assistant Professor of Law and Public Finance, University of Barcelona. *Political Career:* mayor of Ibiza (1970–71); founder member of the Liberal Party of the Balearic Islands (1976); senator for Ibiza and Formentera (1977–82); member of Spanish Parliament for the Balearic Islands (*Alianza Popular* — AP), spokesman for the Popular Group on the Economic Affairs and Finance Committee in the Congress of Deputies, chairman of the AP National Electoral and Economic Affairs and Public Finance Committees and deputy national chairman of AP (1982–85). Became a Commissioner in 1986 with responsibility for small business, credit, investments and financial engineering (1986–89) and responsibility for Mediterranean policy relations with Latin America and North–South relations (1989–93).

Bruce Millan (UK): responsible for regional policies and relations with the Committee of the Regions.

Born in 1927 and is married with one son and one daughter. *Education:* Harris Academy, Dundee. *Professional Career:* national service (1945–48); chartered accountant (1950–59); worked in the gas industry (1950–59). *Political Career:* Labour MP for Glasgow Craigton (1959–83), Glasgow Govan (1983–88); Parliamentary Under-Secretary of State at the Ministry of Defence (RAF) 1964–66, and at the Scottish Office (Health and Education) 1966–70. Opposition spokesman on civil aviation and Scottish affairs (1970–74). Minister of State at the Scottish Office (1974–76); Secretary of State for Scotland (1976–79) and opposition spokesman for Scotland (1979–83); member of the Council of Europe and the WEU (1984–88). Joined the Commission in 1989 with responsibility for regional policy.

Yannis Paleokrassas (Greece): responsible for Environment, nuclear safety and civil protection and Fisheries.

Born in 1934, he is married with three children. *Education:* Graduated from London School of Economics (1956) with a BSc. (Econ.) International Economics and an MSc. (Econ.) Economics of Transport (1958). *Professional Career:* member of the Planning Committee of the Ministry of Coordination (1959–63) and played a key role in designing the first five-year development plan for Greece; joined Doxiadis Associates, consultants in development (1963–68); general manager of Windward Shipping Ltd in London (1968–72); joined American Express Banking International Corporation (1974–77) and ERGOBANK (1975). *Political Career:* Under-Secretary of State at the Ministry of Coordination (1977–80); deputy to the Greek parliament (1978–90); Minister of State for Coordination (1981); Secretary General of his parliamentary party group (*Nea Dimokratia*), chairman of its finance committee and chairman of the ND parliamentary group on the national economy (1981–90). He was one of the seven new members who joined the Commission in 1993.

Antonio Ruberti (Italy): responsible for Science, Research and Development and Education and Training.

Born in 1927, he is married with four children. He graduated as an engineer and taught at the University of 'La Sapienza' in Rome since 1962. He became Minister for Scientific Research and Development in 1987 and then took on the portfolio for Universities and Research. He was elected as a Socialist Deputy in 1992. He joined the Commission in 1993.

Peter Schmidhuber (Germany): responsible for EC budget, financial control, anti-fraud measures and the coordination and management of the cohesion fund.

Born in 1931, he is a widower with one daughter. *Education:* diplomas in economics (1955) and law (1960), University of Munich. *Professional Career:* civil servant in the Bavarian State Ministries of Finance, Economics and Transport (1961–72); attorney, Munich Bar (1965–78) and head of department in an industrial federation (1969–71). *Political Career:* Joined the CSU (Christian Social Union) in 1952; honorary councillor of Munich (1960–66); member of the *Bundestag* (1965–69 and 1972–78); member of the Council of Europe and WEU Assembly (1972–78); member of the Bavarian Parliament, Bavarian Minister for Federal Affairs and Representative of Bavaria to the Federal Government; member of the *Bundesrat;* of the Mediation Committee of the *Bundestag* and *Bundesrat* and of the North Atlantic Assembly (1978–87); joined the Commission in 1987 with responsibility for economic affairs, regional policy and the statistical office (1987–89).

Christiane Scrivener (France): responsible for taxation and consumer policy.

Born in 1925 and is married with one son. *Education:* studied for a degree in psychology at Paris University; graduate of the Harvard Business School. *Professional Career:* businesswoman involved with organising French technical cooperation with developing countries, international trade in technological and industrial goods and promotion of French technology abroad; director of an association for training in France; Director General of ACTIM (agency for technical, industrial and economic cooperation) 1958–76; member of the board of Assurances Générales de France (French General

Insurance Company) 1986–89. *Political Career:* state secretary for consumer affairs (1976–78); MEP (Liberal Group) serving on committees on the budget and budgetary control (1979–88); Rapporteur for the Community Budget (1984). Joined the Commission in 1989 with responsibility for taxation and customs union.

René Steichen (Luxembourg): responsible for agriculture and rural development.

Born in 1942, he is married with three children. *Education:* studied law in Aix-en-Provence and Paris. *Professional Career:* barrister (1969–84). *Political Career:* town councillor for Diekirch (1969); mayor (1974–84); Christian Democrat Deputy (1979–92). Junior minister for agriculture (1984–89); Minister for Agriculture and Wine Production and Minister for Cultural Affairs and Scientific Research (1989–92). Joined the Commission in 1993.

Hans van den Broek (Netherlands): responsible for external political relations, common foreign and security policy and enlargement negotiations.

Born in 1936 and is married with two children. *Education:* Degrees in law from Utrecht University and administration from the De Baak institute in Noordwijk. *Professional Career:* lawyer (1965–68); commerce (1969–76). *Political Career:* Councillor for Rheden (1970–74); member of the second chamber of the Netherlands Parliament (1976–81) sitting on the foreign affairs, cooperation and development, and justice committees; Secretary of State for Foreign Affairs (1981–82); Foreign Minister (1982–84). Joined the Commission in 1993.

Karel van Miert (Belgium): responsible for competition, personnel and administration, translation and information technology.

Born in 1942, he is married with one son. *Education:* degree in diplomatic sciences, University of Ghent (thesis on the supranational character of the European Commission); postgraduate course at the European University Centre, Nancy; traineeship with the European Commission (1967–68). *Professional Career:* research assistant at the National Scientific Research Fund (1968–70); assistant at the Vrije University, Brussels (1971–73); member of Henri Simonet's (Vice-President of the European Commission) *cabinet*, (1973–75); head of the private office of the Belgian Minister for Economic Affairs (1977); part-time lecturer in international law, social law and European Institutes at Free University, Brussels (1978). *Political Career:* co-chairman of the Belgian Socialist Party (1977); vice-chairman of the Confederation of Socialist Parties of the European Communities (1978–80); MEP (1979–85); member of the Belgian Chamber of Representatives (1985) and vice-president of Socialist International (1986). Joined the Commission in 1989 with responsibility for transport, credit control and consumer policy.

Raniero Vanni d'Archirafi (Italy): responsible for institutional matters, internal markets, financial services, enterprise policy (small business and distributive trades).

Professional Career: entered the diplomatic service in 1956, serving in the Italian permanent representation to Brussels (1961–66). Appointed ambassador in 1983 and sent to Madrid and Bonn. Member of the Italian delegation in the Maastricht Treaty negotiations. Minister for Cultural Affairs and Scientific Research (1989–92).

ANNEX C

Delors's Second Commission (1989–1993) and Portfolios

Jacques Delors
France

President; secretariat-general; monetary affairs; Forward Studies Unit; Joint Interpreting and Conference Service; Security Office; Spokesman's Service

Frans Andriessen
The Netherlands

Vice-president; external relations; commercial policy; cooperation with other European countries

Henning Christopherson
The Netherlands

Vice-president; external relations; commercial policy; cooperation with other European countries

Manuel Marín
Spain

Vice-president; cooperation and development; fisheries

Filippo Maria Pandolfi
Italy

Vice-president; science, research, and development; telecommunications, industries, and innovation; Joint Research Centre

Martin Bangemann
Germany

Vice-president; internal market and industrial affairs; relations with the European Parliament

Sir Leon Brittan
United Kingdom

Vice-president; competition; financial institutions and company law

Carlo Ripa di Meana[1]
Italy

Environment and nuclear safety; civil protection

Antonio Cardoso E Cunha
Portugal

Personnel and adminstration; energy; enterprise policy, trade, tourism, and social economy

Abel Matutes
Spain

Mediterranean policy; relations with Latin America and Asia; north-south relations

Peter Schmidhuber
Germany

Budgets; financial control

Christiane Scrivener
France

Customs union and indirect taxation

Bruce Millan
United Kingdom

Regional policy

Jean Dondelinger
Luxembourg

Information, communication, and culture

Ray MacSharry
Ireland

Agriculture; rural development

Karel Van Miert
Belgium

Transport; credit and investments; consumer policy

Vasso Papandreou   Employment, industrial relations, and social
Greece   affairs; relations with the Economic and Social
                              Committee; human resources, education, and
                              training

Delors's Third Commission (1993–1995) and Portfolios

Jacques Delors   President; secretariat-general; monetary
France   matters; Forward Studies Unit; Legal Service;
                              Joint Interpreting and Conference Service;
                              Security Office; Spokesman's Service

Henning Christopherson   Vice-president; economic and financial affairs;
Denmark   monetary matters (in agreement with
                              President Delors); credits and investments;
                              Statistical Office

Manuel Marín   Vice-president; cooperation and development;
Spain   European Community Humanitarian Aid
                              Office

Martin Bangemann   Vice-president; industrial affairs; information
Germany   and telecommunications technology

Sir Leon Brittan   Vice-president; external economic affairs;
United Kingdom   commercial policy

Karel van Miert   Vice-president; competition; personnel and
Belgium   administration policy, translation, and
                              informantics

Antonio Ruberti   Vice-president; science, research and
Italy   development; Joint Research Centre, human
                              resources, education, training, and youth

Abel Matutes   Energy and Euratom Supply Agency; transport
Spain

Peter Schmidhuber   Budgets; financial control; fraud prevention;
Germany   Cohesion Fund: coordination and management

Christiane Scrivener   Customs and indirect taxation; direct taxation;
France   consumer policy

Bruce Millan   Regional policy; relations with the Committee
United Kingdom   of the Regions

Hans van den Broek   External political relations; Common Foreign
The Netherlands   and Security Policy; enlargement negotiations
                              (task force)

João de Deus Pinheiro   Relations with the European Parliament;
Portugal   internal relations with members states with
                              regard to openness, communication, and
                              information; culture and audio-visual; Office
                              for Official Publications

Pádraig Flynn *Ireland*	Social affairs and employment; relations with the Economic and Social Committee; questions linked to immigration, internal, and judicial affairs
René Steichen *Luxembourg*	Agriculture and rural development
Iannis Paleokrassas *Greece*	Environment, nuclear safety, and civil fisheries
Raniero Vanni d'Archirafi *Spain*	Institutional questions; internal market; financial institutions; enterprise policy

[1]Left the Commission in June 1992 to join the Italian government

3. Staff and personnel policy in the Commission

David Spence

Introduction

Despite the brickbats and criticisms levelled at the European Commission, it remains a surprisingly small organisation, especially given the range of tasks and functions for which it is responsible. Nor, despite the public's impression, are its officials particularly highly paid. Yet the myths of 'faceless bureaucrats' or *'technocrats apatrides'*, occupying the fortress building of the Berlaymont (when not out on extended lunches at the taxpayers' expense) persist. The Commission has long been a more open bureaucracy than many at the national level, as Chapter 7 on lobbying suggests. The Commission's headquarters and the majority of its staff may well be in Brussels, but since December 1991, the Berlaymont has been abandoned because of asbestos and the bureaucrats scattered in some dozen or so buildings around a main office, the 'Breydel' building. As one observer has suggested, the shut-up Berlaymont facing the new Council of Ministers building (completed in 1994) symbolises "the Commission's institutional retreat in the face of a more assertive Council" (Dinan 1994, p. 200).

Other Chapters examine the evidence and dispel some of the myths about Commission power and behaviour. This Chapter is concerned with the Commission's current management and staffing practice and the question of its administrative culture. Its theme is the juxtaposition of formal and informal processes in personnel policy and the way in which this is a reflection of an unresolved tension between the aim of supranationalism and the reality of encroaching intergovernmentalism. The Commission's bicephalous nature as a civil service in the classic sense and yet a policy initiator, the motor of integration and guardian of the European interest has, perhaps inevitably, meant that its status is contested. Its recruitment and management procedures underline the originality of Commission officialdom, serving as it does a supranational polity. But they highlight simultaneously the ambiguities arising from the comprehensive and diverse terms of reference of Article 155 (EEC) and, through this, an inherent conflict between supranationalism and intergovernmentalism. There has from the beginning been a tension between the need for a 'European' civil service and the practice of the Member States of seconding or 'parachuting' national officials into it with a resulting exacerbation of divergent administrative cultures. That has inevitably intensified the varying perceptions of Commission officials about the role of their institution. Their seeming inability to promote a clear image to the general public about what their role could, or should be, may be a causal element in the European Union's failure to gain public support.

The origins and ethos of the Commission administration

The internal structure of the European Commission was modelled on the High Authority of the European Coal and Steel Community, set up in 1952. Given the key role played by Jean Monnet, the High Authority's first president, it was no accident that the French civil service served as a model, at least as far as Monnet had been able to manipulate it in setting up the *Commissariat au Plan*. When the European Economic Community and the European Atomic Energy (Euratom) Community were established in 1958, each had its own separate Commission, and these were only merged into one, the European Commission or, more precisely, the Commission of the European Communities, in 1967. Within five years of this merger came the first enlargement to include Denmark, Ireland and the United Kingdom, followed in 1981 with the accession of Greece and in 1986, Spain and Portugal. Each enlargement meant a readjustment of the Commission's staffing and organisation. Each introduced new management styles, adding to the diversity of views on the Commission's role and creating still further management tensions based on diverse cultures and management methods. Enlargements have thus contributed to successive re-definitions of the self-image of the official and the role of the institution itself, and yet the ideal of a neutral European civil service standing above the interests of the Member States has persisted.

To meet this ideal and to ensure from the outset that European officials were independent of national governments, a special category of European civil servant had to be created. Monnet wrote of the growing legend in the 1950s of "un nouveau type d'hommes [qui] était en train de naître dans les institutions de Luxembourg comme dans un laboratoire . . . c'était l'esprit européen qui était le fruit du travail en commun" (Monnet 1976, p. 551). Daniel Strasser captured well the essence of this in terms of staffing and administration when he wrote:

"It was normal to give the status of civil servant to those who are a prefiguration of what will one day be a civil service of a European Confederation. Of course, doing that is more costly and more of a constraint than a system of contracts would be, but it is a modest price paid for the construction of one of the pillars of Europe." (Strasser 1980, p. 429)

The rules of the European public service of the new European Economic Community and Euratom were designed to ensure the quality and independence of Community officials, both on recruitment and in the course of their careers. Given the scope of EU legislation today and the number of domestic policy areas concerned by it, Commission officials' independence of national governments is vital. As the Statutes put it, officials operate "having solely in view the interests of the Communities, without soliciting or accepting instructions from any government authority or organisation or person extraneous to his institution" (European Commission Staff Regulations 1994).

Alternative models were of course possible. The Community could have been staffed by temporary, contractual employees serving for short periods and mainly drawn from national administrations. This was for long a French argument. But after three years of experience in the High Authority, the option was rejected in favour of the creation in July 1956 of a similar civil service to that which existed in most of the Member States. The rationale was the same — the need to guarantee independence in the face of pressures from politicians and interest groups. In the High Authority's case, it was in addition of clear importance to create allegiance to the supranational European Coal and Steel Community and the European ideal itself in order to limit the potential for national influences on policy-making. Yet, the force of the national alternative remained embodied in the special relationship between Member States, 'their' Commissioners and *Cabinets* (Noël 1967; see also Chapter 2) and in the practice of maintaining national balance in terms of staff.

This conscious attempt to endow the Commission with a supranational ideology or mission was confirmed in the establishment of Walter Hallstein's first Commission of the European Economic Community in 1958. Hallstein was unashamed to include "theory, doctrine, utopia, forecasts, planning, futurology (and) vision" in his writing, nor to admit that for him the final stage was "full and complete federation" (Hallstein 1972, pp. 11 and 295). The collective memory of these early halcyon years remains important in the self-perception of Commission staff and contributes strongly to the sense of 'we-ness' and singleness of purpose of officials from the original Six. It can, however, also create barriers to younger generations where the very language used and the symbols of the past, redolent though they may be of early definitions of purpose, and evocative of an identification with building something new, frequently fall flat in the face of the need to deal with continuous technical and administrative details of legislation.

Yet the aim of establishing a European civil service with an ethic and working methods as coherent as those of a national civil service has persisted. The administrative route taken to fulfil the aim followed fairly logically. That a British model with senior levels with high status (Oxbridge; relatively high salaries) and low external visibility was not chosen is not surprising, given both the absence of the British from the ECSC, the role of Monnet and the tasks for which the bureaucracy was designed. The French model included high status (ENA, 'grand corps') but with strong links to party politics, rigid structures but flexible working methods. Not unsurprisingly the Coal and Steel Community was based on the French *Commissariat au Plan*, and Euratom was based on the *Commissariat de l'Energie Atomique*. The German model, more legalistic and rigid, formed the basis of the European Audit Office, which followed the design of the '*Bundesrechnungshof*' (Cassese 1987). The

European Commission of today is a mix of the French and German systems, but French administrative style and practices predominate, notably in the *cabinet* system, the Secretariat General, the personnel structure, interservice groups etc. (Dubouis 1975). The French language also remains the main working language of the Secretariat General. Thus, instructions from the core of the European administration in French imbue the institution with a mentality which looks to French culture and administrative norms as the unstated model of public administration.

The Commission remains a very small organisation given its responsibilities for the development, management and control of Community policies. The total number of permanent Commission officials and temporary staff is under 20,000, with costs representing some 3 per cent of total EU expenditure. The majority of its staff may be concentrated in Brussels and Luxembourg, but the research staff is spread over five centres throughout the Community with smaller numbers of staff attached to some national centres. There are also 20 offices in Member State capitals and the regional centres of Berlin, Munich, Edinburgh, Cardiff, Belfast, Milan, Barcelona and Marseilles. In addition, there are 119 external delegations and sub-offices. It may not be quite as small as envisaged by Monnet, i.e. an élite with a mission, but it is not large and its size is arguably a source of strength, especially when coupled with the close links it maintains with national and regional administrations. Administration is close to the effective players in the Community game and discussion, explanation and lobbying take place within a closely knit web of contacts. But the reverse side of the coin is that combining knowledge of the situation of the individual region, firm or citizen, and managing the enormous amount of contact with the Member States in the administering of policies, inevitably stretches staff resources. It has led inexorably to the creation of various categories of temporary staff and seconded officials in order to ensure the work is done. The established, statutory European civil service is thus flanked by a large number of floating temporary helpers with all the possible dangers and difficulties of the emergence of an almost parallel administrative regime with its own salary scales, promotion prospects and procedures.

Statutory staff

Commission staff are divided into statutory (13,200 in November 1992) and non-statutory or 'external' personnel (4,651 in November 1992 or 26.7 per cent of the total). The total can be divided by function, with more than 10,000 involved with policy and executive tasks, some 3,200 with scientific research, 2,700 with language work and 400 working in the Publications Office. Comparisons with other organizations are difficult, because it is not easy to find any with comparable responsibilities or staff composition. With this caveat, the statistics in Table 1 are nonetheless interesting.

The Commission's policy and executive services are about the same size as the French Ministry of Culture or the Lord Chancellor's Department in the British Civil Service. They are smaller than the total staff of the City of Amsterdam or the Comunidad Autónoma of Madrid (Hay 1989).

Table 1: *Statutory officials — November 1992*

European Commission	13,200
Council of Ministers	2,097
European Parliament	3,310
Economic and Social Committee	500
Court of Justice	693
Court of Auditors	320
Total	20,120

Statutory staff comprise the officials and temporary agents covered by the 'Regulations and Rules applicable to Officials and other Servants of the European Communities' determining their rights and obligations, career structure, pay scales and social security and pension arrangements. The rules were first codified only in 1962 and were based on the experience of the ECSC (Conrad 1992). They are regularly amended by the Council of Ministers on proposals from the Commission and after consideration of the opinion of the European Parliament (European Commission Staff Regulations 1994).

Permanent officials

Permanent officials serve with the Commission until they reach the minimum retirement age of 60 (maximum 65) or 35 years service. They are divided into five categories, each then divided into grades. Category A Staff (about 3,900 officials) comprises staff engaged in administrative and advisory duties which require a university education. They are divided into eight grades, from A6–A8 (Assistant Administrator) to A1 (Director General). A2 officials are either Directors or Principal Advisors and officials of grades A3 (Head of Division) and A5/A4 (Principal Administrator) make up middle management as head of unit, or advisors. In practice, within grades A8 to A4, responsibility has no necessary link with grade, a separation which characterises the Commission in all the categories. It is only at the most senior levels, where management responsibility is specifically allocated, that a link between function and grade is the norm. And even here, the management of a unit may in effect be undertaken by an A5, A4 or A3 official.

Category LA Staff (about 1,600 officials) constitutes the linguistic staff of translators and interpreters, the latter appointed to the Interpretation and Conferences Service common to all institutions of the Union. LA staff must have a university degree and be able to work from at least two languages into their mother tongue. The LA category consists of six grades, from LA8 to LA3.

Category B staff (about 2,700 officials) comprises staff with executive duties, who must have an advanced secondary education, but are not required to have attended university. They are recruited through external and internal competitions open to statutory C staff with experience within their grade. Category B is divided into five grades, from B5 to B1.

Category C staff (about 4,500 officials) are essentially secretarial and clerical staff with secondary education. Like B staff, they are recruited either through external or internal competitions open to category D staff. Category C is divided into five grades, from C5 to C1. Finally, Category D staff (about 800 officials), divided into four grades, is composed of officials with a primary education, mainly employed in manual or service duties.

Recruitment and career structure

Entry of recruits possessing "the highest standard of ability, efficiency and integrity" (European Commission Staff Regulations 1994, Article 27) is by competitive exam, the *concours*, for a limited number of places forming a reserve list from which DGs with a vacant post can trawl. The *concours* system is based on the standard entry route in France to the higher civil service and was the procedure chosen by Monnet in 1953 (Conrad 1992, p. 67). The *concours* involves written and oral tests. It is open only to nationals of Member States from which the Commission recruits yearly some 550 officials — 150 for the A category, 100 for the LA category (i.e. Linguistic A grades), 75 for the B category, 200 for the C category and 20 for the D category. The main competitions are for candidates for the starting grades in the different categories. The 1993 A7/A8 *concours* had 58,000 candidates, of which 1,800 reached the second stage and 600 reached the final oral examination for a total of 200/250 places available on the reserve list. While the Staff regulations provide for competitions to be organised at all levels, the practice of the Commission has always been to limit them to the lowest grade of each category (A8 or A7, B5, C5 and D4). The reason is essentially the attitude of the unions, which have always been hostile to the recruitment of staff at mid-career level, where newcomers compete with existing staff seeking promotion. There are limited exceptions, however; notably at A3 level, where the technical, managerial and political qualifications required for certain jobs justify the organisation of specialised external competitions.

Except for the linguistic test, the *concours* is the same for all candidates and organised on the same day in all the member countries. Thousands apply and this means high administration costs, since the Commission reimburses the travel expenses of candidates, in order to avoid discrimination against those from peripheral member countries or from the regions. High numbers have also led to a much criticised system of elimination tests, based on multiple choice questions of general culture somewhat akin to the board game *Trivial Pursuits*. This provides a lowest common denominator for entry while whittling down to about 2,000 the number of applicants for real consideration. A common criticism is that schools systems vary nationally and *Trivial Pursuits* involves varying cultural criteria. With as many as 58,000 candidates, 12 different nationalities and educational systems to take into account, and with exams to organise in nine languages and in 12 countries, the *concours* are complicated to manage, and inevitably take many months between launch and conclusion. In the past, the cycle has sometimes taken over two years, but new recruitment procedures have now speeded up the process, particularly for the main recruiting competitions to the starting grades of each category. The aim now is to hold competitions in the main sectors of recruitment at regular, pre-announced intervals, and to complete the competitions within 12 months. An improved method of training new recruits has also been introduced.

Although general administrators are needed, lawyers and economists are in particular demand, as are specialist staff from doctors, veterinarians, mineralogists and accountants to nuclear inspectors. For purely administrative tasks, the Commission traditionally favoured competitions for specialists, but lawyers or economists in countries such as the United Kingdom are not particularly attracted to the civil service and are unlikely to be willing to wait after passing the *concours* for years on a "reserve list" to be selected for a post. Since there is also a good deal of evidence suggesting that the UK, with a generalist tradition in the civil service, performs comparatively well in the defence of its interests in EU policy-making (Metcalfe 1987), the Commission was persuaded in 1991 to open competitions for young generalists. For the UK government this was one way of remedying the chronic under-representation of the British much discussed in 1990 (Denman 1990). They had been lobbying for the change for years. An added advantage for the Commission was that increasing the frequency of A8 competitions for generalists was likely to attract more women, as they seem more ready to become expatriates when they are young.

Hierarchy, mobility and career structure

Hierarchy plays an important role in the internal cohesion of the Commission services, though this is one area where national administrative styles make for varied procedures within the Commission services. On the one hand, there are senior managers working on the basis of delegation of responsibility to their staff, using an open flow of information without insistence on a restrictive system of hierarchical management. On the other hand, there are those senior managers who insist on a monopoly of rights to signing letters and other documents (a system well-known in German public and private sector life) and where guarding information is a means of retaining power in a framework where little initiative is delegated to staff lower down the hierarchy. Thus some DGs resemble feudal systems and their most senior staff are often described as the 'barons' of the system. Importantly, however, there is no single agreed management style, as one would expect in a national civil service.

During a career with the Commission, mobility between jobs is normal, though the scope for some very specialised staff to change sectors is limited. In general, staff are encouraged to move between areas of work, at least within a Directorate General and often between them. Indeed, the 1991 'screening' operation suggested extensive redeployment of staff. Movement between categories for B, C and D staff, and beyond A4 for A staff is not the norm, though it does happen. About 20 per cent of the intake into the C and B categories is by internal movement from the categories below, and the share is still significant, if lower, for intake into the A category. Within the A category, all but a small part of A3 staff are now drawn from internal promotion, and a growing share of movement to A2 and A1 also comes from within, although at these levels there is more outside recruitment. Overall, some 12 per cent of A staff move jobs each year. Mobility from LA to A and A to LA also exists, without the need to sit a *concours*, but this is relatively rare because of the different skills or qualifications required. Officials are eligible for promotion after two years in a current grade depending on a combination of experience, age and merit relative to the category and the grade. While experience plays the major role for promotion in the lower categories and grades, merit becomes more important as the grade increases. Thus, it is much easier to be promoted from B5 to B4 or A7 to A6 than from B2 to B1 or A5 to A4. Promotion committees (one for each category) consist of equal numbers of administration and staff representatives. The notable exception is for promotions to A3, where a Consultative Committee for Nominations, composed of a group of Directors General under the chairmanship of the Secretary General, decides. For a number of years the unions have unsuccessfully requested staff representation in this committee, obviously involved in the first level of 'political' appointments discussed below.

Promotion's counterpart, demotion, is practically unheard of. This is partly due to the system of national protection via the *Cabinet* system running through personnel policy in practice. As one official observed "it is theoretically possible (to fire someone) but when I fire someone, I am not firing him, but a nationality, I am not firing a civil servant, but an Italian . . . The only way to get rid of him is to promote him and 'sell' him to someone else" (quoted in Michelmann 1978, p. 489). As to promotion, in order to obtain an interesting post, personal networks and colleagues with influence — usually, but not always of the same nationality — are important. Relying on DG IX or the personnel unit in one's own Directorate General are no guarantee of recognition. Indeed, the extent to which this can demoralise staff was highlighted in a survey carried out by the French opinion pollsters Cegos. In response to a question on how to get ahead at the Commission, employees cited producing results and working hard as the least important. They said the best way to ensure promotion is to have the right connections, followed by seniority, luck, the right nationality, service in a *Cabinet*, the will to succeed, ability, qualifications, knowing when to keep quiet and — last of all — producing results and hard work. In addition, 52 per cent said of their promotion prospects: "It doesn't matter what I do, promotion won't come any faster."

In a letter to Commission officials after the Cegos study was published, David Williamson, the secretary-general, promised changes in the system:

"On promotion and career prospects the result of the survey was not good. Clearly there is some lack of confidence in the present procedures and the way they work. Although many of the fears are in my view not justified, it is nonetheless important that there should be some changes so that real merit should be, and should be seen to be rewarded." (Quoted in *Eurobusiness*, December 1988)

These figures confirm the earlier results of a small survey in the early 1980s. The sample included 150 officials of whom 24 British, 19 Italians, 11 Germans, five Irish, five French, four Belgians, three Danes, two Dutch and one Luxembourger (a total of 74) responded. Though limited in size, the survey showed several of the main points brought out in this Chapter. Officials complained about the lack of mobility, the lack of transparency in selection procedures, lack of adequate personnel management and the problem of *'parachutage'* (Cassese 1987).

Pay

When the Commission was set up, the Member States fixed relatively high salaries in order to attract high-quality staff on a permanent basis from both the private and the public sectors. Indeed, there have often been criticisms of the high rates of pay. However, the differences with national public service salaries and conditions have been reduced over the years, particularly at senior levels. Table 2 gives an international comparison of salaries in the public sector. It is true to say that a Commission official earns roughly 30 per cent more than his equivalent in, say, the French civil service. But the reverse is the case if one takes a French official seconded to a post at the French mission in Brussels where the salary is 30 to 50 per cent higher than that of the Commission official. Such diplomatic staff also receive diplomatic benefits and immunities, not available to Commission staff.

Table 2: *Comparison by grade of the net annual remuneration (in ECUs) of the officials of the European Union, The United Nations and some national civil services**

Equivalent A4		Equivalent B3		Equivalent C3		Equivalent D2	
France	107,769	Denmark	77,951	France	67,221	Denmark	63,470
UK	104,577	UK	75,551	Denmark	63,470	France	51,843
EU	**95,251**	France	74,668	UN	59,251	UN	46,909
UN	87,700	UN	69,104	UK	57,403	UK	46,430
Denmark	85,010	Germany	57,585	Germany	53,246	Germany	41,393
Germany	78,072	**EU**	**54,747**	**EU**	**41,094**	**EU**	**34,784**

At 1st April 1994, 1 ECU = UK £0.775297.

*For official with dependent spouse and two dependent children serving abroad. Does *not* include education allowance or pension payments.

Source: Adapted from European Commission and European Parliament Staff Magazines.

Pay scales for Community officials are decided by the Member States meeting in the Council of Ministers. The rules, known as *'la méthode'*, lay down that pay should be reviewed at least annually, and that levels should be adjusted in accordance with movements in the levels of pay of national public servants. Each official of the same grade and seniority is paid the same, while arrangements are made to ensure that pay has the same purchasing power in different places of work. Each grade is divided into salary steps with advancement every two years. Pay is subject to tax, with rates varying from 10 per cent to 45 per cent. The proceeds are paid directly into the Community budget. Taxation levels are reviewed from time to time and changes in national taxation rates are taken into consideration in calculating salary changes and tax levels for Community staff. There is also a 'crisis levy' — an additional temporary tax, introduced in July 1981, to contribute towards the costs of the (seemingly permanent) 'economic crisis'. This is deducted from salaries at a variable level which for most senior staff is now 5.83 per cent. Allowances are paid for family and housing and all staff receive an expatriate allowance, unless they happen to be working in their own country. The Annex gives current salary figures for all Commission grades.

Staff representation

As the European civil service was originally inspired by the French and German civil services, staff representatives are involved in all aspects of personnel policy and management. Unions thus play an important role in the administrative life of the Commission. However, it has been argued that despite the occasional strike and a formally close relationship between management and personnel representatives, national networking is a more powerful means of redress, as it is for promotion, than the official channels in cases of disciplinary action:

> "the interaction of multinational staffing and cabinet-centred nationality-based internal organisation makes effective disciplinary action difficult. Any such action becomes politicised when the official threatened with punishment takes his case to the *Cabinet* of his nationality to seek backing from powerful compatriots." (Michelmann 1978, p. 488)

Much personnel administration is also a matter of legal interpretation and officials may contest decisions they consider harmful by formal procedures, first within the Commission and, in the final resort, before the Court of First Instance of the European Court of Justice, which decided 30 such cases in 1988 (Hay 1989).

A Central Staff Committee, elected by the staff, is the contact point between the administration and the staff representatives. It appoints staff representatives to a variety of committees, ranging from the management committee of the nursery for staff children, the disciplinary and promotion committees, to selection boards involved in the recruitment competitions. They participate in these committees with a consultative role. If staff representatives disagree with a measure proposed by the administration, the question is then discussed in a meeting between the Director General for Personnel and Administration (DG IX) and staff representatives and, if they continue to disagree, with the Commissioner for Personnel and Administration. There is also a mediator who intercedes between the administration and its officials on working conditions and relations with management. The mediator is supposedly completely independent. Officials seeking advice or pursuing complaints have access in confidence.

Temporary agents (TAs), non-statutory staff and the emergence of a parallel administration

Temporary agents serve under contract with the Commission for a limited period of time and are divided into the same categories and grades as permanent officials. Indeed, the staff statutes apply equally to them. Their conditions of employment are the same, except for the limited period of employment and the fact that, in the A category, they cannot normally be appointed to management functions. In 1994 there were some 520 temporary agents under the operational budget, and about 1,100 employed under the research appropriations. They are divided into four different groups. *Temporary agents on temporary posts* are recruited for specific jobs of a transitory nature. Selection procedures consist of a public call for applications, an evaluation of the candidate's professional experience and an interview with a selection board. *Temporary agents on permanent posts* exist where a permanent post is vacant, there is no internal candidate to fill it and no names are available on a reserve list from a competition. This is a rare occurrence in category A, but is more frequent in the B and C categories. Contracts for these temporary agents are limited to two years, with extension possible for a maximum of one year. *Cabinet Temporary Agents* are recruited from outside the Commission directly by the Commissioner, and serve in his or her private staff for the duration of the mandate. Finally, *temporary agents recruited under the research budget* of the Commission are usually scientific experts recruited on indefinitely renewable five-year contracts.

Internal competitions allow some temporary agents to become established permanent officials, but hitherto while many apply, few are chosen. However, conditions for establishment were relaxed in 1994. The Commission had been under pressure from the unions to integrate a large number of TAs recruited after implementation of the SEA and the so-called 'Delors 1 Package' of 1988 and thus on contracts expiring in 1994. Moreover, budgetary difficulties in 1993 had prevented an increase in personnel to match the expansion in the Commission's responsibilities arising from implementation of the Treaty on European Union. Thus, a more flexible approach to the formal integration of TAs into the permanent staff seemed appropriate. The European Parliament's resolution on the 1994 budget pointed to its readiness to accept the transformation of the relevant temporary posts into permanent ones. The Commission advertised around 100 posts in February 1994 and received 15,000 applications. The intention is now to transfer credits currently used for temporary staff to the general administrative budget in order to finance the establishment of many temporary agents as permanent officials, particularly where temporary personnel had been negotiating policy, representing the Commission outside or supervising EC policy.

The SEA, the single market and the evolution of the situation in Eastern Europe increased the tasks of the Commission considerably, yet few if any provisions were made to increase the human resources necessary to deal with them. As a result, the Commission services were faced with the choice between simply not doing the work, or finding other means to secure the necessary manpower. A device known as the 'mini-budget' arose. It consisted of using part of the Community's operational budget to hire personnel under contract, buy computers, rent office space etc. It thus created quasi-private informal administrations. The budgetary authorities and the Commission's own financial control services turned a blind eye to the practice for some time, despite its highly unorthodox nature; the budgetary procedure reserves administration and personnel expenditure to the central administrative budget. Mini-budgets were condemned by the Court of Auditors in 1990. The Commission subsequently conducted a thorough screening of its services to determine the amount of additional full-time staff needed, if acceptable staff recruitment procedures were to prevail. Following this, it proposed a programme designed to whittle down the number of external personnel and to transfer the sums allocated for external posts to the creation of new permanent posts. The European Parliament also condemned mini-budgets in 1992, arguing that "the 1993 budget must resolve the problem" and recalled its decision to delete the relevant appropriations from the Commission's budget (European Parliament 1992).

The exact number of external personnel was estimated at 4,651 in November 1992 but the real figure was probably substantially higher, as there are many ways in which the services hide recruitment. Apart from the secondment system, most external personnel are 'experts' or 'consultants' under contract with the services (and not with the Commission itself), to perform technically limited tasks. But these frequently turn out to be administrative jobs that would be performed by statutory staff if there were enough of them. It is no secret that in certain areas of the Commission, these 'experts' manage budget lines, commit the Commission in contracts with outside firms or otherwise perform tasks that are undoubtedly of a public service nature. In some instances, this is the result of a genuine shortage of human resources. In others, it has become a convenient way of hiring and firing and introducing a carrot and stick management ethic. The possibility of not having a contract renewed is doubtless an incentive to achievement. The problem in terms of public service ethic is that the system of recruitment of such external personnel is almost totally discretionary, and there is no central control of their qualifications. There is thus much lobbying by would-be recruits. Although the recent creation of a General Inspectorate of Services could provide a sound system of control, it also lacks staff and has little supervisory power over the two main categories of non-statutory staff — auxiliary agents and seconded national officials.

Auxiliary staff are engaged for a period not exceeding one year except in the C category where, in certain cases, they may be employed for a maximum of three years, either to replace an official who is temporarily unable to work, or as a temporary reinforcement. In addition, staff locally recruited in the Commission Delegations in third countries, or in the Commission Offices in the capitals of the Union, form a separate group of 'local agents'.

Seconded national experts are civil servants from Member State administrations and, more rarely, from the private sector, loaned to the Commission for up to three years. They remain paid by their employer, though the Commission covers their living expenses in Brussels. In 1994 they numbered about 600 (compared to about 250 in 1990). This is now considered a maximum unlikely to increase in the coming years. As they are not part of the statutory staff, they have no access to internal competitions and cannot normally be integrated into the statutory staff. The seconded national experts system is primarily conceived as a two-way information system, designed to tighten relations between the Commission and national administrations by allowing civil servants from each side to learn about the other's procedures and administrative culture.

The arrangements are thus one way of ensuring that the Commission is not regarded merely as a collection of 'foreigners' with power to determine the national policy-making agenda. Together with more general attempts at achieving a geographical balance of staff (see below), the Commission has taken seriously the need to ensure that its methods are understood in Member States and that secondees may return to imbue their own administration with an understanding of the purpose and priorities of the Commission. It makes little sense therefore if the system is used as a short cut by national civil servants to join the Commission staff, though a number of them do since nothing prevents them from applying and being recruited on temporary agent posts. It has, in fact, become common practice for such posts to go to deserving national experts.

With subsidiarity and the increasing trend to decentralised management of EU policy, the Commission seems set to develop further its links with national and regional administrations. This partly explains the increase in the number of temporary posts and secondments between 1990 and 1994. Some Commission officials are also sent to Member States for training in political and administrative structures at central and regional levels and in the language of the country. In January 1993 there were 23 Commission officials from 13 DGs on detachment to national or regional administrations in six Member States and two international organisations.

'Piston' *and* 'sousmarins'

Except for seconded national experts, external personnel have no guarantee of employment. They do not benefit from the social and medical coverage of the Commission's statutory staff, they are usually paid less than staff with equivalent qualifications, and they have no protection from the unions or the staff regulations. The duration of their service with the Commission is limited to three years, after which they are not entitled to unemployment benefits as, in the majority of cases, they are self-employed; a situation giving little, if any, social protection under Belgian law. Understandably, many are keen to join the statutory staff but they cannot benefit from waivers of age limits to participate in external competitions and are not allowed to participate in internal competitions. Their only chance for a career in the Commission is to obtain a temporary agent contract. But given the limited number of these and the fierce competition for them, only the very best, or those with the greatest contacts in high places, *piston*, as it is known, are likely to succeed.

Apart from the formal entry method via the *concours*, one informal route to full official status, despite its implications for a *European* civil service, is transit via one or other non-statutory 'atypical contract'. If, for example, an individual, say, a seconded national official, is sought by a Directorate General yet cannot take the normal competition route to official status, e.g. on grounds of age, he or she may be employed on a contract as a consultant, thereafter obtain the status of auxiliary agent, graduate to a full temporary agent contract and thus be eligible for the internal competition for establishment, for which the age requirements are waived. The various stages give the person concerned the epithet *sousmarin* (submarine) in the Commission jargon. The point is that such individuals are from the outset destined to join the statutory staff of the Commission, though avoiding some of the more difficult formal hurdles involved.

Since *sousmarins* avoid the rigours of laborious official recruitment procedures, they are the bugbear of the unions as well as posing a challenge to coherence and efficiency. Some external personnel, such as language teachers for staff, nurses for the staff kindergartens or seconded national experts are legitimate and pose no specific problem. But it has increasingly become impossible for the Commission to carry out its routine tasks without recourse to outside personnel, and the implications are therefore more serious in terms of a European civil service ethic and continuity of efficient management. The unions also make much of the demoralisation resulting from the uncertainty of the duration of outside help, the apparent inability of guaranteeing a proper career structure as a national civil service would, the need for constant training for new recruits and the consequent obstacles to the creation of a longer-term *esprit de corps.* The Commission is not solely responsible for this curious situation. The Council, the Parliament and Member States' governments have preferred limiting the ceiling on official employment to ensuring the Commission is given the means to match their own expectations, though this now seems set to change.

National balance and *'parachutage'*

The diversity of nationalities and professional origins of Commission staff is an area of obvious originality in terms of administrative culture (Willis 1982). Allegiance to the European ideal and a high level of competence were originally the two basic criteria of selection of Commission staff. Even after 40 years, the ideal remains and is an integral part of the Commission official's self-perception. However, while his or her work may be infused with the spirit of independence and neutrality essential both to the self-esteem of the institution and to the maintenance of respect for its policy-making methods and political priorities, there are tensions over the proper balance between resource allocation and power-sharing between the state, region and 'Europe', which can pose problems for officials and the services. National experts, for example, may well retain allegiance to their home administration while seconded to the Commission. This is perhaps also the case of some members of Commissioners' *Cabinets,* whose role involves being a channel of communication between Commissioner and home governments. It may also be the case with those officials who arrive in the Commission by the much abhorred but nevertheless common practice of *parachutage,* the process whereby posts are filled by appointments from outside the regular career structure. Member States may, therefore, whether deliberately or not, effectively undermine any coherent philosophy of loyalty to the supranational Commission. Certainly, the continued existence of national quotas as a criterion for staff recruitment in the Commission services indicates Member States' concern to ensure that their national interests may be expressed, *inter alia,* in the Commission's staffing structure.

Recruitment of national officials, *parachutage* and national balance do not, of course, necessarily mean a loss of independence of the Union's own civil service. The great majority of detached national experts for example seem to find little difficulty in working for the Commission while keeping an allegiance to their home administration. There are, perhaps, national parallels where a Scot or a Bavarian can retain loyalty to his or her regional origins as well as to the Member State. The Commission services are actually content to hire experienced civil servants providing direct access to the national administrations with which they work on a permanent basis. After all, since the Commission's prime role is as initiator of Community policy, it makes sense to ensure that the spread of administrative cultures is such that differing national styles of policy-making and administration are fully taken into account when legislation is drafted. And it also makes sense to start from within the agenda-setting process. So, if nothing else, the system has certainly contributed to the general improvement of the collaboration between national governments and the Commission and mutual comprehension of the national and supranational stakes at issue. But it has also indisputably contributed to a dilution of the idea of a totally independent European civil service — a danger Monnet had pointed to in the early days of the ECSC, when he refused to incorporate some of the best of the many national experts who came to Luxembourg to advise the small corps of officials during the early days: "La tentation était forte de retenir les meilleurs d'entre eux, mais nous eûmes la sagesse de les remettre en train" (Monnet 1976, p. 550).

If avoiding bureaucracy and increasing efficiency is the rationale for the employment of external staff, the different but generally accepted principle of national balance in staffing also clearly affects the careers of officials and produces widespread frustration. Michelmann noted in 1978 the existence of "nationality-based intelligence networks" run by the *Cabinets* with an informal system of "credits" for officials negotiable at promotion time (Michelmann 1978, p. 482). Quotas existed as early as the High Authority (Conrad 1992, p. 68), the aim from the outset (*pace* Monnet) being that Member States had a modicum of certainty that their interests were respected, or at least that their national administrative concerns and methods were recognised. Thus, in a game where the autonomy of the Commission was and is the *sine qua non* of effective performance, it is also part of the very definition of the 'European interest'. Yet, there is no statutory system of nationality quotas in the Commission. The Statutes state that officials are to be recruited "on the widest possible geographical basis amongst the nationals of the Member States" (European Commission Staff Regulations 1994, Article 27), but there are no formal arrangements to ensure balance. The task falls to individual *Cabinets* which keep a data-bank on staff contingents (Michelmann 1978, p. 483). Coombes describes how a gentleman's agreement existed to divide posts between the original six Member States on the basis of proportions to the Community budget (Coombes 1970, p. 141). This meant that for the original Six, the French, Germans and Italians provided 25 per cent and Benelux provided the rest. On enlargement, the UK was to have joined the other three large states and Benelux with 18.4 per cent each, leaving Ireland and Denmark with 4 per cent each. As was the case with the Six, the proportions applied only for the top three grades. There are three possible ways of establishing a fair system of national balance of Commission staff, as Table 3 illustrates. Population figures and the corresponding percentages are an objective, apolitical test. The number of members of the European Parliament and QMV (qualified majority voting) allows for some political factors to be taken into account. There is no formally recognised system aimed at ensuring a fair distribution of posts. Efforts are made to avoid too great a disparity, but as Tables 4a–d show, some considerable imbalance exists.

These tables illustrate several interesting themes. First, the balance between population totals and the number of officials fluctuates over time, with the UK and Belgium contrasting most sharply. The UK is severely under-represented across the board, but particularly in the B, C and D grades, and Belgium is very over-represented in all grades, but particularly in the B, C and D grades. Of the big five only Italy is over-represented. Over-representation of the smaller countries in staffing follows the same principle as that for qualified majority voting in the Council or the attribution of seats

Table 3: *National allocations of Commission staff — potential calculation methods*

	Pop. 1989*	%	Pop. 1992	%	EP seats pre-1994	%	EP seats post-1994**	%	Votes in Council	%	Commission Staff % Total			
											74	80	89	94
Germany	61.7	19.0	80.3	23.3	81	15.6	99	17.5	10	13.2	16.3	14.6	11.0	10.5
Italy	57.5	17.7	56.8	16.4	81	15.6	87	15.3	10	13.2	16.7	17.6	14.7	13.8
United Kingdom	57.2	17.6	57.7	16.7	81	15.6	87	15.3	10	13.2	8.4	9.4	7.7	8.0
France	56.0	17.2	57.2	16.6	81	15.6	87	15.3	10	13.2	14.9	14.0	11.0	11.0
Spain	38.9	12.0	39.1	11.3	60	11.6	64	11.3	8	10.5			8.5	8.7
Netherlands	14.8	4.5	15.1	4.4	25	4.8	31	5.5	5	6.6	6.0	5.7	4.4	4.3
Belgium	9.9	3.0	10.0	2.9	24	4.6	25	4.4	5	6.6	26.2	26.8	26.6	26.6
Greece	10.0	3.1	10.2	3.0	24	4.6	25	4.4	5	6.6			4.3	4.7
Portugal	10.3	3.2	9.8	2.8	24	4.6	25	4.4	5	6.6			3.5	4.1
Denmark	5.1	1.6	5.2	1.5	16	3.1	16	2.8	3	3.9	3.7	3.8	3.1	3.2
Ireland	3.5	1.1	3.5	1.0	15	2.9	15	2.6	3	3.9	1.9	1.9	2.2	2.6
Luxembourg	0.4	0.1	0.4	0.1	6	1.2	6	1.1	2	2.6	5.1	5.2	3.0	2.5
Total	325.3	100.0	345.3	100.0	518	100.0	567	100	76	100.0				100.0

*Figures before German unification.
**Following decision at Edinburgh Council December 1992, seats were increased (largely to take account of German unification).

Source: (Population figures): Eurostat Basic Statistics of the Community, 28th (1991) and 20th (1993) editions.

in the European Parliament. They are over-represented as a matter of course.

Table 4a: *Percentage of 'A' Grade staff by nationality*

	74	80	89	94
UK	14.9	14.5	11.7	11.4
Germany	18.7	19.0	14.9	13.8
France	18.5	20.2	16.5	16.5
Italy	18.2	17.4	13.4	13.1
Spain			10.1	10.5
Netherlands	6.3	6.0	5.4	5.5
Belgium	13.1	13.5	12.1	12.0
Portugal			3.9	4.1
Greece			4.7	5.4
Denmark	3.8	3.0	2.4	2.9
Ireland	3.9	2.9	3.3	3.4
Luxembourg	3.1	2.9	1.6	1.0

Table 4b: *Percentage of 'B' Grade staff by nationality*

	74	80	89	94
UK	7.3	8.4	6.9	6.8
Germany	19.7	16.2	10.5	9.0
France	17.2	16.5	11.4	11.2
Italy	14.0	13.5	11.4	11.2
Spain			9.0	9.1
Netherlands	7.6	7.7	6.4	6.2
Belgium	23.2	27.8	30.0	33.2
Portugal			2.7	2.8
Greece			3.4	2.8
Denmark	2.9	2.5	1.9	2.0
Ireland	1.5	1.2	2.5	2.5
Luxembourg	5.8	5.3	3.4	2.0

The Commission has attempted to achieve balanced representation of the different nationalities among junior officials through the *concours*, but it is also recognised that there is a political need to maintain balance between different nationalities in top management posts. Hence the use of *parachutage*. In the lower grades, factors influencing the choice of candidates relate more obviously to competence, personal networks and the interest of the service. At senior levels, where appointments can be made from outside, career civil servants and their unions keep a watchful eye to ensure that appropriate permanent staff are not overlooked in the Member States' attempts to reserve particular jobs for a given nationality.

Table 4c: *Percentage of 'C' Grade staff by nationality*

	74	80	89	94
UK	3.3	4.9	4.8	5.6
Germany	13.6	11.0	9.3	8.6
France	12.9	11.0	8.1	8.0
Italy	13.8	15.0	14.7	13.4
Spain			5.3	5.4
Netherlands	4.1	3.4	2.5	2.2
Belgium	39.8	39.9	39.0	39.6
Portugal			2.3	3.6
Greece			3.3	3.5
Denmark	2.5	3.2	2.9	2.9
Ireland	1.9	2.1	2.3	2.8
Luxembourg	7.1	8.2	4.4	3.8

Table 4d: *Percentage of 'D' Grade staff by nationality*

	74	80	89	94
UK	1.7	2.4	1.1	1.0
Germany	5.5	4.3	1.6	1.0
France	6.6	3.8	7.0	7.8
Italy	42.7	43.5	34.6	32.8
Spain			3.6	5.4
Netherlands	1.2	1.2	1.4	1.0
Belgium	34.6	35.7	36.7	36.4
Portugal			2.5	3.0
Greece			3.3	4.6
Denmark			0.6	0.7
Ireland			0.2	0.2
Luxembourg	7.2	8.2	6.5	5.3

Sources: 1974: Strasser (1980); 1980: Willis (1982); 1989: DG IX-European Commission; 1994: DG IX-European Commission.

France has often been taken as the model of astute placement of key French officials. Clearly placement can have wider implications than mere recognition of national practices but can also include the promotion as well as defence of national interests (Michelmann 1978; Hesse and Goetz 1992). Willis (1982, p. 8) quotes a House of Lords report on development policy, which found contracts to Member State companies within the framework of the Lomé Convention had gone largely to French companies (33 per cent), with UK companies picking up a mere 11 per cent. One reason for this was seen to be the fact that "the key posts in the upper echelons of the administration in Brussels were staffed predominantly by French nationals". In Germany, realisation of the importance of strategic placements came somewhat later and the UK's worries over imbalance took some 15 years to become acute.

The issue of national quotas became prominent in the UK largely because it has proved consistently unable to ensure adequate representation. In 1990 only 8 per cent of junior (A7) staff were British, while an extrapolation from population figures would justify a 16.7 per cent share. The implications in simple terms of the availability of British officials for promotion to more senior posts are obvious. With a smaller catchment area, the likelihood of a 'fair' British share of the senior jobs without *parachutage* is slight. But 'parachuting' is only usual in the most senior grades of A1, A2 and (less frequently) A3, and there is even a growing trend to promote to these senior posts from within the existing staff. Willis already noted in 1982 that 70 per cent of the two top grades were recruited from within (*ibid.*). It is for this reason that the Cabinet Office makes a concerted effort to boost British access to Commission officialdom through preparation seminars for the entry competition and a 'European Fast Stream' in the domestic civil service, aimed at recruiting 30 British civil servants per year to be groomed for entry to the European civil service (Civil Service Commission 1990).

There are two riders to a simplified attempt at national balance: first, the acknowledged desirability of staff immediately below or above a given senior post being of a different nationality; and, secondly, the pressure from some Member States to retain staff in certain key policy areas. This means brokerage and package deals are part of a round of new appointments made necessary when one or two staff leave or are promoted. It also means that a way has to be found of ensuring a fair tally of posts on a national basis and the consequent resort to periodic national appointments circumventing the statutory recruitment procedures. Hence the system of parachuting in senior staff from outside the ranks of Commission officialdom, and its criticism.

The Court of First Instance of the European Communities (Case T-58/91) was asked to decide whether the Commission's decision to appoint outsiders of the same nationality to fill three posts previously held by a Spaniard, a Frenchman and an Italian was fair to two internal candidates of German and Belgian origin who had applied for the posts. The Court indicated that while Article 27 of the Statutes provides for a wide geographical distribution of posts, there could be no justification for an appointment on nationality grounds alone. Article 27 provides that no post be reserved for a specific nationality, even for grades A1 and A2. Thus, if there is general acceptance that an element of national balance must exist, reserving a post under national quotas and thus eliminating otherwise excellent candidates actually breaks the rules (European Court 1993).

Parachutage is a phenomenon well known in the civil services of states where political appointees become managers in the public service during the life-span of a government. As has been suggested, it takes two forms in the Commission. Parachuting from the 'outside' occurs at senior level (A1 and occasionally A2), when Directors General return to their own countries and are replaced (sometimes as part of an overall shuffle of senior posts) by a new national nominee. In addition, after having served four years, and sometimes more, on the staff of a Commissioner, *Cabinet* members without statutory status in the Commission frequently join the Commission staff at the highest possible grade. There is no particular difficulty for the highest ranking members. The *Chef* and deputy *Chef,* respectively A2 and A3 grade, are often appointed by the Commission to directorial functions. It is more problematic for more junior members, who can be anywhere from A8 to A4, where it is difficult to transfer from temporary agent status into that of a permanent official. It has become common practice to organise special internal competitions to promote the integration of desirable temporary agents into the permanent staff, despite the complaints of the unions about such rigged exams or *concours bidons,* as they are known.

'Internal' parachuting is also frequently used by permanent officials to short-cut the normal promotion procedures, and reach managerial functions. Statutory officials who have served in a *Cabinet* commonly seek appointment on promotion. This is considered normal practice; a reward for serving in a *Cabinet* with a heavy workload, unsocial hours and no weekends. Even the unions accept that there may be a fast stream for particularly competent and hard-working staff. Thus, an official returning to his service after a spell in a *Cabinet* is usually welcomed, whereas someone from outside the regular staff who parachutes into a service (usually at a fairly senior level) after a spell in a *Cabinet* will be welcomed with a degree of cynicism or even reluctance. The practice becomes especially controversial when several career stages are jumped, as was twice the case when an A5 official was promoted to A2 because he had served as *Chef de Cabinet.* It further contributes to the lack of regard for the *Cabinets* by career staff.

Parachuting can occur at any time, but is particularly common in the period preceding the appointment of a new Commission when *Cabinet* staff begin looking for a *point de chute* after their Commissioner departs. Two elements then come to the fore; senior posts may be kept vacant for a long period and new posts created. The resulting number of vacancies forms the basis of a distribution of jobs for the parachutists. One staff association calculated in spring 1994, for example, that the Commission would need at least 30 posts by the end of 1994 to integrate *Cabinet* staff into the services. The reorganisation of DG X (Audiovisual, Information, Communication and Culture) was cited as an example. Initially decided in July 1992 as a result of a management review, the reorganisation was suspended until 1993, when the new Commission took office. After some delay, a further review decided in November 1993 to shuffle a number of heads of unit posts and create two directors' posts. The latter, it was argued, were reserved for two staff with *'piston'* from the Cabinets of President Delors and Commissioner Pinheiro (*Renouveau and Democratie,* 16.3.1994). As one newspaper commented, one of them, a former journalist, had "no degree and would not even qualify to take the recruitment examination, the grapevine says" (*The European 8 —* 14.4.1994). The two candidates were, in fact, appointed.

This is not to say that *parachutage* is without advantages. It does sometimes make sense to take outsiders for senior posts. Experience of *Cabinet* work on the one hand or high management responsibilities in a national administration on the other are of obvious relevance to efficient performance in the higher echelons of the Commission services. Moreover, the practice was established early in the history of the ECSC before the establishment of formalised recruitment procedures. Recruitment was originally a direct responsibility of members of the High Authority themselves, who naturally favoured people and administrative styles they knew and respected. It was perhaps inevitable that on occasion such knowledge was coterminous with political and personal allegiance rather than such principles as recognition of competence and fair play. It is precisely in this respect that the practice creates such ill will amongst staff. Indeed, even the European Parliament confirms this. Here, it has been argued, Parliament:

"has the means and the obligation to redress the injustice caused to the Community's civil servants as a whole by some unfair nominations or promotions and some blatant cases of incompetence. It can and should use the power of inquiry, formally recognised in Article 138c of the Maastricht Treaty to publicly stigmatise any case of contravention or maladministration." (European Parliament 1994)

Finally, achieving a national balance in staffing policy has required more than recruitment competitions and *parachutage* when faced with the further complications of periodic enlargement of the Community. Further adjustment is needed to allow officials from the new Member States to take up posts and with each enlargement — as with the fusion of the executives in July 1967 — some staff have been invited to resign. In particular 'Taking Article 50' (of the staff regulations), as it is colloquially known, involves special arrangements for A1 and A2 officials to take voluntary early retirement. But, in addition, each new enlargement or 'widening' has also coincided with, if not led to, a 'deepening' of the Community, requiring new tasks of the Commission. Just as the Portuguese and Spanish enlargement occurred in conjunction with the SEA, so implementation of the Maastricht Treaty coincided with the negotiations for enlargement of the Union to include Austria, Finland, Norway and Sweden and preparation for a further IGC in 1996. The combined administrative consequences have inevitably been extensive and complex.

Over the three-year period 1986–88, the Commission recruited 1,320 Spanish and Portuguese officials, who were selected as a result of 106 competitions. To make these recruitments possible, about 446 officials chose early retirement, while an extra 939 posts were created (Hay 1989). In 1994 a Task Force for recruitment was created to manage the process by which 1,976 new officials and 455 linguists from the four new Member States were to be recruited over a period likely to extend to three years after their scheduled entry in 1995. The operation goes well beyond the mere recruitment of administrative staff, since it will include the political bargaining brought about by the need to invent four new portfolios for Commissioners, appoint several new Directors General and Directors, while simultaneously organising the retirement of officials thus rendered supernumerary. The process is seemingly non-problematic for the unions, although it demands considerable flexibility and adaptability in the Commission's internal organisation. Meeting such new demands while retaining continuity and stability is no mean feat. There are a number of implications arising from this, together with some general conclusions to be drawn from the foregoing analysis of mixed recruitment procedures and formal versus informal promotion methods.

The question of the mix of statutory Commission staff and staff employed from outside does not only raise the issue of potentially undermining the ethic of a European civil service. The effects of national balance and national influence on recruitment policy and the undermining of career prospects by parachuting senior staff from outside into top jobs also need to be considered. The existence of an important body of external staff is one of the most serious problems of personnel management in the Commission. In some services, particularly those involved in the management of new policies, external staff outnumber permanent officials. This may be less a threat to the independence of the Commission than a sign of a potential lack of control of the Commission over its services. It is certainly a result of a clear shortage of personnel. The distribution of external staff was long based on the availability of funds from the operational budget rather than on the effective needs of the services. In other words, the 'richer' the DG, the more personnel it could afford, regardless of its actual needs. This was a source of conflict with Member States both over the budgetary implications and over the fact that the Commission seemed reluctant to redeploy staff, preferring to increase external staff numbers instead of 'biting the bullet' of internal reform.

Though the policy was changed in 1992, it is still a major source of conflict with the unions, which see the refusal until 1994 to boost the statutory staff numbers and the increase over time in the recruitment of external staff as an undercover attempt to 'privatise' the European civil service and rob it of its *raison d'être*. The increasing number of European agencies created to take on tasks arguably the legitimate province of the Commission is seen as a further illustration of the endeavour to weaken the *esprit de corps* of the statutory staff, especially when recruitment to the new agencies is by local or temporary contract. Indeed, the recommendation by the Commission that statutory C and D posts should be excluded from the permanent staff of the new Community agencies was criticised by the Central Staff Committee as "contrary to correct application of the Statutes, a degradation of the European Civil Service and a threat to the independence, the competence and the personnel of the Institutions" (Staff Committee 1994).

Women in the Commission

The situation of women within the Commission has long been the subject of strong criticism. The college of Commissioners was a male bastion until 1986 when the first two women Commissioners were appointed (Christiane Scrivener from France and Vasso Papandreou from Greece). In the 1993/94 Commission, only one, Christiane Scrivener, remained. While women represent 48 per cent of total Commission staff and, in 1993, figures show that 48 per cent of all recruitment were women, this is due mainly to their heavy representation in the lower grades (see Figures 1 and 2). In 1993 in the A grades, they still numbered only 13.5 per cent compared with 11.3 per cent in 1992 and 6.1 per cent in 1982. Only 3 per cent in the four higher grades are women (*Courrier du Personnel*: 11.2.1993.) There are only five women at A2 level and since the retirement of the long-serving head of interpretation René van Hoof in 1993, one at A1 level, the former Luxembourg Foreign Minister,

COMMISSION OFFICIALS (1.1.94)

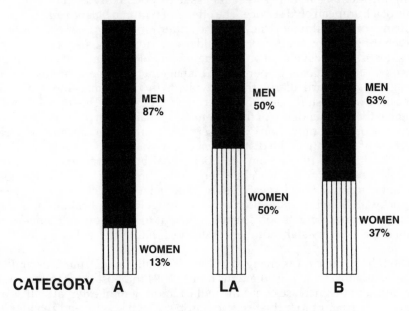

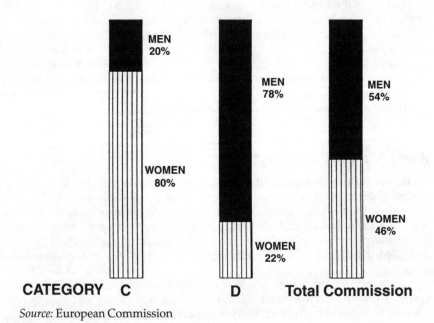

Source: European Commission

Figure 1: *Commission officials 1.1.94*

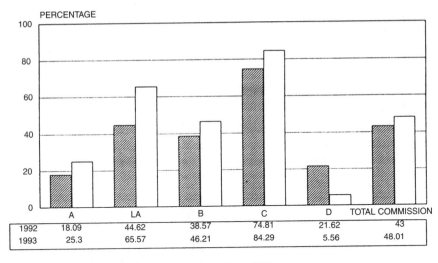

	A	LA	B	C	D	TOTAL COMMISSION
1992	18.09	44.62	38.57	74.81	21.62	43
1993	25.3	65.57	46.21	84.29	5.56	48.01

▨1992 ☐1993

Source: European Commission

Figure 2: *Female recruitment at the Commission*

Colette Flesch. As recruitment for the most senior levels is largely by *parachutage,* Member States' appointment policies rather than the Commission's recruitment procedures may explain the imbalance. But it is not set to change for the others — at least from within — because of the relative absence of women at lower levels of the A grade. However, numbers are growing and so the catchment areas for promotion to higher grades is expanding, but only slowly.

Under-representation of women in the lower grades is the result of women being less successful than men in the Commission recruitment competitions. In the 1992 A8 competitions, for example, women represented 50 per cent of all candidates but only 25 per cent of those successful. Poor results have been attributed by some to the logical reasoning tests (arguably designed to suit male logic) which used to be part of the eliminatory stage of the competitions. But the test has been discontinued without any improvement in the outcome. Nevertheless, the Commission does attempt a fair mix between men and women in all grades by recruiting female candidates in preference to males where the candidates are otherwise equal, encouraging career progression for younger women officials and giving preference to women in promotions from category to category. This involves a pro-active information policy, making women aware of the opportunities and openings available to them and running training programmes to enable them to enter higher categories. The framework for this is currently the second five-year positive action programme, monitored by an equal opportunities unit. While the aims are of necessity long-term, some results for the short term are already apparent.

Trainees

The traineeship scheme started in 1960. By 1994, over 1,000 trainees or *stagiaires* were spending five months working in the Commission every year. *Stagiaires* are university graduates, for the most part from the Member States, but also from more than 50 countries outside the Union. Approximately 13 per cent of those who apply to the *'bureau de stages'* are successful. In the first half of 1994, for example, there were 5,102 applications, while the total number accepted was 613. Table 5 gives an idea of the evolving size of the arrangement.

Traineeships were sometimes a fast route to a job in the Commission, since extensions to the traineeship period or part-time contracts often replaced the formal *stage* period, thus forming a further category of *sousmarins* to those discussed above. The growth in demand for extensions was enormous, but this informal system of recruitment ended in 1993, when extensions were discontinued and a lapse of one year was introduced before temporary contracts could be offered to former *stagiaires* (an exception being made for interpreter *stagiaires* who are trained in-house and who are guaranteed a job provided they pass a series of tests). For the private sector, maintaining close contacts with *stagiaires* or employing them at a later date provides privileged access to information and inside knowledge. *Stages* and *stagiaires* are thus much sought after.

Table 5: *Stagiaires — evolution from 1960 to 1994*

Period	Member States	Others	Total
1960–1972 (EUR 6)	2,369	300	2,669
1973–1980 (EUR 9)	2,737	743	3,480
1981–1985 (EUR 10)	1,933	614	2,547
1986–1990 (EUR 12)	3,053	485	3,538
1991	878	157	1,035
1992	1,008	173	*1,181
1993	980	203	**1,183

* Plus 151 }
** Plus 213 } Officials on special programmes (EFTA, PHARE etc.)

Language

Everything the European Union does, especially its directly applicable legislation, must be accessible to people in the 12 Member States. Commission officials may agree to use French or English in internal meetings, but documents addressed to other European institutions, the Member States, the social partners and the general public are made available in the nine official languages of the Community: Danish, Dutch, English, French, German, Greek, Italian, Portuguese and Spanish. To these nine will soon be added Norwegian, Swedish and Finnish. The principles are outlined in Article 217 of the EC Treaty and in Council Regulation No 1 of 15 April 1958. The fact that EU legislation covers most areas of traditional domestic legislation in Member States makes matters more difficult than in traditional international organisations. EFTA, after all, worked only in English, the 16- member NATO works in English and French, and the 180+ United Nations uses only six (see Table 6).

During the first months of the High Authority, Monnet actually refused to sign decisions in languages he did not understand (Morgan 1992, p. 7). Today, in the internal work of the Commission there is hardly ever recourse to translation or interpretation in all languages, but the fact that most people are working in a language other than their own undoubtedly makes it more difficult to communicate. Meetings take longer and more effort is required to achieve understanding. Outside, the dangers of alienating public opinion are many, as the difficulties encountered with the ratification of the Treaties on European Union in 1992/93 underline. Publications thus need to be available in all EU languages simultaneously. MEPs and others are quick to question the Commission if this rule is not followed.

Table 6: *International institutions and language*

International Organisations	Member States	Languages	Pairs	Number of interpreters
United Nations	180	6	30	18
NATO	16	2	1	6
Council of Europe	32	2	1	6
EFTA	9>6	1	0	0
EU	12	9	72	27
EU	16*	12	132	36
EU	22**	18	306	54

*Assumes four further members — Finland, Sweden, Norway, Austria
**Assumes six further members — Cyprus, Czech Republic, Hungary, Malta, Poland, Turkey

As a result, the Commission has a large language staff. With more than 400 interpreters and 1,200 translators, nearly 30 per cent of university graduates employed by the Commission are directly engaged in language work. In addition, the Commission's language services have a large support staff — 650 clerical staff typing the different language versions of each document and providing technical support for meetings. In fact, this total of 2,250 staff seriously underestimates the number of those engaged on language work because many other officials undertake some translation and typing of different language versions of texts as part of their routine tasks. A rough estimate is that at least another 500 could be added to this figure, bringing total staff involved in the language area to at least 2,700 (Hay 1989) plus an average of 250 freelance interpreters per day.

The translation service of the Commission is the largest in the world. It not only translates texts from their original language into eight (soon 11) languages but also ensures that the end result is as if it were the original text. Legislation in this area is not without difficulty, as a report by the Commission in 1993 showed (European Commission 1993). The number of cases before the European Court concerning different interpretations of Community law in Member States because of linguistic differences in texts shows the importance (and difficulty) of accuracy (Braselmann 1992; Usher 1992). Indeed, the Commission itself was sued by an official invoking the absence of a Greek version of the staff regulations to justify his action. The Court held that since all Commission staff were required to know another language and since a French version was available, the argument did not hold (Case 276/85 Kladakis v. Commission (1987) ECR 495).

Interpretation is equally as important. The Commission's Joint Interpretation and Conference Service provides interpreters at all meetings attended by representatives of Member State governments or specialist interest groups and at many other meetings each week. Table 7 gives details of the evolution over time. They are responsible for meetings both of the Commission and of Commission bodies (committees, etc.) involving people from Member States, but also of the other Brussels and Luxembourg-based European institutions (Council of Ministers, Economic and Social Committee, Committee of the Regions and the European Investment Bank).

Table 7: *Interpretation and Community meetings*

	Meetings	Interpreter days	of which freelance
1959	2,081	4,438	36.9%
1965	3,260	17,785	29.3%
1970	5,516	29,551	28.0%
1980	8,423	75,472	29.1%
1989	10,270	109,279	35.3%
1991	9,601	110,237	41.5%
1993	10,558	121,122	39.5%

At meetings of the Commission itself and for some Council working groups French and English tend to dominate in practice, even if interpretation is provided from and into other languages. For example, out of 18 Commission meetings with interpretation each day, 14 manage with fewer than six languages. In the Council, however, eight out of 12 meetings are provided with interpretation covering more than six languages. Those able to use their native language — the French, the British, the Irish and the French-speaking Belgians and Luxembourgers — are at a clear advantage. The fear of institutionalising this advantage was one of the reasons for Gaston Thorn's failure when Commission President to formalise the principle of French and English as the two official working languages (Hemblenne 1992). French has long been the norm for intra-Commission business, but whether it will remain the *lingua franca* of the Commission is beginning to be subject to doubt. While there may be no concerted effort to establish the dominance of English, there has been an increasing frequency of intra- and inter-service meetings in English since as early as 1974 (Michelmann 1978, p. 490). The tradition of using French for meetings has clearly been somewhat eroded after over 20 years of British and Irish membership and the process is likely to be encouraged by the addition of the Nordic states. There has been pressure to use German more frequently, but though it is the most widely spoken first language in the European Union, it does not rank high as a second language, which is the obvious criterion for *lingua franca* status.

The total cost of the language services of all Community institutions is 2 per cent of the total Community budget and about a third of the total budget for administration. The Commission accounts for a quarter of these costs (Brackeniers 1993). This may seem high, but with 12 Member States and nine languages, there are 72 different possible pairs of official languages. After the 1995 EFTA enlargement, assuming all four candidates enter, there will be 132. Beyond this phase of enlargement lies Central and Eastern Europe and the Mediterranean countries of Turkey, Cyprus and Malta. The European Parliament's view is that "with the increase in the number of official languages in the European Union, agreement must be reached restricting the number of working languages for internal use, in line with the varying requirements of each institution" (European Parliament 1993).

Those in a situation where they do not share a working language with their staff or superiors are clearly at a distinct disadvantage. As for situations where interpreting is needed, one solution to the resulting problems and costs might be to create a system where national delegates could *speak* their own language, but only expect to *receive interpretation* in one of two or three 'core languages'. This so-called asymmetric system, tailored to the real rather than political needs of the delegates at each individual meeting, has been applied by the Commission with mixed success since 1985, though the Germans and the Spanish have never accepted it.

Conclusion: a European Civil Service?

Jacques Delors has said that a Commission official has six professions (Hay 1989):

1. to innovate, as the needs of the Community change;
2. to be a law maker, preparing the legal texts needed for Community decisions;
3. to manage the growing number of Community policies;
4. to control respect for Community decisions at all levels;
5. to negotiate constantly with all the different actors in the Community process;
6. to be a diplomat in order to be successful in the five other professions.

This is a demanding list of accomplishments which, added to the mix of policy styles and management methods in the Commission, indicates the complexity of its day-to-day work. The basic assumption is that the

Community needs a permanent public service made up of highly qualified officials who spend their career in its service and identify closely with its goals. In a national framework there is more or less agreement about what the 'national interest' might signify and a general consensus on the role of the civil service in its achievement. But in the affairs of the Union, the notion of a 'European interest' is constantly contested. Governments, the Commissioners themselves and public opinion are divided on the essential question of whether the European interest is best served with the Commission as a key institutional player, or whether the Commission's role should be closer to that of a national civil service. In practice, as Chapters 7 and 8 make clear, the Commission is at once a broker of interests, a source of political dynamism and an administration in the service of the Council of Ministers and the Member States. In practice these roles have become inseparable and the debate about reform of the Commission largely concerns the resolution of the tension between them.

The problem is that the Commission was set up, as Chapter 1 outlines, to perform a political function. It thus contributes publicly to the definition of its own tasks and enjoys a political independence allowing it to provide its own delineation of the 'European interest'. This is no arbitrary power; it is a power vested in the Commission by Article 155 (EEC), which states *inter alia* that the Commission should "formulate recommendations or deliver opinions on matters dealt with in this Treaty, if it expressly so provides or if the Commission considers it necessary".

One such opinion, expressed by Commission President Delors in 1988, is that the Commission is the "amorce d'un gouvernement européen" (*Eurobarometer*, May 1994). This may be disputed, but the Commission has certainly achieved a profile quite unlike a national civil service and this affects both its image outside and its administrative culture within. For officials working in the Commission, the 'European idea' is the abstract political goal which justifies their commitment, but this very commitment is open-ended and subject to constant questioning and revision. And the role of the European civil service undergoes constant and vigilant re-definition at the same time. The fundamental ambiguity in the Commission's role, as bureaucracy and as political power broker, is reflected in the self-perception of those who work in it. In terms of their relations with the outside world and their status within the Commission itself, DGs rise and fall in importance in line with the budget they are able to command (DG XVI, DG VI), the high political nature of their responsibilities (DG I and DG IA) and the respect enjoyed by their Commissioner. Senior officials' attempts to link this internal, bureaucratic power to the enhancement and politicisation of their own service's status indicate the importance of the stakes. They jostle for power in the attempt to ensure that their DG coordinates policy and to construct a privileged access to information so that it becomes a power base enabling their DG to lead in the articulation of the Union's goals. This search for bureaucratic power is politicised by the tensions analysed above between national and *ad hominem* criteria in staff management and the criteria of efficient public service management. This Chapter has pointed to key elements in this regard; the potential for conflicting national clusters of staff; the tensions arising from the requirement for national balance and its corollary — the need to deny the existence of national quotas.

But all this takes place in a vacuum of which the general public is unaware. It is not surprising, therefore, if media coverage of and public support for the Commission is low, yet scathing when it does occur. A traditional national civil service is linked more closely to the public and certainly held accountable for what it does or does not do for the public, as Chapter 1 underlines. The Commission appears on the national horizon only when its President causes controversy (by visiting the British Trade Union Conference or expressing a view about the outcome of the Danish referendum), or when a newspaper publishes an article critical of EU policy or when a national politician attributes blame to the Commission rather than to the Council. Small wonder that Commission officials are little understood and little liked.

The administration itself is, therefore, at once part of the national political power stakes and those between Commissioners and Directors General, with the Commission's bicephalous status increasingly a source of stress as the Union itself evolves, as its competence increases and as its political profile is enhanced. A continuing theme in terms of its administrative culture is a dialectic between two traditions. On the one hand are the centripetal forces of traditional French administrative methods, with senior management politicised and closely linked to the party in power and information retained as a constituent element of a bureaucratic and political power base. On the other hand is the tradition of human resource management common in the Anglo-Saxon tradition, typified by civil service neutrality, the formal absence of nepotism, a high degree of delegation and the principle of sharing information with colleagues. Whether the two can be resolved in a synthesis containing the positive features of both is a moot point, given three potential problems now looming.

The first issue is an emerging divergence between the innovating idealism of the founding generation of administrators who identified their role almost as missionary, and the pragmatism of a new generation of officials for whom the existence of the European Community has been a fact throughout their adult life. Some officials are no longer in the Commission for the big ideas of the previous generation, but for more sober career-oriented reasons. Significantly, as we have seen, as the areas of Community competence have expanded, the Commission has been forced to employ increasing numbers of national civil servants on a temporary basis, simply in order to get the work done. This contributes to an identity crisis in the European civil service, as the staff associations' literature makes evident. The ideology of the newcomers and the outsiders is rarely perceived as so integrationist as that of the permanent staff. Indeed, the prospects for more federalising integration in a European Union enlarged to include the former EFTA states are questionable, given the likely size of the 'no' vote in their referendums and the likely attitudes of the arriving staff. In the debate on the evolving role of the Commission in the run-up to the inter-governmental conference of 1996, a significant feature is thus the fact that it is still a relatively young bureaucracy subject to changes in its power, composition, influence and role and apparently unable to achieve a harmony of views within its own ranks on the criteria of the ideal-type of European administration. It is ripe for change and its role is in need of re-definition.

The second emerging issue results from the dilemmas posed by the first. There is a need for a decision on the deontology of the European civil service itself. Among the various rites of passage into the upper reaches of European officialdom, the ability to come into the system from outside causes the most concern to career officials. Committed to the European ideal and to the defence of an independent European civil service, they see in the flexible recruitment procedures of the Commission the risk of dilution of the ideal through the addition of rival, national ideologies. While the ethic of the European public service must be impartiality in regard to outside interests, it does not stretch the imagination too far to see that a management system based on personal networking, political influence and *parachutage* may bring less than objective criteria into the recruitment and promotion process and instil cynicism and alienation where idealism was a driving force of staff culture. After all, if capability and ambition have little influence in terms of promotion, it is not surprising that those who do not succeed in using the system to their personal advantage become disabused. Indeed, their discontent may become the subject of general concern. The IGC of 1996 will doubtless consider such factors in considering the reform of the Commission.

Finally, some implications for the role of administration in further European integration emerge from the foregoing analysis. The Commission has clearly been successful in becoming the focus of a form of 'internationalised pluralism' as it draws to its constituency pressure and interest groups and the unbounded concern of national governments and administrations. By doing so, the Commission has created and captured a whole new level of pluralist politics in Western Europe and appears in a para-governmental light. Yet, while such factors are an undoubted impetus to further integration, the continued existence of parallel administrative methods to the official procedures is disconcerting. There are thus opposing potentially disintegrative trends; national quotas and balance, *parachutage, sousmarins, Cabinets, piston,* seconded national experts, posts reserved for certain nationalities, etc. are all signs of disintegrative seeds lurking in the fruit of apparent integration.

The Commission thus hovers on the brink of a re-definition that will come largely from outside. The Council, the European Parliament and the parliaments of the Member States may require the Commission to adapt to the increasing intergovernmentalism implied by the triumph of the three-pillar model produced by Maastricht. If an alternative, federal, model is chosen, the Commission could evolve towards a more powerful, political role. For its administration the challenge is acute.

References

Bangemann, M. (1992) quoted in 'La Commission refuse d'être le bouc émissaire', in *La Libre Belgique,* 24.9.1992.

Brackeniers, E. (1993) 'Europa bleibt mehrsprachig', in *EG-Informationen,* Bonn: the European Commission.

Braselmann, P. (1992) 'Ubernationales Recht und Mehrsprachigkeit: Linguistische Uberlegungen zu Sprachproblemen in EuGH-Urteilen', in *Europarecht* 27/01, pp. 55–74.

Cassese, S. (1987) *The European Administration,* Maastricht: EIPA.

Civil Service Commission, 'The European Fast-stream', a regularly updated brochure.
Conrad, Y. (1992) 'La Communauté Européenne du Charbon et de l'Acier et la situation de ses agents. Du régime contractuel au régime statutaire (1952–1958),' in Heyen, E.V. and Wright, V. (q.v.).
Coombes, D. (1970) Politics and Bureaucracy in the EEC, London: Allen and Unwin.
Courrier du Personnel of the Commission.
Denman, R. (1990) 'There are not enough Sir Humphreys in Europe', in The Independent, 6 March 1990.
Dinan, D. (1994) Ever Closer Union, London: Macmillan.
Dubouis, L. (1975) 'L'influence française sur la fonction publique communautaire' in La France et les Communautés Européennes, Paris.
Economist (1990) 'The British Problem', 7 April 1990.
Economist (1992) 'Why Brussels Sprouts', December 26 1992–January 8 1993.
Eurobarometer (May 1994).
Eurobusiness (December 1988).
European Commission (1991) Twenty-fifth General Report, Luxembourg: EC Commission.
European Commission (1993) 'Communication from the Commission to the Council and the European Parliament Concerning Language Use in the Information of Consumers in the Community', COM (93) 456.
European Commission 1994 Staff Regulations.
European Court, Decision of the Court of First Instance 3 March 1993 in Case T – 58/91.
European Parliament 1992: Resolution A3-0124/92 voted on 13 May 1992. PE 161.068.
European Parliament 1993: Resolution on the Structure and Strategy for the EU with Regard to its Enlargement and the Creation of a Europe-wide Order 20/1/93 OJ C42 15/2/1993 p. 124.
European Parliament 1994: Report of Committee on Institutional Affairs on the Independence of Members of Community Institutions PE 201.997/fin 28 Jan. 1994.
Hallstein, W. (1972) Europe in the Making, London: Allen and Unwin.
Hay, R. (1989) The European Commission and the Administration of the Community, Luxembourg: OPOCE.
Hemblenne, B. (1992) 'Les problèmes du siège et du régime linguistique des Communautés européennes', in Heyen and Wright (op. cit.).
Hesse, J. and Goetz, K. (1992) 'Early Administrative Adjustment to the European Communities: the Case of the Federal Republic of Germany', in Heyen and Wright (eds.) (q.v.)
Heyen, E. V. and Wright, V. (1992) Early European Community Administration, Baden-Baden: Nomos.
Metcalfe, L. (1987) 'Comparing Policy Coordination Systems: Do the Differences Matter?', unpublished paper at the Vth Erenstein Colloquium on Action or Reaction? The Role of the National Administrations in European Policy-Making 30–31 Oct 1987, Kerrade: the Netherlands.
Michelmann, H. (1978) 'Multinational Staffing and Organisational Functioning in the Commission of the EEC', International Affairs, Spring 1978, Vol. 32 No. 2.
Monnet, J. (1976) Mémoires, Paris: Fayard (Livre de Poche edition).
Morgan, R. (1992) 'Jean Monnet and the ECSC Administration' in Heyen, E.V. and Wright, V. (eds.) (q.v.)
Noël E. (1967) 'The Committee of Permanent Representatives' in Journal of Common Market Studies, Vol. V, 1967, No. 3.
The Observer, 2 December 1990, 'On a Fast Track to Brussels'.
Official Journal of the European Communities (L 328) December 1993: Council Regulations (Eurotom, ECSC, EC) No. 3608/93 of 20 December 1993 adjusting, with effect from 1 July 1993, the remuneration and pensions of officials and other servants of the European Communities and the weightings applied thereto.

Staff Committee 1994 Resolution of 22 April 1994 (Com/pers/IX/0651/94/F).

Strasser, D. (1980) *Les Finances de l'Europe*, Paris: Nathan Labor.

Usher, J. (1992) 'General Course on the European Community: the continuing development of law and institutions', in *Collected Courses of the Academy of European Law Vol. 2*, Book 1, Kluwer, p. 371.

Willis, V. (1982) *Britons in Brussels: Officials in the European Commission and the Council Secretariat*, London: PSI.

ANNEX

COUNCIL REGULATION (EURATOM, ECSC, EC)
No 3608/93
of 20 December 1993
adjusting, with effect from 1 July 1993, the remuneration and pensions of officials and other servants of the European Communities and the weightings applied thereto

THE COUNCIL OF THE EUROPEAN UNION,

Having regard to the Treaty establishing a Single Council and a Single Commission of the European Communities,

Having regard to the Protocol on the Privileges and Immunities of the European Communities, and in particular Article 13 thereof,

Having regard to the Staff Regulations of Officials and the Conditions of Employment of Other Servants of the European Communities laid down by Regulation (EEC, Euratom, ECSC) No. 259/68 ([1]), as last amended by Regulation (EEC, Euratom, ECSC) No. 3947/92 ([2]) and in particular Article 63, 64, 65, 65a and 82 of the Staff Regulations, Annex XI to the Staff Regulations, and the first paragraph of Article 20 and Article 64 of the Conditions of Employment,

Having regard to the proposal from the Commission,

Whereas a review of the remuneration of officials and other servants carried out on the basis of a report by the Commission has shown that the remuneration and pensions of officials and other servants of the Communities should be adjusted under the 1993 annual review,

HAS ADOPTED THIS REGULATION:

Article 1

With effect from 1 July 1993:
(a)   the table of basic monthly salaries in Article 66 of the Staff Regulations shall be replaced by the following:

Grade	Step							
	1	2	3	4	5	6	7	8
A1	412 056	433 946	455 836	477 726	499 616	512 596		
A2	365 667	386 555	407 443	428 331	449 219	470 107		
A3/LA 3	302 840	321 110	339 380	357 650	375 920	394 190	412 460	430 730
A4/LA 4	254 416	268 677	282 938	297 199	311 460	325 721	339 982	354 243
A5/LA 5	209 757	222 183	234 609	247 035	259 461	271 887	284 313	296 739
A6/LA 6	181 267	191 157	201 047	210 937	220 827	230 717	240 607	250 497
A7/LA 7	156 033	163 797	171 561	179 325	187 089	194 853		
A8/LA 8	137 999	143 565						
B1	181 267	191 157	201 047	210 937	220 827	230 717	240 607	250 497
B2	157 053	164 416	171 779	179 142	186 505	193 868	201 231	208 594
B3	131 734	137 857	143 980	150 103	156 226	162 349	168 472	174 595
B4	113 941	119 250	124 559	129 868	135 177	140 486	145 795	151 104
B5	101 847	106 144	110 441	114 738				
C1	116 217	120 902	125 587	130 272	134 957	139 642	144 327	149 012
C2	101 078	105 374	109 670	113 966	118 262	122 558	126 854	131 150
C3	94 293	97 972	101 651	105 330	109 009	112 688	116 367	120 046
C4	85 196	88 648	92 100	95 552	99 004	102 456	105 908	109 360
C5	78 560	81 779	84 998	88 217				
D1	88 780	92 662	96 544	100 426	104 308	108 190	112 072	115 954
D2	80 949	84 397	87 845	91 293	94 741	98 189	101 637	105 085
D3	75 344	78 569	81 794	85 019	88 244	91 469	94 694	97 919
D4	71 041	73 955	76 869	79 783				

[1] OJ No. L 56, 4.3.1968, p. 1.
[2] OJ No. L 404, 31.12.1992, p. 1

Note: The above monthly sums are in Belgian Francs. Exchange rate on 1 May 1994: £1 = BF51.64. Thus, a Director (A2) in mid-career (step 4) would earn £8,295 (monthly) while starting salary at A8 grade would be £2,672 (monthly).

4. Structure, functions and procedures in the Commission

David Spence

Introduction

Throughout this book reference is made to Directorates General (DGs), to the multiple functions of the Commission and to decision-making procedures. This Chapter provides both a general description of the Commission's structure and working methods and an insight into the daily workings of the Commission Services. The first section deals with the Directorates General, the Services and their internal structure, the second with the Secretariat General, decision-making and coordination. This leads to some conclusions on some 'parallel' administrative methods which actually make the Commission work.

The Directorates General and the Services

As its current Secretary General has put it, the Commission is "basically a structure of mini-Ministries called Directorates General" (Williamson 1991). But, one of the prime problems in terms of Commission efficiency is that the departments or 'Services', as they are known, are not defined in the same way as national ministries, reporting to one minister. As the examples discussed below illustrate, portfolios of Commissioners include several Services and vary from one Commission to the other. This makes for a lack of continuity and, given the short history of the Commission, a certain sense of impermanence resulting from the changing structures and status of some Services. Such changes result from the expansion of Community competence and the concomitant increase in the number of Services over time. But the changes have simultaneously led to disruption in hierarchical patterns, as individual Services change Commissioner and portfolios are created to match the ambitions of new Commission presidents and national government pressures. When to these trends are added the staff problems described in

Chapter 3, it will be readily understood that the creation of a European civil service and of an efficient management system has been fraught with difficulties.

Relations between Commissioners and their Services

Commissioners are customarily of a different nationality from their Directors General, who are usually of a nationality in turn different from their assistant and their directors. The purpose, clearly, is to ensure a wide spread of nationalities in senior positions and the avoidance of nationality clusters. The latter could lead to charges of complicity in the defence of one national interest (Willis 1983, p. 8). A more generous view would be that such clusters would prevent the expression of other national administrative styles and viewpoints in the articulation of Commission policy. There are, however, some exceptions to the rule. Thus, in the Delors III Commission, the Belgian Commissioner, Karel Van Miert, whose responsibilities included personnel and administration, had a Belgian Director General, Frans de Koster. While the criticism may be unfounded that this Belgian duo avoided discussions and official reviews of national balance in staffing because of the relative advantage of Belgian nationals, particularly in the B grades, the existence of the criticism itself underlines the public relations importance of maintaining balance in the upper echelons.

It is not unknown for Directors General to be required to leave the service after the appointment of a new Commissioner, usually for reasons of incompatibility. Disagreement over policy and an inability to communicate satisfactorily in a common language was reputed to be the reason for the departure of a German Director General from DG VIII (Development) after the appointment in 1993 of the Spanish Commissioner Manuel Marin. The resignation of the Director General for Agriculture and his replacement on the appointment of Commissioner Andriessen in 1985 is a similar case. The staff regulations allow for this in Article 50, which states "An official holding a post in Grades AI or A2 may be retired in the interests of the Service by decision of the appointing authority". Thus, it may be made clear to a senior official that there is no suitable employment available for him and that the "interests of the Service" require his retirement. The technique is also used when posts are required after enlargements. Since the financial consequences of the measure are quite advantageous, it has also been known for senior staff to seek, or at least hope for, Article 50 to apply to themselves.

The political interest in periodic restructuring operations is worth underlining. From a Member State's point of view, reshuffles of Commissioners and of Director Generals need to be closely supervised so that national interests are defended. But politics is not the whole story. Over time, an overall structure has emerged where the 'vertical' DGs with responsibility for a given policy in terms both of legislative initiative and of subsequent management have created fiefdoms and management structures of a typically bureaucratic nature. It is not surprising that these DGs resist the necessary coordination of policy and collaboration with rival/partner DGs in specific areas and form a bulwark against root and branch reform.

Structures and roles of the Services

Each Commissioner is then responsible for several Services with 'vertical' responsibilities, of which the Directorates General are formally and permanently constituted, while other 'Services' are often forerunners of full DGs. Some, such as the Legal Service, the Secretariat General and the Spokesman's Service have 'horizontal' responsibilities and, though equivalent to DGs, are not known as Directorates General. In addition there are various 'task forces'. Some of these, for example enlargement task forces, are by their very nature transitory. They might be expected to disappear when their negotiating role is over. Yet, enlargement task forces are put under the direct authority of a Commissioner, figure in the official Commission organigramme and have traditionally formed the basis of new directorates charged with the next enlargement wave. The enlargement task force dealing with British, Irish and Danish membership in 1973 was subsequently converted into Directorate (H) within DG I, and made responsible, under Commissioner Natali, for the enlargement negotiations with Greece and then Spain and Portugal. The Enlargement Task Force (TFE) in the Delors III Commission is the latest example. The TFE was under the direct authority of the Commissioner for External Political Relations, Hans van den Broek. The Head of the Task Force, the Dane Steffen Smidt, enjoyed Director General status during the negotiations, which lasted one year from March 1993 to March 1994. The important feature here is the relative independence of such 'horizontal' teams in the 'vertical' structure of the DGs and the fact that they report directly to a Commissioner as opposed to a Director General in the typical hierarchy of a Directorate General. An exception to this model was the Task Force for German Unification (TFGU), constituted under the chairmanship of the Deputy Secretary General, the Dutchman Carlo Trojan. The TFGU never entered the organigramme, lasted a mere seven months and resembled an *ad hoc* inter-service group rather than a fully constituted task force with offices, secretaries and seconded staff.

Other Task Forces, while enjoying an equivalent status to a DG, prefigure later establishment as a full DG, such as those in the early 1980s dealing with information and telecommunications technology, which reported directly to Commissioner Narjes, or the Task Force for Small and Medium Enterprises, which later became DG XXIII. Whether such transformations are planned or simply emerge, given the factors discussed below, is a moot point. One task force, 'coordination of structural funds', did become a DG, but its role was short-lived, since DG XXII disappeared in the Delors III Commission. Significantly, it was, by definition, a 'horizontal' DG, rather than the longer-lived vertical DGs which were subject to its coordinating ambition.

There are, essentially, three key elements in the *raison d'être* of a Directorate General; administrative logic and the politics of the College and the Member States. Administrative logic might be thought to be the prime feature. One would expect the expansion of Community competence described in Chapter I to lead to a concomitant and parallel expansion of DGs. This is partly the case, as the example of environmental affairs demonstrates (Berlin 1987). But in the area of consumer affairs, a full DG has not yet replaced the Service despite considerable legislation in the field. Given the expansion of the Commission to 21 members after the enlargement to include Austria, Finland,

Norway and Sweden, it is conceivable that this 'Service' might become a full DG, as portfolios for four new Commissioners are created. Clearly a second major reason for the creation of new DGs is the need for Commissioners to have a structure at their command. How much such factors played a role in the separation of fisheries (now DG XIV) and the harmonisation of food production standards (until 1993 DG III and since then DG XV) from DG VI (Agriculture) in 1977 would be interesting to research. Likewise, the division in 1967 of the former DG IX from purely 'administration' into three separate DGs, DG XIX Budgets, DG XX Financial Control and DG IX Personnel and Administration may make operational sense, yet it seems likely that finding posts for the increase in numbers of Commissioners after the merger of the institutions in 1967 may have played some part.

A factor in the ability of DGs to survive intact may well be Member States' wish to see a sector of political interest maintained and their own national remaining in charge. This is not the place to repeat the exhaustive evaluation of the many structural changes since the Commission's inception undertaken by Berlin (ibid.). Suffice to say that it seems clear that most restructuring operations take place when new Commissions take office (ibid., p. 54), rather than as a result of perceived management need. The question of whether the 'screening' of 1991 was a response to an internally perceived need to restructure and enhance efficiency or whether pressure from outside the Commission was the catalyst is relevant here. Criticism had been rife, in particular from the Court of Auditors and some Member States (particularly the net contributors to the Community budget) owing to the apparently large numbers of under-employed staff in the Commission, the clear lack of staff in key areas of emerging policy responsibility, the inability hitherto of the Commission to decide a rational redeployment policy and the large numbers of external staff employed on a range of temporary contracts in order to cope with the resulting staff shortfall in key areas. The Economist epitomised the criticism, claiming:

"Sloppy management means that the Commission cannot ensure that the best people are used where they are most needed. Some departments (directorates general or 'DGs' in Euro-speak) are overworked, while others take it easy. Officials in charge of external relations, agriculture and some bits of competition policy have too much to do. Those at fisheries, information and administration have time to twiddle their thumbs." (Economist 1990)

Senior management structure and hierarchy in the Directorates General

Each DG, headed by a Director General, is divided into directorates, headed by directors reporting to the Director General or, as an intermediary in the larger DGs, a Deputy Director General, whose role is to coordinate, mediate and filter demands on the Director General himself. In the Delors II Commission, in DG III (Internal Market and Industry), for example, the Italian Ricardo Perissisch was Director General, with the German Schaub and Briton Mogg as Deputies. In the Delors III Commission, DGI (External

Economic Relations) had a German Director General, four Deputy Directors General of differing nationalities and a Chief Advisor of Director General grade. Such chief advisors (conseiller principal) usually have responsibility for a precisely determined area of policy with quasi-independent status within the DG. In the case of DG I, during the Delors III Commission the Briton Alan Mayhew supervised relations with the newly independent states of the former Soviet Union, relations with the countries of Central and Eastern Europe and the trade and aid programmes in these areas.

Each directorate is composed of several divisions, or units, headed by an A3, though since David Williamson succeeded in achieving it in the 1980s, staff of A grades 4 and 5 may also head up such units. Each DG varies, of course, in size. DG X (Audiovisual Media, Information, Communication and Culture) has no Deputy Directors General and functioned with only two directors until May 1994, when a reorganisation created two new director posts. In the Delors II Commission, the Luxembourger Colette Flesch reported (unusually) to a Commissioner of her own nationality, Jean Dondelinger, with the Dane Niels Thogersen and Italian Marco Piccarolo as her directors. In the Delors III Commission, after the reorganisation, she reported to the Portuguese Commissioner, or Professor as he wished to be called, João de Deus Pinheiro, and acquired two further directors, the French former Delors *Cabinet* member and subsequent head of the Commission's Paris office, Jean-Michel Baer, and the former deputy-head of the Pinheiro *Cabinet*, Fernando Balsinha, parachuted into the new post in May 1994. This relatively light management structure is clearly very different from that of DG I, with its four deputies, one advisor and 11 directors, or from that of DG VI (Agriculture), with its four deputies, seven advisers and 11 directors. One simple reason is the distinction between those DGs with a large or small legislative programme (DG X only has responsibility for one Community directive, the Television without Frontiers directive) and a large burden in terms of the management of policy, with all the concomitant demands in terms of comitology, line management and responsibility to the Council and Parliament. Lists of all DGs in the Delors II and Delors III Commissions are to be found in the Annex.

The Secretariat General, decision-making and coordination

The Secretariat General

The Secretariat General, the Legal Service and the Spokesman's Service each report to the President of the Commission and provide an administrative, political and public relations power base of enormous skill and intellectual agility. Since, as Chapter 1 outlines, President Delors has created a tight management system run by his *Cabinet*, it is not surprising that these 'horizontal' Services have seen their influence grow since the mid-1980s. The Secretariat General is of particular interest since it provides the administrative means of the Commission's, and particularly the President's, ambitions.

The Secretariat General is the Commissioners' own secretariat, and the Secretary General and his Deputy are the only non-Commissioners allowed to participate in the Commission's formal meetings on a regular basis, unless a *Chef de Cabinet* is standing in for a Commissioner or a Director General is present to assist his Commissioner with technical advice. The Secretary General also presides over the regular Monday morning meeting of *Chefs de Cabinet* and the regular Thursday meeting of Directors General. He attends European Councils with the Commission President, and his Deputy coordinates and defends the Commission position in COREPER II (full ambassadors).

There have only been two Secretaries General of the Commission, the Frenchman Emile Noël and the Briton David Williamson. Both were the epitome of their national civil service traditions. After Ecole Normale Supérieure Noël worked for the Council of Europe from 1949 to 1958 and was secretary of the Constitutional Committee of the *ad hoc* assembly asked by governments of the six to draft the project for a European Political Community. He was subsequently *Chef de Cabinet* of Guy Mollet both during his spell as President of the Consultative assembly and later when Mollet was President of the Council of Ministers in France. Noël's functions included representing France in the negotiations leading to the two Treaties of Rome. His reign as Secretary General of the Commission lasted from 1958 to 1987. He was clearly a brilliant administrator and a close confidant of several Commission Presidents. Monnet greatly appreciated Noël's collaboration with the Action Committee for Europe. He wrote of Noël, that he always found him:

> "appliqué avec autant de tenacité que de modestie à mettre de la rigueur dans la structure des institutions communautaires et de la souplesse dans leur fonctionnement." (Monnet, p. 617)

David Williamson became Secretary General during the final stages of the Delors I budgetary dispute and was instrumental in achieving a settlement. Based on his previous position as Head of the European Secretariat in the Cabinet Office in London and prior to that Deputy Director General of DG VI (Agriculture), he helped persuade Margaret Thatcher to accept a settlement agreeable to the British at the February 1988 Brussels Summit. Williamson was close to Delors, helping to provide "the administrative base of the Presidential regime" (Ludlow 1991, p. 120). Clearly aware of the advantages to the UK of its excellent system of coordination of UK policies on European affairs, Williamson set up efficient lines of communication not only between the Commission's feudal Directorates General, but also between the Commission, the Parliament and the Council Secretariat. He presided over the most important of the inter-departmental committees established in the late 1980s in the aim, as he once confided, "not to mould a technically perfect administration, but one that will work" (Leonard 1990). Under Williamson, the Commission saw an enormous expansion of its role and responsibilities after 1989 when it was set to become, as Williamson argued, part of the "future administration of the central institutions of the greatest civil power in the world" (Williamson 1991). As one of the few incisive recent studies of the Commission underlines, compared with the past, Williamson's Commission is better coordinated, shares more information and monitors more efficiently progress in implementing the Commission's targets as laid out in its yearly programmes (Ludlow 1991).

The Secretary General has Director General (AI) rank and is considered *primus inter pares*. The heads of the various divisions within the Secretariat General reporting to him have a status somewhere between that of a deputy Director General and a Director. The Secretariat General is in one sense the brain of the Commission Services, the Commission's "memory, principal advisor, its mediator and general supervisor" (Berlin 1987, p. 69). It is "discreetly omnipresent, indispensable but intervening rarely in an ostensible manner" (*ibid.*, p. 292). Largely modelled on the French Secretariat du Conseil de Ministres, the Secretariat General is responsible for the Commission's agenda, the control of legislative texts and formal communication with the other institutions (see Wessels and Rometsch, Chapter 8; Westlake, Chapter 9). It is here that the vital coordination functions are placed and where information is centralised and redistributed. As Berlin has observed "Son efficacité est à la mesure de sa discrétion, et si rien ne peut se faire contre lui, fort peu se fait sans lui" (*ibid.*, p. 293). The Secretariat General has also been the staging post for the treatment of issue-areas outside the framework of the Community, such as European Political Cooperation, which became the nucleus of the new DG IA (External Political Relations) in the Delors III Commission (see Nuttall, Chapter 11), once Maastricht had given the Commission a clear power of initiative in this area. It remains to be seen whether the other areas of Maastricht's third pillar, justice and home affairs, which remained within the Secretariat General in the Delors III Commission, follow the same course in the 1995 Commission.

Decision-making — from initiation to first draft

A distinction needs to be made between three main kinds of Commission proposals. Attempts to articulate the European interest by statements or white papers on policy issues achieve no legal status until they become legislative initiatives. As Chapter 1 argues, the Commission may or may not be the catalyst of proposals for policy-making, but legislative proposals to the Council fall broadly into two categories, where the Commission is the drafter; those proposing the creation of completely new legislation and thus, potentially, with politically debatable content; and those proposing technical legislation merely amplifying existing rules. In addition, the Commission is called upon to decide policy with regard to its own legislation in the framework of delegated powers discussed by Docksey and Williams in Chapter 5. Procedures decided within the framework of the Commission's role as "guardian of the treaties", discussed by Usher in Chapter 6, are also of relevance in terms of the decision-making process.

Legislative initiatives and decisions to take Member States to court are highly political. The College debates proposals, and one Commissioner will be required to defend the proposals in discussions with the Council of Ministers. In both institutions, there are voting, negotiation, coalition-building and package deals. As for the more technical legislation, officials from the Commission services debate the issues with national officials and the Commission and Council are often called upon only to rubber stamp their officials' decisions — on the Commission side by written procedure, rather than oral discussion in the College, and on the Council side as an 'A' point in a Council meeting. Wessels and Rometsch elaborate on the latter in Chapter 8.

In terms of the Commission's procedures, there are six phases in the process of policy formulation; the initiation phase, the drafting phase, inter-service coordination, agreement between specialised members of *Cabinets*, by *Chefs de Cabinet* and finally by the College itself. The adoption of proposals for action follows the same administrative procedure, whether the decision concerns new policy orientations, minor amendments to existing legislation, the management of agricultural markets or a decision to bring (or threaten to bring) a legal action in the European Court of Justice. The adoption of the proposal by the College under Article 2 of the internal rules of procedure is the outcome, but it is the journey, rather than the arrival of the proposal that requires explanation.

The originator of a policy proposal in any given area can be either the Commission or the Council (here including the European Council as well as the Council of Ministers). Once the germ for a policy has been sown, however, the Commission has responsibility for the formal draft and enters discussions with actors inside and outside the Community institutional framework. Mazey and Richardson describe the resulting 'policy networks' in Chapter 7. The usual internal route for new proposals is for Directorates General of the Commission to set up consultative committees of 'technical experts', some of whom are independent consultants from academia or interest groups, while others are desk officers from the national governments, who may well turn up later in the Council working group to discuss the resultant proposal. Often, to the irritation of Commission officials, they may then argue a somewhat different case, since inter-ministerial coordination in the national capital may have introduced nuances in the original (technical) national position.

There is a view in some government circles that time is too short to attend all of these committees (there are several in progress at any time) and that, in any case, the key debate will take place when the proposal is actually on the table. This can be a risky strategy. An element of pre-negotiation actually takes place in the Commission's committees, with the main lines of the ultimate intergovernmental bargain beginning to emerge and thus setting the parameters for subsequent discussion by indicating, as it were, the lowest common denominator likely to prevail in the formal negotiations. So it is unwise to let others make the running and better to influence the Commission early in order to obviate the need for tiresome negotiations later. The point is to ensure a national viewpoint gets due consideration in the Commission proposal. For the private sector, squaring the lobbying circle means influencing all governments early in the initiation process as well as the Commission itself. There are thus many varied and competing pressures on the Commission in the initiation phase, as national officials take on a role of representation of the same group interests, which, if they have prepared the ground thoroughly, will have lobbied the Commission Services too.

The drafting stage takes place when consultation is complete. Here, middle-ranking officials in the Directorate General in the lead begin the process. The temptation is great for strong positions emerging in technical experts groups to be incorporated in the text. Clearly, under qualified majority voting, if only a minority of Member States persists in a given view, pressure will not be high on the Commission to dilute its position. The draft finds its way up the 'hierarchy' in due course to Director General level for endorsement. On the way, inter-service meetings and consultation procedures in principle ensure consistency of overall policy by taking the views of other Directorates General into account. In addition to *ad hoc* inter-service consultations, there were 48 formalised inter-service groups in 1990. By 1993 there were 63 groups.

Coordination

As mentioned above, one problem of coordination arises from the fact that there is often no precise hierarchical structure in terms of relations with the responsible Commissioner. In the case of DG I, for example, there are two Commissioners responsible, the Briton Sir Leon Brittan responsible for external economic affairs and trade policy and the Spaniard Manuel Marin, mainly responsible for cooperation and development policy, the province of DG VIII (Development), but also responsible within DG I for North–South Relations, Mediterranean policy and relations with Latin America and Asia. As for external political relations, these are the responsibility of yet another Commissioner, Hans van den Broek, operating through a completely different DG, DG IA, which also has responsibility for the Commission's delegations abroad, as Smith explains in Chapter 10. Rivalry between the three Commissioners and the three Directors General involved has slowed considerably the creation of a unified foreign service in the Delors III Commission and led to some cynicism and embitterment of staff.

In 1988 the Commission held a seminar in Erenstein to debate the need for increased coordination and for simplification of procedures. The resulting committee continued to stress the ongoing need to improve inter-departmental coordination. It is rare that a DG is solely responsible for a legislative proposal, so coordination with other DGs is thus a constant feature of the daily routine of the DG, though it is not without difficulty. The problem of coordination is undoubtedly one common to every modern administration (Debbasch 1987.) Yet, within a national governmental structure, the coordinating mechanism forms part of the official command structure of government. Not so in the Commission. Here, coordination *within* a DG may be compared to a national governmental structure, since there is a distinct hierarchy and the possibility for directors or the Director General to impose a line. Coordination between competing DGs is a different matter, except, of course, in the rare cases when both report to the same Commissioner and cabinet structure. The Commission's rules of operational procedures stipulate that:

> "Any department preparing a Commission decision or proposal must take account of the fact that the Commission as a whole will bear responsibility for the measure in question and must act accordingly, i.e. in conjunction with other departments as appropriate. Underlying this requirement is the principle that the administration is 'one and indivisible': although each sector is the responsibility of a different Member, the administration as a whole serves the Commission as a whole." (Manual of Operational Procedures 1992)

The lead department is obliged to make informal contact with other departments as soon as drafting begins. But there are various formal procedures by which coordination is, in principle at least, provided for. At the weekly meeting of Directors General and at the weekly meeting of assistants of Directors General, the schedule of implementation of the Commission's work programme is reviewed and issues about to be brought to the College are flagged. This ensures against a potential lack of coordination between the Services, but coordination ought already to have taken place. The formally constituted 'inter-service groups' build a permanent coordination structure. The Secretariat General is responsible for supervision of coordination meetings and ensuring the appropriate departments are indeed consulted. A full list of inter-service groups is kept by the coordination unit in the Secretariat General. Formally subject to a Commission decision, inter-service groups are now set up only with the authorisation of the Secretariat General, though the numbers of such formally constituted groups belies the extent to which coordination on an *ad hoc* basis is routine.

Despite this obvious commitment to interdepartmental coordination, it is often argued that the system is flawed. On this analysis, some DGs, such as DGs I, III, VI or IX, are more powerful than the others. Their status is based on the preponderance of their issue areas in the history of the Commission since its inception, their large staffs, their contribution to budgetary considerations and finally the excellence, professionalism and commitment of staff in these areas. Thus, the argument goes, these DGs are able to impose their will and avoid the essential purpose of coordination mechanisms, since the Secretariat General provides monitoring mechanisms for coordination but no command structure. Though it might be argued that the Cabinet Office plays a similar role in Whitehall, the essential difference is the respect enjoyed by the Cabinet Office, its generally recognised impartiality between Whitehall departments and the fact that it serves a Prime Minister and a government with an agreed ideology and programme. As Donnelly and Ritchie argue in Chapter 2, all of these elements are absent in the Commission.

The College, argue the cynics, only has cognisance of issues in the final stage of a dossier's journey through the system. Despite the fact that Commissioners may vote on proposals and that a simple majority suffices to carry a measure, the principle is consensus, so the justified case of the specialist official may be drowned by bureaucratic power structures on its way up the hierarchy and in the political compromises emerging from *Cabinet* and College discussion. Methods used, according to the detractors of present arrangements, include the setting of time limits for coordination proceedings which obviate any real preparation and discussion, and the organisation of meetings without due notice or at such a high level of officialdom that the detail may remain undiscussed as the lead department attempts to achieve a political settlement. In addition, where a strong DG is in the lead, it may not attempt to seek consensus, but simply try to impose its view. In doing so it may restrict access to information, so that DGs with a marginal interest are, in fact, marginalised. Be these arguments as they may, and it is not stretching the imagination too far to suppose that similar methods might exist in some national systems, there is a formal requirement for coordination at the highest level between DGs before the proposal finally reaches the Commission agenda, as was outlined above.

Internal rules of procedure provide for a series of formalities to be completed before submission to the College and for the text to be circulated no later than noon on the Thursday before the Commission meeting. The

Secretariat General's registry division, known by its French term *'greffe'*, is responsible for the formalities involved. But it is the lead department or departments which prepare the text itself on the responsibility of the lead Commissioner. Differences of opinion remaining after inter-departmental consideration are outlined in an explanatory note which accompanies each document. In case of such differences of opinion between Directorates General the decision cannot be based on a written or delegation procedure (see below).

Several Commission services are involved as a matter of routine in the decision-making process. The Directorates General for Budgets (DG XIX) and Financial Control (DG XX) must be consulted on any proposals with financial implications. Likewise, the Directorate General for Personnel and Administration (DG IX) must be formally involved if a proposal has personnel implications. The Commission's Legal Service must be consulted before a proposal reaches the agenda of the College or enters a written procedure. The role of the Legal Service is formally to ensure conformity with the Treaties, coherence with existing legislation and with agreed procedures in other areas of Community business. While these requirements may be considered a routine task, the third relates to political desiderata such as the maintenance of a line on competence, on legal base or on comitology (see Chapters 1, 5 and 6). Ensuring the Legal Service is in agreement with the principle at issue is clearly, therefore, one way of commanding respect and acceptance for the proposal.

The current head of the Legal Service is the French lawyer, Jean Louis Dewost. The Legal Service reports directly to the Commission President and collaboration between the President's *Cabinet* and senior officials from the Legal Service can provide a vital agenda-setting function. A favourable opinion from the Legal Service on the text concerned is a clear political advantage. An unfavourable opinion means either that the text must be amended or an accompanying explanatory statement must be provided and that proposals may not follow the written or delegation procedures described below. For new legislation, the lawyer-revisers *(juristes-linguistes)* must also be involved to ensure coherence of the proposal in the nine official languages of the Union. Preparation of the text by the translation service may not have covered all the legal nuances.

Decision-making — College and Cabinet *procedures*

The final stage in the decision-making process is formal submission of the draft to the College of Commissioners. Often, this occurs by written procedure, but where this is not possible the text is placed on the agenda of the Commission's weekly meeting. The relevant Commissioner's *Cabinet* may well have been involved in the drafting process, and will certainly have closely vetted the text. But the other *Cabinets* are now an important port of call for the draft. The text goes via the Secretariat General to all other *Cabinets* for vetting and control. At this stage the process of inter-*Cabinet* negotiation begins. This is the highest level of coordination. It should be remembered that the *Cabinets* will seek to defend their own Commissioner's interest, but the responsible *Cabinet* officials will naturally also look to the national interests involved and will be fully briefed by 'their' permanent representation and national officials about what is at stake.

As Donnelly and Ritchie describe in Chapter 2, the key preparatory meeting for the College is the *Chef de Cabinet* meeting on Mondays. The Secretary General (who chairs this meeting) submits the text for discussion and, just as in COREPER before a Council meeting, agreement on most issues may already emerge. This enables non-controversial issues to proceed to the Commission as 'A points', which are not formally discussed, as opposed to 'B points' which require discussion. Textual amendments arising from prior *'specials chefs'* meetings or the meeting of Heads of Cabinet can be dealt with in the remaining time before the College meet to formalise the resulting decision. Commissioners debate major issues still unsettled, which they can agree in the meeting, put on the agenda of a future meeting or have referred back to the services and *Cabinets* for re-drafting. 'A points' are simply agreed as a formality.

In addition to meetings of the full Commission which adopt texts, there are two kinds of formal meetings of Commissioners to settle policy lines where the whole Commission need not be involved. The first 'restricted' group *(groupe restreint)* would be composed of a small number of Commissioners, mandated by the College on grounds of the specificity of the subject at issue. In the period immediately following the announcement that the unification of the two Germanies was likely, a group restricted to President Delors, the External Affairs Commissioner Frans Andriessen, the Commissioner for Economic Affairs, Henning Christopherson and the Internal Market Commissioner Martin Bangemann met frequently to decide a coordinated Commission strategy in the ongoing debate about the nature of the unification process and the overall implications for the Community. Subsequently, an 'open group' *(groupe ouvert)* was constituted under the chairmanship of Commissioner Bangemann to analyse the implications of German unification for all aspects of the *acquis communautaire*. An open group is 'open' to all Members of the Commission who wish to participate. The system resembles the original system of the ECSC and the early days of the EEC when groups of Commissioners fell into eight or so categories approaching each of the issue areas as a mini-College, rather than the more individualised approach of today. It was only after 1970 that the current system of individual portfolios began to emerge.

In addition to full meetings of the College, there are two other procedures by which decisions may be taken; *'habilitations'* and written procedures. A short case study involving both procedures is provided below. Given the collegial nature of the Commission and the resulting collective responsibility for decisions, sensitive matters must come before the full Commission at its weekly meetings. The Commission cannot delegate powers for decision-making akin to those enjoyed by a member of a national government minister. But if all decisions in Community life had to be discussed in a full meeting of the Commission, there would be administrative overload, paralysis of the decision-making process and the submergence of important subjects in the myriad of managerial and administrative decisions for which formal Commission decisions are required. Hence the need for alternative procedures.

Habilitations

The purpose of the delegation procedure, known internally in the Commission by the French word *'habilitation'*, is to relieve the College of discussion of decisions on routine matters, usually with a narrow margin of discretion and which present no political problems. Article 27 of the internal rules of procedure allows the Commission to delegate a power of attorney to one Commissioner, formally to commit the Commission. The *habilitation* procedure is usually used in areas of managerial or administrative nature. A condition of the exercise of the mandate remains the ultimate collective responsibility of the College. Questions of principle or general policy, as mentioned above, are customarily dealt with in the Wednesday meeting and cannot be the subject of *habilitation* procedures. Typically, *habilitations* occur either for purely technical issues, often in the agricultural sphere, or where political and substantive differences on a text have been removed by previous discussion and compromise, so that all that is required is a final adjustment of the text. Personnel and financial decisions are excluded from the procedure.

Written procedures

Written procedures are a much used decision-making process for items not requiring discussion at the weekly meeting and where a delegation procedure is not necessary. It is used where the relevant Directorates General have agreed the proposal and the legal service has given its approval. Written procedures are initiated by the Secretariat General at the request of one or more Members of the Commission. The request is submitted by the lead Directorate General to the registry service in the Secretariat, known inside the Commission by its French name, the *greffe*. The *greffe* ensures that formal requirements have been completed as follows:

1. approval of associated DGs
2. favourable opinion of legal service
3. examine legal form and terminology
4. prepare summary list and memo indicating agreement at appropriate levels
5. set time limit
6. send different language versions to lawyer-revisers
7. circulate proposal after completion of formalities to Commissioners and concerned DGs

Thereafter, if no reservations are made by Commissioners through their *Cabinets* before the expiry of the time limit, the Secretary General records approval of the measure, draws up the final text incorporating drafting changes by lawyer-revisers and includes mention of the decision in a daily memorandum to Commissioners listing all items agreed by written procedure.

There are two basic types of written procedure; ordinary and expedited. 'Ordinary' written procedures allow five working days for agreement after distribution of the text. Allowing for the administrative work of the *greffe* to take place, this means a decision by ordinary written procedure occurs 10 days after receipt of the request. The 'expedited' written procedure (*procédure écrite accélerée*) is authorised by the President on a request from the Secretariat General. Here, three days is allowed for texts where legislation is urgently required. The 10-day ordinary procedure is thus reduced to five. Expedited written procedures 'for finalisation' enable urgent measures agreed by the *Chefs de Cabinet* meeting or by the College to be adopted rapidly. The time limit can be as little as one day. 'Expedited written procedure by special circulation' enables the Commission to take decisions at short notice in response, for example, to natural disasters or requests for emergency aid etc. A 'special' version of this procedure is reserved for Commission responses to Council common positions under the cooperation procedure. Forty-eight hours are allowed in order to enable Commission officials immediately to continue discussions in the inter-institutional context.

Procedures in the framework of the Commission's role as Guardian of the Treaties

As Usher outlines in Chapter 6, under Article 169 of the Treaty (see p. 168), the Commission may institute legal proceedings against a Member State before the Court of Justice for alleged non-fulfilment of Treaty obligations. Member States generally respect the Treaty and most violations are due to misunderstandings, misinterpretations or to delays in transposing Community legislation into national law. Deliberate non-compliance nonetheless exists, either because the Member State concerned has intentionally misread the terms of a directive, believing it has a case for an exemption from the legislation or because it may wish to gain time before full implementation. The areas of competition and environment policy and the internal market are prime examples. Member States and the Commission are generally reluctant to pursue cases before the Court of Justice and most disputes are thus resolved at an early stage; albeit 'early' can sometimes mean years, since the procedures leading to a full court action take several months and, given the current overload on the European Court itself, thereafter a wait of some years can ensue before a case comes to court.

The Commission may become aware of an infringement for a number of reasons: an individual, a company or a Member State may complain, or an investigation by Commission officials may uncover possible violations. The Commission needs then to decide whether to take action. Such a decision would be subject to the procedures described above — either a decision in the Wednesday meeting of the College, or a written procedure. Thereafter, the Commission sends a 'letter of formal notice' — there are approximately one thousand letters of notice annually — requesting the Member State concerned to explain the alleged breach. The Member State then has approximately two months to reply. If it fails to reply or provides an unsatisfactory explanation, the Commission issues a 'reasoned opinion' outlining why it considers the Member State to be in violation of the Treaty. Again, the Commission usually gives the Member State two months to comply. Most cases end with such a letter of notice or a reasoned opinion.

The prime purpose of the infringement procedure is not to secure a court ruling that the infringement has taken place, but to persuade the Member

State to conform. In almost 85 per cent of cases the infringement proceedings are terminated after the first two stages — formal notice and reasoned opinion — and thus before a reference to the Court of Justice takes place. Litigation is thus the final resort. Member States are reluctant to let legal proceedings begin and the Commission is similarly reticent for fear of alienating opinion in Member States, where its role is often contested by large parts of public opinion. On the other hand, non-compliance by one Member State does require formal action and a refusal by the Commission to prosecute may alienate precisely those interest groups whose sympathy the Commission needs in its more general task of creating legitimacy for the European institutions and European integration itself. Nevertheless, political deals between the Commission and Member States are common. To save the British government possible embarrassment and to help establish good relations with London during the UK Presidency in the second half of 1992, for instance, the Commission reputedly requested the Court to postpone a number of highly-publicised environmental law cases against the UK. On the other hand, under pressure from environmentalists, the Commission made threatening noises, which reached the media, over the famous Twyford Down issue just prior to a British general election.

Case study: Proposal for a Council Directive on Articles of Precious Metals COM(93) 322 final — SYN 472, 14 October 1993

The drafting of a proposal for a directive concerning the jewellery industry was made by the Commission after representations from several Member States and European manufacturers. The Commission's proposal was to approximate national regulations under Article 100a (EEC) (see p. 167). The point of the proposal was to protect consumers from differences in national laws regarding the standards and content of articles made of precious metals, i.e. gold, palladium, platinum and silver. The Commission had found that standards of precious metal content varied enormously and that the external appearance of goods did not allow a customer to verify the quality. Further problems resulted from varying national certification and inspection procedures. The proposal's objectives were the achievement of product quality assurance, a declaration by producers of conformity to the directive and agreed verification procedures by third parties.

In an area where total EC production in 1989 surpassed the combined output of America and Japan and ran to 5.6 billion Ecus, with the production of fine gold alone exceeding 630 tonnes, the issue was clearly of interest to the trade. In addition, 1,700 businesses were involved in industrial production and 13,000 on a small craft basis. The jewellery sector alone employed over 56,000 people, with a total of 120,000 people involved more generally in the production of articles involving precious metals; and there were even higher numbers involved in distribution.

The Commission consulted over more than a year representatives of all parties affected by the proposed legislation and claimed in its explanatory memorandum that it had the agreement of those consulted, with some reservations expressed by, for example, the European Bureau of Consumers Unions and the Association of European Assay Offices. Such remaining conflicting interests would need to be resolved in Council. Clearly, the existence of reservations meant that the College needed to agree a position in areas of sensitivity and it is not surprising that the written procedure was held up by some *Cabinets* and that the issue went to a full meeting of the College. The fact that Commissioner Bangemann received an *habilitation* shows agreement was rapidly and conclusively reached on the broad lines of policy. Table 1 sets the final administrative stages the proposal went through.

Table 1:   *Progress of a proposal through the College*

1993	Stage	Comment
14 June	Written Procedure request to Secretariat General	
	1. File checked for completed formalities	Lead department DG III. Associated departments:
	2. Concerned *Cabinets* consulted	DGs I, 1X, XV, XIX, XX, XXI, XXIII, SPC, Sec. Gen. Consulted Departments: Legal Service
7 July	Written procedure begins with distribution of document (E/938/93)	
14 July	Date for finalising document	
14 July	Suspension of procedure by the following *Cabinets:*	
	1. Brittan and Millan	"for further examination" "to examine implications for consumers"
20 July	2. Flynn and Pinheiro	"pending further information"
	3. Suspension note distributed	"to examine implications"
26 July	1. *Cabinets* agree to close procedure	Item placed on Commission agenda
28 July	1. Issue becomes a point of oral procedure at Commission meeting no. 1163	Point postponed
1 Sept	Commission approves text with amendments at meeting 1165	In agreement with Commissioner Vanni d'Archirafi and President Delors, Commissioner Bangeman "habilitated" to

		establish a new text for transmission to Council, Parliament and Ecosoc.
24 Sept	1. *Habilitation* procedure arrives in Secretariat General 2. File checked and *Cabinets* consulted	
14 Oct	1. *Habilitation* signed by responsible Commissioner	End of decision-making process Formal proposal goes to Council.*

* *In March 1994, the Council was still working on the proposal.*

Conclusions

This Chapter has reviewed some of the most common, everyday procedures in the Commission. Yet, despite the seeming simplicity of the procedures described, there seems to be broad agreement that what makes the Commission work in practice, as with staffing (see Chapter 3) is the existence of a layer of procedures designed almost to ensure that real power remains outside the services and is focused in the *Cabinet* system. It is almost as if Commissioners and their *Cabinets* let the Services play the game of policy-making, consultation of interest groups and inter-institutional relations, while reserving both judgement and the exercise of real power to themselves. When speed and efficiency are required, task forces can be set up independently of DGs. When issues are tactically inconvenient, a view from the legal service can stymie a proposal's progress. Inter-service groups function effectively on one reading, but they are unable to sway a powerful DG 's view on another reading. In any case, the best coordination by the Services often runs foul of *Cabinet* objections at a later date. If a draft proposal is inconvenient or unacceptable to one or other Commissioner, *Cabinets* may re-draft it, often running roughshod over their own Services. As the Spierenburg report commented:

> "although the usefulness of these private offices is not disputed, some aspects of their operation are starting to cause difficulties and are even threatening to disrupt, quite substantially, the smooth running of the Commission Services: *Cabinets* 'shielding' Members from their Services, *Chefs de Cabinet* usurping the responsibilities of Directors General, meetings of *Chefs de Cabinet* (and indeed of junior *Cabinet* staff) questioning proposals without consulting the officials responsible for them, interference in appointment procedures with undue weight being given to nationality factors, and so on." (Spierenburg 1979)

Indeed, within the structure of the *Cabinet* system, the President's *Cabinet* is much more than *primus inter pares*. Delors' *Chef de Cabinet* during all three Delors Commissions was Pascal Lamy, of whom one observer writes "He ran 'the house' through his control over the Commission agenda (with Williamson) and his ability to command attention from General Directors of the administration" (Ross 1993). Moreover, the President's *Cabinet* "had to be willing to break through official chains of command and responsibility" by "reaching around" Commissioners and "reaching into" the work of both the services and the other *Cabinets*. It is important to note that what makes the Commission function is precisely the existence of what Berlin calls an "informal parallel administration" (Berlin 1987, p. 301), where personal networks and the privileged place of the *Cabinets* in an extremely hierarchical command structure form the basis of a set of informal rules of procedure, which command the respect, despite the resentment, of the Commission staff. This latter point is dealt with in Chapter 3. If the reason, as some argue (Berlin 1987; Spierenburg 1979), is the clash between the verticality of command structures in the DGs and the horizontality of the collegial system of Commission decision-making, one might expect to see a future increased role of the Secretariat General. It is a Service with a horizontal mission, yet it enjoys a degree of respect in DGs that produces a *de facto* verticality in its operational style. The test will perhaps come when a Commission is appointed with two significantly different features from those of the Delors/Noël/Williamson Commissions; first, the absence of a dramatic-political President and second, the absence of an ever-expanding administrative agenda, thus allowing for internal administrative reform and the consolidation of the resulting civil service ethic.

References and bibliography

Berlin, Dominique (1987) 'Organisation de la Commission', in Cassese, S. *The European Administration*, EIPA, Maastricht 1987.

Debbasch, Charles (1987) *Administrations Nationales et Integration Européenne*, Aix en Provence, CNRS.

Economist (1990) 'Waste a lot, want a lot', 6 October 1990.

Leonard, Dick (1990) 'The Man at the Top', in *The Bulletin*, 6 September 1990.

Ludlow, Peter (1991) 'The European Commission', in Keohane, Robert and Hoffmann, Stanley (eds.) *The New European Community; Decision-making and Institutional Change*, Oxford: Westview.

Manual of Operational Procedures, European Commission internal document 1992.

Monnet, J. (1976) *Mémoirs*, Paris: Fayard.

Ross, George (1993) 'Sidling into industrial policy: inside the European Commission', *French Politics and Society* 11 No. 1 (Winter).

Spierenburg, Dirk (1979) *Proposals for Reform of the Commission of the European Communities and its Services*, Brussels: European Commission.

Williamson, David (1991) Redcliffe-Maud Memorial Lecture, 10 October 1991.

Williamson, David (1993) Brandon Rhys Williams Memorial Lecture, 4 March 1993.

Willis, Virginia (1983) *Britons in Brussels*, London: PSI.

ANNEX

Directorates General in the Delors II and Delors III Commissions

Delors II Commission *06.01.89 – 05.01.93*		*Delors III Commission* *06.01.93 – 05.01.95*	
DG I	External Relations	DG I	External Economic Relations
		DG IA	External Political Relations Enlargement Task Force
DG II	Economic and Financial Affairs	DG II	Economic and Financial Affairs
DG III	Internal Market and Industrial Affairs	DG III	Industry
DG IV	Competition	DG IV	Competition
DG V	Employment, Industrial Relations and Social Affairs	DG V	Employment, Industrial Relations and Social Affairs
DG VI	Agriculture	DG VI	Agriculture, Veterinary and Phytosanitary Office
DG VII	Transport	DG VII	Transport
DG VIII	Development	DG VIII	Development
DG IX	Personnel and Administration	DG IX	Personnel and Administration
DG X	Audiovisual, Information, Communication and Culture	DG X	Audiovisual Media, Information, Communication and Culture
DG XI	Environment, Nuclear Safety and Civil Protection	DG XI	Environment, Nuclear Safety and Civil Protection
DG XII	Science, Research and Development Joint Research Centre	DG XII	Science, Research and Development Joint Research Centre
DG XIII	Telecommunications, Information, Industries and Innovation	DG XIII	Telecommunications, Information, Market and Exploitation of Research
DG XIV	Fisheries	DG XIV	Fisheries
DG XV	Financial Institutions and Company Law	DG XV	Internal Market and Financial Services
DG XVI	Regional Policy	DG XVI	Regional Policies
DG XVIII	Credit and Investments	DG XVIII	Credit and Investments
DG XIX	Budgets	DG XIX	Budgets
DG XX	Financial Control	DG XX	Financial Control
DG XXI	Customs Union and Indirect Taxation	DG XXI	Customs and Indirect Taxation

DG XXII   Coordination of
              Structural Policies
DG XXIII Enterprise Policy,   DG XXIII Enterprise Policy,
              Distributive Trades,   Distributive Trades,
              Tourism and   Tourism and
              Cooperatives   Cooperatives
Task Force for Human Resources,   Task Force for Human Resources,
   Education, Training and Youth   Education, Training and Youth
Secretariat General   Secretariat General
Forward Studies Unit   Forward Studies Unit
                                                          Inspectorate General
Legal Service   Legal Service
Spokesman's Service   Spokesman's Service
Joint Interpreting and Conference   Joint Interpreting and Conference
   Service   Service
Statistical Office   Statistical Office
Translation Service   Translation Service
                                                          Informatics Directorate
Security Office   Security Office
Consumer Policy Service   Consumer Policy Service
Euratom Supply Agency   Euratom Supply Agency
                                                          European Community
                                                             Humanitarian Office
Office for Official Publications   Office for Official Publications
   of the European Communities   of the European Communities
European Foundation for the   European Foundation for the
   Improvement of Living and   Improvement of Living and
   Working Conditions   Working Conditions
European Centre for the   European Centre for the
   Development of Vocational   Development of Vocational
   Training (Cedefop)   Training (Cedefop)

5. The Commission and the execution of Community policy

Christopher Docksey and Karen Williams

Introduction

It is widely understood that the European Commission is the executive body of the European Community — indeed it is not uncommon, especially in the more popular press, for the Commission, or 'Brussels', to be considered omnipotent, with scant if any attention paid to the other institutions. Curiously, there is nothing in the original Treaties to suggest that the Commission should have the exclusive right to manage Community policy. To the contrary, the EC Treaty provides for management powers to be exercised by both the Council and the Commission.

The EC Treaty confers management powers upon the Council both with regard to decisions of general import, as in the case of Article 94 on state aids and Article 103 on conjunctural policy, and decisions relating to specific cases, an example being the third indent of Article 93(2) concerning the exceptional authorisation of a state aid. Similarly, the Commission is empowered by the Treaties to take decisions which are not only individual in scope but also in exceptional cases of general application. The Treaty allows for individual decisions under Article 89 on competition (now virtually redundant), Article 93(2) on illegal state aids, and Article 79(4) on discrimination in transport. Articles allowing for decisions of general application include Article 48(3)(d) on the right of migrant workers to remain (see Commission Regulation (EEC) No. 1251/70 of 29 June 1970, OJ No. L 142/30 of 30 June 1970), Article 91(2) on dumping, and Article 90(3) on public undertakings (see Joined Cases 188–190/80, *France and UK v. Commission* [1982] ECR 2545).

However, Community policies are normally managed by the Commission under management powers conferred by secondary legislation adopted by the Council. This role is specifically provided for under the fourth indent of Article 155 and now under the third indent of Article 145. Legislation conferring management powers in specific areas may be expressly provided for by the Treaty, as in the case of the agricultural and competition regulations under Articles 43 and 87 respectively, or adopted on the basis of more general provisions such as Articles 100, 100a and 235 (see Annex to Chapter 6).

As a result, the Commission is required to exercise a wide range of executive functions relating to the management, supervision and implementation of Community policies. This executive role has grown considerably as the scope and intensity of Community activities has developed beyond those originally envisaged under the EEC Treaty. The intensive internal market programme is one example. Another is the Commission's responsibilities beyond the scope of Community action, such as the coordination of aid to Central and Eastern Europe under programmes such as PHARE and TACIS. This Chapter analyses these functions of the Commission in light of the debate about how much power should be vested in the Commission and the tussle between the institutions and Member States for a right to increase supervision of the process. In particular, this Chapter highlights the interplay with representatives of Member States and the emerging supervisory role of the European Parliament.

The nature of the management role of the Commission

The Commission's executive functions may be divided into four main categories: direct implementation of policy; rule-making to flesh out policy laid down under primary Treaty or derived Council legislation; supervision of policy implementation by national front-line bodies; and the management of Community finances.

Direct implementation of policy

For the most part, the Commission cannot normally be compared to a national agency carrying out a front-line policy management function. However, in some limited areas, notably the management of competition policy, the Commission is able to pursue a 'hands on' role in implementing the relevant Community rules. Within these areas the Commission may even enjoy exclusive executive powers. But such powers tend to be exceptional and subject to significant reservations by Member States, as can be seen in the history of the powers conferred on the Commission under Council Regulation (EEC) 4064/89 of 21 December 1989 relating to merger control. These exclusive management powers took more than 16 years to be adopted and are limited to much larger-scale (and hence fewer) mergers than the Commission itself had sought.

Negotiations over merger control also involved negotiation over a key feature determining the nature of the Commission's role — resources. The Commission does not have the staff to play a front-line role in all the areas of Community policy, and thus will do so only in exceptional situations where resources are allocated to allow it to carry out that function. Indeed, even in the area of competition policy it is generally acknowledged that the Commission's resources are inadequate (House of Lords: 1993–94 paras. 125–127). Staffing issues are considered in Chapter 3, but in understanding the nature of the Commission's executive role it has to be borne in mind that the staff available to carry out that role is comparable in number only to a large European city administration.

Rule-making

It is therefore unsurprising that the Commission's best known executive function, and that to which it allocates a significant part of its resources, is the exercise of rule-making powers, laying down the ground rules to be followed by national administrations and those subjected to Community rules. The vast majority of conferred rule-making powers concern day-to-day management decisions. They can be made by the Commission acting alone where they are a matter of routine and involve little or no exercise of discretion. This is the case, for example, where reduction percentages are fixed, if necessary, to equate demands for import licences of agricultural products from outside the Community with the quantities available of those products. Where an exercise of discretion is concerned, however, such as the opening and deciding upon tenders to sell quantities of agricultural products held by intervention agencies or to grant aids to reduce market prices, the Commission will act following one of the committee procedures discussed below.

A second category of decisions permits minor modifications of Community legislation to be carried out more informally. Thus Article 12 of Regulation (EEC) No. 1765/92 introducing the 'set-aside' scheme, specifically permits the Commission to amend the list of minor arable crops covered by set-aside via the management committee procedure, whereas an amendment concerning a major crop would have to be adopted by the Council itself.

Finally, some decisions which are quasi-legislative and of great economic or political significance are designed to flesh out the framework Council legislation concerned in particular cases. Thus Article 12 of the set-aside Regulation 1765/92 grants the Commission the power to adopt general rules via the management committee procedure and sets out an extensive list of particular areas where rules had to be adopted by the Commission. Areas to be fleshed out by the Commission in this way include those enabling the various arable 'quotas' and the amount of land to be set-aside to be determined and those governing the way set-aside is to be applied.

The express or implied scope of rule-making powers of implementation can be extremely controversial. Both the Council and the Parliament may feel that their legislative prerogatives are threatened by an overbroad use of powers of implementation. For example, in January 1993 the Commission adopted Regulation (EEC) No. 207/93 in which it took the power to authorise in the future the use of genetically modified micro-organisms (GMMOs) as ingredients of organically produced food or as processing aids. This was based on powers of implementation conferred by Council Regulation (EEC) No. 2092/91 on organic production of agricultural products. Parliament felt that the Commission Regulation had in effect modified the scope of the Council Regulation, which should have been the role of the Council, and which would then necessarily have involved re-consulting the Parliament. As a result Parliament felt it had been deprived of this right to be re-consulted and opened proceedings in April 1993 alleging that the Commission had exceeded the powers conferred upon it under the Council Regulation (Case C-156/93, *Parliament v. Commission*). In such contexts, the wish of Member States to influence such decision-making and the interest of the European Parliament in being able to follow the work of such committees can be well understood.

Supervision of policy implementation by national bodies

The Commission's supervisory role is based on the fact that the bulk of Community policy is implemented by national bodies and their officials. National bodies such as customs and excise, agriculture and intervention agencies, fisheries inspectorates and even the police all play a role in implementing Community policy and combating attempts to defraud the system.

In this respect, the Commission has a significant supervisory function, both as a line manager and, if necessary, as a prosecutor, since it is the "guardian of the Treaties". However, despite these powers it must rely heavily on the goodwill and cooperation of national agencies. Its role as the guardian is fully treated in Chapter 6, but it is useful to note here that the question of resources again plays a determinative part in the way that the Commission must choose to exercise this function. The Court of Justice and the Court of First Instance have both recognised in very different contexts the limits on the Commission's ability to scrutinise closely all aspects of Community policy. In the *Automec II* case, the Court of First Instance recognised that the Commission has discretion whether or not to take up particular competition complaints, and may prioritise its investigations and allocate its resources accordingly (Case T-24/90 [1992] ECR II–2223). This judgment complements an earlier judgment by the Court of Justice that the Commission has general discretion in managing alleged infringements of Community law (Case 247/87, *Star Fruit* [1989] ECR 291 at 301).

In a similar vein, the Court of Justice has recognised the limited extent to which the Commission can supervise national authorities. In a case concerning the issue of special licences to import 'GATT' beef under low import levies the Court found that:

"a Community ... management method does not presuppose that all the decisions should be taken by the Commission but may equally be achieved by decentralised management .... Nor do the requirements of Community management entail that the Commission ought necessarily to be able to correct wrong decisions taken in specific cases by the national authorities." (Joined Cases C-106/90, C-317/90 and C-129/91, *Emerald Meats* [1993] ECR I–290 at paragraphs 39–40)

These decisions are a valuable recognition of the practical constraints placed upon the Commission by its relative lack of resources, allowing it to prioritise its work without being harassed by legal actions alleging maladministration in a situation where, as one commentator points out, "the Commission is not, in general, well enough resourced for the job" (Nugent 1992, p. 83).

Management of Community finances

The role exercised by the Commission as the manager of the Community's finances has features of the three other roles. The Commission is the manager of the budget itself, responsible for ensuring that the approved annual budget and the guidelines for expenditure are observed. It takes general management decisions concerning disbursement of the budget, principally within the two main areas of agricultural support and the structural funds. And finally it supervises implementation of payments by national authorities acting on behalf of the Community, such as intervention agencies, exercising specific powers to withhold refunds as a sanction for payments in breach of the rules laid down.

The exercise of rule-making powers by the Commission

A feature common to all the implementing powers conferred upon the Commission by the Council is that they come with 'strings attached'. These strings relate to the involvement of the Member States or the Council itself in the Commission's internal decision-making process. In certain cases, this includes the possibility to amend or even to block Commission decisions. As a result, the Commission is not totally free to act independently, although in practice it will be able to exercise its management powers as it wishes in most cases.

The various forms of committee structure imposed upon Commission decision-making are known collectively as 'comitology', a set of arrangements which have developed parallel to but outside the original Treaty provisions. The first attempt to codify committee structures occurred as late as 1985 in the Single European Act, when comitology was very much regarded as the 'management' counterpart of the expanded qualified majority voting procedures introduced in the Act itself. Outside the Community institutions and national government departments, comitology remains a subject which is little known or understood. However, a knowledge of its basic elements is crucial to a proper understanding of the role of the Commission as the manager of Community policy and of the inter-institutional debate between the Commission, Council and Parliament. The arcane comitology procedures in fact embody two distinct power-struggles, between the Commission and the Council for the power to make implementing rules, and between the Council and the Parliament for the power to supervise the Commission. In fact, the same struggle to establish an acceptable institutional balance (Bradley 1992, p. 699) or separation of powers (Lenaerts 1991, pp. 30–31) is taking place in both the legislative and the executive arenas.

The Council, the Commission and comitology

In essence, comitology constitutes an institutional compromise between the need for more effective Community decision-making and Member States' desire to preserve national influence over Commission decision-making.

From the Community perspective, the aim of the exercise is to "speed up decision-making in the Community by more frequent delegation to the Commission of powers to implement Community legislation" (House of Lords 1986, para. 2). From a national perspective, the aim is to retain as much influence for Member States over the Commission as is felt to be necessary when the latter exercises powers of implementation. As a result, the Council has consistently sought to adopt stricter forms of committee procedure than those proposed by the Commission, so as to maximise Member States' influence over the Commission when exercising powers of implementation (Engel and Borrmann 1991, pp. 55 and 151).

Many aspects of the comitology procedures are no more than the technical or administrative preparation of a decision by the Commission. They are rendered necessary by the EC system of devolved national implementation and administration of EC policies, whereby each Member State is responsible for the implementation of most Community policy within its territory. Indeed, one commentator has concluded that the real impetus behind comitology is Member States' responsibility for the national implementation of policy decided at EC level. Comitology allows for the necessary coordination between the EC and national levels of responsibility:

> "The committees . . . have the purpose both of sensitising and of associating national administrations with the EC legislative and executive rules which they will have to implement." (Blumann 1992, pp. 93–94)

Thus, objections to a Commission draft decision by national representatives on a management or regulatory committee may point to difficulties of implementation at national level, and must if possible be taken into account before adopting that decision. In such circumstances, there will always be a need for procedures to involve national authorities.

The lead-up to the Single European Act

Powers of implementation were first subjected to committee procedures in the guise of management committees in agriculture in 1962 and as regulatory committees in customs, health and veterinary legislation in 1968. A classic basic formula for the organisation of committees has been developed. Their members are drawn from Member States but they are chaired by a Commission representative, and their secretariats are provided by the Commission, normally the unit dealing with the particular policy area concerned. In 1980, the Commission listed four categories of committee members: representatives of Member States (the category concerned with the committee procedures imposed by the Council); representatives of professional and economic milieux; scientists, scientific experts or highly qualified persons; and mixed groupings of representatives of Member States and of professional and economic milieux (European Commission 1980).

As early as 1978 the 'Three Wise Men' in their Report on the European Institutions emphasised the need to simplify the range of procedures and to use a much more limited number of procedures when considering powers of implementation (Committee of Three 1979). In 1986, the European Parliament identified 310 such committees divided into 31 categories of procedure (European Parliament 1986). The House of Lords commented that the range of procedures and variants available to the Council "defied description" and resulted in a considerable waste of time and energy (House of Lords 1986 para. 26). Codification did not take place until 1987. Numbers of committees, however, continued to grow, reaching 1,000 by 1989. They were then reduced. Even so, the range of Community activities continued to expand; some 361 committees being identified in the report on the draft 1994 budget (European Parliament 1993).

The key feature of these committees, apart from advisory committees, is that an unfavourable opinion, or in certain circumstances even a failure to adopt an opinion, can result in the decision being referred back to the Council, where it is possible for the measure to be blocked by the Member States.

The creation of such committees was controversial, and the Court was obliged to lay down the ground rules early on in two leading cases. In Case 9/56, *Meroni* ([1958] ECR 139) it held that the High Authority of the ECSC had no right to delegate discretionary powers to subsidiary bodies. It was subsequently argued on the basis of that judgment that committee procedures were unlawful in the sense that they interfered with the powers of both the Council and the Commission. A positive committee vote meant that the Commission, not the Council, exercised the power in question, which arguably should have been exercised by the Council. A negative vote meant that the Commission was deprived of the power conferred upon it, and in effect infringed Article 155 EC, fourth indent. This provides that "the Commission shall . . . exercise the powers conferred upon it by the Council for the implementation of the rules laid down by the latter". It was claimed that the provision only contemplated two possibilities — either the Council should confer executive powers upon the Commission, or it should exercise them itself. The committee procedures were unacceptable because they involved a conferral which was only conditional.

However, in Case 25/70, *Köster* ([1970] ECR 1161), the Court recognised the validity of committee procedures, in that case the cereals management committee. It held that there was no infringement of the powers of the Council or the Commission. With regard to the Council, the Court distinguished between measures based directly on the Treaty and implementing measures and found that, since the Council cannot cover everything in its basic legislation, some matters have to be covered by implementing legislation, either by the Council itself or by the Commission under Article 155, fourth indent. With regard to the Commission, the Court held that Article 155 *authorises* but does not *oblige* the Council to confer executive powers upon the Commission subject to detailed rules concerning their exercise. It may subject powers of implementation to a committee procedure, so long as there is no conferment of any decision-making powers to the committees themselves.

"The function of the Management Committee is to ensure permanent consultation in order to guide the Commission in the exercise of powers conferred upon it by the Council and to enable the latter to substitute its own action for that of the Commission". (*ibid.* at 1171 para. 9; Schindler 1971)

Thus the Court left the Council and the Commission free to develop this particular aspect of institutional decision-making. The Court has subsequently established that, where management powers are conferred upon the

Commission, it enjoys a broad discretion in the exercise of those powers: in the agriculture area, "the concept of implementation must be given a wide interpretation . ... [because] . . . only the Commission is in a position to keep track of agricultural market trends and to act quickly when necessary" (Joined Cases 279, 280 and 286/84, *Rau* [1987] ECR 1069 at 1120 para. 14, affirming Case 23/75, *Rey Soda* [1975] ECR 1279 at 1300 paras. 10 and 11).

The Single European Act

The Single European Act (SEA) did not settle the differences between the Commission and the Council over comitology, despite strong recommendations to that effect in the preparatory work and a recommendation by the European Parliament in its Draft Treaty (Articles 28 and 40) that the Commission be awarded all executive power. However, the SEA did provide for the primary executive role to be exercised by the Commission, subject to the compromises discussed below.

Article 10 of the SEA introduced a new third indent to Article 145 EEC:

> "the Council shall . . . confer on the Commission, in the acts which the Council adopts, powers for the implementation of the rules which the Council lays down. The Council may impose certain requirements in respect of the exercise of these powers. The Council may also reserve the right, in specific cases, to exercise directly implementing powers itself. The procedures referred to above must be consonant with principles and rules to be laid down in advance by the Council, acting unanimously on a proposal from the Commission and after obtaining the Opinion of the European Parliament."

In one sense, this was a step forward in that it obliged the Council for the first time to confer implementing powers upon the Commission. However, this progress was qualified by two features. The Council was allowed to impose requirements in respect of the exercise of those powers (subsequently adopted in the 1987 framework Decision discussed below) and even to reserve for itself the exercise of such powers in specific cases. The only caveat to the latter power was the obligation to ensure that procedures are compatible with general rules and principles laid down in advance by the Council.

Article 10 of the SEA was accompanied by a Declaration on the powers of implementation of the Commission by the Member States in the Intergovernmental Conference (IGC):

> "The Conference asks the Community authorities to adopt, before the Act enters into force, the principles and rules on the basis of which the Commission's powers of implementation will be defined in each case. In this connection the Conference requests the Council to give the Advisory Committee procedure in particular a predominant place in the interests of speed and efficiency in the decision-making process, for the exercise of the powers of implementation conferred upon the Commission within the field of Article 100a of the EEC Treaty."

Thus the Council was mandated to adopt overall rules and to give special prominence to the advisory committee procedure.

The 1987 Comitology Decision (Council Decision 87/373 of 13 July 1987)

The Commission duly followed up the adoption of the SEA by a proposal (COM(86)35 Final) for a regulation to the Council to define procedures for the exercise of implementing powers conferred by the Council upon the Commission (Nicoll 1987, p. 185). Its aim was to codify and simplify existing practice by streamlining the multitude of existing procedures into three well-established procedures — advisory committee, management committee and regulatory committee. It was assumed after the SEA and especially in view of the IGC Declaration that the normal procedure would be the advisory committee, the most efficient means of decision-making, and that implementation by the Council itself would be exceptional.

However, the Council proceeded to adopt a decision which was disappointing for a number of reasons. First, it provided for a set of seven rather than three alternative procedures. Among these were two procedures, the 'safety-net' and one of the 'safeguard clause' procedures, which allowed decision-making not only to be taken over but even to be blocked by the Council. The Commission and Parliament were strongly opposed to these devices on the grounds that they could lead to paralysis in decision-making (European Commission 1987). Secondly, the Decision did not define the 'specific cases' where the Council might reserve the exercise of executive powers to itself, and did not specify the areas to which the committee procedures might be applied. Nor did it oblige the Council to modify existing procedures to bring them into line with the Decision.

The procedures laid down in the Comitology Decision

All the various types of committee which have to be consulted by the Commission are chaired by a senior Commission official, normally at director level, who controls the agenda and submits draft measures to the committee for its opinion subject to a deadline laid down by the chair. The deadline is mandatory in the case of the management and regulatory committees. Where opinions are adopted by qualified majority (54 votes), votes are weighted in analogous fashion to Council voting,[1] i.e. 54 of 76 votes.

The 1994 draft budget report identified 294 committees which had to be consulted by the Commission. Of these, according to the classification laid down by the Comitology Decision, there were 156 advisory committees (Procedure I), 63 management committees (42 Procedure IIa and 21 Procedure IIb) and 81 regulatory committees (61 Procedure IIIa and 20 Procedure IIIb) (European Parliament 1993, p. 10). As will be seen below, these committees form only a part of all the committees and groups organised by the Commission.

The advisory committee — Procedure I

The advisory committee procedure represents the most diluted form of Member State influence. If the committee adopts an opinion, the Commission is obliged to take the "utmost account" of it, but in the final resort it may decide as it thinks fit and there is no referral to the Council. However, Member States retain some measure of influence by using devices reinforced by provisions of the Comitology Decision (Blumann 1988, pp. 53–54). They may force a vote to establish an Opinion by the Committee, if necessary by simple majority (second indent); they may record their (minority) objections in the Minutes (third indent); and they may insist that the Commission respect its obligation to report on how it has taken the "utmost account" of the Committee's opinion (third indent).

In the competition area, advisory committees are the traditional method by which Member States retain influence over the Commission's decision-making powers. Consultation of the advisory committee before the adoption of individual decisions on breaches of Articles 85 and 86 is long-established (under Article 10 of Regulation 17), as it is in the exercise of more general legislative powers delegated to it by the Council, such as in the adoption of block exemptions. The influence of the Comitology Decision can be seen in the Merger Regulation, which for the first time requires the Commission to take the "utmost account" of the opinion of the Committee on a draft merger decision following a full investigation by the Commission. By contrast, there is no provision for consultation of the advisory committee where the Commission decides to clear a merger following an initial examination of the case. It is, however, required in general terms to carry out procedures under the Regulation in "close and constant liaison" with the competent authorities of the Member States. Since the overwhelming majority of cases are, in fact, cleared on this basis the power of Member States to scrutinise potential decisions is severely limited. Similarly, under Article 85, the majority of cases notified to the Commission are settled informally rather than by decision, at least those where the Commission clears or exempts the agreement in question. In such circumstances, the advisory committee is not involved at all.

In cases where the Committee is formally consulted, however, the Merger Regulation grants it the possibility to recommend publication of its opinion (though there is no equivalent provision under Regulation 17 in relation to Articles 85 and 86). In practice all opinions of the advisory committee have been published to date, and the Commission itself has advocated even greater transparency in its decision-making process by accelerating publication of such opinions.

It is interesting to note that the Council was finally prepared to accept the advisory committee structure despite the long-held concern of Member States about handing over powers on merger control to the Commission. Given the jurisdictional structure of the Merger Regulation, which confers exclusive jurisdiction on the Commission to deal with mergers falling within turnover thresholds set out in the regulation itself, this is quite remarkable. The Regulation contains the notion of the 'one stop shop', whereby industry should in principle have to deal with only one set of regulatory bodies — national or Community — rather than both. This contrasts with cases of alleged restrictive practices or agreements or monopolies affecting trade between Member States contrary to Articles 85 and 86. However, it must be recalled that the actual thresholds for Community competence were set extremely high, and much higher than the Commission itself wanted.

Nevertheless, analysis of the other procedures and variants, progressively subjecting Commission decision-making to greater Member State influence, shows that the retention of the advisory committee structure by Member States marks the success of the system in the field of competition law.

The management committee — Procedure II

The management committee procedure originated in, and is typical of, the agriculture area (Bertram 1967–68, pp. 247–248). As has been seen, some particular instruments may be extremely important in filling out Council framework legislation, but for the most part the management committees are concerned with decisions implementing the day-to-day management of the common agricultural policy. A management committee exists for each main group of agricultural products, including cereals, rice, beef, milk and dairy products, fruit and vegetables, wine, hops and tobacco. These committees must be consulted across a whole range of possible market management measures such as managing intervention, fixing levels of import levies and export refunds, and opening and deciding upon tenders.

After the advisory committee, this procedure leaves the Commission the greatest degree of autonomy, because a committee can only trigger referral of a proposed Commission measure to the Council by adopting an unfavourable opinion by qualified majority. If a committee adopts a favourable opinion or fails to adopt any opinion within the deadline laid down by the chair, the Commission may adopt the measure with immediate effect. However, if the committee adopts an unfavourable opinion by qualified majority, the Commission must communicate the proposal to the Council. There are two variants on the consequences of this referral.

Under variant (a) of the procedure, the Commission may, but does not have to, defer implementation of the measure pending its reconsideration by the Council. Otherwise the decision may be adopted and enter into force immediately. The Council then has one month in which to take a different decision by qualified majority. This variant is the norm for agriculture committees, where it would be counter-productive to delay the implementation of market management measures which must be implemented quickly to be of any use.

Under the stricter variant (b) of this procedure, the Commission *must* defer implementation of the measure pending its reconsideration by the Council, and the Council has the period laid down in the enabling legislation, subject to a maximum of three months, in which to take a different decision by qualified majority. The Commission will propose this variant, in preference to the regulatory committee, for areas other than agriculture which are less concerned with decisions of day-to-day management. Thus, decisions on aid to Eastern Europe under the PHARE programme are taken under this variant (Council Regulation (EEC) 3906/89, Article 9). A negative opinion on a draft PHARE measure would trigger a six-week deferral period in which the Council may itself act (though, so far, there have been no such references).

The strength of either variant of the management committee procedure is that the negative opinion required to trigger referral to the Council can be difficult to achieve in the face of inevitable differences between Member States. The first variant has the additional strength that the Commission may immediately implement its decision, even if a referral to the Council is triggered, and thus put the Council in the difficult position of reversing or reworking a *fait accompli*. A third strength which applies to both variants is that it may well not be possible to find the same negative majority in the

Council which existed in the management committee due to the political rather than technical approach at the higher level.

The regulatory committee – Procedure III

The regulatory committee procedure was developed and refined over 1967–68 to cover matters outside agriculture where Member States wished to control the Commission more closely than under the management committee procedure. The Commission may only adopt measures which accord with an opinion adopted by the committee. Otherwise, even if there is only a failure to adopt an opinion within the deadline laid down by the chair, the measure is referred to the Council and cannot enter into force.

The Commission initially attempted to employ the management committee procedure in areas such as Customs legislation, veterinary and plant health, and food, but met strong opposition from Member States who objected in particular to the Commission's ability under that procedure to bring measures into effect immediately, notwithstanding strong national opposition. The Commission finally agreed to this procedure in these areas in view of the longer-term nature of the legislation proposed and the absence of the same urgency for action as in agriculture (Olivier 1974, p. 169). For example, it is also used for the adaptation of certain internal market and environmental directives to take account of technical or scientific progress. The Commission finally felt obliged to propose the regulatory committee procedure in the Comitology Decision, despite the European Parliament's opposition to its continued use (as in Parliament's Opinion of 9 July 1986 and its subsequent Resolution of 23 October 1986).

Under variant (a) of the procedure, known as the 'net' or *'filet'*, if the committee adopts a favourable opinion by qualified majority, the Commission may adopt the measure with immediate effect. However, the Commission must submit its measure to the Council if the committee simply fails to reach such a majority and does not adopt any opinion within the deadline laid down by the chair. Naturally, the measure is also referred if the committee adopts an unfavourable opinion by qualified majority against the proposal. As a result, the matter ceases to be delegated, and has to be addressed under the Treaty itself, that is, by way of a formal Commission proposal and Council decision. However, the Council only has the period laid down in the enabling legislation, subject to a maximum of three months, to take a decision either amending the proposal by unanimity or adopting or rejecting it by qualified majority. If no decision is taken within the time limit, the matter returns to the Commission, which may then adopt the proposed measures itself. This is the 'net', which guarantees that a decision will be taken. The 'net' is commonly used for customs legislation.

Under the stricter variant (b) of the procedure, known as the 'safety-net' or *'contre-filet'*, the Council may reject the proposal by *simple* majority and thereby block subsequent adoption by the Commission. The 'safety-net' is commonly imposed in the more sensitive veterinary area.

An analysis of the use of the 'net' and the 'safety-net' is carried out below. However it may be asked at this juncture why the Council should need to impose the 'safety-net' even in sensitive areas, when a qualified majority would be sufficient to adopt its own decision in place of the Commission's and thus to avoid the 'net'. In this respect it should be borne in mind that opinions within the Council itself may be very divided on sensitive issues. Indeed, Member States may well disagree with each other on such issues as much, if not more than they disagree with the Commission. In such cases, the ability under the 'safety-net' to block decisions which they oppose by simple majority affords a greater protection for their interests than variant (a), which requires Member States to arrive at a qualified majority to reject a Commission proposal.

Safeguard measures — Procedure IV

Under Article 3 of the 1987 Decision on comitology the Commission may be empowered to take safeguard measures to protect the interests of the Community or individual Member States. The Commission is obliged to notify the Council and Member States beforehand of any measures to be taken under this provision. It may also be required to consult Member States before adopting such decisions. Any Member State may refer the Commission decision to the Council within a deadline laid down by the enabling legislation, and the Council will have a certain period in which to take a different decision, confirming, amending or revoking the decision by qualified majority vote. In the absence of a vote within this period, the Commission's decision may either be adopted — variant (a) — or is deemed to have been revoked — variant (b). In practice, the details of many of the safeguard procedures adopted under this rubric may vary from the precise requirements of Article 3.

Safeguard measures under Article 3 will normally relate to some action which is urgently required arising out of trade or commercial policy. Variant (a) coupled with an advisory committee has been used in the context of association agreements with EFTA Member States. A version of variant (a) has also been used in the transport sector, combined with consultation of the Member States directly (in practice by letter) or via the relevant advisory committee (see Article 4 of Council Regulation EEC 3916/90 of 21 December 1990 on measures to be taken in the event of a crisis in the carriage of goods by road). Variant (b) has been used in the external trade sector, most recently with regard to restrictions on imports of aluminium from CIS Member States (Commission Regulation (EEC) 2227/93 of 6 August 1993). Safeguard measures may also be adopted in the context of other procedures. Thus in 1991 the Commission reacted to the cholera epidemic in Peru by prohibiting the importation of certain products originating in or coming from Peru, acting via the Veterinary Committee under the IIIb procedure (Decisions 91/146/EEC and 91/147/EEC of 19 March 1991, adopted under Article 19 of Council Directive 90/675/EEC).

"Procedure" V — the Council itself in specific cases

Article 1 of the Decision excepts specific cases where the Council reserves the right to exercise directly implementing powers itself. As will be seen below, the Council tends to exercise this right either in specially sensitive areas such as health or financial institutions, or where it has been unable to impose the 'safety-net' procedure, as in the veterinary, plant health and food sectors.

From the Parliament's point of view, the possibility of using this exception at any time, even at the last stage of the legislative procedure, may make it impossible for it to know, when voting on the enabling Council legislation, whether the Commission or the Council will adopt the necessary implementing measures. Moreover, if it is the Council, then the Parliament's power of supervision over the Commission concerning those measures is removed. It has been argued that these infringements of Parliament's legislative and supervisory prerogatives constitute a violation of Article 145(3) of the Treaty, and that the only correct course would be for the Council to indicate at the outset in the enabling legislation the specific cases in which it itself would adopt implementing measures (Bradley 1992, pp. 712–719). Whilst logical, these arguments might presently go further than the Court of Justice could accept, particularly since the Council's practice is undoubtedly based on precedent.

From the Commission's point of view, the major problems with the use of this device are both principled and practical. The threat to use this device at any time can be used to force the Commission to concede a less satisfactory committee procedure, and when it is used there is a danger that serious inconsistencies in Community decision-making can take place. The existence and scope of this exceptional power therefore involves a wide difference in approach between the Council on the one hand and the Commission and Parliament on the other.

Conclusions on the working of the procedures

It has been seen that there are significant differences between the different types of committee procedure. In brief, advisory committees can only *advise;* management committees can *block,* and regulatory committees must *approve* (Nugent 1992, p. 84). The procedures constitute a continuum of power to make or block decisions, with the Commission deciding alone or in the advisory committee at one end and the Council alone or via the safety-net at the other. The choice of procedure with regard to a particular subject area will show the extent to which the Council is prepared to confer powers of implementation upon the Commission.

These procedures may be compared, at least with respect to the result, to the three main procedures available to the UK Parliament when it wishes to reserve a power of direct control over the adoption of delegated legislation by the executive (House of Lords 1986, paras. 15–18). The simplest procedure provides for the instrument of delegated legislation to be laid before Parliament before its entry into force, but without further provision for action by Parliament. Alternatively, the enabling legislation may provide for the 'negative resolution' procedure, whereby the instrument of delegated legislation is laid before Parliament for a period of 40 days, after which it may be put into effect unless either House of Parliament adopts a resolution praying against it. Or the instrument may be subjected to the 'positive resolution' procedure, whereby it is laid before Parliament for a period of 28 days and may only enter into effect if approved by a resolution of each House during that period.

The comitology procedures have three main strengths: the Commission controls the agenda of the committees; the Commission's draft must be voted upon by the national representatives; and, subject to the two specific exceptions noted above, the effect in practice of the procedures is to guarantee that a decision will be taken within the deadlines laid down (Olivier 1974, p. 175).

The weakness of the procedures is that they allow Member States total control over powers of implementation in practice in two situations — either directly, where the Council itself acts, or indirectly in procedure IIIb cases, where in case of doubt or disagreement a measure can easily be referred to the Council and if necessary blocked, using the 'safety-net'. In these two situations, there is no guarantee that the deadline will be respected, or that there will be any decision at all.

Litigation challenging the Council on comitology

After the adoption of the Single European Act and the Comitology Decision, there were two attempts to persuade the Court to address the perceived inadequacies of the system.

In Case 302/87, *Parliament v. Council* ([1988] ECR 5615), Parliament attacked the Comitology Decision itself, on the grounds that it infringed Article 145 EEC, as amended by the SEA, in failing to respect the distinction between decision-making by the Council, acting in consultation with Parliament, and decision-making by the Commission using implementing powers, now vested in the Commission as a matter of principle. In breach of this principle, the Council could have the last word in four of the seven procedural variants. Moreover, variants (b) of procedures III and IV, could lead to no decision being taken at all.

Parliament also challenged the Decision on the basis that it permitted existing procedures to be maintained and that it infringed the principle that reservation of powers should be exceptional. This disregard for the rights of the Commission also encroached on Parliament's right to exercise political control over the Commission.

However, the Court simply held that the action was inadmissible, on the grounds that Parliament had no capacity to bring an action for annulment under Article 173 of the Treaty. As a result, it simply did not deal with the substance. It may be noted in passing that the Court has subsequently reconsidered its position and has held that Parliament may bring proceedings for annulment of actions by the Commission or the Council which allegedly infringe its prerogatives, particularly those concerning its participation in the drafting of legislative measures (Case C-70/88, *Parliament v. Council* [1990] ECR I-2041 at 2073-4, see Mancini and Keeling 1994, pp. 180-1).

Secondly, the Commission attempted to tackle infiltration of its exclusive budgetary powers by the Council, which had adopted the practice of inserting committees into financial instruments. In Case 16/88, *Commission v. Council* ([1989] ECR 3457), the Commission attacked an attempt to insert a management committee procedure into Regulation No. 3252/87 on the coordination and promotion of research into the fisheries sector. As the regulation was an instrument with financial aspects, the Commission took the view that it had the right to adopt such an instrument, pursuant to its sole responsibility under Article 205 EEC to execute the budget, including all decisions relating to the use of budgetary appropriations. In answer to the argument that the Council had the right to pass such legislation under general institutional rules, including the power under Article 145 EEC to confer powers of implementation, the Commission argued that Article 205 constituted a *lex specialis* conferring exclusive power on the Commission.

Advocate General Darmon supported the Commission, taking the view that it "enjoys a sphere of activity which is shielded from interference, whether direct or indirect, by the Council" (at p. 3480, para. 48).

However, the Court found in favour of the Council, and held that the power in question was of a legislative rather than a financial nature. In doing so, it gave the general institutional provisions in Part I of the Treaty, including Articles 145 and 155, priority over the financial provisions in Part II, such as Article 205.

Other aspects of the judgment supported the Commission's position. The Court held that the Council may impose new committees only in the form provided for in the Comitology Decision (at p. 3486, para. 13). It also held that the Council's right to exercise powers itself is exceptional and must be justified each time it is used:

> "after the amendments made to Article 145 by the Single European Act, the Council may reserve the right to exercise implementing powers directly only in specific cases, and it must state in detail the grounds for such a decision." (at p. 3485, para. 10)

The Court may well have been hesitant to confer sole jurisdiction upon the Commission in a situation where the Treaties had left open the possibility for both the Council and the Commission to act as executive bodies, a situation which the SEA and the Comitology Decision had left unchanged. The Court has interpreted those provisions to establish a presumption that the Commission should exercise implementing powers, together with a wide discretion in that exercise, and has characterised the exercise of such powers by the Council as exceptional. That is as far as it has felt able to go. As a result, the present position is that set out by Advocate General Jacobs:

> "the provisions of the Treaty and the 'comitology decision' . . . do not lead to the conclusion that the Council's power to delegate the power to draw up implementing provisions must be interpreted strictly; rather they suggest the contrary. There seems to be a presumption that the Council delegates to the Commission the power to adopt all measures necessary to implement the rules laid down by it, except in the specific cases where it decides it is more appropriate for it to exercise such power itself." (Case C-240/90, *Germany v. Commission* [1992] ECR I–5383 at 5416, para. 36)

Other forms of committees

A discussion of the committees organised by the Commission would not be complete if it omitted two areas of committee work which fall outside the comitology structure. The Commission exercises its right of initiative in close collaboration with interest groups on both an informal and formal basis. Mazey and Richardson review the relations between the Commission and the lobby in Chapter 7. The following discussion illustrates the more formal committee procedures involved which do not fall under the Comitology Decision.

(a) *Commission committees and expert groups*

The Commission has set up many committees and expert groups to assist it in implementing policy. These fall conceptually into three main categories (Glatthaar 1992, p. 180). The largest category concerns agriculture, where Commission-created committees tend to be set up by formal decision as 'advisory committees'. There will normally be an advisory committee of representatives of the sector concerned for each sector or common market organisation having a management committee. Thus the Cereals & Rice and Milk & Dairy Products Management Committees are shadowed by Advisory Committees (see generally OJ No. L 45 of 14.2.87). Members of committees are appointed every three years by decision of the Commission[2] on the basis of special interest bodies or associations specified in the Decision setting up the Committee. Thus the cereals advisory committee is composed of representatives of producers, cooperatives, food processors and manufacturers, traders, workers in agriculture and processing and food-manufacturing, and consumers. Its mandate is to advise the Commission of the views of producers, traders and consumers on the issues arising from the operation of the common market organisation in cereals "and in particular on measures to be adopted by the Commission". Such committees provide invaluable expertise to the Commission when contemplating the need for or effect of proposed measures. They are precluded from voting, but the views expressed by the various interests represented are reported to the Commission, and on request may be passed on to the Council and to the relevant Management Committees.

The second main category mainly concerns the social area, where advisory committees or groups have been created both by formal decision and by informal administrative practice. The Commission has set up a number of joint and tripartite committees where representatives of government and the two sides of industry or the two sides of industry alone meet to advise the Commission on the planning and implementation of social policy.

The Advisory Committee on Equal Opportunities for Women and Men was established by Commission Decision 82/43/EEC of 9 December 1981 to provide an institutional framework for consultation of specialised national equal opportunities bodies or their equivalents. Its members range from representatives of autonomous equality bodies such as the Equal Opportunities Commissions in the UK and the Employment Equality Agency in Ireland to officials in national ministries handling equality issues in the absence of such specialised agencies.

Such bodies may also be found in the field of competition policy in the few areas where no formal consultation requirement has been imposed in relation to procedural legislation adopted by the Commission, in particular, early legislation providing for the notification form (Form A/B) to be completed by companies requesting exemption from the prohibition imposed in Article 85(1). In practice, the Commission has always convened such meetings of its own volition (they are generally referred to as meetings of national governmental experts to distinguish them from meetings of the advisory committee, although the same people are normally involved) and it has also sought to pay equal attention to the views expressed therein. In more recent legislation, however, such as the regulation implementing the Merger Regulation, the advisory committee has been formally constituted.

The Commission has recently set up an advisory committee within this category aimed at the coordination of fraud prevention (Commission Decision 94/140/EC of 23 February 1994, OJ No. L 61/27, 4.3.94). This committee will be used to complement the work of existing committees by providing a horizontal view of the whole area of fraud against the Community budget and to assist in coordinating the action taken by Member States to protect the interests of the Community and to counter fraud.

The third category consists of groups of experts who provide scientific and technical advice to the Commission in carrying out its policies. Such groups may be set up formally or informally. Examples of the latter are the so-called 'equality networks' composed of diverse specialists such as lawyers, specialists on child care, education and training and small business creation, and representatives of European television organisations (Docksey 1987, p. 1). These various networks are a source of expert advice to the Commission in their fields of expertise and carry out pilot projects in their sectors.

Scientific groups set up by formal decision are normally intended to back up the rule-making function. The recent judgment of 25 January 1994 in Case C-212/91, *Angelopharm v. Hamburg*, has revolutionised the status of such groups in the decision-making process. The Scientific Committee on Cosmetology was established by the Cosmetics Directive 76/768/EEC to bring together a group of scientists in disciplines related to cosmetics, such as medicine, toxicology, biology and chemistry, to aid the Commission in establishing whether particular substances could be injurious to human health and so should be prohibited for use in cosmetic products. The Commission could adopt such prohibitions acting through a regulatory committee, variant (a). In that case the Commission prohibited the use of a particular substance in a cosmetic product to combat hair loss. The regulatory committee had been consulted, but not the scientific committee.

The Court held, contrary to its Advocate General, that it was impossible to divine from the wording of the Cosmetics Directive whether the scientific committee had to be consulted in all cases or only "at the initiative of" the Commission or a Member State. It accordingly looked to the scientific committee's role in adapting the Cosmetics Directive and found that it was intended to ensure that measures adopted were scientifically accurate in assessing what prohibitions were necessary to protect human health. In view of this objective, consultation of the scientific committee was found to be mandatory. The prohibition adopted without consulting the scientific committee was accordingly found to be invalid.

As a result of this case, the Commission will have to consider carefully the role of such expert groups in the future when deciding whether they should be consulted and what account to take of their opinions.

(b) *Intergovernmental bodies*

There exist various intergovernmental bodies set up by Member States to deal with issues of common interest falling outside the scope of the Treaties. Such bodies include the *ad hoc* Working Group on Immigration set up in October 1986 and the Coordinator's Group on the free movement of persons set up following the Rhodes European Council in December 1988. Various bodies of the Trevi Group work on police cooperation, and the European Committee to Combat Drugs (ECCD), set up in 1989, reported on the implementation of the European Programme for Combating Drugs, adopted in December 1990. These bodies are very different to the structures described above, and the Commission obviously does not have the same status in them. However, it is normally represented on such bodies, though only with observer status on the Trevi bodies.

With the coming into force of the Treaty on European Union, the activities of such bodies now fall within the ambit of cooperation in the fields of justice and home affairs. They fall under the authority of the Coordinating Committee provided for under Article K4 of the Treaty, which has the power to restructure them if it wishes (Commission reply to Written Question No. 830/92, OJ C 297/3, 3.11.93).

The Council's follow-up of the Comitology Decision

Returning to the procedures under the 1987 Decision, the Parliament and the Commission have made it clear that, on the one hand, they greatly prefer the first two types of committee and, on the other hand, they are very much opposed to the 'safety-net' variants because there is no guarantee that a decision will be taken at one level or the other. Both bodies would like to see powers of implementation subjected to only two formulas, advisory committee or management committee, and had wanted reform in that direction to be implemented at Maastricht (European Commission 1991, p. 11, para. 39).

In practice, since the Commission has the right to propose legislation to the Council, it will normally choose the lightest appropriate procedure, which the Council can only change acting unanimously. However, Member States can put pressure on the Commission to change its proposal itself by threatening to block adoption of the proposal, where there are enough Member States to constitute a blocking minority, or threatening to use the Council's own implementing powers. Thus the Commission will often be forced to negotiate with the Council as to the type of procedure to be adopted, as occurred over German unification (Spence 1991, pp. 30–35).

Similarly, the type of procedure adopted may influence the content of the measure itself. In the case of German unification, the most difficult negotiations between the Commission, the Council and Parliament concerned the type of procedure to be adopted. Only when the Commission and Parliament tacitly conceded the regulatory committee procedure in exchange for greater involvement of Parliament in considering new issues that might arise was the Council willing to adopt the necessary measures.

The Commission and Parliament have complained that the Decision and subsequent practice have shown that comitology practice has been regressing rather than progressing. In 1991, the Commission adopted a report on the comitology procedures, pursuant to Article 5 of the 1987 Decision. It reiterated criticisms made in 1988 (22nd General Report 1988, p. 33, No. 9) and 1989 (23rd General Report 1989, p. 32, No. 6) that the situation was "far from satisfactory" because of developments which ran counter to the spirit of the Single European Act and which were likely to compromise the efficiency of Community action in the lead-up to the single European market. The report pointed out that problems had persisted at three main levels (European Commission 1991, pp. 1, 7–10).

Firstly, the Council had restricted selection of the advisory committee procedure, contrary to the IGC Declaration calling for use of that procedure in the internal market area. It had stuck to the status quo by almost systematically replacing the proposals for advisory committees by regulatory committees, only adopting 12 out of 37 such proposals in the internal market area (see Annex). Secondly, the Council had shown a preference for the 'safety-net' procedure, and had even started using it in setting up new committees in areas such as research, banking and the environment. Moreover, despite the existence of a 'safety-net' procedure, the Council had conferred only limited powers on the Commission in the environmental directives on genetically-modified organisms and quality of water, and had reserved to itself the power to adapt to technical progress. Similarly, in the RACE and ESPRIT II research programmes, the Council had imposed the 'safety-net' procedure for specific matters such as adaptation of the annual programme and derogations from general rules. Thirdly, the Council had decided not to confer powers of implementation in a number of cases, for two main reasons. The area concerned may have been one of special sensitivity, such as health or financial institutions. Thus in the financial institutions sector, the Council either retained powers of implementation for itself ('own funds' directive) or conferred only limited powers on the Commission, despite the existence of a 'safety-net' procedure (direct life insurance, access to the activity of credit institutions, the 'solvency ratio').

Alternatively, the Council may have found that it was easier in practice to reach agreement on a decision not to confer than to confer powers subject to the 'safety-net' procedure. For example, in certain cases in the veterinary, plant health and food sectors, the Commission refused to introduce the safety net into its proposal to allow adoption of the proposal by qualified majority. As a result, the Council, which could have obtained a qualified majority but not unanimity in favour of the 'safety-net' procedure, found it easier to decide not to confer any powers at all.

The Commission itself claims that its conduct where powers had been conferred has given no cause to the Council to be so hesitant. In agriculture, there had only been 10 referrals to the Council from management committees, and of these only two had resulted in the Council amending the Commission decision. In regulatory committee areas, 98 per cent of proposed decisions had been approved by the committees, and almost all of the remaining 2 per cent of measures sent to the Council had been reformulated by the Commission so as to aid the Council to reach agreement.

In fact, the only example cited by the Commission where it successfully refused to change its position was the BSE or 'mad cow disease' affair in 1990. In this case, the Commission's draft measures received an unfavourable opinion from the Standing Veterinary Committee, which triggered a referral of the proposed instrument to the Council on 22 January 1990. Under Article 13 of the enabling legislation Directive 64/432/EEC, the Council had a maximum period of 15 days in which it itself could adopt the proposed instrument. However it was unable to act within the time limit, and the Commission immediately used the 'net' to adopt its Decision on 7 February 1990. The Commission therefore concluded that there was "no objective reason for the Council's hesitancy" and that it was:

> "deeply concerned by developments in this area which, to its mind, run counter to the spirit of the Single Act and are likely to compromise the efficiency of Community action in the lead-up to the single European market." (European Commission 1991, p. 1)

The major areas of difference in approach between the Council and the Commission

The above discussion shows that the main difference of approach between the Council and the Commission is the type of procedure to be used when adopting implementing powers. The Commission takes the view that the advisory committee procedure is the norm, at least with regard to the implementation of the Single Market, and that all other types of procedure should be regarded as exceptional. It bases this view on the IGC Declaration accompanying the Single European Act. In contrast, Member States seem to take the view that any of the whole range of procedures may be used as appropriate, depending upon the sensitivity of the matter being dealt with. In sensitive areas, where the Council does not decide to exercise executive powers itself, the extreme 'safety-net' procedure is regarded as the norm.

A second area of disagreement concerns the status of committee procedures existing before the entry into force of the 1987 Decision on comitology. The Commission feels that it is essential to bring them into line with the Comitology Decision over a reasonable period of time so as to clarify and simplify those procedures. It is not a real simplification if the plethora of existing procedures is simply allowed to continue (European Commission 1991, pp. 3 and 11–12). However, Member States seem to take the view that they should be continued unless there is good reason for change. They point to Article 4 of the Comitology Decision, which allows existing procedures to be continued where legislation is amended or extended, and to the preamble, which states that existing procedures are not directly affected by the Decision.

Thirdly, the two Institutions are divided on the question of implementation by the Council itself. The Commission takes the view that the Council can decide to act as the executive only in exceptional circumstances, and subject to the criteria in the Comitology Decision. Moreover, this should be interpreted in the light of Article 10 of the Single European Act introducing Article 145 third indent, which transfers administrative competence to the

Commission and states that the Council can only award itself such powers in "specific cases".

In contrast, Member States will consider exercising this right wherever necessary in sensitive areas and do not regard themselves as bound by the Decision criteria. In this respect, the holding in Case 16/88, *Commission v. Council*, that the Council may only exercise this right in specific cases and that it must give detailed reasons justifying its exercise, would favour the Commission's approach on this point.

The European Parliament and comitology[3]

The European Parliament has taken a particular interest in comitology since the adoption of its first major report in 1968. After initial doubts as to the legality of the procedures (Olivier 1974, p. 164), it has supported the Commission against the Council, indeed taking a stronger view than the Commission on the flaws in the 1987 Comitology Decision. Parliament seeks to assert its own legislative prerogatives (Bradley 1992, p. 717) and its supervisory and political powers over the Commission pursuant to Articles 137, 142 and 144 EC. Any infringement of the rights of the Commission accordingly infringes its own rights to supervise that body. Put bluntly:

> "Since the Parliament's ultimate power of control lies in sacking the Commission, the committee procedure offering maximum power to the Commission simultaneously offers the largest degree of parliamentary censure." (Spence 1991, p. 32)

In its Resolution of 22 November 1990 adopting the Roumeliotis Report (European Parliament 1990), Parliament deplored the Council's practice of subjecting powers of implementation to the most restrictive committee procedures. It urged that procedures should be limited to the advisory and management committee procedures, and that only the advisory committee procedure should be used in matters concerned with implementation of the budget. It concluded that only a reform of the Treaty would guarantee effective Community decision-making and proposed a new Article 155, fourth indent. This would expressly state that the Commission is the Community's executive body and would provide Parliament with a right to refer implementing measures back to the Council, for adoption in cooperation or consultation with Parliament. However, no such provision was adopted by the European Council at Maastricht in December 1991.

In practice, the major concern of Parliament is to receive timely information from the Commission on the work of the committees. It regards such information as an essential element in reducing the "democratic deficit", since it cannot react politically and effectively to influence draft decisions if it is not informed in good time. It has therefore developed a policy of seeking broad equivalence with the Council *vis-à-vis* the Commission.

In 1986 following the Hänsch Report (European Parliament 1986), Parliament proposed that it should be informed of all documents submitted to committees at the same time as the committees. This demand was unrealistic, not least because of the mass of routine documents that would have swamped Parliament. It did however lead to the Commission setting up internal arrangements for informing Parliament, which led to a formal agreement on procedures between the two Institutions in March 1989, following an exchange of letters between their then respective Presidents Plumb and Delors. The details are described by Westlake in Chapter 9.

Under the Plumb-Delors agreement, the Commission undertook to forward to Parliament, for information, draft decisions of a legislative nature forwarded to a committee in the working language or languages in which they were forwarded to that committee. Routine management documents with a limited period of validity were excluded from the procedure, to avoid overloading Parliament with unnecessary administrative documents. In addition, documents whose adoption was complicated by considerations of secrecy or urgency were excluded.

There have been certain specific circumstances in which these two types of exceptions — routine and secrecy/urgency — have not been used. In November 1990 the Commission undertook to communicate to Parliament all draft implementing measures without exception relating to transitional measures on German unification. Drafts would be forwarded to Parliament at the same time as the relevant committee and would indicate the date upon which the draft measure would be discussed. Parliament set up a Temporary Committee on German Unification, which met practically every week and was able to examine Commission and German officials on implementing measures. It is also notable that the Council allowed the Commission considerable discretion in this area and agreed to procedures which guaranteed effective decision-making. In particular, it refrained from resorting to the safety-net (European Commission 1991, p. 11).

However, these procedures were temporary and highly exceptional. Otherwise, there have only been two areas where the Commission has gone further than the Plumb-Delors agreement and has undertaken to forward to Parliament all the implementing measures concerned: with regard to food aid to Romania, Bulgaria and Soviet Union; and with regard to the specific research programmes within the 1990–94 research framework programme, together with background information on the development of those programmes, subject to the exception of measures involving confidentiality (PE 150.483, 18 April 1991).

The significance of Parliament being informed of Commission draft measures is to allow an issue to be taken up by Parliament and pressure to be put on the Commission to change a disputed text. Apart from the specific and exceptional procedures set up to deal with German unification, the following practical or procedural avenues are open to Parliament to exert political influence. It can put oral questions to the Commission in Plenary Question Time at any time and on any subject; it can put written questions to the Commission; it can informally question members of the Commission or their officials in Committee; it can send a letter to the Commission from its President or the President of the relevant Committee. It can also adopt resolutions which are not legally binding, but which do have undoubted political effect.

The major precedent showing the type and speed of reaction which is possible concerns Commission Directive 321/91/EEC of 14 May 1991 on infant formulae milk. The draft measure was received by the Environment Committee in February 1991, which put down a question to the Commission for Committee Question Time and subsequently drew up a motion for a resolution which was adopted by Parliament on 19 April 1991. The measure finally adopted by the Commission on 14 May 1991 was thus able to take account of Parliament's concerns.

However, in its Resolution adopting the Roumeliotis Report (European Parliament 1990), Parliament expressed its concern at how few Commission proposals were being transmitted to Parliament and insisted that the Commission ensure that its services were aware of their duties in this respect.

As the Council and the Commission increasingly resort, for reasons of efficiency, to entrusting implementation powers to the Commission, the democratic aspect of the debate is becoming more significant. For example, the Council has abolished its right to adopt so-called 'second generation' regulations in the cereals sector allowing it to lay down detailed rules, leaving this exclusively to the Commission.[4] The European Parliament is aware of the danger that only the Council will supervise decision-making by the Commission, or that the Council will carry out such decisions itself, unsupervised. To that end, it has been pressing the Council to return to the matter of comitology after the entry into force of the Treaty on European Union, and obtained undertakings from the Council to that effect in February 1992 and again in October 1993 upon the occasion of the ratification of the 1993–1999 inter-institutional agreement, including a declaration on comitology.

The Parliament has also argued that its representatives should attend committees dealing with powers of implementation. The Commission has opposed this approach on the legal grounds that it would fall outside the terms of the Comitology Decision and on the principal grounds that members of the legislature are neither fitted to be members of technical committees nor is their political role consistent with such a function.

The entry into force of the Treaty on European Union has brought the issue to a head over the co-decision procedure introduced under Article 189b. Parliament set out its position in its Resolution of 16 December 1993 adopting the De Giovanni Report (European Parliament 1993) on comitology and the Treaty on European Union. Having become a co-legislator together with the Council, the Parliament claims that the conferral of powers by instruments adopted under the co-decision procedure is a joint conferral by the Council and the Parliament, and that Article 145(3) EC and hence the Comitology Decision does not apply to acts adopted under the new co-decision procedure. As a result, Parliament claims it has corresponding rights to receive information provided to the Council on the work of the committees and to trigger referral back to the Community legislator, the Council and the Parliament. The report accordingly proposes far-reaching negotiations between the three institutions on the consequences for comitology of the new co-decision procedure and the adoption of a new Comitology Decision by the Parliament and the Council.

In the meantime, several legislative proposals changed their legal base from the old cooperation base, now Article 189c, to the new co-decision base under Article 189b. To give teeth to its position, Parliament began to propose ad hoc comitology procedures for these instruments whereby the conferral of powers by Parliament and Council could be referred back to both co-legislators rather than to the Council alone. An unsatisfactory situation developed where each of the three legislative institutions would have its own proposal for a committee procedure. For example, in the case of the draft directives on sweeteners and colourings, the Commission proposed the advisory committee procedure, the Council opted for the regulatory committee 'net' procedure, and the Parliamentary rapporteur proposed a completely new procedure involving Parliament as co-legislator. The positions of the Council and Parliament were poles apart and were in danger of becoming virtually irreconcilable. When discussing the proposed directive on the application of open network provision (ONP) to voice telephony, the issue of comitology and the accompanying question of institutional balance became so sensitive that for the first time under the co-decision procedure the conciliation phase failed. This failure made it possible for the Parliament to exercise its new veto power under that procedure.

To resolve this increasingly intractable situation, the Commission proposed a temporary Inter-institutional Agreement to cover acts adopted under the co-decision procedure until the 1996 IGC (Commission 1994). The procedure divides decisions into two categories, normative and non-normative. Measures which are not of a rule-making nature may be adopted under the advisory committee or management committee — variant (a) —procedures laid down by the comitology decision. As a result, Parliament is not involved in supervising administrative decisions.

In contrast, rule-making measures are to be adopted under the special procedure laid down by the draft Inter-institutional Agreement. This procedure is the advisory committee procedure adapted to provide a parallel procedure for the Parliament and providing that the co-legislators, the Council and Parliament, acting together, may abrogate a decision adopted by the Commission under this procedure. Parliament would be sent the draft measure at the same time as the members of the advisory committee; any deadline laid down to give an opinion would apply to both the advisory committee and to Parliament; and the Commission would inform both parties of how it had taken account of their views. The Commission may adopt its decision with immediate effect and inform Parliament and the Council, or it may choose to defer its effect until two months from the date of communication of its adoption.

Within one month of communication either of the co-legislators (Parliament by simple majority or the Council by qualified majority) may request the other to agree to the repeal of the measure. If the other institution decides by the appropriate majority to agree to that request within a further month, the act is annulled and has no retroactive effect. In such a case, the Commission may choose either to submit a new measure under the same procedure, or to propose an act for adoption by the Council and the Parliament.

If the institutions accept the Commission's proposed Inter-institutional Agreement, the immediate causes of conflict between the Council and Parliament would be removed. However, both may have reservations. Parliament may take the view that it is inadequate because it does not provide that Commission measures that are rejected by the co-legislators return automatically to them, but gives the Commission discretion as to what subsequent action to take.

The Council may object to the fact that only the advisory committee procedure is available rather than the full range of procedures under the 1987 decision, a distinction is made between normative and non-normative acts, and Parliament for the first time enjoys equal status with the Council over control of the Commission's exercise of its implementing powers. All these aspects may well be thought to be overdue, but the Council may prefer to attempt to hold the situation until the 1996 IGC or to devise a temporary solution providing greater flexibility.

Much will depend upon the attitude of the newly elected Parliament in the second half of 1994 and its willingness to confront the intransigence of the Council in the run-up to the 1996 IGC. Far from being an abstruse issue for institutional conflict, comitology is likely to be the major battle-ground between the two institutions. Parliament now has the power under the new co-decision procedure to reject measures which are unsatisfactory with regard to comitology.[5] If Parliament does not win its campaign for broad equivalence with the Council in supervising the Commission, it will be in a weak position in 1996.

Conclusion

It is clear that the Community is in a state of considerable transition in this area. Issues which the Member States failed to tackle in 1986 and 1992 will have to be taken on board by the IGC in 1996 when it takes up the theme of reform of EC legislative measures postponed by the Maastricht IGC.[6] The progressively greater emphasis on the implementation of policy by the Commission will inevitably involve further consideration by Member States and Parliament of the supervision of that implementation.

No doubt it will again be urged that the new Treaty should confer sole executive power upon the Commission, as repeatedly demanded by the European Parliament. At the very least, the areas should be specified where the Commission would have sole executive jurisdiction. These questions will be linked with the question of the hierarchy of norms, which is already formally on the agenda for 1996. It will be necessary to distinguish between legislative rules with a general and abstractly defined scope ('lois matérielles') and the administrative application of those rules to individual or specific categories of cases (Lenaerts 1991, p. 141).

It will also be necessary to grasp the nettle on the linked question of 'institutional balance', the balance of powers under the new institutional structure. There may well have been significant developments under the present structure by then, to provide a more amenable context for the changes required under the new structure. The Council will have been forced to look hard at its reluctance to confer implementing powers upon the Commission and to sharing the supervision of the Commission with the Parliament; the Commission has already taken a position on the supervisory role of Parliament over its implementation of normative legislation enacted under the co-decision procedure, but will have to ensure that its practice with regard to the involvement of Parliament meets up to its principles; and Parliament will have to decide how far it is prepared to go to be able to supervise the management function of the Commission.

Notes

1   See Article 148 (2) EC, whereby Germany, France, Italy and the UK have 10 votes; Spain eight votes; Belgium, Greece, the Netherlands and Portugal five votes; Denmark and Ireland three votes; and Luxembourg two votes. Agreement at the European Council held in Brussels in December 1993 will mean that with enlargement to include the EFTA candidate countries, Finland and Norway will have three votes, Austria and Sweden four votes (*Bulletin of the EC* No. 12 1993, p. 18).
2   Current appointments are set out in OJ No. C 96 of 5 April 1993.
3   The authors would like to thank Francis Jacobs for his support and advice on this topic.
4   Compare the former common market organisation, Regulation (EEC) No. 2727/75 and its replacement adopted during the agricultural reform, Regulation (EEC) No. 1716/93.
5   The newly elected Parliament rejected the ONP Directive at the first plenary in July 1994.
6   The IGC adopted a Declaration on the hierarchy of Community acts, agreeing that "the Inter-governmental Conference to be convened in 1996 will examine to what extent it might be possible to review the classification of Community acts with a view to establishing an appropriate hierarchy between the different categories of act" (OJ No. C 191/101, 29.7.92).

References

Bertram, C. (1967–68) 'Decision-making in the EEC: the Management Committee procedure' 5 *Common Market Law Review*, 246.

Blumann, C. (1988) 'Le pouvoir exécutif de la Commission à la lumière de l'Acte unique européen', 1 *Revue Trimestriel du Droit Européen* 23.

Blumann, C. (1992) 'La Comitologie: L'exercice de la fonction exécutive dans la Communauté Européenne', in Engel, C. and Wessels, W. (eds.) *From Luxembourg to Maastricht: Institutional change in the European Community after the Single European Act*, Bonn: Europa Union Verlag, 1992, pp. 89–108 (quoted translation by the authors).

Bradley, K. (1992) 'Comitology and the law: through a glass, darkly', 29 *Common Market Law Review*, 693.

Commission Decision 82/43/EEC of 9 December 1981 relating to the setting up of an Advisory Committee on Equal Opportunities for Women and Men, OJ No. L 20/35, 28.1.82.

Commission Decision of 7 February 1990 amending Decision 89/469/EEC concerning certain protection measures relating to bovine spongiform encephalopathy in the United Kingdom, OJ No. L 41/23, 15.2.1990.

Commission Directive 321/91/EEC of 14 May 1991 on infant formulae and follow-on formulae, OJ No. L 175/35, 4.7.1991.

Commission Draft Inter-institutional Agreement between the European Parliament, the Council and the Commission on the rules for exercising the powers to implement acts adopted jointly by the European Parliament and the Council in accordance with the procedure laid down in Article 189B EC, SEC (94) 645 final/2 27 May 1994.

Commission Regulation (EEC) No. 570/88 of 16 February 1988 on the sale of butter at reduced prices and the granting of aid for butter and concentrated butter for use in the manufacture of pastry products, ice-cream and other foodstuffs, OJ No. L 55/31, 1.3.1988.

Commission Regulation (EEC) No. 548/92 of 6 March 1992 concerning import licences for milk products from certain East European countries, OJ No. L 62/34, 7.3.1992.

Commission Regulation (EEC) No. 1765/92 concerning the 'set-aside' scheme, OJ No. L 181/12, 1.7.92.

Committee of Three (1979) *Report on European Institutions* (Report presented to the European Council, October 1979), Brussels.

Council Decision 87/373 of 13 July 1987 laying down the procedures for the exercise of implementing powers conferred on the Commission, OJ No. L 197, 18.7.87, p. 33.

Docksey, C. (1987) 'The European Community and the promotion of equality,' in McCrudden (ed.) *Women, Employment and Equality Law,* Eclipse 1987, p. 1.

Engel, C. and Borrmann, C. (1991) *Vom Konsens zur Mehrheitsentscheidung. EG-Entscheidungsverfahren und nationale Interessenpolitik nach der Einheitlichen Europäischen Akte,* Bonn: Europa Union Verlag.

European Commission (1980) *Bulletin of the EC:* Supplement 2/80.

European Commission (1987) *Bulletin of the EC* 6 No. 2.4.14, pp. 111–12.

European Commission (1990) *Opinion on the proposal for amendment of the Treaty,* COM (90) 600 final.

European Commission (1991) *Communication to the Council on the conferment of implementing powers on the Commission,* Brussels, 10 January 1991, SEC (90) 2589 final.

European Parliament (1968) Jozeau-Marigné Report Doc. 115/1968–69.

European Parliament (1986) Hänsch Report Doc. A2 78/86 and 2nd report Doc. A2 138/86, OJ No. 2-341/138, 9 July 1986, OJ No. C 227/54.

European Parliament (1990) Roumeliotis Report Doc. A3 0310/90, 19 November 1990.

European Parliament (1993) De Giovanni Report for the Committee on Institutional Affairs on questions of comitology relating to the entry into force of the Maastricht Treaty, PE 206.619/fin p. 10, cited in the Opinion of the Committee on Budgets.

Glatthaar, C. (1992), 'Einflußnahme auf Entscheidungen der EG durch die Ausschüsse der EG-Kommission', *Recht von Internationalen Wirtschaft,* Heft 3, p. 179 at 180.

House of Lords Select Committee on the European Communities (1986) *Delegation of powers to the Commission,* Session 1985–86, 19th Report.

House of Lords Select Committee on the European Communities (1994) *Report on Enforcement of Community Competition Rules,* Session 1993–94, First Report.

Lenaerts, K. (1991) 'Some reflections on the separation of powers in the European Community', 28 *Common Market Law Review* 11.

Mancini, G. F. and Keeling, D. T. (1994) 'Democracy and the European Court of Justice', 57 *Modern Law Review,* 175.

Nicoll, W. (1987) 'Qu'est-ce que la comitologie?' *Revue du Marché Commun,* No. 306, April.

Nugent N. (1992) *The Government and Politics of the European Community,* London: Macmillan.

Olivier, G. (1974) *Les pouvoirs de gestion de la Commission,* in *La Commission des Communautés Européennes et l'Elargissement de l'Europe,* Université Libre de Bruxelles.

Schindler, P. (1971) 'The problems of Decision-Making by way of the Management Committee Procedure in the European Economic Community', 8 *Common Market Law Review* 184.

Spence, D. (1991) 'Enlargement without accession: the EC's response to German unification', RIIA Discussion Paper No. 36.

ANNEX

Committee procedures

Committee procedures proposed by the Commission and adopted by the Council in all areas, including the internal market, since the entry into force of the Single European Act and published in the Official Journal up to 30 November 1990.

		Commission	Council
I	Advisory Committee	88	60 .
	Technical standards committee*	11	10
IIa	Management Committee, variant (a)	64	67
IIb	Management Committee, variant (b)	3	10
IIIa	Regulatory Committee with 'net'	70	72
IIIb	Regulatory Committee with 'safety-net'		
IVa	Safeguard Procedure, variant (a)	8	2
	other (revised ESF, Codest)	2	2
	Total — committee procedures	253	267
	Total — measures	223	223

*Advisory-type technical standards committee laid down under Directive 83/189/33C

Source: European Commission (1991).

6.   The Commission and the law

John A. Usher

Introduction

Politicians critical of 'creeping federalism' in the Community have sometimes pointed to the European Court of Justice (ECJ) as the most 'federal' of the Community's institutions and the most effective locomotive of European integration (Heseltine 1989). But it is argued here that as regards the legislative and administrative functions in the Community, it is still true to say (perhaps even more than it was in 1970 when Commission President Malfatti so informed the European Parliament) that "the Commission is, at one and the same time, the guardian of the Treaties and the motive force of integration" (Lasok and Bridge 1991).

Under Article 155 of the EEC Treaty, the first duty of the Commission with regard to the proper functioning and development of the Common market is to "ensure that the provisions of this Treaty and the measures taken by the institutions pursuant thereto are applied". In its unique position as proposer and enforcer of Community legislation, the Commission has the opportunity to fulfil this duty both in the legislative process and subsequently in ensuring the observance of the legislation itself. Moreover, this Chapter argues that Article 155 has conferred on the Commission both legislative powers and enforcement duties that are not apparent from the substantive Treaty provisions.

The Commission and the legislative process

(a) Council legislation

The fundamentals of the Commission's position in the legislative process under the EEC Treaty are set out in Article 149(1) and (3) (Article 189a(1) and (2) following the Maastricht amendments). Here, the Commission's sole right of legislative initiative is set out. Under these provisions, the Council, on the one hand, must act unanimously if it wishes to amend a Commission proposal, and the Commission, on the other hand, may alter its proposal at any time during the procedures leading to the adoption of a Community act. Of course, in the day-to-day process of negotiation in the Council of Ministers and its subsidiary bodies, the Council Working Groups and COREPER, there is a constant process of negotiation involving a collaborative process of adjustment of the Commission's proposals. The Commission is an equal partner in the process, albeit deprived of a vote on the outcome, but it nevertheless retains a veto power in its ability to withdraw the proposal itself unless satisfactory compromise is reached.

Discussion of the changes in the legislative process brought about by the cooperation procedure introduced by the Single European Act and the co-decision procedure introduced by the Maastricht Treaty has concentrated on the relationship between Parliament and Council. While the cooperation procedure has hardly diminished the role of the Commission — indeed it might be argued that it has enhanced it — it remains to be seen whether the co-decision procedure will. Of course, at first sight, the cooperation procedure appears always to give the Council the last word. But if the Commission retains the right (under the terms of Article 149(3)/189a(2)) to alter its proposal at any time during the whole procedure, judging when the 'last word'comes remains a further issue on which to compromise.

The Commission's right, as long as the Council has not acted, to alter its proposal at any time would appear to be a general authority to the Commission to amend its proposal whenever and at whatever stage a proposal by the Commission is a prerequisite to action by the Council. However, this general power must be read in conjunction with the specific power set out in Article 149(2)(d)/189c(d), to re-examine its proposal in the light of amendments put forward by the European Parliament.

Three important questions also arise. First, in the situation envisaged in Article 149(2)(b)/189c(b) second indent, where the Parliament has agreed with the Council's common position, it would hardly accord with the purpose of that article if the Commission were able to amend its proposal before the Council adopted an act in accordance with the common position. Second, the practice of the Commission appears to be that it may not only amend an act before adoption, but also (despite the surprising silence of the Treaties on the matter) withdraw the proposal and thus prevent its adoption, particularly if it dislikes amendments made (or proposed) in the Council. Indeed, if the precedents under the original system of legislation are followed, the Commission could, if it believed that amendments pursued by the Council effectively changed the nature of its proposal, simply withdraw its proposal. It did precisely this in November 1986 with regard to the Erasmus scheme for student exchanges. According to Commissioner Marin, who was responsible for the matter, this was done to prevent the Council from depriving the scheme of all significant content (EC Commission 1986). It could presumably do the same if it took exception to the Parliament's amendments on the second reading (though this would be unnecessary unless the Council was pressing for the inclusion of the EP's amendment). Third, as with amendments made by the other institutions, the question arises of when an amendment is so fundamental as to constitute a new proposal. In the context of a dispute between Parliament and the Council, it has now been held that where a

Council amendment altered the substance of a proposal compared with the version seen by Parliament, it must be resubmitted to the Parliament unless the change was requested by Parliament itself (Case C-65/90, 1992).

Given the apparent generality of the Commission's right of amendment under Article 149(3)/189a(2), what useful purpose is served by Article 149(2)(d)/189c(d), the requirement that the Commission re-examine its proposal in the light of the European Parliament's proposed amendments? On the assumption that there is a useful purpose, it must represent a special rule derogating from the general rule of Article 149(3)/189a(2) in the circumstances to which it applies. At the very least, therefore, it means that when the Parliament has amended the common position on the second reading, the Commission is required to consider those amendments when re-examining the proposal. The important question, however, is whether the *only* amendments the Commission may make at this stage are those based on amendments proposed by the Parliament. The wording of the provision does not appear necessarily to lead to this conclusion. It seems to imply that the Parliament's amendments form the starting point for the Commission's re-examination, but do not necessarily limit it. If the Commission were so limited, it would have to be argued that a purposive interpretation of the provision leads to the conclusion that after the second reading the Commission has no power to introduce its own amendments. This conclusion is difficult to reconcile with the apparent generality of Article 149(3)/189a(2) discussed above. It might also have unfortunate consequences if the Commission were prevented from putting forward its own amendments during the final discussion in the Council.

It is clear that the Commission retains a vital role in the cooperation procedure. It is still the Commission that drafts the original proposal and in the second reading stage, whether or not the Commission decides to accept a Parliamentary amendment will determine the majority required in the Council to accept or reject that amendment. Furthermore, the Commission retains its original power to amend or, in practice, withdraw its proposals at any stage during the procedure, which is a powerful negative weapon.

(b) Treaty base

Differences of opinion on the appropriate Treaty base under which proposals for Community legislation are made are a regular source of conflict between the Commission and Member States. Indeed, officials from some national administrations are given explicit instructions to check whether proposals (and even impending proposals or 'gleams in the Commission's eye') do not establish precedents leading to an increase in the Commission's power or the spill-over of responsibility from an exclusively national arena to the sphere of Community competence. Arguments about competence are matters of day-to-day negotiation in Community business. They are practical evidence of the continuance of the dispute between supporters of supranationality and intergovernmentalism.

According to Article 4 of the EEC Treaty, "each Community institution shall act within the limits of the power conferred upon it by this Treaty". Further, Article 190 provides that acts of Community legislation "shall state the reasons on which they are based". The European Court's role is to ensure these articles are respected and, in this context, it is interesting to note that the express grounds for annulment of acts of the Community institutions under Article 173 are "lack of competence, infringement of an essential procedural requirement, infringement of this Treaty or of any rule of law relating to its application, or misuse of powers".

"Competence" is thus a crucial issue. It is an area where the tension between the Commission's two main roles is clearly articulated. As a civil service, the Commission would naturally give way to its political masters. As an independent political animal, the Commission is keen to extend its power and play a politically strategic role in setting the goals of the Community itself. For that purpose, it clearly suits the Commission to choose a Treaty base enabling it to expand Community competence and to enhance its own power. This means a constant quest to identify potential for new areas of competence. In tactical terms it means the Commission will seek legal justification for the selection of Treaty bases requiring qualified majority voting (QMV) rather than unanimity. This not only removes the potential for one or two Member States to block the Commission's proposals. Choosing a QMV Treaty base implies that compromises resulting from negotiations are likely to be based somewhere above the lowest common denominator of agreement between Member States and thus somewhat closer to the Commission's initial proposal.

Some Member States have not shared the Commission's view, and argue that the Treaty base should be determined by the policy objective being pursued, which may in turn lead to arguments as to what the policy objective is. Disputes between the Commission and some Member States occur frequently. A classic example is the Commission's longstanding proposal to ban all forms of tobacco advertising. Some Member States argue that the policy objective is the reduction of the incidence of cancer and is thus purely a health policy issue, for which the Community had no direct competence until the Treaty of Union. On this argument, any legislation would have to be under Article 235 EEC, which provides for measures necessary to achieve the aims of the Community, where the Treaty has made no explicit provision for the policy area concerned. Article 235 requires unanimous decision-making in Council. However, the Commission would claim that its proposal is justified under Article 100a of the EEC Treaty, covering the internal market and providing for QMV and the cooperation procedure with the European Parliament. The Commission's argument is that different legislation in the Member States on tobacco advertising might lead to distortions in the market, say, for periodicals carrying tobacco advertising.

To sum up, the Commission's power to propose legislation gives it the further power to indicate the Treaty base under which it is to be enacted. Determining the Treaty base has important consequences in two respects: the legislative procedure (and majority) to be used; and the question of substantive competence. As to existing jurisprudence, a clear example in the area of legislative procedure is that of health measures relating to agricultural products. This was traditionally dealt with by legislation made jointly under Article 100 on the approximation of laws and Article 43 on agricultural legislation. While Article 100 requires unanimity, Article 43 allows a qualified majority decision to be taken. The United Kingdom challenged two pieces of

Council legislation adopted under Article 43 alone, which it thought should have been adopted under Article 100 by unanimity as well (Case 68/86 and Case 131/86). These pieces of legislation related to the hormone content of meat and to the treatment of battery poultry (Council Directives 85/649 and 86/113). Although the United Kingdom 'won' because of procedural irregularities, on the substantive issue the European Court made it clear that a mere practice of the Council could not create a binding precedent with regard to the correct legal base, and that agricultural legislation could, and should, take account of requirements such as the protection of the health and life of humans and animals.

There is some authority for saying that there is an additional factor to take into account in determining whether to enact legislation under Article 100a (or another provision involving QMV in Council and the cooperation or co-decision procedure with the European Parliament) where the alternative legal base does not involve an enhanced role for the European Parliament. This arose from a dispute between the Commission and the Council on the appropriate legal base to be used in a case concerning environmental legislation. The issue (Case C-300/89) arose from the enactment of a Directive on titanium dioxide waste by unanimity under Article 130s, when the Commission had proposed that it should be adopted by QMV under Article 100a. The Court's view was that it was not possible to use procedures involving both unanimity and the cooperation procedure for the same legislation. To do so would defeat the very object of the cooperation procedure, which was to increase the Parliament's participation in the legislative process as a matter of fundamental democratic principle. Requiring the Council to act throughout by unanimity would certainly diminish Parliament's influence, since under the cooperation procedure unanimity is normally only necessary where the Council wishes to override Parliament or the Commission. It normally only requires a qualified majority in Council to carry the Parliament's view. The Court in fact found that Article 130r envisaged that legislation under other provisions could (indeed should) have the aim of protecting the environment, and that Article 100a envisaged the need for a high level of environmental protection for single market legislation (see also Chapter 7). The Court therefore held that the Directive should have been enacted under Article 100a, but the message may be taken to mean that where alternative Treaty bases are available, preference should be given to that which enhances the democratic role of the Parliament.

However, this would appear not to be an absolute rule, and it is not illegitimate to use Article 130s where the internal market effects of environmental legislation are subordinate in nature. This appears from Case C-155/91 *Commission v. Council* (1993), where the Commission and Parliament claimed, on the basis of the judgment in the titanium dioxide case, that Council Directive 91/156 on waste should have been enacted under Article 100a rather than Article 130s. It might have been thought that since the Court had held in Case C-2/90 *Commission v. Belgium* (1992) that each region, commune or other local authority could take measures to ensure the treatment and elimination of its own waste as near to its place of production as possible so as to limit its transport, questions of the movement of goods did arise. However, the Court took the view that the Directive was intended to achieve the precise opposite of the free movement of waste within the

Community, that is, that each Member State should eliminate its own waste at the nearest point of disposal. While admitting that certain aspects might affect the internal market, the Court held that these effects were subordinate to the overall aim of protecting the environment through effective waste management. Attractive as the democratic appeal of the titanium dioxide case may be, it is the policy objective which remains the main determinant of Treaty base, though there is often scope for more than one view of the predominant policy objective. Indeed, in the particular area of environmental legislation, the new Article 130s introduced by the Maastricht Treaty amendments would in principle allow environmental legislation to be adopted by cooperation procedure with qualified majorities in the Council, as under the original version of Article 100a, making the distinction of less practical value. Indeed, to the extent that legislation under Article 100a will become subject to the more complex co-decision procedure by virtue of the Treaty on European Union (TEU), the Commission might even be tempted to prefer Article 130s as a legal base.

Ironically, while the Commission may perhaps claim some responsibility for extending the bounds of Community competence by proposing the use of general Treaty provisions such as Articles 100 and 235 (see Annex), those provisions do require unanimity in the Council. So it can hardly be claimed that the Commission is solely responsible for expanding Community competence and thereby expanding its own power. On the other hand, since the Single European Act, the Commission has consistently sought to justify use of Article 100a, which allows for qualified majority voting. This enhances the chances of early acceptance of the Commission's proposal or, at worst, acceptance of a compromise solution somewhat further from the lowest common denominator that might otherwise have been the case. Article 100a was introduced by the Single European Act for the purpose of swift completion of the internal market, where Article 100 had previously been used.

To take a particular example, the Community legislation on consumer protection was largely developed under the old Article 100, on the basis that differences in national legislation with regard to the protection of consumers could lead to distortions of competition. This is the case even with the fundamentally important Council Directive 85/374, on liability for defective products and Council Directive 87/102 on consumer credit. The prevention of distortion of competition is not mentioned amongst the attributes of the internal market as defined in Article 8a, yet consumer protection legislation has now been enacted under Article 100a. The Council Directives on consumer protection in the indication of the prices of non-food products (88/314) and of foodstuffs (88/315) were both made under the Article 100a procedure (see Annex). These Directives are in fact concerned with the indication of prices to the final consumer, arguably involving retail trade within a Member State rather than trade between Member States. However, the only justification given in the recitals is that the indication of the selling price and the unit price of the products makes it easier for consumers to compare prices at places of sale, so that it accordingly increases market transparency and ensures greater protection for consumers. While the Maastricht Treaty introduces a Title on consumer protection into the Treaty, one of the expressly mentioned methods of achieving that aim is the use of

Article 100a. Thus, Article 100a has served in the way Article 235 was intended and its use has extended Community competence into areas unforeseen by the original Treaty. In terms of the expansion of Community competence, the procedure has served the Commission well.

(c) Delegated powers

There is a further important provision relating to the Commission's legislative powers in Article 10 of the Single European Act (SEA) supplementing Article 145 of the EEC Treaty. This sets a framework within which the Council may delegate powers to the Commission (Chapter 5 gives details of the administrative procedures involved). The Council has, of course, been delegating powers to the Commission from the outset. The best-known example is the system of management committees used in the common organisation of agricultural markets. Management committees enable the Council to delegate discretionary powers to the Commission with a requirement to consult a committee representing the interests of the Member States (see, for example, Council Regulation 2727/75). This pattern has been followed in other areas, but with variations, so that there are nowadays many different committee procedures. The committees must either be consulted by the Commission, have their approval sought by the Commission or must be informed by the Commission in particular circumstances. The basic aim of Article 10 of the SEA was to provide an overall framework for such delegation of powers and for the committees to which the Commission should refer its proposals. This would prevent the creation of *ad hoc* systems, each marginally different from the other. Article 10 required the structure of such "comitology" to be laid down in advance by the Council, so that the system used in any particular legislation follows one of the patterns laid down beforehand (Nicoll 1987).

The relevant Council Decision (87/373), adopted in 1987, provides for just three basic types of committee procedure: an advisory committee, a management committee and a regulatory committee. The advisory committee is just that: the Commission may seek the opinion of the committee and its members, but is not bound by it. The management committee system is mainly used in the agriculture sector. The Commission presents to the committee a draft of the measures it wishes to take, but it is able to implement its measures immediately even if the committee votes against them, subject to the possibility of the Council taking a different decision within a fixed time limit. Under the third procedure, the regulatory committee, the Commission may only introduce its measures if the committee has approved them. If the committee does not approve, the Commission is required to refer the matter to the Council, which again has a time limit within which to act. Only if the Council does not act within that time limit may the Commission adopt its own measures.

When the proposal for this Council Decision came before the European Parliament in October 1986, the Parliament decided by a majority of 235 to 36 to reject that part of the proposal allowing for regulatory committees. The Parliament took the view that the existence of such committees diminished its own power of control over the Commission. Following the enactment of the

Decision, Parliament sought its annulment, but was held not to have *locus standi* (Case 302/87). Parliament's rules of procedure require amendments to proposed legislation on the internal market to foresee advisory committees, with management committees acceptable at second reading. This view is shared by the Commission. In its opinion of October 21, 1990 on amendments to the Treaty, the Commission argued that "as far as delegation of powers to the Commission is concerned, efficiency demands that both the letter and the spirit of the Single European Act be fully applied in practice . . . only two formulas should be allowed under the Treaty; the advisory committee and the management committee" (COM (90) 600 final).

The important point of principle in this seemingly recondite issue is that the European Parliament is not involved in any of the committees, which are composed of Member State representatives. These are usually the same people who sit in the Council Working Groups which prepare the Council decision. Since the Parliament's ultimate power of control lies in censuring the Commission, the committee procedure offering maximum power to the Commission simultaneously offers the largest degree of Parliamentary control and censure. Needless to say, the Council takes the opposite view, opting frequently for the regulatory committee.

In practice, the Council was not willing, notwithstanding the scrutiny and supervision afforded by the comitology, to limit itself to the adoption of the framework legislation for the achievement of the internal market by the end of 1992, and leave it to the Commission to enact the detailed implementation. It was, however, prepared to do so in the areas of agriculture, the customs tariff, and the updating of technical standards. In the Commission's submission to the Council in 1991 on the operation of the comitology decision, the Commission commented bitterly on the fact that despite the commitment to speed and efficiency in implementing the internal market, the Council had been extremely reluctant to accept the Commission's adherence to the principle of advisory committees for all internal market matters.

(d) Original legislative powers

Whatever express legislative powers the Commission may enjoy under the ECSC Treaty,[1] it is commonly held that under the EEC Treaty "the Commission proposes but the Council disposes". Like most generalisations, it is subject to exceptions, notably in Articles 13(2), 33(7) and 90(3) of the EEC Treaty. The first two of these were transitional powers related to charges equivalent to quantitative restrictions. The third relates essentially to the application of the competition rules to public undertakings. It was nevertheless perhaps belief in the generalisation that led the United Kingdom to challenge Commission Directive 80/723 on the transparency of financial relations between Member States and public undertakings, issued under Article 90(3)EEC, on the basis that under the scheme of the Treaty only the Council could issue directives containing general legislative provisions imposing new obligations on Member States. The aim of Commission directives, it was argued, was merely to deal with a specific situation in one or more Member States. This argument did not find favour with the European Court. In its judgment in Cases 188–190/80 [1982], the European Court held that the limits of the powers conferred on the Commission by a specific provision of the Treaty are to be inferred not from a general principle but from the wording of the provision in question, analysed in the light of its purpose. The purpose, in this case, was found to be to enable the Commission to perform effectively the duty of surveillance imposed upon it (i.e. with regard to the payment of unlawful State aids, which it treated as a matter of competition policy in the structure of the EC Treaty).

A similar broad view of the Commission's powers under Article 90(3), which were stated to be "normative", i.e. law-creating, was taken in Case C-202/88 *France v. Commission* with regard to a Commission Directive on competition in the market in telecommunication terminals. It was stated that the possibility that there might be Council legislation under other provisions did not restrict the powers of the Commission under Article 90(3). On the other hand, in interpreting that provision, the Court held that while the Commission could require *exclusive* rights of importation etc. to be abolished, it could not require *special* rights to be abolished in the absence of further precision, and could not use Article 90(3) to deal with the unilateral conduct of undertakings.

Even where the only express power of the Commission is to make proposals there have also been interesting developments. Specific examples may be cited from the agricultural sector in situations where the Council failed to do what it should have done. One illustration relates to the common fisheries policy. Under Article 102 of the 1972 Act of Accession, the Council should have adopted legislation "with a view to ensuring protection of the fishing grounds and conservation of the biological resources of the sea" by the end of 1978. Such legislation was not in fact adopted until 1983. In the meantime, the Commission had put forward proposals for a common fisheries policy suggesting total allowable catches (TACs), and amended these proposals from time to time. It would appear that the Commission was prepared to authorise national catch quotas which followed the proposals, as is evidenced by Case 287/81. Eventually, the Council issued a series of Decisions on fisheries activities in waters under the sovereignty or jurisdiction of Member States. These required Member States to observe the TACs laid down in the Commission's proposals, as e.g. in Council Decision 82/739. More contentious, however, was the fact that the Commission itself published a declaration (OJ 1981 C224/1) to the effect that it considered its proposals to be legally binding on the Member States. Whatever the view of the Council in the matter, no published retraction of this declaration was ever made.

The ramifications of accepting that Commission proposals may eventually become legally binding in themselves are immense, but the tactic did not meet with the approval of the Court. The European Court had to consider the matter in Case 346/85 *United Kingdom v. Commission*. This arose from the Commission's refusal to allow the European Agricultural Guidance and Guarantee Fund (EAGGF) to meet United Kingdom expenditure in relation to fisheries activities not in accordance with the Commission's TAC proposals. In its judgment, the Court stated categorically that unilateral proposals by the Commission were not rules of Community law. It emphasised, in particular, that legislation with financial consequences should be certain and of foreseeable application. A similar view was taken in Case C-

303/90 *France v. Commission* where the Commission appeared to impose obligations on Member States by a 'Code of Conduct' on the implementation of a Council Regulation. It was found that the Code went beyond what was required by the Regulation, and that in any event the Regulation did not confer implementing powers on the Commission.

Matters have, however, gone somewhat further in the cereals market, where 1985 saw the basic prices being set by legislation adopted unilaterally by the Commission. Under Article 43(2) EEC, legislation on the common organisation of agricultural markets is adopted by the Council acting by a qualified majority on a proposal from the Commission. It is further provided in Article 3 of Council Regulation 2727/75 on the common organisation of the market in cereals that the target and intervention prices for each marketing year should be fixed by the Council under the same procedure. In 1985 the Commission proposed for the first time that some of these prices expressed in ECUs should actually be reduced. The Council was unable to reach agreement on the matter by the appropriate date. This is not unusual. Indeed, it has often been necessary to "stop the clock" when prices were likely to rise or stay the same, which meant paying the previous year's prices on a temporary basis. But much greater difficulty arises if the aim is to reduce the guaranteed prices. If the previous year's prices were to be paid in such a case, producers would be paid an excess which would have to be recovered (with considerable administrative rigmarole) once the new lower prices were agreed. The matter came to a head in June 1985. Under the version of Article 3 of Regulation 2727/75 then in force, the intervention prices valid on June 1 in Greece, Italy and certain regions of France had to be adjusted in the light of the intervention prices fixed for August. This was the first month of the new marketing year. In the light of the Council's failure to act on its proposals, on June 20, 1985 the Commission adopted Decision 85/309 on "precautionary measures" with regard to the buying-in of cereals in Greece, Italy and those regions of France requiring the Member States to reduce certain of the previous year's prices by 1.8 per cent. This was replaced by Commission Regulation 2124/85 adopted on July 26, 1985 (i.e. just before the start of the marketing year) applying general "precautionary measures". These fixed lower prices in the cereals sector other than for durum wheat. In October 1985, the Commission exercised its express power under Article 13 of Regulation 2727/75 to fix import levies on cereals, adopting in Regulation 2956/85 levies calculated from the basic prices it itself had enacted. Interestingly, no Council legislation was adopted in the matter until Council Regulation 1584/86 of May 23, 1986 fixing the cereal prices for the 1986–87 marketing year. This expressly continued some of the prices fixed by the Commission.

In adopting its "precautionary measures" the Commission declared in the recitals to the Decision and to the subsequent Regulation that it was acting under Articles 5 and 155 of the EEC Treaty. Article 5 requires the Member States to take all appropriate measures to ensure fulfilment of the obligations resulting from the action taken by the institutions of the Community, to facilitate the achievement of the Community's tasks, and to abstain from any measure which could jeopardise the attainment of the objectives of the Treaty. Article 155 empowers the Commission, *inter alia,* to ensure that the provisions of the Treaty and the measures taken by the institutions pursuant thereto are applied. This is the 'guardian of the Treaty' function. Presumably, therefore, the rationale of the Commission's action was that the failure of Member States in Council to fix the cereal prices in due time constituted a breach of their duties under Article 5 and that the Commission's duty under Article 155 was to ensure the application of the common organisation of the market in cereals. That no direct challenge to the Commission's legislation was mounted either by the Council as such or by any of the Member States is particularly remarkable.

Certainly, the cereals price issue is not the only case of the use of this technique. Subsequent examples of the same technique may be found, for example, in the sheep meat market in 1990. Likewise, in 1991 in the market in oils and fats a Council Regulation gave the Commission express power to act if the Council had not taken a Decision by a specific date.

Inaction on the part of the Member States in agricultural price-fixing cases forms an interesting contrast to the alacrity with which Germany, France, the Netherlands, Denmark and the United Kingdom sought the annulment of Commission Decision 85/381. This established a prior communication and consultation procedure with regard to migration policies concerning nationals of non-Member States which the Commission claimed to be able to issue under Article 118 of the EEC Treaty (see, for example, Case 281/85). It could well be that in the price-fixing case the Commission's legislation provided a mutually convenient solution to a difficult political problem. Nevertheless, if the legal basis for the Commission's action does indeed authorise the enactment of legislation by the Commission in circumstances where the Council should have acted but has not done so, the potential scope for such Commission legislation is enormous. It might, on the other hand, be argued that such legislative power should be restricted to matters such as the common organisation of agricultural markets which are entirely subject to rules of Community law.

In any event it is clear from Case 63/83 *R v. Kirk* that where the Council's failure to act does not leave a legal vacuum but leads to the cessation of a derogation from the basic rules contained in other Council legislation (in this case the principle of equal access to the waters of other Member States), the Commission has no power to breach that Council legislation.

Enforcement of Community Law

(a) Against Member States

Under Article 169 of the EEC Treaty (see Annex), if the Commission considers that a Member State has failed to fulfil an obligation under the Treaty, it *shall* deliver a reasoned opinion on the matter after giving the State concerned the opportunity to submit its observations, and if the State concerned does not comply with the opinion within the period laid down by the Commission, it *may* bring the matter before the Court of Justice. As the EEC Treaty was originally drafted, there were two significant differences from Article 88 of the ECSC Treaty. Under the ECSC Treaty the Commission itself could find a Member State in breach, subject to review by the Court. Under the EEC Treaty it is the Court which determines whether there is a breach.

Further, while the ECSC Treaty provides for financial penalties to be imposed (though this never seems to have occurred), the original version of the EEC Treaty did not.

The Commission's powers in this respect have been changed by virtue of the amendment introduced by the Maastricht Treaty in the shape of the new Article 171 of the EC Treaty (see Annex). This now provides a supplementary procedure if a Member State has breached the Treaty and has not taken the necessary measures to comply with a judgment of the Court of Justice. In such a case, the Commission shall, after giving that State the opportunity to submit its observations, issue a second reasoned opinion specifying the points on which the Member State concerned has not complied with the judgment of the Court of Justice. If the Member State concerned fails to take the necessary measures to comply with the Court's judgment within the time limit laid down by the Commission, the latter may bring the case for a second time before the Court of Justice. In so doing it must specify the amount of lump sum or penalty payment which it considers appropriate for the Member State concerned to pay. If the Court of Justice finds that the Member State concerned has not complied with its judgment it may impose a lump sum or penalty payment.

It remains to be seen how frequently this provision will be used, but it has anyway long been the case that the Commission itself may impose indirect financial sanctions where Community money is involved. Cases 15 and 16/76 *France v. Commission* involved a Community aid for the distillation of table wine. The French government had taken the view that the aids payable under Council Regulation 766/72 were inadequate, and supplemented them with national aids. The Commission then initiated the procedure under Article 169 EEC against France in relation to the breach of a Treaty obligation involved in the payment of national aids, but did not pursue the matter when the aids ceased to be paid. However, when it came to the discharge of the EAGGF accounts, the Commission refused to accept liability for the amounts of aid payable under Community law, on the grounds that the national measures had had the effect of distorting the distillation operation by extending it. Before the Court, the French government claimed that the EAGGF should meet the proportion of the aid granted which corresponded to the rates fixed by Community rules. But it was held that it was impossible to ascertain the extent of the effect of the combined national and Community aid due to one or other component part and that it was impossible to establish with certainty what quantities of wine would have been distilled in France if the national measure had not been adopted. With regard to the discontinuance of the proceedings under Article 169, the Court pointed out that this did not constitute recognition that the contested conduct was lawful. So, by adding a national element to a Community aid, France found itself having to finance the whole amount.

On the other hand, if a Member State does not add its own national aid, but pays a Community aid to recipients falling outside its scope, the Member State will not necessarily lose the whole aid. In Case 49/83 *Luxembourg v. Commission* it was held that where the Member State had acted in good faith it might still obtain reimbursement to the extent that it could prove that the aid was properly paid — but the burden is on the Member State.

In the context of state aids, recourse by the Commission to Article 169 is not necessary. The Commission has power under Article 93(2) itself to decide that a Member State should abolish or alter an aid. Moreover, the Commission may go to the Court directly if the Member State does not comply.

Article 169 proceedings have not always been automatic. The Commission enjoys a certain discretion under Article 169 if a Member State appears to be in breach of its Treaty obligations. However, it would appear from the statistics in the annual Reports to the European Parliament on Commission monitoring of the application of Community law that a change in attitude occurred in 1979. Before then, a positive decision was required to take action. Since 1979, it seems that a positive decision is required not to take action. Be that as it may, from 600 to 700 Article 169 letters a year give rise to considerably fewer than 100 cases a year before the Court.

Any legal challenge to the Commission's exercise of its discretion in this matter is very difficult to mount directly, although indirect remedies may be available. Article 169 does not require the Commission to issue a binding decision. Rather it requires it to issue a reasoned opinion to a defaulting Member State, an act which has no binding effect under Article 189 of the EEC Treaty and which is not susceptible to judicial review under Article 173. The conclusion drawn from this in Case 48/65 *Lutticke v. Commission*, was that since the opinion itself could not be challenged, a letter sent to a complainant refusing to issue such an opinion could not be subject to an action for annulment either, although it did constitute a "definition of position" so as to block an action for failure to act under Article 175 of the EEC Treaty. If the Member State does not comply with the opinion, the Commission is then empowered, but not required, to bring the matter before the Court. Hence the Commission has a discretion which does not appear to be susceptible to direct challenge, although a complainant Member State could bring an action against the defaulting State in its own name once the Commission had issued an opinion, or has failed to do so within three months, under the terms of Article 170, as in Case 141/78 *France v. UK*.

On the other hand, indirect challenge to the exercise of the Commission's discretion may be mounted by invoking the direct effect (if such there be) of the relevant Community rule before a national court against the defaulting Member State or one of its agencies. The practical result may well be that the validity of national legislation is put indirectly at issue before the European Court. The Court recognised this possibility of private policing in the leading case of *Van Gend en Loos* itself, stating that "the vigilance of individuals to protect their rights amounts to an effective supervision in addition to the supervision entrusted by Articles 169 and 170 [of the EEC Treaty] to the diligence of the Commission and the Member States". One effect of this has been to prevent a settlement of enforcement proceedings brought by the Commission against a Member State from being final, if private interests are involved. In Joined Cases 80 and 81/77 *Ramel v. Reçevoir des Douanes*, French wine importers were able to invoke the direct effect of the relevant provisions of EEC law to challenge levies imposed by the French authorities on imports of Italian wine in 1975–76. They did so before the French courts and thence on a reference for a preliminary ruling before the European Court (Article 177), even though the Commission had withdrawn an action it had brought against France under Article 169 alleging that the imposition of such levies was in breach of France's Treaty obligations. Further, in Joined Cases 142 and 143/80 *Italian Finance Administration v. Essevi*, it was recognised that an individual may invoke the direct effects of a Treaty obligation even against conduct of a Member State which the Commission had regarded as permissible in its opinion given under Article 169.

Indirect challenge may also be mounted through an action for damages. In Case 14/78 *Denkavit v. Commission,* it was alleged that the Commission had failed to act sufficiently urgently to require the abolition of certain Italian measures, thereby incurring liability to the applicants. The Court in its judgment was apparently willing to accept that if there was no justification for the Commission's conduct, and this improperly contributed to the maintenance of an obstacle to trade between Member States, then the Commission could incur liability. It was, however, held that in the circumstances, since the Italian measures related to additives in animal feeding-stuffs, it was reasonable for the Commission to wait to receive the respective reports of a standing committee and of a scientific committee on animal feeding-stuffs.

(b) Against individuals

The power of the Commission to enforce Community law against individuals relates essentially to competition law. Again there are differences between the Treaties, since the Commission's powers in this area were trimmed after the initial year's experience of the ECSC. Unlike Articles 65 and 66 of the ECSC Treaty, which clearly give the Commission sole jurisdiction to apply their rules, the EEC Treaty does not confer on the Commission exclusive powers with regard to the competition rules it contains. Rather, Article 87 of the Treaty provides for the Council to take measures to give effect to the substantive rules contained in Articles 85 and 86. The point, *inter alia,* was to define the functions of the Commission. Until such measures were adopted, EEC competition rules were to be enforced either by the national authorities, under Article 88, or by the Commission "in cooperation with the competent authorities of the Member States" under Article 89. The Commission's powers to enforce the competition rules alone were conferred on it by Council Regulation 17/62. Although this Regulation confers exclusive power on the Commission to grant exemptions under Article 85(3), it otherwise maintains the competence of the national authorities to apply the prohibitions in Article 85(1) and Article 86 unless proceedings have been initiated before the Commission itself (under Article 9 (3)). Furthermore, the regulation was not universal in its application. Council Regulation 141/62 excluded transport from its scope, and although specific rules for road, rail and inland waterway transport were enacted in 1968, air and sea transport remained excluded until power to enforce the competition rules in the context of sea transport was eventually conferred on the Commission by Regulation 4056/86. This was done with regard to air transport by Regulations 3975 and 3976/87.

Thus, in its 1980 *Report on Competition Policy,* the Commission noted that when it was faced with a complaint from a Danish airline, Sterling Airways, alleging abuse of a dominant position by Scandinavian Airlines System (SAS), it had to fall back on the system envisaged in Article 89 of the EEC Treaty and seek the cooperation of the competent national authorities in order to be able to investigate the complaint (Commission 1980, pp. 94–96).

Of greater practical importance is the fact that it has been clearly established by the European Court that the prohibitions contained in Articles 85(1) and 86 of the EEC Treaty produce direct effects, and hence may be invoked by parties to litigation before national courts irrespective of the terms of Regulation 17/62 (or the Merger Regulation) (see Cases 127/73 and the second *Brasserie de Haecht* case. Indeed, much of the case-law on competition rules has evolved in the context of questions referred for preliminary rulings by national courts rather than in direct actions seeking the annulment of Commission competition decisions.

Nevertheless, the role of the Commission remains of fundamental importance for those subject to general EEC competition rules. The Commission is the only body which directly enforces those rules at the Community level in the interests of Community policy, rather than national policy or private interest. It is the only body which may grant exemptions under Article 85(3), and it may, under Article 15 of Regulation 17/62, impose fines of up to one million ECU or 10 per cent of turnover where that is greater. The example might be taken of the fine of 75 million ECU imposed on the packaging firm Tetra PAk for an abuse of a dominant position (Commission Decision of 24 July 1991).

Be that as it may, in 1992 the Commission indicated both in 'soft' legislation[2] and in its formal decisions, a desire for a greater role to be played by national courts and authorities in the application of Community competition rules. In December 1992, the Commission adopted a Notice on the Cooperation between National Courts and the Commission in applying Articles 85 and 86 of the EEC Treaty (OJ 1993 C39/6). For the most part the Notice appears simply to codify the case-law of the European Court on the matter, while indicating the remedies available at the national level (for example, damages) which the Commission itself cannot give. On the other hand, the Commission does offer, in the context of Articles 85 and 86, to advise any national court which wishes to consult it, as to its "customary practice" in relation to the Community law at issue (Commission 1992 para. 38). This might appear to create an unofficial system of references for preliminary rulings parallel to that created by Article 177 of the EEC Treaty in relation to the European Court, though the Commission does emphasise that the answers it gives are not binding on the courts which requested them (*ibid.* para. 39). The clear underlying aim, justifiable within the framework of subsidiarity[3] now anchored in the Treaty of Union's Article 3b, is that the Commission should be able to concentrate on cases of Community interest.

In the context of decisions given in individual competition cases, in November 1992, in the *SACEM* case, which involved complaints about fees charged by a French copyright agency, the Commission made public (in *Agence Europe* No. 5868, November 30, 1992) the fact that it had referred the matter to the French competition authorities to deal with. The basis for the referral was that the effects of any abuse of a dominant position in that case would mainly be felt on French territory.

The area of mergers is somewhat different. Here, it seems an exclusive competence has been created by secondary legislation, albeit in the guise of the Commission's exclusive jurisdiction to administer the system. The EEC Treaty was silent on mergers, although certain types of takeover were eventually held to constitute an abuse of a dominant position (see Case 6/72).

More generally, in 1990, a system of merger control under the EEC Treaty came into operation by virtue of Council Regulation 4064/89. Under this legislation, notably Articles 1 and 21, the EC Commission has exclusive competence with regard to mergers with a "Community dimension" and Member States are in principle prohibited from applying their national legislation. "Concentrations with a Community dimension" are defined as those where the aggregate worldwide turnover of all the undertakings concerned is more than 5,000 million ECU and the aggregate Community-wide turnover of at least two of the undertakings involved is more than 250 million ECU, unless each of the undertakings concerned achieves more than two-thirds of its aggregate Community-wide turnover in one Member State. In the present context, Article 21(2) of the Regulation prohibits Member States from applying their national legislation to such "concentrations". Member States are, however, entitled under Article 21(3) to protect legitimate interests, defined as including "plurality of the media", by measures compatible with the general principles and other provisions of Community law. This may prove of particular importance in the context of the special United Kingdom rules on newspaper mergers, which prohibit the transfer of a newspaper to a newspaper proprietor whose newspapers have an average daily circulation, together with that of the newspaper concerned in the transfer, of 500,000 or more, unless the transfer is made with the written consent of the Secretary of State (Fair Trading Act 1973 ss 57–62).

Furthermore, by virtue of Article 9 of the Regulation, the Commission may refer a notified concentration to the national authorities with a view to the application of national competition law. It may do so where it considers that a concentration threatens to create or strengthen a dominant position, which might impede effective competition within that Member State's market, where that market presents all the characteristics of a distinct market, whether or not it constitutes a substantial part of the common market. The reason for this is that in the context of the EC's internal market, the area of a particular State is not necessarily a relevant criterion in determining whether competition is adversely affected. Conversely, however, under Article 22(3) of the Regulation, a Member State may request the Commission to take a decision with regard to a concentration which has no Community dimension. It may do so where such concentration creates or strengthens a dominant position as a result of which effective competition would be significantly impeded in the Member State concerned and where such concentration affects trade between Member States. It would appear that Belgium referred the 1992 takeover of Dan-Air by British Airways to the Commission under this provision (*Agence Europe* No. 5880, December 16, 1992).

Duties on the Commission

That the Commission's status as guardian of the Treaties may lead to the imposition of duties as well as the conferment of powers in its relationships with the Member States has been clearly shown in Case C-2/88 *Imm. Zwartveld*. This involved a request by a Dutch court for the European Court to give it assistance in a case before it. The judge was investigating an alleged fraud involving breaches of the Community fish quota system and the fish marketing system and claimed that in order to proceed with his investigation he needed access to certain reports prepared by Commission officials and required those officials to give evidence before him.

The Commission refused to transmit the reports to him. He then sent a request to the European Court asking it to order the Commission to produce the documents and to order the inspectors to give evidence. The Dutch judge was obviously aware of the difficulty of finding a legal base on which the European Court could act and invoked Articles 1 and 12 of the Protocol on the Privileges and Immunities of the European Communities. Article 1 provides that the property and assets of the Communities shall not be subject to legal measures of constraint without the authorisation of the Court of Justice, while Article 12 provides, among other things, that the immunity of Community officials with regard to acts performed by them in their official capacity is subject to the jurisdiction of the Court in disputes between the Communities and their officials and other servants. The judge also invoked the Council of Europe conventions on assistance in criminal matters, arguing that, although the Community itself was not a party to these conventions, they should, nonetheless, be considered as an integral part of the Community legal order. This, in itself, indicates an interesting development of the Court's well-known case law holding that the principles underlying the European Convention on Human Rights are general principles which must be recognised within the Community context, even though the Community itself is not a party to the Human Rights Convention (see, for example, Case 36/75 at p. 1232).

The Commission's view was that the Dutch judge's application was inadmissible. It argued that the Treaty must be regarded as exhaustive with regard to the remedies available before the European Court, and it emphasised that the only way a national court could bring a matter before the European Court was by a reference for preliminary ruling under Article 177 of the EEC Treaty, but that in this case Article 177 was not relevant because the Dutch judge was not seeking the interpretation of a provision of Community law. The Commission also suggested that Articles 1 and 12 of the Protocol on the Privileges and Immunities of the European Communities were not relevant in this context.

Asked by the Court as to its substantive reasons for refusing to produce the reports or to allow its inspectors to give evidence, the Commission took the line that its inspectors' reports were internal documents which did not necessarily reflect the Commission's position. In addition, their communication could harm relations between the Commission and Member States in the delicate area of supervision of the fisheries market. In addition, the Commission invoked Article 2 of the Protocol on Privileges and Immunities, which provides that the archives of the Communities shall be inviolable, claiming that it contained no exemptions so that the Court had no power to lift that immunity.

With regard to the appearance of its inspectors as witnesses, the Commission indicated that it was neither willing to indicate the identity of its inspectors nor authorise them to give evidence, for it might affect their work and the degree to which they were able to exercise effective supervision on behalf of the Community. On the other hand, the Commission did declare its willingness to prepare a report for the Dutch judge to the extent that this would not compromise the Commission's supervisory functions. The

Commission also indicated that it might designate specific officials to give evidence before the Dutch judge, but he in turn refused to accept this offer.

Following a procedure analogous to a reference for a preliminary ruling under Article 177 of the EEC Treaty, the Court invited the Community institutions and the Member States to submit observations. The case aroused a great deal of interest with observations received from the Council, the Parliament, Germany, France, Greece, Ireland, Italy, The Netherlands, Portugal and the United Kingdom.

The Court's own reasoning began with a reference to the famous case of *Costa v. ENEL*, emphasising the passage in that judgment which held that the EEC Treaty had created its own legal system which became an integral part of the legal systems of the Member States. The Court then referred to its judgment in the *Les Verts v. European Parliament*. Here, despite the silence of Article 173 of the EC Treaty which refers only to acts of the Council and the Commission and not to acts of the European Parliament, it had held that the general scheme of the Treaty was to make direct action available against all measures adopted by the institutions which are intended to have legal effect. Therefore, an action for annulment must lie against measures adopted by the Parliament intended to have legal effects with regard to third parties. It pointed out that the EC is a Community based on law. Neither the Member States nor the institutions might escape from judicial control over the conformity of their actions to the Treaty, which the Court described as a constitutional charter.

It argued that the relationship between the Member States and the Community institutions is governed, by virtue of Article 5 of the Treaty, by the principle of loyal cooperation. This not only requires that Member States take all necessary measures to guarantee the effective implementation of Community law, including the use of criminal penalties. The principle also requires the Community institutions to observe reciprocal duties of loyal cooperation with the Member States. The Court argued that this duty to cooperate was of particular importance in the relationship with national judicial authorities responsible for ensuring respect for Community law within the national legal order.

In the light of these arguments, the Court held that the privileges and immunities of the Communities were not absolute and that the specific privileges and immunities accorded to Community officials were for their own personal protection. The Protocol could not therefore be used to avoid the duty of loyal cooperation owed to national judicial authorities. The Court suggested that where a request for information or evidence came from a national judge investigating alleged breaches of Community law, it was the duty of any Community institution to give active support to the national judge by handing over the documents and authorising the officials to give evidence. This was particularly so in the case of the Commission, since it is entrusted with ensuring that the provisions of the Treaty are applied.

In seeking to establish its own authority to order the Commission to comply with this basic duty of loyal cooperation, the Court invoked Article 164 of the Treaty, under which the Court is required to ensure that in the interpretation and application of the Treaty the law is observed. The Court held that by virtue of this provision it must ensure that an appropriate remedy be available to enable it to exercise judicial control over the Commission's performance of its duty of loyal cooperation towards a national judicial authority. The Court therefore held that it had jurisdiction to examine whether the refusal to cooperate was justified in the light of a need to avoid interference with the operation and independence of the Communities. The Commission was ordered to deliver the documents requested by the Dutch judge and to authorise its officials to give evidence before him, unless it could show that there were imperative reasons relating to the operation or independence of the Communities which would justify the refusal to deliver the documents or to authorise the giving of the evidence. The duty of the Commission in this respect was thus clearly established.

Conclusion

The intention of this Chapter has been to illustrate the pivotal role in the Community legal framework, albeit one subject to the jurisdiction of the European Court (and, in competition matters, to that of the Court of First Instance). In some areas the Commission has made bold innovations, such as its 'precautionary' legislation. On the other hand, the current attempts by the Commission to divest itself of some work in the competition area is evidence of caution, and perhaps even an example of the principle of subsidiarity being applied in practice. A more prosaic explanation, however, is that it reflects the fact that the Commission has not been given the level of staffing necessary to carry out its myriad supervisory duties. In the light of this, the fact that the European Court, through the doctrine of direct effect, has allowed the private policing by interested individuals of certain breaches of Community law which fall within the supervisory jurisdiction of the Commission, may be seen as offering a degree of relief to the Commission, rather than as a challenge to its pivotal role as guardian of the Treaties.

Notes

1 Where, under Article 14 the only defined "acts" are those of the Commission. The Treaty is drafted in some detail, and the Member States presumably thought that legislative activity would be administrative rather than policy-making in nature.

2 Here used to describe an act of a Community institution which does not take a legally binding form but which is nonetheless likely to guide the conduct of those concerned.

3 Although here it is a question of subsidiarity in the administration of Community law, not subsidiarity with regard to the exercise of legislative competence.

References

Heseltine, M. (1989) *The Challenge of Europe*, London: Weidenfeld and Nicolson, p. 21.

Lasok, D. and Bridge, J.W. (1991) *Law and Institutions of the European Community* (5th edition) p. 219–20.

Ludlow, P. 'The European Commission' in R. Keohane and S. Hoffmann (1991) *The New European Community: Decision-making and Institutional Change*, Oxford: Westview, p. 104.

Nicoll, W. 'Qu'est-ce que la comitologie?' *Revue du Marché Commun* 306, 1987.

Case 26/62 *Van Gend en Loos* [1963] ECR 1, 13.
Case 6/64 *Costa v. ENEL* [1964] ECR 585.
Case 48/65 *Lutticke v. Commission* [1966] ECR 19.
Case 48/72 *Brasserie de Haecht* [1973] ECR 77.
Case 6/72 *Continental Can v. Commission* [1973] ECR 215.
Case 127/73 *BRT v. SABAM* [1974] ECR 51.
Case 36/75 *Rutili* [1975] ECR 1219.
Cases 15 and 16/76 *France v. Commission* [1979] ECR 321.
Cases 80 and 81/77 *Ramel v. Reçevoir des Douanes* [1978] ECR 297.
Case 14/78 *Denkavit v. Commission* [1978] ECR 2497, 2505.
Case 141/78 *France v. UK* [1979] ECR 2923.
Cases 142 and 143/80 *Italian Finance Administration v. Essevi* [1981] ECR 1413.
Cases 188 to 190/80 *France, Italy and UK v. Commission* [1982] ECR 2545.
Case 287/81 *Kerr* [1982] ECR 4053.
Case 49/83 *Luxembourg v. Commission* [1984] ECR 2931.
Case 63/83 *R v. Kirk* [1984] ECR 2689.
Case 294/83 *Les Verts v. European Parliament* [1986] ECR 1339.
Case 281/85 *Germany v. Commission* [1987] ECR 3203.
Case 346/85 *UK v. Commission* [1987] ECR 5197.
Case 68/86 *UK v. Council* [1988] ECR 855.
Case 131/86 *UK v. Council* [1988] ECR 905.
Case 302/87 *European Parliament v. Council* [1988] ECR 5615.
Case C-2/88 *Imm. Zwartveld* 13 July 1990.
Case C-202/88 *France v. Commission* 19 March 1991.
Case C-300/89 *Commission v. Council* [1991].
Case C-2/90 *Commission v. Belgium* [1992] ECR I-4431.
Case C-65/90 *European Parliament v. European Council* [1992] ECR NYR.
Case C-303/90 *France v. Commission* 13 November 1991.
Case C-155/91 *Commission v. Council* [1993] 1. 13 July 1990.

Commission Decision 85/309 (OJ 1985 L198/1).
Commission Decision 85/381 (OJ 1985 L217/25) on migration policies.
Commission Decision of 24 July 1991 (OJ 1992 L72/1).

Commission Declaration prior to the Council's final decision on a common fisheries policy (OJC 224, 3.9.1981).

Commission Directive 80/723 (OJ 1980 L195/35) on the transparency of financial relations between Member States and public undertakings.
Commission Directive 85/309 (OJ 1986 L163/52) on 'precautionary measures' with regard to the buying in of cereals in Greece and elsewhere.

Commission Regulation 2124/85 (26 July 1985) on general "precautionary measures".
Commission Regulation 2956/85 (OJ 1985 L285/8) on import levies.
Commission Regulation 3890/90 (OJ 1990 L367/154) on the sheep meat market.

Council Decision 82/739 (OJ 1982 L312/17).
Council Decision 87/373 (OJ 1987 L197/33).

Council Directive 85/374 (OJ 1985 L210/29) on liability for defective products.
Council Directive 85/649 (OJ 1985 L382/228) on the hormone content of meat.
Council Directive 86/113 (OJ 1986 L95/45) on the treatment of battery poultry.
Council Directive 87/102 (OJ 1987 L42/48) on consumer credit.
Council Directive 88/314 (OJ 1988 L142/19) on consumer protection in the indication of the prices on non-food products.

Council Directive 88/315 (OJ 1988 L142/23) on consumer protection in the indication of the prices on foodstuffs.
Council Directive 91/156 (OJ 1991 L78/32) on waste.

Council Regulation 17/62 (OJ Sp.Ed. 1959-62 p. 87) on the enforcement of competition rules.
Council Regulation 141/62 (OJ Sp.Ed. 1959-62 p. 291).
Council Regulation 2727/75 Articles 25-27 (OJ 1975 L281-2/1) on the organisation of the market in cereals.
Council Regulation 1584/86 (OJ 1986 L139/41).
Council Regulation 3975/87 (OJ 1987 L374/1) laying down the procedures for the application of competition rules in the transport sector.
Council Regulation 3976/87 (OJ 1987 L374/9) on the application of Article 85(3) EEC to certain categories of agreements and practices in the air transport sector.
Council regulation 4056/86 on rules of competition in the maritime sector.
Council Regulation 4064/89 (OJ 1989 L395/1) on merger control.
Council Regulation 1720/91, Art.4 (OJ 1991 L162/27) on the market in oils and fats.

European Commission (1986) 'The Week in Europe' 4 December 1986 (ISEC/WT42/86).
European Commission (1991) 'Conferment of implementing powers on the Commission' (SEC (90) 2599989 final).

ANNEX

Treaty on European Union

Article 100*

The Council shall, acting unanimously on a proposal from the Commission and after consulting the European Parliament and the Economic and Social Committee, issue directives for the approximation of such laws, regulations or administrative provisions of the Member States as directly affects the establishment or function of the common market.

As amended by Article G(21) TEU

Article 100a

1. By way of derogation from Article 100 and save where otherwise provided in this Treaty, the following provisions shall apply for the achievement of the objectives set out in Article 7a. The Council shall, acting by a qualified majority on a proposal from the Commission in cooperation with the European Parliament and after consulting the Economic and Social Committee, adopt the measures for the approximation of the provisions laid down by law, regulation or administrative action in Member States which have as their object the establishment and functioning of the internal market.**

2. Paragraph 1 shall not apply to fiscal provisions, to those relating to the free movement of persons nor to those relating to the rights and interests of employed persons.

3. The Commission, in its proposals envisaged in paragraph 1 concerning health, safety, environmental protection and consumer protection, will take as a base a high level of protection.

4. If, after the adoption of a harmonisation measure by the Council acting by a qualified majority, a Member State deems it necessary to apply national provisions on grounds of major needs referred to in Article 36, or relating to protection of the environment or the working environment, it shall notify the Commission of these provisions.

   The Commission shall confirm the provisions involved after having verified that they are not a means of arbitrary discrimination or a disguised restriction on trade between Member States.

   By way of derogation from the procedure laid down in Articles 169 and 170, the Commission or any Member State may bring the matter directly before the Court of Justice if it considers that another Member State is making improper use of the powers provided for in this Article.

5. The harmonisation measures referred to above shall, in appropriate cases, include a safeguard clause authorising the Member States to take, for one or more of the non-economic reasons referred to in Article 36, provisional measures subject to a Community control procedure.

**Paragraph 1 as amended by Article G(22) TEU*

Article 169

If the Commission considers that a Member State has failed to fulfil an obligation under this Treaty, it shall deliver a reasoned opinion on the matter after giving the State concerned the opportunity to submit its observations.

If the State concerned does not comply with the opinion within the period laid down by the Commission, the latter may bring the matter before the Court of Justice.

Article 171

1. If the Court of Justice finds that a Member State has failed to fulfil an obligation under this Treaty, the State shall be required to take the necessary measures to comply with the judgment of the Court of Justice.
2. If the Commission considers that the Member State concerned has not taken such measures it shall, after giving that State the opportunity to submit its observations, issue a reasoned opinion specifying the points on which the Member State concerned has not complied with the judgment of the Court of Justice.

    If the Member State concerned fails to take the necessary measures to comply with the Court's judgment within the time-limit laid down by the Commission, the latter may bring the case before the Court of Justice. In so doing it shall specify the amount of the lump sum or penalty payment to be paid by the Member State concerned which it considers appropriate in the circumstances.

    If the Court of Justice finds that the Member State concerned has not complied with its judgment it may impose a lump sum or penalty payment on it.

    This procedure shall be without prejudice to Article 170.

Article 235

If action by the Community should prove necessary to attain, in the course of the operation of the common market, one of the objectives of the Community and this Treaty has not provided the necessary powers, the Council, shall, acting unanimously on a proposal from the Commission after consulting the European Parliament, take the appropriate measures.

7. The Commission and the lobby

Sonia Mazey and Jeremy Richardson

Introduction

This Chapter focuses upon the links between EC Commission officials, who are responsible for the formulation and implementation of Community policies, and the growing number of interest groups affected by these policies. The founding Treaties of the EC state that the European Commission is the initiator of Community policies and has the sole right to propose Community legislation. The Commission is also the executive arm of Community governance, responsible for ensuring the effective implementation of the policies decided upon by the Council of Ministers. Administrative officials within the Commission are thus centrally involved in the formulation, management and application of Community policies. This fact is now widely appreciated by the burgeoning numbers of lobbyists in Brussels who — while not ignoring other EC policy-making institutions and national administrations — sensibly direct their energies towards the Commission as their first port of call. This is, of course, not to understate the important role in policy initiation played by other EU institutions, especially the Council of Ministers and the European Parliament (EP) (Judge *et al.* 1994) and indirectly by the European Court of Justice. National governments also continue to play a key role in the initiation of European policy proposals (Moravcsik 1991). This complex array of actors (which increasingly includes regional governments) makes the EU policy process especially difficult to characterise. The EU is an extreme case of the US example cited by Kingdon in which a Washington official argued that it was very difficult to identify the actual origin of any policy — the policy process was not like a river, the origin of which could be located (Kingdon 1984, p. 77). Thus, in concentrating on the Commission in this Chapter, we are conscious that we are excluding the role played by other institutions in policy initiation. Our focus is on the role that the Commission plays as a broker or clearing-house for the now high levels of interest group mobilisation within the EU. Wherever policy is initiated, it is Commission officials who are charged with the task of drafting legislative proposals which are acceptable to affected interests and governments within the Community.

Not only do groups and other policy-watchers recognise the key role played by the Commission, but their actions also directly influence the position of national governments in what Putnam has described as two-level games (Putnam 1988). The result is a sometimes symbiotic relationship between the Commission and groups in favour of policy change. It is unsurprising, therefore, that the Commission is the focus of so much lobbying by interest groups, independent experts, national administrations, and, increasingly, quasi-non-governmental organisations (QUANGOS). Of course, the phenomenon of European Lobbying is not at all new (Kirchner and Swaiger 1981; Butt Philip 1985). Some fairly stable 'policy networks' involving ECSC officials and corporatist interests were apparent as early as the mid-1950s (Mazey 1992). However, the considerable expansion of the Community's legislative competence following the adoption of the 1986 Single European Act prompted a sharp increase in the numbers and range of regional, national and European-level organisations seeking to influence EC policy outcomes.

In practice, there is considerable variation between sectors in the precise nature of the relationships between Commission officials and groups. The Commission is involved in a wide variety of types of policy networks, many of them so loose and unstructured that the term network may have little utility other than to suggest that there are lots of actors involved. While some interests — for example, in agriculture or information technology — have managed to become part of an identifiable 'policy community' (Smith 1990; Peterson 1992), most are involved in ill-defined and rather loose 'issue networks' of the type identified in the US by Heclo.[1] Both the recent growth of EC lobbying and the existence of significant links between the European Commission and organised interests in and beyond the EC has been well-documented in a number of sectoral and national case studies (Greenwood *et al.* (eds.) 1992; Mazey and Richardson (eds.) 1993b; M.P.C.M. Van Schendelen (ed.) 1993; S.S. Andersen and K.A. Eliassen 1991). There is, however, as yet no single, definitive characterisation of the nature of the relationship between the Commission bureaucracy, interest groups and other policy actors (Greenwood and Ronit 1994; Mazey and Richardson 1994a; Peterson 1994). To some extent, differences in policy-making styles within the Commission can be explained by the particular features of different policy sectors. However, the unique structural characteristics of the EC policy-making process do inhibit the establishment of stable policy communities similar to those typically found at the national level in countries such as the UK, Germany, Denmark and the Netherlands (Richardson 1993). In particular, the multinational nature of the EC policy-making institutions and their openness to outside interests renders the decision-making process extremely pluralistic. The Commission is at the centre of this extremely complex and varied web of relationships and can act as a *'bourse'* where problems, policies and interests are traded. Somewhat less flatteringly, it may be at the centre of a classic 'garbage can' decision-making process (Cohen *et al.* 1972; Mazey and Richardson 1994a).

Paradoxically, however, the peculiar features of the EC policy process may also render the establishment of reasonably stable policy networks essential to the effective functioning of the Community. Popular mythology notwithstanding, the European Commission is a very small administration;

fewer than 5,000 senior officials are collectively responsible for the drafting of EC legislation (though this number is supplemented by short-term, contract staff, expert consultants and secondees — see Chapter 3). In carrying out this role, officials have somehow to accommodate diverse and often conflicting demands of national governments and sectoral interests within and beyond the European Union. Consequently, there exists a powerful 'logic of negotiation' (Jordan and Richardson 1979) and Commission officials are necessarily 'brokers of interests' trying to mobilise transnational coalitions of interests and institutions in favour of policy change. Of course, similar pressures exist at the national level, but they are significantly greater in the multinational context of European policy-making. The recent extension of Community competence has thus both increased the need for group consultation and — because of the proliferation of Euro-lobbyists — given rise to a new problem, namely how to manage that consultation process. The proliferation of Euro-lobbying is now recognised as a 'problem' by senior Commission officials, who are anxious to rationalise the system of group consultation. In particular, they wish to establish more stable and manageable relations with those groups upon whose expertise and cooperation they are — as initiators and managers of EC policies — increasingly dependent. If the Commission can achieve this, its bargaining position with other institutions such as the Council, the EP, and national governments will be strengthened.

Evidence of the desire to create stable constituencies is reflected in the emergence of new consultation procedures within some Directorates General. However, the development of such practices, though functionally effective, has further fuelled the mounting concern among MEPs and senior Commission officials about the growing importance of corporatist interests in the European decision-making process. Public debate about the Community's 'democratic deficit' has thus far focused primarily upon the weakness of the European Parliament. However, the absence of formal regulations governing relations between Commission officials and interest groups raises equally pertinent questions concerning administrative transparency within the Commission. More generally, the active participation of interest groups in the EC policy-making process suggests that neo-functionalist theories of integration were perhaps rather too hastily abandoned by their erstwhile supporters in the 1970s. In several sectors, key interests have indeed played a leading role in the implementation of the 1992 programme. As Peters has observed:

> "the tendency [in the Commission] of bureaucratic decision-making to occur within policy communities (especially those of a technical nature) has been able to depoliticise what could have been highly divisive issues, and thereby the less overt politics of the EC has been able to force, or perhaps cajole, integration along." (Peters 1992, p. 15)

The following discussion is divided into three parts. The first section highlights the organisational and cultural characteristics of the Commission bureaucracy and the implications of these characteristics for groups seeking to develop effective lobbying strategies. All bureaucracies are to some extent shaped by the nature of the environment in which they must operate. The European Commission is no exception. Its historical development as a segmented and pluralistic administration — though contrary to Jean

Monnet's ambitions — is perfectly consistent with its role as multiple-interest broker and policy initiator. The second section examines the growth of the EC lobby and examines whether these developments might result in the appearance of a European 'policy style'. The concluding section considers the wider political and theoretical implications of the integration of special interests into the EC policy-making process.

The European Commission bureaucracy: cultural and organisational characteristics

In many respects, the EC administration resembles a typical bureaucracy. However, its peculiar status, composition and role within the decision-making process creates special problems for officials and groups alike. The multinational composition of the Commission, the absence of any uniform administrative procedures, democratic mandate, or governing ideology in the political sense of the word (Donnelly 1993) give rise to an extremely pluralistic and in some respects "leaderless" executive. Moreover, the pluralistic structure and functioning of the Commission bureaucracy is further reinforced by the fragmentation of political authority within the Community as a whole. Unlike many national executives, the Commission shares power with democratically elected governments and the European Parliament. Page thus uses the term "leaderless pluralism" to describe the EC Commission, on the grounds that this term "acknowledges the fact that in the absence of a focus of political authority, such as provided by a cabinet within a nation state, a variety of institutions, some dominated by politicians and others by officials share it" (Page 1992, p. 193). Within this environment, the Commission performs a pivotal political brokerage role, without which few EC policies would ever be agreed upon in the Council of Ministers. In order to perform this role effectively, however, the European Commission needs to be able both to draw upon the technical expertise and secure the support and compliance of those interests directly affected by EC legislation. This need explains in part at least the bureaucratisation of the Commission — a development much feared by Jean Monnet, who believed it would undermine the supranational nature of the Commission (Monnet 1978, p. 384).

The bureaucratisation of the European Commission

The founding fathers of the European Coal and Steel Community (ECSC) were motivated by a shared commitment to the principle of supranationalism (see also Chapter 1). The creation of the High Authority was an attempt to 'operationalise' this principle. Jean Monnet, in particular, hoped to avoid the divisive effects of nationalism by means of collegiate decision-making and the separation of administrative and executive functions within the High Authority. Somewhat unrealistically, Monnet drew a distinction between the 'political/decision-making' function of the latter (i.e. the equivalent of the present College of Commissioners) and the 'preparatory/technical' role of the administrative services. Previous experience of national and international administrations had also convinced him of the need to prevent the development of sectoral hierarchies, which he believed would similarly threaten the supranational and collegiate nature of the High Authority. Thus, his ambition was to build up gradually, a small, non-hierarchical administration composed of highly qualified (technically and linguistically) officials to support and assist the supranational European executive (Monnet 1978, pp. 384–385). It was not to be. As Gerbet (1992) has observed, the supranationalist principle of the High Authority was, in fact, rapidly eroded by national cleavages and sectoral conflicts within the executive. Such divisions were most visibly reflected in the development of *Cabinets* within the High Authority, which tended to be used by member governments and sectoral interests as a vehicle for promoting national interests within the ECSC (Ritchie 1992). Predictably, the internal divisions which developed within the High Authority reached down to the administrative level. Here, national and sectoral cleavages were reflected in the introduction of national quotas governing the allocation of administrative posts, and increasing functional specialisation within the bureaucracy (Mazey 1992).

This development was inevitable. As theorists such as Max Weber (1962 ed.) and Anthony Downs (1967) have convincingly argued, bureaucracies have an inexorable tendency to grow, both in size and complexity. In terms of its genesis and subsequent development, the administration of the High Authority offers a good example of Down's model of bureaucratic dynamics. By 1954, the rudimentary administrative structures established by Monnet had become ineffective. Increasingly, there were problems of administrative coordination, delays and overlapping responsibility as all divisions sought in isolation from each other to extend as far as possible their sphere of competence. Administrative reorganization, undertaken in 1954 in the name of efficiency, created a more hierarchical, functionally segmented bureaucracy. This was entirely predictable. As Downs (1967) has argued, most bureaux have a notion of "policy space" and are determined to defend and extend the existing borders of their territory. The benefits of expansion far outweigh the disadvantages to the bureaucrat, added to which the pressures for growth are likely to be particularly strong in new bureaux (McKenzie and Tullock 1975). This development was accompanied by the blurring of the distinction made by Monnet between the political and administrative functions of the High Authority. As the scope and complexity of the tasks performed by the ECSC expanded, administrative officials became increasingly involved in the daily management — i.e. the execution — of Community policies (Mazey 1992).

Since 1957, this process of bureaucratisation has continued within the European Commission. The creation of the European Economic Community (EEC) and Euratom in 1957, piecemeal enlargement of the Community in 1973, 1981 and 1986, and incremental expansion of the Community's sphere of competence have prompted continual growth and readjustment of the Commission's staffing and structure. More importantly for the purposes of this Chapter, each division and Directorate General has become — to varying degrees and in different ways — associated with a number of 'client groups'. Again, this fits the Downsian prediction of the behaviour of new bureaucracies — they encourage the development of 'constituencies' loyal to the agency and in some senses dependent on it. The newly-created constituency can then be expected to defend the agency in times of threat. In the case of the Commission, for example, we might expect a range of interests to defend it against the threat of subsidiarity.

In those sectors where the Commission has no specific mandate to initiate EC policies, officials have over the years gradually acquired for themselves a *de facto* policy role. EC Information Technology policy, for example, has been characterised by the almost symbiotic relationship between officials in DG XIII and the powerful IT companies. The Commission's objective in this sector has been to increase its own importance by playing a key role in defending and promoting an internationally competitive 'European' industry (Peterson 1992; Cram 1994). It has sought to achieve this by actively encouraging cooperation between EC companies within the framework of the ESPRIT programmes (European Strategic Programme for Research and Development in Information Technology) and by bringing together the 12 leading IT companies in the EC in a 'European Round Table'.[2] Meanwhile, in the field of EC social policy, much of the work of DG V has been directed towards mobilising a constituency of support for policies which the Commission would like to pursue, but which have to date been blocked by some national governments (Cram 1993, p. 11–13; Mazey 1994). For instance, since the late 1980s, the European Commission has funded six specialised anti-poverty networks, all of which arose from groupings which participated in the Commission's Second Programme against Poverty of 1986–89 (Harvey 1993, p. 190).[3] More generally, DG V has since the mid-1980s promoted and funded research in the fields of poverty, preventive health-care provision, and the social position of women. Though the Commission has no legislative competence in these areas, it has (in keeping with Down's model of bureaucratic development) assiduously cultivated an important constituency among voluntary associations. In so doing, DG V has gradually acquired increased policy-making importance in areas formerly the preserve of national governments. As Peters has observed, "the politics of the European Community is best understood as bureaucratic politics"(Peters 1992, p. 15).

In consequence, as with all bureaucracies, there are often jurisdictional disputes between different parts of a supposedly unified bureaucracy and problems of horizontal coordination across related policy sectors. A classic example is the lack of coordination between DG XI (Environment) and DG XVI (Regional Affairs). As a Court of Auditors' report in 1992 confirmed, several DGs have responsibility for specific aspects of EC environmental policy. The report went on to conclude, "this spread of responsibility requires substantial coordination which is far from being achieved" (Court of Auditors 1992, p. 6). In fact, several policies initiated by DG XVI, and funded by EC structural funds, actually contributed to the deterioration of the environment and were directly at odds with EC environmental policy. Territorial clashes between Commissioners can also encourage their *Cabinets* to run rough-shod over the Commission civil servants who work in the Directorates (*Financial Times*, June 21, 1993).

The overlapping responsibilities of different parts of the Commission undoubtedly complicate the Commission's brokerage function, in that interests may find it difficult to discern just who the broker is on any one issue. The 'lead' DG can be identified easily, but this still leaves the problem of how to interface with other relevant DGs and leaves interests to cope with the general lack of coordination within the Commission. In some sectors, notably environmental policy, groups are themselves beginning to play an important coordinating role at the EC level, bringing together officials and funds from different parts of the Commission (Mazey and Richardson 1994b). Thus, we should note that interest groups themselves may be brokers between different parts of the Commission and between different EU institutions and may even facilitate the brokerage function across national boundaries.

The European Commission: a multinational and multi-cultural bureaucracy

As highlighted above, the EC bureaucracy in many respects resembles any other administration. In other respects, however, it is unique. A major difference, discussed earlier in this Chapter, is the absence of political leadership within the Commission. The former Secretary General of the Commission, Emile Noël, described the European administration as "une administration engagée", motivated by a commitment to European integration (Noël 1981). In this sense, the European Commission may indeed be described as an administration with a mission. Moreover, as Ross's research has confirmed, the impact of the Delors Presidency upon the pace and direction of EC policy since 1984 has been considerable (Ross 1993).[4] Nevertheless, the Commission's role within the EC policy-making process differs significantly from that of national administrations. In most national bureaucracies, the policy agenda is set by the elected government and any changes to it tend to be relatively infrequent and signalled well in advance. At the EC level, no such government exists and there is no single or obviously dominant policy initiator. Formally speaking, the Commission *is* the executive and each year it publishes its work programme for the forthcoming session. This document reflects the formal status of the Commission as EC policy initiator. In practice, however, this schedule is often blown off-course, either by European summit decisions or by pressure from individual Commissioners, MEPs or even interest groups themselves. Indeed, all Commissioners and their *Cabinets* are expected by their national governments to promote national interests within the context of the EC policy process (Donnelly 1993; Spence 1993). Similarly, each Member State seeks to promote favoured projects during the six months it holds the Council presidency (Edwards 1985). Commission proposals are thus often the result of demands from other sources.

Of equal importance are the constraints imposed on officials by existing EU policies. The volume of EU legislation has reached a critical mass where yesterday's policies become today's problems (Wildavsky 1980). Existing programmes and policies inevitably restrict the opportunity for genuinely new European policy initiatives just as they do at the national level. Thus, the Commission will be increasingly subject to policy-making at the margins, a trend which will further underline the fact that the 'stuff' of European integration will be about technical detail — i.e. precisely those issues most susceptible to group influence. However, the permeability of the EC policy process and institutional competition mean that the agenda-setting process is likely to remain fluid. Relative to the national level, the EC policy agenda is therefore extremely unpredictable (Mazey and Richardson 1994a; Peters 1994).

This uncertainty is in large part a consequence of both the schizophrenic relationship that exists between the Commission and the Member States, and the pluralistic, multinational nature of the EC policy-making structures and processes. There has, for instance, been a growing tendency within the context of the 1992 programme for national policy issues to appear — often quite unexpectedly — on the Community's own agenda. One reason for this is the concern among sectoral interests and/or national governments that there should be a 'level playing field' within the SEM. Much Euro-lobbying by groups and national officials is thus designed to ensure that similar technical standards, employment costs, environmental regulations etc. exist throughout the Community. In September 1990, for instance, the Commission revised proposals for EC legislation on recycling in response to more stringent legislative plans announced earlier that year by the German government (Mazey and Richardson 1992a, p. 99). Such changes occur because within the framework of the SEM, national interests and governments are anxious to gain a comparative advantage over their EC counterparts. One way of achieving this is to persuade Commission officials to adopt their existing national standards as the basis of EC standards. Thus, EC policy initiation and formulation is characterised by 'competitive agenda-setting', a process which can be extremely frustrating for those groups which 'lose'. In May 1993, for example, John Rimington, Director General of the UK Health and Safety Executive, complained that the health and safety EC framework directive had been "entirely written to serve the French system" (*The Guardian*, May 12, 1993). Groups and governments also lobby the EC in an attempt to make sure the playing field slopes in their favour, such as the campaign led by UK employers' associations and the UK government against the Social Chapter of the Maastricht Treaty. The opt-out clause secured by the UK Prime Minister with respect to this part of the agreement means that UK employers will not have to provide the same level of social protection for UK employees as their EC counterparts. Thus, groups seeking to monitor policy developments at the EC level need to take account of the fact that the EC policy agenda is to a considerable degree driven by national policy agendas within the 12 Member States.

The multinational composition of the administration also influences the manner in which the Commission functions and its relations with groups in the policy-making process. At national levels, there are usually unified recruitment and training procedures with bureaucrats drawn from a pool of applicants from a common cultural and educational background. European officials are drawn from all the Member States. As a multinational bureaucracy, the European Commission has not yet developed a coherent bureaucratic or operational style. In consequence, there are at present no standard operating procedures with regard to interest-group consultation. New procedures are only now beginning to emerge. Arguably, the diversity of administrative practices and styles within the Commission is in part due to its relative immaturity, but it is also in part a consequence of the multinational character of the bureaucracy. In reality, there are 12 national bureaucratic cultures at work within the Commission, each with its own style of policy management. Christoph's research, for example, confirmed that British Commission officials "saw themselves as products of an *administrative tradition* quite different from what they encountered in Brussels" (Christoph 1993, p. 321). David Williamson, the (UK) Secretary General of the European Commission has also commented on the "quite marked differences in style between Whitehall and Brussels":

> "I won't say that Whitehall is a club but there's a common approach to a large number of things, and an enormous amount of consultation. Here, people are more detached, more proud of their specific responsibilities. So consultation here is a more difficult business." (Quoted in R. Collis,'Two Men and their Dog', *In Flight Magazine*, British Midland, January 1991, p. 29)

Different cultural styles are also important in determining the rhythm of the Commission's work. The British sense of humour, the German and Danish tendency to lunch early, the Italian habit of working late, French formality, nine official languages, and the continental (but not British) tradition of appointing economists and lawyers as senior civil servants combine to create an extremely diverse Euroculture within the Commission (J. de la Guérivière 1992; Christoph 1993). The disparate nature of the Commission's administrative style is often unappreciated by interest groups, many of whom develop a generalised view of the Commission based upon their experiences with one division or section of a DG. In practice, the 'rules of the game' vary quite markedly between different parts of the Commission and may change if a policy sector or DG is taken over by an official of a different nationality.

The Commission as a marketplace for ideas and interests

In order to be effective initiators and managers of policies, all bureaucracies need to secure the cooperation of those interests directly affected by and/or responsible for the implementation of those policies. This helps policy design and strengthens a bureaucracy in its dealings with other policy-making institutions. Thus, part of a bureaucracy's expertise is knowing the affected interests and their likely reaction to policy change. Also, having consulted widely, the bureaucracy's legitimacy is thereby increased when dealing with elected legislatures and ministers. This is especially true at the EC level where all policy-makers are to some degree operating in a political vacuum largely devoid of effectively articulated public opinion, mass media, and effective European-level political parties. Conventional channels of representation, familiar at the national level, are weak, leaving the interest-group channel (however limited) as one of the most effective channels of representation available (Mazey and Richardson 1994c). In short, in order to be heard, European public opinion must be organised and mobilised. Being at the centre of this representational channel gives the Commission some advantages in the European policy game. Yet the incoherence and bias in the lobbying system places officials under pressure to seek practical ways of structuring, organising and stabilising interest-group intermediation. Essentially, they need to secure a 'negotiated order' in which to formulate policy.

Not surprisingly, Commission officials often lack the necessary detailed technical expertise and knowledge of sectoral practices and problems in the 12 Member States (let alone those in other non-member countries) and are thus heavily dependent on outside expertise. To some extent, this expertise can be obtained by bringing national officials into the Commission on a temporary basis. Increasingly, however, Commission officials have become dependent upon the relevant interest groups for information and expertise as well as the various epistemic communities, i.e. networks of knowledge-based experts (Haas 1992). Officials also know that they need to mobilise the support of those interests directly affected by EC legislative proposals since the legislation is otherwise unlikely to be adopted by the Council or implemented effectively. Most groups therefore experience little difficulty in gaining access to Commission officials. Insofar as access is a problem, it is precisely because almost everyone gains access. This means that it is very difficult for particular sectoral or national interests to gain privileged access to Commission bureaucrats, who are generally anxious to consult as widely as possible. This bureaucratic openness is an important cause of the sometimes quite dramatic changes in EC policy as draft Directives are revised following diverse representations from affected groups or because of a bias in the selection of so-called independent experts. Thus, the market for policy ideas is both large and varied.

In recent years, the growth of Euro-lobbying has placed considerable strains upon officials. The key issue, therefore, is how do Commission officials 'manage' the brokerage process? In fact, there is no single or straightforward answer to this question. The nature of the relationship between officials and interest groups at the EC level varies considerably between policy sectors. The differences are the result of the different structural characteristics of individual sectors, diverse bureaucratic interests and administrative styles within the Commission on the one hand, and differences between groups themselves in terms of their size, resources, ideology and objectives. Notwithstanding this diversity, it is nevertheless possible to identify some important trends.

First, in responding to increased interest-group mobilisation, the Commission's approach to consultation has been essentially pragmatic and — until recently — undirected. A few individual officials have simply resorted to the technique of 'closure', i.e. they either terminate the consultation process at the point they judge it to be dysfunctional to effective policy-making, or they are reluctant to engage in it at all. Thus, the brokerage function is not essential in all sectors. Increasing numbers of officials have begun to be more discriminating in their attitude towards lobbyists. Professional consultants, for instance, are not generally highly regarded by officials. This is partly because of their poor reputation and partly because pressed officials prefer to negotiate directly with interested parties. There does exist a 'procedural ambition' within the Commission that wherever possible, officials should consult with the relevant European associations for each particular policy sector. This can be seen as an attempt to sub-contract or privatise the most difficult aspects of the brokerage function — namely the formation of a Euro-level consensus within the relevant industry or sector. To facilitate this process, the Commission Services have drawn up directories which list Community trade, agricultural, industrial and professional associations (Commission of the European Communities 1992b, p. 4 — see Annex A). Where such groups do not exist, the Commission itself has been active in helping to create and sustain them. Unfortunately, most Euro-groups are in many cases unable to be of much assistance to the Commission since they tend to be internally divided, poorly resourced and unable to respond quickly to Commission requests for information (McLaughlin and Jordan 1993). In reality, therefore, Commission officials regularly consult individual companies and national associations for information and advice, and are forced to deal with a disparate set of interests within and beyond the Member States.

Secondly, consultation structures and processes which are commonly employed by national bureaucracies such as the publication of Green and White Papers, information seminars, advisory committees, working groups, and informal negotiations with interested parties, are widely used at the European level (Commission of the European Communities 1992a, p. 2 — see Annex B). By this means, big, politically sensitive issues can be unpacked into technical and therefore more manageable, depoliticised policy problems. Trade-offs and an exchange relationship can be developed into 'bargainable' problems. These problems can then be processed within something akin to the policy community model cited earlier. Officials from most policy-orientated DGs habitually use various advisory bodies (e.g. expert committees, industry groups) and regularly convene seminars, workshops and conferences of the relevant interests. These structures provide an opportunity for selected groups (i.e. those groups who 'matter') and officials to exchange information, define problems and negotiate mutually acceptable policy compromises. The accommodation of group demands at this early stage of the EC policy-making process also reduces the likelihood of more public (and therefore potentially more damaging) disputes when the proposals reach the European Parliament or the Council of Ministers. The Commission is able to take an overview of the different positions, formulate and reformulate possible solutions which can attract a winning coalition of groups, individuals and institutions. Given their participation in all stages of the EC policy process, Commission officials are also uniquely placed to identify likely sources of opposition at either the Member State or European level (see also Chapter 8).

The third characteristic of the EC policy-making process which is in many respects a function of the close links which exist between groups and officials concerns the *type* of policy instrument typically employed by the Commission. As Majone (1991a; 1991b) has convincingly argued, the peculiar institutional and political context of EC policy-making has prompted "the rise of the regulatory state in Europe". In the environmental sector, for instance, the European Commission has in recent years employed a regulatory mode of policy-making (e.g. with regard to drinking-water quality, waste-water disposal). A similar approach is evident in the field of EC social policy (e.g. notably with regard to health and safety in the workplace, worker protection) (Cram 1993; Mazey 1994). The reasons for the growth of Community regulation have to do with the EC policy-making structures and the strategic interests of those actors involved in the policy process. As Majone writes:

"any satisfactory explanation of the remarkable growth of Community regulation must take into account both the desire of the Commission to increase its influence — a reasonable behaviourial assumption — and the possibility of escaping budgetary constraints by resorting to regulatory policy-making." (Majone 1991a, p. 96)

In short, European policy-making has, in practice, become increasingly bound up with European regulation. In part, this is because a small European Commission with relatively few financial resources to hand out is, almost inevitably, going to turn to regulation as a cost-effective means of securing European integration. European regulation of industrial and commercial sectors may also be more acceptable to EC member governments if it means that they, in turn, can pass on the costs involved to the groups themselves. Since Commission proposals need to be endorsed by the Member States, this is an important consideration in favour of this type of policy. Crucially, regulation provides the Commission with an alternative resource to money in terms of legitimising and strengthening its brokerage role. By using regulation instead of money, it can distribute costs and benefits and is bound to attract the lobbying attentions of those likely to be affected.

In addition, multinational, export-oriented firms may also have an interest in Community regulation. Groups often support EC-wide regulations since this is one means of ensuring that rival interests within the Community do not enjoy an unfair comparative advantage. Moreover, by supporting a single European standard, companies often hope to prevent the imposition of more stringent national standards. Indeed, since groups themselves are typically involved in both the formulation and implementation of the policies, EC regulatory policies might even be regarded as being more akin to 'self-regulation'. The emergence of 'regulatory communities' and, under certain circumstances, coherent 'policy networks' at the EC level, within which affected interests play a key role, means that national governments increasingly find themselves reacting to an EC policy agenda which has effectively been set and/or 'processed' elsewhere. Thus, as Van Schendelen concluded from a study of EC lobbying practices in 12 European countries, "the tendency all over the Community is for Member States to become less successful in coordinating national public and private interests regarding the EC agenda" (Van Schendelen 1993, p. 277).

Conclusion: brokering and a European policy style

That there is a complex *mélange* of non-governmental actors in Brussels is beyond dispute. A Commission study showed that there are now approximately 3,000 special-interest groups of varying types in Brussels, with up to 10,000 employees working in the lobbying sector. These figures include more than 500 European and international federations, whose constituent members belonging to national associations number more than 5,000. In addition, there are 50 offices in Brussels representing regional and local authorities, more than 200 firms with direct representation, about 100 consultancies in Brussels itself and 100 law firms in Belgium specialising in Community law (Commission of the European Communities 1992b, p. 4). Diverse and numerous interest groups within and beyond the European Community have established close links — informal as well as formal — with the European Commission. The primary catalyst for this lobbying explosion was, of course, the 1986 Single European Act, which committed EC Member States to complete the internal market by the end of 1992 and reformed the EC decision-making process in such a way as to reduce the power of individual national governments to block EC policies. The further extension of the Community's legislative competence and changes to the EC decision-making process introduced by the Maastricht Treaty will give fresh impetus to this trend. The pluralistic nature of the EC decision-making process, combined with the reliance of Commission officials upon outside expertise (be it from conventional interest groups or from epistemic communities) will further encourage the development of sectoral (and increasingly cross-sectoral) policy networks centred upon the European Commission as the heart of the EU's 'nervous system'.

These developments represent an unplanned and pragmatic response to the growing importance of European policy-making. In terms of the policy process, the development of effective EC level policy networks would be functionally beneficial, if only because it might stabilise and regularise the policy process.

Regulated and structured participation in the policy process might be preferable to 'garbage-can' politics, even though the latter clearly presents the Commission with opportunities both to initiate policy ideas and to encourage in a rather subtle way the formation of 'advocacy coalitions' (Sabatier 1987; Sabatier and Jenkins-Scott 1993). However, the considerable influence wielded by organised interests within the European Commission and the close — often informal — links which exist between some groups and Commission officials have served to increase public unease about the Community's 'democratic deficit'. The European Parliament began in 1991 to debate the need for a register of lobbyists. Partly in response to these pressures the Secretariat General of the European Commission in 1992 reviewed Commission procedures regarding group consultation. Allegations concerning the political influence of corporate groups and other special interests are, of course, not unique to the European Community. Liberal democratic theorists and political scientists have for many years studied and debated the impact of organised interests on public policy-makers. However, unlike national executives, the European Commission is not an elected government, democratically accountable to the electorate. Nor is the EU policy-making process as transparent as many national-level procedures. Indeed, the debate over links between special interests and EC Commission officials forms part of a much wider, current debate within the Community on the need to increase the openness and transparency of the EU decision-making process (Commission of the European Communities 1993; Commission of the European Communities 1992a).

There are at present no explicit Commission regulations (such as accreditation, registration, code of conduct) with respect to interest groups. Paradoxically, this is due to the Commission's longstanding commitment to maintaining an open dialogue with as many special interests as possible. As a general policy, therefore, it has consistently refused to grant formal privileges such as the issuing of entry passes and favoured information to selected groups. However, the growth of EC lobbying, aggressive lobbying styles and 'misdemeanours', such as lobbyists selling draft documents and misrepresenting themselves to the public by the use of Commission symbols, has persuaded the Commission Secretariat General of the need "to clarify and better structure the Commission's relations with special interest groups" (Commission of the European Communities 1992b, p. 6).

The same Commission report recommended a series of guiding principles defining the Commission's future relations with interest groups, proposed the creation of a single directory of non-profit-making groups and drew up a list of minimum requirements for a code of conduct between the Commission and special-interest groups. In an attempt to rationalise the consultation process, the Commission also proposed the establishment of one or more organisations (open to all representatives of special-interest groups), through which groups would communicate with the Commission. In substantive terms, the changes proposed are far from radical. The guiding principles defining relations between Commission officials merely reiterate the Commission's adherence to the principle of an open administration, its preference for dealing with European (con)federations and the need for transparency. The proposed directory of groups will only include details of non-profit-making organisations; the profit-making sector is merely encouraged to draw up its own directory. All organisations are similarly invited to draw up and enforce their own codes of conduct with regard to EC lobbying. Such codes should include rules governing misrepresentation, honesty, competence and openness. The rights and obligations of Commission officials remain unchanged (Commission of the European Communities 1992b, pp. 6–7).

Group representatives reacted favourably to the idea of self-regulation involving a voluntary code of conduct, a directory for profit-making organisations and the establishment of one or more organisations to act as communication channels between groups and the Commission. Yet, by June 1993, no steps had been taken in this direction (Commission of the European Communities 1993, p. 9). In order to accelerate implementation of these proposals the Commission organised a series of consultation meetings to reiterate its intentions. Meanwhile, the Commission and European Parliament have joined forces to prepare a common database (which will be publicly available) of groups which maintain relations with them (Commission of the European Communities 1993, p. 10).[5] The proposals are in themselves unlikely to have much impact. However, the fact that they have been introduced at all confirms the degree to which lobbying is now perceived to be a problem within both the Commission and the European Parliament. Increasing numbers of Commission officials feel rather 'exposed' and would welcome the introduction of guidelines governing contacts with group representatives.

Whatever rules may be introduced in the future governing links between the Commission and special interest groups, their integration (in growing numbers) into the EC policy-making process is now an established fact. In view of this development, it is appropriate to end this discussion by considering once again the suggestion made some 30 years ago by neo-functionalist theorists that groups would play a key role in the process of European integration (Haas 1958; Lindberg 1963). As we have argued elsewhere (Mazey and Richardson 1993a), there is more and more evidence that organised interests (notably the multinational companies) are increasingly active in pressing for standardisation, harmonisation and the establishment of a 'level playing field' within the Community. They recognise that in terms of world competition there is little alternative to cross-national collaboration if European industries are to be able to compete with those of the Pacific rim in the next century. Their desire to reduce uncertainty might also lead them to press for greater political as well as economic union within Europe. The European Round Table (ERT), for instance, argued in 1991 that "the unification of Europe is the only practical way to realise its potential and to harness its resources" (European Round Table 1991, p. 13). It would be wrong, of course, to see this type of pressure as *necessarily* leading to more European integration. However, in his discussion of the concept of "community sentiment", Haas suggested that two of the six necessary conditions for this sentiment to flourish are that:

> "Interest groups and political parties at the national level endorse supranational action and in preference to action by their national government ... [and] interest groups and political parties organise beyond the national level in order to function more effectively as decision-makers *vis-à-vis* the separate national governments or the central authority and if they define their interests in terms of longer than those of the separate nation-state from which they originate." (Haas 1958, pp. 9–10)

Haas goes on to define political integration as "a process whereby political actors in several distinct national settings are persuaded to shift their loyalties, expectations and political activities toward a new centre, whose institutions possess or demand jurisdiction over the pre-existing states" (Haas 1958, p. 16). This process is underway; interest groups often press for wider EC jurisdiction over the pre-existing nation-states. The administrative and transaction costs of operating under 12 different sets of VAT or pollution control regulations, for example, are now regarded as being too high — and anachronistic — by companies which have become 'Europeanised' (partly as a result of European Commission initiatives) in terms of their market.

Writing in 1963, Lindberg suggested that European associations were relatively ineffective and that interest groups generally were playing only a limited role in the integration process. However, he went on to argue that:

> "one can expect that over time the necessity for lobbying will force groups to emphasise collective needs rather than national differences. Such a development can be expected as the central institutions of the EEC become more active, as the types of actions taken involve the harmonisation of legislation and the formulations of common policies (rather than the negative process of . . . barriers to trade), and as . . . groups become aware that their interests can no longer be adequately served at the national level alone."(Lindberg 1963, p. 101).

Most of the available evidence suggests that groups now recognise that supranational decisions are required for many policy problems and that it is often in their interests to participate in the formulation of such policies. Groups are therefore beginning to play a significant role in the process of European integration, as predicted by the neofunctionalists. At the European level, their primary means of doing so is to develop direct relations with the Commission and to participate in the usually messy process by which agreed

European policies eventually emerge. Our central argument here has been that the Commission is unusually well-placed to massage and orchestrate this process via its brokerage role.

Notes

1   The State-group relations typology based on the concept of policy networks was initially developed in the context of the British policy-making process by G. Jordan and J. Richardson (1979). For more recent elaborations of the typology see R. A. W. Rhodes and D. Marsh (1992). A policy network brings together public officials and those groups with an interest in a particular policy sector. Various types of network exist. A 'policy community' is characterised by an intimate relationship between groups and government department(s), the development of common perceptions and the existence of a common language for describing policy problems. Membership is relatively stable and selective and an exchange relationship exists between members. By contrast, 'issue networks' are more pluralistic. They are characterised by loose links between officials and groups. There are few shared values and competition over policy objectives. Membership of the network is unstable and open, and relationships between members based on competition and bargaining (see Heclo 1978).
2   Members included ICL, GEC and Plessey of the UK; Thomson, Bull and CGE from France; AEG, Nixdorf and Siemens from Germany; Olivetti and STET from Italy; and Philips from the Netherlands.
3   These include: Women in Poverty, Eurolink Age (elderly people), European Federation of National Organisations working with the Homeless (FEANTSA), Network for One-Parent Families, Trans-European Rural Network and ATD Quart Monde.
4   Sir Roy Denman, former EC ambassador in Washington, described the Delors regime as "Tammany Hall with a French accent", likening it to the powerful political machine that once ran New York City (*Financial Times*, 21 June 1993).
5   The Commission has stated that inclusion in the directory will not imply any form of official recognition or confer any privileges.

References

Andersen, Svein S. and Eliassen, Kjell A. (1991) 'European Community Lobbying', *European Journal of Political Research*, Vol. 20 (2), pp. 173–87.
Butt Philip, Alan (1985) *Pressure Groups in the European Community*, London University Association for Contemporary European Studies, Occasional Papers No. 2.
Christoph, James B. (1993) 'The Effects of Britons in Brussels: the European Community and the Culture of Whitehall', Paper presented at the annual Meeting of the Midwest Political Science Association, Chicago, April 9–11.
Cohen, Michael, March, James and Olsen, Johan P. (1972) 'A Garbage Can Model of Organizational Choice', *Administrative Science Quarterly*, Vol. 17, pp. 1–25.
Commission of the European Communities (1992a) *Increased Transparency in the work of the Commission*, Brussels, 2 December, SEC (92) 2274 final (see Annex B).
Commission of the European Communities (1992b) *An Open and Structured Dialogue between the Commission and Special Interest Groups*, Brussels, 2 December, SEC (92) 2272 final (see Annex A).
Commission of the European Communities (1993) *Openness in the Community, Communications to the Council, the Parliament and the Economic and Social Committee*, Brussels, 2 June. COM (93) 258 final.

Court of Auditors (1992) Special Report No. 3/92 concerning the Environment together with the Commission's replies, *Official Journal*, 92/C245/01, Vol. 35, 23 September.

Cram, Laura (1993) 'Calling the tune without Paying the Piper? Social Policy Regulation: the Role of the Commission in European Community Social Policy', *Policy and Politics*, Vol. 21 (2), pp. 135–46.

Cram, Laura (1994) 'Breaking Down the Monolith: the European Commission as a Multi-Organization: Social Policy and IT Policy in the EC', *Journal of European Public Policy*, Vol. 1(1), pp. 45–67.

de la Guérivière, Jean (1992) *Voyage à l'Intérieur de l'Eurocratie*, Paris: Le Monde Editions.

Donnelly, M. (1993) 'The Structure of the European Commission and the Policy Formation Process', in Mazey, Sonia and Richardson, Jeremy J. (eds.), *Lobbying in the European Community*, Oxford: Oxford University Press, pp. 74–81.

Downs, A. (1967) *Inside Bureaucracy*, Boston: Little, Brown and Company.

Edwards, G. (1985) 'The Presidency of the Council of Ministers of the European Communities: the Case of the United Kingdom' in C. O'Nuallain, *The Presidency of the European Council of Ministers*, London: Croom Helm, pp. 237–591.

European Round Table (1991) *Reshaping Europe*, Brussels: European Round Table.

Greenwood, Justin, Gröte, Jurgen R. and Ronit, Karsten (eds.) (1992) *Organized Interests and the European Community*, London: Sage Publications.

Haas, E. (1958) *The Uniting of Europe — Political, Social and Economic Forces 1950–57*, Stanford: Stanford University Press.

Haas, Peter (1992) 'Introduction: Epistemic Communities and International Coordination', *International Organization*, Vol. 46, pp. 1–35.

Harvey, B. (1993) 'Lobbying in Europe: the Experience of the Voluntary Sector', in Mazey, Sonia and Richardson, Jeremy J. (eds.), *op. cit.*

Heclo, Hugh (1978) 'Issue Networks and the Executive Establishment', in King, Anthony (ed.) *The New American Political System*, Washington DC: American Enterprise Institute.

Jordan, Grant, McLaughlin, Andrew M. and Malone, William A. (1993) 'Corporate Lobbying in the European Community', *Journal of Common Market Studies*, Vol. 31(2), pp. 191–212.

Judge, David, Earnshaw, David, and Cowan, Ngaire (1994) 'Ripples or Waves: the European Parliament in the European Community Policy Process', *Journal of European Public Policy* Vol. 1 (1), pp. 27–51.

Kingdon, John (1984) *Agendas, Alternatives and Public Policies*, Boston: Little Brown.

Kirchner, E. and Swaiger, K. (1981) *The role of Interest Groups in the European Community*, Aldershot: Gower.

Lindberg, L. (1963) *The Political Dynamics of European Economic Integration*, Stanford: Stanford University Press.

Majone, Giandomenico (1991a) 'Cross-national Sources of Regulatory Policy-making in Europe and the United States', *Journal of Public Policy*, Vol. 11(1), pp. 79–106.

Majone, Giandomenico (1991b) *Market Integration and Regulation: Europe after 1992*, EUI Working Papers, SPS No. 91/10, Florence: European University Institute.

Mazey, Sonia (1992) 'Conception and Evolution of the High Authority's Administrative Services (1952–56): from Supranational principles to Multinational Practices', in Morgan, R. and Wright, V. (eds.) *The Administrative Origins of the European Community*, Baden: Nomos.

Mazey, Sonia (forthcoming 1995) 'The Development of EC Equal Opportunities Policies: Bureaucratic Expansion on Behalf of Women?', Paper presented at 'ESRC Research Seminar: State Autonomy in the European Community', Oxford University, 14–15 January 1994.

Mazey, Sonia and Richardson, Jeremy J. (1992a) 'British Pressure Groups in the

European Community: the Challenge of Brussels' *Parliamentary Affairs*, Vol. 45 (1), pp. 92–107.

Mazey, Sonia and Richardson, Jeremy J. (1992b) 'Environmental Groups and the EC: Challenges and Opportunities', *Environmental Politics*, Vol. 1(4), pp. 109–128.

Mazey, Sonia and Richardson, Jeremy J. (1993a), 'Interest Groups in the European Community', in Jeremy J. Richardson (ed.) *Pressure Groups*, Oxford: Oxford University Press, pp. 191–213.

Mazey, Sonia and Richardson, Jeremy J. (eds.) (1993b) *Lobbying in the European Community*, Oxford: Oxford University Press.

Mazey, Sonia and Richardson, Jeremy J. (1994a) *Promiscuous Policy-Making: a European Policy Style?* European Public Policy Institute, occasional paper No 8. Warwick: EPPI.

Mazey, Sonia and Richardson, Jeremy J. (1994b) 'Policy Coordination in Brussels: Environmental and Regional Policy', *Regional Politics and Policy*, Vol. 4(1), pp. 22–44.

Mazey, Sonia and Richardson, Jeremy J. (1994c) 'Interest Groups as a channel of representation in the European Union', Paper presented to the European Consortium of Political Research Joint Sessions Workshops, Madrid, 17–22 April.

McKenzie, R.B. and Tullock, G. (1975) *The New World of Economics: Explorations in Human Experience*, Homewook III: Richard Irwin Inc.

McLaughlin, A. and Jordan, G. (1993) 'The Rationality of Lobbying in Europe: why are Euro-groups so Numerous and so Weak? Some Evidence from the Car Industry', in Mazey, Sonia and Richardson, Jeremy (eds.) (1993b) *op. cit.*

Monnet, Jean (1978) *Memoirs*, London: Collins.

Moravcsik, Andrew (1991) 'Negotiating the Single European Act' in Keohane, Robert and Hoffmann, Stanley (eds.) *The New European Community*, Oxford: Westview Press, pp. 41–84.

Noël, Emile (1981) 'La Fonction publique européenne', speech given on 25 October 1981, published in European Commission (1988) *Hommage à Emile Noël*, Luxembourg: European Commission, pp. 153–57.

Page, Edward C. (1992) *Political Authority and Bureaucratic Power: a Comparative Analysis*, London: Harvester Wheatsheaf.

Peters, Guy (1992) 'Bureaucratic Politics and the Institutions of the European Community', in Sbragia, A.M. (ed.) *Euro-Politics, Institutions and Policy-Making in the "New" European Community*, Washington DC: The Brookings Institute, pp. 75–122.

Peters, Guy (1994) 'Agenda-Setting in the European Community', *Journal of European Public Policy*, Vol. 1 (1), pp. 9–26.

Peterson, John (1992) 'The European Technology Community: Policy Networks in a Supranational Setting' in Marsh, David and Rhodes, R.A.W. (eds.) *Policy Networks in British Government*, Oxford: Oxford University Press.

Peterson, John (1994) 'Understanding Decision-Making in the European Union: towards a Framework for Analysis', Paper presented to the Ninth Annual Conference of Europeanists' Council for European Studies, Chicago, 1 April 1994.

Putnam, Robert (1988) 'Diplomacy and Domestic Politics: the Logic of Two-Level Games', *International Organization*, Vol. 42(3), pp. 427–60.

Rhodes, R.A.W. and Marsh, David (1992) 'New Directions in the Study of Policy Networks', *European Journal of Political Research*, Vol. 21(1), pp. 181–205.

Richardson, Jeremy J. (ed.) (1993) *Pressure Groups*, Oxford: Oxford University Press.

Richardson, Jeremy J. and Jordan, Grant (1979) *Governing under Pressure: the Policy Process in a Post-Parliamentary Democracy*, Oxford: Martin Robertson.

Ritchie, Ella (1992) 'The Development of *Cabinets* within the High Authority', in Morgan R. and Wright, V. (eds.) *The Administrative Origins of the European Community*, Baden Baden: Nomos.

Ross, George (1993) 'Sidling into Industrial Policy: Inside the European Commission' *French Politics and Society*, Vol. 11, Winter, pp. 20–45.

Sabatier, Paul A. (1987) 'An Advocacy Coalition Framework of Policy Change and the Role of Policy-Oriented Learning', *Policy Sciences,* Vol. 21, pp. 129–68.

Sabatier, Paul A. and Jenkins-Scott, Hank C. (eds.) (1993) *Policy Change and Learning: an Advocacy Coalition Approach,* Oxford: Westview.

Smith, M. J. (1990) *The Politics of Agricultural Support in Britain: the Development of the Agricultural Policy Community,* Aldershot: Dartmouth Press.

Spence, D. (1993) 'The Role of the National Civil Service in European Lobbying: the British Case', in Mazey, Sonia and Richardson, Jeremy (eds.) (1993a) *op. cit.,* pp. 47–73.

Van Schendelen, M.P.C.M. (ed.) (1993) *National Public and Private EC Lobbying,* Aldershot: Dartmouth Press.

Weber, Max (1962) 'Bureaucracy', in *idem, Essays in Sociology,* translated by H. H. Gerth and C. Wright-Mills, Oxford: Oxford University Press.

Wildavsky, A. (1980) *The Art and Craft of Policy Analysis,* London: Macmillan.

This Chapter is based upon research undertaken as part of a longer study of interest groups and EC policy-making, funded by the Economic and Social Research Council.

ANNEX A

An open and structured dialogue between the Commission and special interest groups
(93/C 63/02)

I. INTRODUCTION

The Commission has always been an institution open to outside input. The Commission believes this process to be fundamental to the development of its policies. This dialogue has proved valuable to both the Commission and to interested outside parties. Commission officials acknowledge the need for such outside input and welcome it.

The Commission has in particular a reputation for being accessible to interest groups and should of course retain this ease of access. Indeed, it is in the Commission's own interest to do so since interest groups can provide the services with technical information and constructive advice. The present communication arises from the belief that by placing these relations on a slightly more formalized footing the Commission will make them more transparent to the benefit of all concerned.

This Communication aims to implement the commitment contained in the Commission's work programme for 1992, indicating that 'relations between the Community's institutions and interest groups, useful though they are, must be more clearly defined. Consideration will therefore be given to the preparation of a code of conduct designed to govern relations with those organizations set up with the specific purpose of liaising with the Commission. This step will in no way compromise the freedom of trade or professional groupings, or hinder essential dialogue with institutional committees'.

The present Communication should be seen in the context of the larger debate on the declaration on the right of access to information as annexed to the Treaty on European Union and on the Birmingham Declaration which called for a more open Community to ensure a better informed public debate. However, it addresses in detail only one of the issues related to these declarations, i.e. the relations with special interest groups.

Of particular relevance to special interest groups are the wider issues linked to both declarations on broadening participation of Commission proposals and on the wider availability of Commission documents. These questions are dealt with in a separate communication on transparency.

II. SPECIAL INTEREST GROUPS

The Commission is frequently contacted by the representatives of special interest groups. These groups can be divided into non-profit making organizations (European and (inter)national associations/federations) and profit making organizations (legal advisers, public relations and public affairs firms, and consultants). The former are largely, but not solely, professional organizations. The latter are persons who often act on the instructions of a third party to set out and defend the interests of that third party. Such a distinction between profit and non-profit special interest groups is somewhat arbitrary. Nevertheless, it is considered practical for the purposes of this communication.

The present situation

At present there are thought to be approximately 3 000 special interest groups of varying types in Brussels, with up to 10 000 employees working in the lobbying sector. Within this total there are more than 500 European and international federations (whose constituent members belonging to national associations number more than 5 000). In addition, there are 50 offices in Brussels representing *Länder,* regional and local authorities (some of which may of course participate in the institutional framework of the Community and it is only their other activities which are concerned by this communication). There are more than 200 individual firms with direct representation, and about 100 consultants (management, and public relations) with offices in Brussels and many others dealing with Community affairs. There are 100 law firms in Belgium specializing in Community law and many more in other countries (both Member States and beyond).

The Single European Act, coupled with the progress of the White Paper programme, prompted a sharp increase in lobbying at Commission level. At the same time there was a shift in the need for information from a general to a specific level. Evidence of this is that independent consultants began to obtain monitoring contracts from clients. Moreover, organizations sought to exert influence directly and/or through intermediaries such as consultants. For similar purposes, large firms from third countries increasingly set up offices in Brussels.

In addition, some of these special interest groups serve as a channel to provide specific technical expertise to the Commission from a variety of sectors, such as in the drafting of technical regulations.

There are basically two forms of dialogue between the Commission and special interest groups: through advisory committees and expert groups which assist the Commission in the exercise of its own competences; and through contact with interest groups on an unstructured, *ad hoc* basis. The nature and intensity of these contacts vary.

Explicit Commission rules (such as accreditation, registration, code of conduct) towards special interest groups do not exist. However, the Commission has a general policy not to grant privileges to special interest groups, such as the issuing of entry passes and favoured access to information. Nor does it give associations an official endorsement by granting them consultative status. This is because the Commission has always wanted to maintain a dialogue which is as open as possible with all interested parties without having to enforce an accreditation system. Commission services have drawn up directories which list Community trade, agricultural, industrial and other relevant professional associations as a first tool in the search for increased understanding of special interest groups.

While there are no general problems with such contacts, there have been cases where more aggressive styles of lobbying have been encountered. Misdemeanours have occurred, such as lobbyists selling draft and official documents; lobbyists misrepresenting themselves to the public by the use of Commission symbols; lobbyists who are in possession of a press card and therefore have direct access to press conferences and press releases. One of the reasons cited for the success of the trade in Commission documents is the length of time it takes to obtain them through official channels (this is partly due to the unavoidable delays inherent in the translation process). Some problems of confidentiality also exist.

Other Community institutions

Contacts were also made with other Community institutions (European Parliament and Council of Ministers), and with the Economic and Social Committee, on the question of relations with interest groups. The Committee on the rules of procedure of the European Parliament has issued (3 October 1992) a recommendation to the Enlarged Bureau on rules governing the representation of special interest groups at the European Parliament. This proposal envisages a register, a code of conduct, rights in connection with registration, such as access to the European Parliament and its documents, and an enforcement procedure.

Member States, third countries and international organizations

In the majority of Member States formal procedures for lobbying are not laid down. In those cases where rules do exist, they deal mainly with the relationship between the Parliament and lobbyists. Some formal framework on lobbying exists in the Federal Republic of Germany, the United States, Canada and the United Nations. In the United Kingdom a similar policy is under preparation. The policy is most developed in the United States (see Annex I). Key elements in the various existing procedures include rules on accreditation, registration, directories, codes of conduct, management and the enforcement of fixed rules.

Guiding principles

A number of guiding principles need to be followed in order to define the Commission's future relations with interest groups:

- preservation of the open relationship between the Commission and special interest groups, adhering to the principle of an open administration, which has been the well established practice built up over many years but which could still be extended further,
- while the Commission tends to favour European (con)federations over representatives of individual or national organizations, it is nevertheless committed to the equal treatment of all special interest groups, to ensure that every interested party, irrespective of size or financial backing, should not be denied the opportunity of being heard by the Commission,
- it should be possible for Commission officials, when dealing with representatives of special interest groups, to know exactly who is who and who does what,
- while the Commission can pursue its own approach to dealing with special interest groups, it should remain open to the possibility of fitting in with the policy of other Community institutions in this field,
- the adoption of simple procedures calling for a minimum amount of human and financial resources and administrative effort.

III. FUTURE POLICY

As a first step, a series of measures are taken in order to clarify and better structure the Commission's relations with special interest groups.

Directory

Information regarding non-profit making organizations is currently held within the Commission in a dispersed and fragmented way by individual departments and is consequently difficult to consult. It is desirable to integrate this data into a single directory and to thereby make this information tool complete. The new directory will include reference to relevant information on special interest groups held by other institutions, for example the Economic and Social Committee and the European Parliament.

This instrument will be useful both for Commission officials and outside parties. The setting up, production and maintenance of the Directory could best be contracted out to the private sector but entries should be supervised by the Commission.

The Directory could contain the following information:

– name of the organization,

– address/telephone/telefax,

– date of foundation,

– legal status and structure,

– names of senior officials,

– names of member organizations,

– principal objectives of the organization.

Inclusion in the Directory will not confer any form of official recognition by the Commission, nor the granting of any other privileges such as special access to information, buildings, officials, etc. Responsibility for the information provided, as well as for its accuracy, will necessarily remain that of the organization listed.

With regard to profit making lobby organizations, such as consultancies, legal advisors, public relations/public policy and other private firms, it is difficult for the Commission to define exactly those which should or should not be included in a directory. The Commission therefore encourages the lobby sector to draw up its own directory, containing all the relevant information. Above all, the register which the European Parliament intends to create on lobbies will undoubtedly provide the Commission's staff with another useful source of information.

The Commission intends to work closely with the European Parliament on the subject of special interest groups. In this collaboration the Parliament could emerge as the driving force in the establishment and management of the above instruments.

The objective is to construct a common database for both institutions even if this means that the data in question is used for different purposes by each institution.

The Commission's data gathering exercise on non-profit making organizations and the European Parliament's one will therefore be consolidated in a single data-base.

Code of conduct

There should be a broad understanding between the Commission and special interest groups on some basic rules of conduct. Over the course of many years, both have followed principles of conduct which the Commission would like to see the special interest groups (profit and non-profit making) continue to adhere to. The Commission therefore encourages the sectors concerned to draw up their own code of conduct. Many of these organizations already have experience in this field and are consequently best placed to establish and enforce such a code. The minimum requirements for a code should include the principles listed in Annex II. Should individual lobbying organizations wish to operate according to a stricter code of conduct than the one outlined, they are clearly free to do so.

The Commission feels that special interest groups have to be given a chance to organize themselves freely and without interference from the public sector. The Commission reserves the right to review the situation, however, particularly as far as profit making organizations are concerned.

Commission staff's rights and obligations

Title II of the Staff Regulations provides a sufficient and appropriate means of regulating the behaviour of Commission employees in this context. Provisions under this Title of particular importance in relation to lobbyists are: receiving gifts (Article 11); engagement in outside activities (Article 12); employment after leaving the service (Article 16); discretion with regard to information and documents (Article 17) and the declaration of a spouse's employment if a conflict of interest arises (Article 13). In addition to a recently published administrative notice, more specific guidelines have been prepared and these will shortly be circulated for the attention of all Commission staff.

DG IX will clarify Commission contracts with temporary staff in order to make them conform with the provisions under Title II of the Staff Regulations.

In line with the proposals of a working group on Article 16 of the Staff Regulations, a committee will be established, as from 1 January 1993, to prepare the Commission's position on each instance of a possible conflict of interest between a member of staff's employment after leaving the Commission and his or her responsibilities whilst at the Commission. In due course, the committee will evolve its own criteria for assessment as a result of handling successive individual cases. This committee will be composed of the Secretary-General, the Directors-General of DG IX, the Legal Service, and two other Directors-General. The Director-General of the employee's service will also be called upon by the committee on an *ad hoc* basis.

IV. MEASURES

The Commission will continue to promote an open and structured dialogue with special interest groups. It had adopted the following measures as a further step towards this goal:

Special interest groups

The Commission will set up a single directory of non-profit making organizations by drawing together the data that already exists and will thereby make this information tool more complete.

It will encourage the profit making sector to draw up its own directory. In general, the Commission will pursue a close collaboration with the European Parliament. The latter could be the driving force in the establishment and management of a database for special interest groups.

The Commission will encourage special interest groups (both profit and non-profit making) to draw up voluntarily codes of conduct which should include the minimum requirements as listed in Annex II. Contacts will be made with the International Press Association to discuss the issue of journalists who are also working as lobbyists.

The Secretariat-General will ensure appropriate implementation of this.

Commission staff

Staff will be reminded of their obligations and rights under Title II of the Staff Regulations. A notice has been drafted to this effect. DG IX will clarify Commission contracts with temporary staff in order to make them conform to the provisions under Title II of the Staff Regulations.

As from 1 January 1993, a committee composed of the Secretary-General, the Directors-General of DG IX, the Legal Service, two other Directors-General, and the Director-General of the employee's service, will be established to prepare the Commission's position on each instance of a possible conflict of interest between a member of staff's employment after leaving the Commission and his or her responsibilities whilst at the Commission. This procedure will reinforce the implementation of Article 16 of the Staff Regulations.

The Commission will maintain its strict security policy towards lobbyists. The Security Committee will monitor developments closely.

The package of measures outlined above should be seen as a first step towards a better structure for an open dialogue between the Commission and special interest groups. Mid next year, a progress report will be made containing an assessment of the adequacy of the measures put forward in relation to their adoption by the private sector. It will also provide an update on developments in other Community institutions. Any additional measures considered necessary in the light of this assessment will subsequently be taken.

ANNEX I

GENERAL OVERVIEW

A fact-finding exercise has been carried out on special interest groups. Its results are summarized below.

A. MEMBER STATES

Federal Republic of Germany

At federal level, a registration procedure exists which is open to associations with federal representation. Those wishing to lobby at either the Bundestag or the Federal

Government (or both) may register. The procedure is overseen by the President of the Bundestag. The register is published annually and a registered association has access to buildings and may participate in the preparation of federal legislation. In addition, various types of less formal procedure exist to involve interest groups in the preparation of federal or regional legislation.

United Kingdom

An informal proposal has been circulated within both Houses of Parliament on the establishment of a register and code of conduct, mainly aimed at professional lobbyists engaged in the lobbying of Members of Parliament. This suggests that each firm specializing in lobbying should be registered. The question of whether the registration procedure should also be extended to associations (i.e. trade unions), private companies, etc., is still under discussion. It is intended that the register will be made public and managed by the Parliament.

B. OTHER COMMUNITY INSTITUTIONS

Contacts were established with other Community institutions with regard to the question of relations with interest groups. Letters on the subject have been sent by the Secretary-General to his counterparts in the other European institutions.

European Parliament

As the Community's directly elected institution, the European Parliament is anxious to maintain its open relationship with the general public, and with lobbies in particular. The European Parliament has in the past issued passes to lobbyists allowing them to enter the premises. However, the increase in the number of lobbyists and the abuse of this privilege have led the European Parliament to reconsider its policy towards lobbyists.

The European Parliament Committee on the rules of procedure adopted on 3 October a recommendation of the Bureau on rules governing the representation of special interest groups at the European Parliament.

The recommendation is therefore at present under discussion in the Bureau. It will be for the Bureau to lay down the extent of rulemaking by adopting all or some of the Committee's proposals.

Content of the recommendation of the European Parliament's committee on the rules of procedure

The main contents of the recommendation are:

- the creation of a public register of lobbyists to be managed by the Bureau of the European Parliament. Admission criteria are to be drawn up by the Bureau,

- the establishment of a code of conduct to be approved by the European Parliament, on a proposal from its Bureau and after consulting its committees. The European Parliament may ask lobbyists to set up one or more professional organizations. Its representatives may serve as interlocutors with the European Parliament,

- the attribution of the following privileges to a registered lobbyist:

  - a pass granting access to public areas of the buildings, valid for one year, renewable on submission of an annual report,

  - access to public meeting of committees,

  - access to the library, subject to prior authorization,

  - documents published by the European Parliament should be issued at cost price. The Bureau may decide to provide other facilities at cost price,

- Parliamentary documents should be available to lobbyists at a price to be determined,
- the establishment of sanctions by the European Parliament, on a proposal from its Bureau after consulting Parliament's committees.

Moreover, Members of Parliament will be obliged to update the declaration of their financial interests (at least annually) ('volet interne').

C. THIRD COUNTRIES

United States

All lobbyists (individuals, associations and private companies) are subject to compulsory registration and must adhere to a code of conduct in order to lobby at Congress. A registered lobbyist is required to submit detailed quarterly reports on his activities to Congress. The registry office manages the procedure and all information concerned is published and publicly available.

Legal provisions and rules on procedure for lobbyists dealing with federal government agencies also exist. A code of conduct is applied.

Canada

Canada's policy is similar to that of the United States. Registration is necessary in order to lobby at the federal government and a proposal to register lobbyists at the Parliament is under consideration.

D. OTHER INTERNATIONAL INSTITUTIONS

United Nations

The United Nations has established two main sets of procedures to deal with the relationship between non-governmental organizations (NGO) and the Economic and Social Council (Ecosoc) and its subsidiary organs.

The first procedure comprises accreditation in order to obtain a consultative status within the Ecosoc system. This procedure is managed by the Council's committee on NGOs. Consultative status grants NGOs a number of privileges such as a greater opportunity to participate at hearings. It also allows the organization to propose items for discussion at Ecosoc as well as to submit written statements. NGOs with consultative status deliver a report on their activities every four years.

The second procedure contains the registration of NGOs. This register (or roster, as it is known) is a public document. The NGO committee mentioned above manages the register. The advantages of being included on the register are similar to those outlined above but are more limited in scope; in particular, the opportunity to submit written statements is more restricted. The adherence to a code of conduct for NGOs is a part of both procedures.

ANNEX II

MINIMUM REQUIREMENTS FOR A CODE OF CONDUCT BETWEEN THE COMMISSION AND SPECIAL INTEREST GROUPS

The Commission has always been an institution open to input from special interest groups. The Commission believes this process to be fundamental to the development of sound and workable policies. This dialogue has proved valuable to both the Commission and to interested outside parties. The Commission acknowledges the need for such outside input, welcomes it and intends to build further on this practice in future. To this end the Commission is taking a series of measures intended to broaden participation in the preparation of its decisions.

In the context of this wider dialogue, the Commission believes that there should be a broad understanding with special interest groups on some basic rules of conduct. Over the course of many years, both have followed principles of conduct which the Commission would like to see the special interest groups continue to adhere to. The Commission feels that special interest groups are best placed to establish and enforce codes of conduct. The Commission therefore invites the sectors concerned to draw up such codes, which should include the following minimum requirements.

1. **Public presentation**

    Special interest groups should not misrepresent themselves to the public by the use of any title, logo, symbol or form of words (particularly those employed by the Commission) designed either to lend false authority to the representative or to mislead clients and/or officials as to his or her status.

2. **Behaviour**

    Special interest groups should behave at all times in accordance with the highest possible professional standards. Honesty and competence in all dealings with the Commission are specifically viewed as being of the greatest importance.

    Special interest groups should avoid working in situations where a conflict of interests is either inevitable or likely to arise.

    The representative should declare the name of the client for whom he or she is working each time he or she consults the Commission.

    In any communication with the Commission (either written and/or oral), the representative should declare all previous contact he or she has had with other representatives of the Commission regarding the same or a related subject.

    Special interest groups should neither employ, nor seek to employ, officials who are working for the Commission. Nor should they offer any form of inducement to Commission officials in order to obtain information or to receive privileged treatment.

3. **Dissemination of Commission information**

    Special interest groups should not disseminate misleading information.

    Special interest groups should not obtain information by dishonest means.

    Special interest groups should not seek to trade copies of Commission documents for profit.

4. **Organizations**

    The establishment of one or more organizations, through which special interest groups would communicate with the Commission, would be welcomed. Such an organization should be open to all representatives of special interest groups and it is therefore hoped that an individual firm's subscription can be in proportion to its relative size.

ANNEX B

Increased transparency in the work of the Commission
(93/C 63/03)

1. INTRODUCTION

The declaration on the right of access to information annexed to the Treaty on European Union states that 'transparency of the decision making process strengthens the democratic nature of the institutions and the public's confidence in the administration'. The conference accordingly recommended that the Commission submit to the Council no later than 1993 'a report on measures designed to improve public access to the information available to the institutions'.

Moreover, the declaration issued by the European Council held in Birmingham on 16 October 1992 called for 'a more open Community, to ensure a better informed public debate on its activities'.

The objective of this communication is to allow an initial discussion of the Commission's contribution to greater openness. It is specifically addressed to those members of the public who, because of their professional of academic activities, follow Community affairs more closely. It is important to underline that it does not concern itself with the wider question of how to communicate with the public at large nor does it attempt to address the issue of improved public access to information available to the Commission. The importance of these issues necessitates a detailed and thorough examination, which the Commission intends to undertake in the very near future.

The present communication should be seen as a parallel document to the communication on 'An Open and Structured Dialogue between the Commission and Special Interest Groups'. These groups would benefit greatly from an intensified Commission policy on transparency.

2. TRANSPARENCY

General awareness of Commission policies will increase if advanced information about initiatives and a broader opportunity to participate in their preparation are given. A number of existing practices could be improved to achieve these aims:

(a) *Annual work and legislative programmes*

The Commission's annual work programme was developed as a direct response to the need for a listing of priorities. The programme defines priority areas and sets out the major measures which the Commission intends to propose or wishes to see carried out by other institutions. Under the present system, the programme is adopted by the Commission at the beginning of the year before being debated and subsequently voted on by the European Parliament.

For the purposes of increased transparency, the Commission has proposed that the work programme should be ready by October.

In addition to the Commission's work programme an inter-institutional legislative programme exists. A greater involvement of the Council of

Ministers in the implementation of the legislative programme could be envisaged. An effort should be made to draft the programme in a clearer and more accessible style. The objectives of each legislative proposal will be explained in simple language.

Both the Commission work programme and the inter-institutional legislative programme should receive more general publicity. It is proposed that, henceforth, both programmes should be published in the *Official Journal of the European Communities*. Updated versions of the legislative programme should also be published at regular intervals;

(b) *Participation in the preparation of Commission decisions and proposals*

Specific attention must be paid to the preparation of Commission decisions and proposals. More public participation in the work of the Commission enhances more open government and can increase public confidence.

Whilst the Commission already has a reputation for openness, based on such existing mechanisms as the submission of draft proposals on key policy issues to the advisory committees, it is believed that widening the fact finding exercise (especially for initiatives with wide ranging implications) may be appropriate in some cases. This would provide opportunities for a broader range of interested persons to express their views. It is for the competent service to decide the appropriate moment when and from whom it should seek advice. Measures should be taken to ensure that all groups with an interest in a given subject should have the opportunity to express their views. This will enable the Commission to draw up balanced proposals.

For initiatives with broad implications, it is recommended that a more extensive and transparent preparation should take place. These initiatives should be carefully selected to avoid overburdening the Commission's work load by including matters which do not need such extensive treatment, i.e. activities which relate to the day to day management of existing Community policies. Such a selection will be made on a provisional basis in the framework of the Commission's annual work and legislative programme. Those initiatives on which the Commission seeks more wide-ranging advice will be earmarked in this document. The work programme will thus provide a first opportunity for interested parties to structure their activities.

The Commission has to date used the publication of Green and White Papers, hearings and the organization of information seminars to stimulate a more general debate on its draft proposals. It could be worthwhile in some cases to introduce a notification procedure. The Commission would publish a brief summary of the proposed policy initiative in the C series of the *Official Journal of the European Communities*, information on how to obtain copies of the document, a deadline for interested parties to respond, and the name and address of the person to whom any such response should be sent. If considered appropriate, commencement of the notification procedure should be simultaneous with the submission of a draft proposal to an Advisory Committee.

The competent Director-General, under the authority of the Commissioners concerned, would decide the way in which more wide-ranging advice should be sought. The use of Green Papers in particular should be encouraged. Hearings and information seminars could also be organized. In other cases the use of the proposed notification procedure would be the best way of increasing participation. The appropriate form of extensive advice would take place after interservice consultation on the proposal.

In the process of exercising the powers conferred upon it by the Council, the Commission is assisted in its work by a great number of committees composed of representatives of the Member States (Comitology). It is proposed that the rules governing access to information for this type of committee should remain unchanged, i.e. the minutes of the meetings and the individual points of view expressed by the Commission and by representatives of the Member States remain confidential. The present practice whereby the opinion of the committee concerned is mentioned in a recital of Commission legislation remains unchanged.

However, with regard to other committees of an advisory nature and expert groups, the Commission should give careful consideration to the question of how the granting of access upon request to these bodies' activities and the increase in transparency this represents, balanced against the additional claims on human and financial resources which will result from such a policy. In examining this it should give full weight to:

- the importance of not undermining the effectiveness of the committees or expert groups and their usefulness to the Commission,
- preserving the confidentiality of the workings of these bodies, where necessary, for instance to protect certain public and private interests;

(c) *Dissemination of existing information*

There is considerable interest amongst the citizens of the Community in obtaining documents, in the nine official languages of the Community, shortly after they have been adopted by the Commission. In this context it should be recalled that, in accordance with the rules determining the languages to be used as well as their implementation, documents which a Member State or a person subject to the jurisdiction of a Member State sends to institutions of the Community may be drafted in any one of the official languages selected by the sender. The reply shall be drafted in the same language. Documents which an institution of the Community sends to a Member State or to a person subject to the jurisdiction of a Member State shall be drafted in the language of such State. Regulations and other documents of general application shall be drafted in the nine official languages. Staff should be reminded of the internal guidelines on the submission of documents in the several Community languages before they can be approved by the Commission; This notice will also remind staff of existing procedures concerning correspondence.

Moreover, more publicity should be given to those existing possibilities to obtain information which is already present in the form of databases (Celex, Rapid, INFO 92). For some of these bases user guides are under preparation designed to simplify access to them. Secondly, it is proposed that documents should be made more immediately accessible to the public once existing procedures have been completed, such as formal submission to the other

Community institutions and/or the formal notification of the Member States. The various possibilities for improving the present situation should be examined by the Secretariat-General, the Translation Service, DGs IX, X, XIII and the Office for Official Publications. In particular, they should look into the possibility of extending a relay information approach, the daily transmission of information (through the use of such automated modern technologies as electronic mail, etc.) to the Commission's offices and some external delegations, and the implementation of a publications and documentation pricing policy.

Under the present system of classification, all documents covering broad subjects are classified as COM documents. These documents are made widely available and are published in the C series of the *Official Journal of the European Communities*. Documents which have a more sectoral focus are classified as SEC documents. The designation of COM and SEC documents is decided on a case by case basis by the Secretariat-General, following consultation with the services. To provide greater access to information held by the Commission, it is proposed that, in future, more documents will be classified under the COM heading: even if they deal with apparently specialized topics. This would result in a wider distribution for documents which, at first sight, appear to have a more sectoral focus. Furthermore, in order to enhance public access and transparency, initiatives have been taken to publish, at regular intervals, a list of COM documents in the C series of the *Official Journal of the European Communities*. The entries include the catalogue number of the Community office of publications and the address of the offices where such documents are available.

3. LEGISLATIVE POLICY

The Commission views consolidation and constitutive codification of existing and new Community legislation as important tools with which to make legislation more accessible to the public.

Consolidation consists of regrouping various Community measures in one text to improve accessibility, clarity and transparency of Community law. The text as such is not legally binding and is published in the C series of the *Official Journal of the European Communities*. Progress has been made in the area of consolidation by the information system managed by the Office of Official Publications which will become operational from the beginning of next year. Additional access to legislation could be provided through updates and a better use of Communitatis Europeae Lex (Celex).

Constitutive codification consists of regrouping existing Community legislation in a new text which is published in the L series of the *Official Journal of the European Communities*. Consequently, the existing legislation which forms part of codification will be repealed when the codified legislation enters into force. The Commission will include proposals on this codification in its annual legislative programmes.

4. PROPOSALS

The following proposals should be seen as a step to increase transparency. They are particularly aimed at those members of the public who, because of their professional or academic activities, follow Community affairs more closely.

It is therefore proposed that the Commission takes the following decisions:

- to prepare the Commission's work programme by October each year; to seek greater involvement of the Council of Ministers in the implementation of the legislative programme; to draft both programmes in a clearer and more accessible style and to publish them in the *Official Journal of the European Communities;*

- to seek wider ranging advice on certain key proposals at an early stage; to this end the Commission will:

  - earmark such proposals in the annual work and legislative programmes;

  - encourage the use of Green Papers and in certain cases have recourse to a notification procedure;

  - consider where and when more access should be given to information on work carried out by advisory committees;

- to ensure that Commission documents are made directly available to the public, in the nine official languages of the Community, once they have been adopted by the Commission and circulated to the other EC institutions; to this end the Commission will:

  - give more publicity to the databases which already exist;

  - ensure that all documents of public interest are classified under the COM heading rather than the SEC;

  - give a mandate to the Secretariat-General, the Translation service, DGs IX, X, XIII and the Office for Official Publications to propose other specific improvements for the dissemination of information;

- the Commission will pursue its work in the area of consolidation and constitutive codification of legislation; to this end it will include proposals in its annual legislative programme.

It is proposed to implement these steps towards increased transparency by 1 January 1993.

In the meantime work will have to continue on a number of other issues. These will include how to improve access to information held by the Commission, and on its communication and information policy. It is requested that the competent services carry out a detailed study and come up with concrete proposals, including the consequences with regard to resources, by 31 March 1993.

It is proposed that the Commission transmits this communication to the Council of Ministers, European Parliament and the Economic and Social Committee. This should be done simultaneously with the communication on 'An Open and Structured Dialogue Between the Commission and Special Interest Groups'.

8. The Commission and the Council of Ministers

Dietrich Rometsch and Wolfgang Wessels

Introduction

The relationship between the Commission and the Council is of crucial importance in understanding the polity and the politics of the European Community (EC). In particular, all legislative and budgetary acts require concerted action between the two bodies. The interactions between Commission and Council are a constituent element of decision-making and implementation within the EC. Commission and Council depend on each other and neither institution can act without the support of the other. This mutual dependence can lead to tension since each institution in a sense seeks to dominate the other: it is in the interest of the Commission to push through its proposals and it is in the interest of the Council to have proposals from the Commission which accord with its own views. It is a relationship of give and take in which power plays a central role.

When discussing the role of the Commission in its relationship with the Council, there is always a danger of drawing naïve analogies to existing institutions whether in traditional nation-states or in classic international organisations. But the Commission's role and behaviour cannot easily be compared to either a national government or an international secretariat. The EC system is a unique political system which does not follow any existing constitutional models. It is a system that produces binding legislative acts by a process in which each institution has specific and unique features.

The Commission has often been seen as the most original part of this system (Hallstein 1979, p. 82). It has, for example, been described as the "heart of the Community system"(Louis and Waelbroek 1989). At the same time, the Council of Ministers is the "Community's decision-making centre" (Wessels 1991). It is clear, in other words, that a major part of the Commission's peculiar role is its multi-faceted and complex relationship with the Council and its administrative substructure. Even if that role has changed over the years due to Treaty or constitutional amendments or reforms, this bilateral relationship has remained at the core of the EC system. It largely determines the overall role, influence and power of the Commission.

The Commission's role

If the Commission's position in the political system of the Community has been and remains crucial, it may well be even more critical in the future European Union. The Commission's role — especially in relation to that of the Council and the European Council — has been a major topic of political and academic controversy. Two opposing views have often been presented. In one, the Commission is seen as the dynamic engine of the Community's legislation and action, the real symbol of a supranational or even federal Community, representing the common interest of the European people. According to this view, the Council is the blocking institution, representing parochial national interests and preventing the Commission from becoming an effective government of the Community.

The opposite view posits the Commission as the "aéropage technocratique apatride et irrésponsable", as General de Gaulle put it at a press conference in September 1965 (de Gaulle 1970, p. 379). Here, the Commission is constantly trying to centralise all political power in a European bureaucracy away from the direct immediate interests of the citizens of Europe. According to this view, echoed more than 20 years later by Margaret Thatcher (Thatcher 1988), the Council, and especially the European Council, represents the common will of the European peoples since their political position is made legitimate through national elections.

Given the similar rhetoric of de Gaulle and Thatcher, the debate might appear somewhat repetitive, yet the relationship between Commission and Council has certainly evolved during the history of the Community. From the early days of the High Authority through the Rome Treaties, the Single European Act and up to the Maastricht Treaty, the procedural and implicit political powers of the Commission in its relationship with the Council have changed. Additional actors have also entered the game, including the European Council as well as the European Parliament and, in a way that was not clearly foreseen, the European Court of Justice. At the administrative level, the increase of the powers of COREPER and the Council Secretariat have also affected the Commission's position (Ludlow 1991, p. 115).

The continued existence of the two opposing views suggested above, redolent though they are of past battles, clearly oversimplifies the present position. A number of different concepts and images of the Commission's role in the Council are discernible (Wessels 1985), each representing different assumptions and national practices (Aberbach et al. 1981, Stillman 1988, Timsit 1985), pre-existing mental "maps" (Wallace 1990) or intellectual "baggage" (Mayntz 1985, Ott 1989). Among the different roles or models that have been suggested, four are of particular significance: the Commission as a dynamic and enlightened technocracy, with the Council as a body of ratification; the Commission as a federal government, the Council becoming a second chamber; the Commission as an expert and administrative secretariat to the Council; and finally, the Commission as the 'promotional broker' within the Council.

The Commission as a dynamic and enlightened technocracy

One of the earliest conceptualisations of the Commission was that expressed by Jean Monnet of the "Haute Autorité (High Authority) dont les décisions lieront . . . les pays qui y adhéront" (Monnet 1976, pp. 351–3). The basic assumption underlying this image was that the Commission possesses superior insights into the common European interest and, through it, transposes the "volonté générale" into action. In this way, its all-embracing knowledge of facts and procedures provides a basic legitimation, which is placed at the service of an integrating Europe — a process considered both positive and necessary.

With this expertise and basic legitimation, the Commission would come to dominate the decision-making of the Council which would remain a kind of 'sounding board' or ratification body without any major role of its own. The Council would not itself seek compromise among different national positions, but would support a common European view which had essentially been worked out by the Commission (*ibid.* p. 446). Figure 1 illustrates this pattern of relationships. The European Council of heads of government would become symbolic in character while the European Parliament would serve as a forum for discussion. Both would be clearly dominated by and dependent on the 'enlightened expertise' of the Commission.

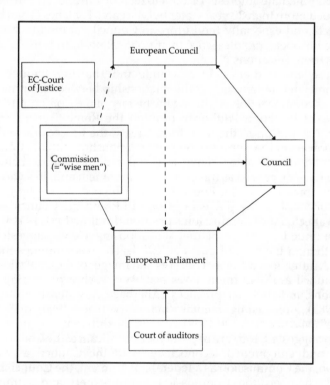

Figure 1: *The Technocracy Model*

This image of the Commission reflects the convergence of several sources to provide a common approach (Berlin 1987): a French political and administrative culture, characterised by the strong position of the bureaucratic élite, symbolised by Jean Monnet, himself, who had been Secretary General of the Commissariat au Plan (which had played a leading role in the French economy and in the politics of the post-war period). To this French tradition came a strong legalistic German bureaucratic tradition of which the German law professor, Walter Hallstein, was a leading representative. A further element in the make-up of the image was the Hallstein concept of a 'Sachlogik' (Hallstein 1979, pp. 22–27), a kind of automatic endogenous dynamic, similar to the neo-functionalist concept of 'spill-over' (Haas 1964 and 1968, Lindberg and Scheingold 1970). By stressing an in-built logic leading to further integration in Europe, the Commission was given the historic task of pushing for and executing an inevitable 'law' of European evolution.

One of the prerequisites for such a process is a high degree of homogeneity among the Commission's civil servants in the sense that they have a common interest in working for a common European goal (Monnet *op. cit.*). Another is the need to have at the head of the Commission a person able — by his or her intellectual capacity and personality — to exert a leadership that energises the Commission internally as well as externally. In a general sense, the Commission, according to this image at least, is less a 'political' institution with direct legitimation by the people than a body that, like Plato's 'wise men', governs by its superior understanding of the subject and all the procedures of decision-making.

Although elements of the model are to be found in the Treaty of Paris establishing the European Coal and Steel Community, the Treaty of Rome pursued a somewhat divergent path in giving more power to the Council of Ministers. The Maastricht Treaty, as far as Economic and Monetary Union is concerned and — even more — as far as the Commission's role is defined in the second and third 'pillars' of the Union relating to a Common Foreign and Security Policy and to justice and internal affairs, has continued the EEC trend of underlining the role of the Council. It was certainly little inspired by this first image of the Commission.

With the establishment of the European Council, the Commission was confronted by a body representing the highest national political authorities. In COREPER, the Commission found bureaucratic 'rivals' in the sense that the Ambassadors and their Deputies not only knew Community procedures but were also a powerful body of experts. With the working groups of the Council, as well as the various types of committee established to control the implementation of EC legislation, the Commission and its civil servants were confronted with national colleagues expert in their various fields. Nor has the growing importance of the Community in a widening range of policy areas increased the dominance of the Commission and its services. On the contrary, new institutions and administrative bodies have been created which are competent both in terms of procedures and political substance. The competition or rivalry between these administrations is as a result part of the institutional system in which the Commission operates.

The Commission as a federal government

From the very beginning of the process of European integration, the technocracy model was rivalled by the federal model, of a United States of Europe built on the institutional structures of classical federations (see Figure 2). According to this, the Commission was to develop into the 'government', the head of which would be elected by, and would be responsible to, the European Parliament. The Council would have only a limited or possibly no say in the election. The head of government would then appoint his or her own ministers. In terms of the relative weight of legislative bodies, the European Parliament would become the 'first' chamber, directly representing the people of the Community, while the Council — as the representation of the Member States — would only be the 'second' chamber. The Council might have equal status in certain areas of competence, such as foreign policy, but those areas would be limited. However, in contrast to the technocracy model, the Commission as government would be controlled politically by the European Parliament and legally by the Court of Justice. Within the triangle of Commission as government, the European Parliament as first chamber and the Council as second chamber, the Council would be the weakest institution. The European Council would play only a symbolic role within this model, restricted to matters of protocol.

In this model, the basic source of legitimation is the election of the European Parliament directly by the European people, from which the Commission as a government would draw its democratic mandate. The Commission as government would not only be responsible for initiating legislation, but also for establishing an efficient and effective policy network in order to push its policies through both chambers.

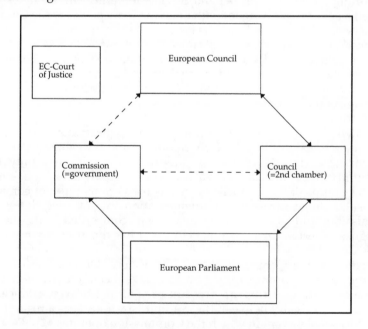

Figure 2: *The Federal Model of a United States of Europe*

Though the concept was launched by federalists such as Altiero Spinelli (Spinelli 1958; Lipgens 1985) during World War II and the period immediately following it, it never really got off the ground. Few constitutional elements of the present treaties can be linked to the model, although there have been concrete proposals leaning in its direction, such as the Draft Treaty on the European Union voted by the European Parliament in 1984 or the Herman Report of the European Parliament of January 1994. So far, the procedural control and, even more importantly, the political prestige and legitimacy of the Commission have rarely begun to approach those of a government in the traditional sense of the word. The increased role of the European Parliament in the (s)election of the Commission (under Article 158.2 of the EC Treaty as amended by Maastricht) could be interpreted as a first step in such a direction, but the overall trend in the EC's institutional balance over the last decade or so has certainly not been wholly in the same direction. And yet the image of the Commission as government is part of the debate about integration, serving as a yardstick as well as a possible potential model. It cannot therefore be excluded from further debate and consideration.

The Commission as an expert and administrative secretariat to the Council

Another alternative to the technocracy model is that of the Commission as an expert and administrative secretariat within an intergovernmental model of a confederal Europe (see Figure 3). Confederal Europe is based on the pooling of national sovereignties leaving the ultimate responsibility with the Member States as the 'masters of the game'. The only legitimacy involved in policy-making is that of national governments obtained through national elections.

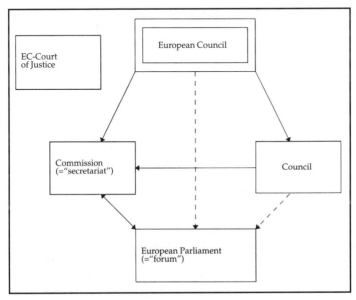

Figure 3: *Intergovernmental Model of a Confederal Europe*

In terms of any institutional evolution, this emphasis on national authorities finds its ultimate representation in the European Council. Accordingly, the European Council becomes the *de facto* or even the *de jure* centre of decision-making, able to take decisions only on the basis of unanimity. Similarly, the Council together with its Secretariat and COREPER and its working groups would be of primary importance. The Commission would be given only modest functions comparable to those exerted by the secretariats of more traditional international organisations. It would become akin to an expert secretariat providing the necessary 'neutral' information on which the European Council or the Council could take their decisions. It would also be involved — on the model of a classical bureaucracy — in the implementation of those decisions which have been taken by the Council or the European Council. The Commission would not play an independent role in either providing information and analysis or in implementing decisions, but would be strictly controlled by national politicians and administrations. Some of the committees in the Community's 'comitology', in which the Member States tightly control the Commission's executive actions, are a good example in this respect. The limitations on its authority are derived from national power and strictly limited to those functions which the Council delegates to it. The Commission would have no procedural rights of its own, but it would be used to contribute to specific questions, especially when invited by the Presidency of the European Council or the Council. The Council Presidency would play a major role in deciding whether or not to use the knowledge and expertise of the Commission.

This kind of role has also been attributed to the Commission in the framework of European Political Cooperation (da Costa Pereira 1988; Nuttall 1992), where the Commission was for a long time invited only as an 'expert guest', its role to a considerable degree dependent on the goodwill of the Presidency. Increasingly, however, the Commission gained a legal position of its own even in this framework (see Chapter 11). With the Single European Act and even more with the Common Foreign and Security Policy Chapter in the Maastricht Treaty, the Commission has obtained the procedural right to submit initiatives of its own. Thus, even in those areas of intergovernmental procedure, the Commission's role is — at least on paper — different from that presented by the image of an expert and administrative secretariat.

The Commission as the 'promotional broker' within the Council

A fourth image of the Commission tries to take into account the development and evolution of the Commission over the last few decades. It attempts to identify certain specific functions in the multi-level game that exists within the European Union. This image is part of what might be called a 'cooperative model' of a new Europe. It is one based on the concept of dual legitimacy, i.e. the legitimacy of both the Member States and the Community. Institutions on both levels participate in preparing, making, implementing and controlling binding decisions for the combined use of public policy instruments (see Figure 4).

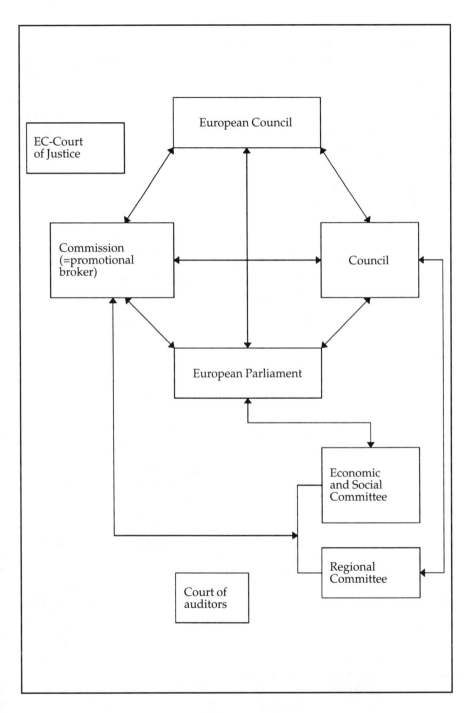

Figure 4: *Cooperative Federal Model of a Merged Europe*

Accordingly, the Commission becomes a co-player with specific attributes. It would employ certain procedural rights, such as the right of initiative and the right to call for a vote within the Council. It would possess expertise both in terms of policy substance and decision-making procedures. Its specific power would be based on its ability to use these rights in the complex bargaining central to a multi-level system.

The Commission would be more than just a 'neutral broker' in relation to the roles attributed to the Presidency of the Council and to the Council Secretariat (Wallace 1985; de Bassompierre 1988). Its position would not be based on the need to reach a consensus in the Council, whatever the substance of the issue. Rather, it would be one geared to promoting common European interests — as well as to promoting its own position. It would be oriented towards 'promotional brokerage', trying to push the member countries represented in the European Council and in the Council to accept policies that go beyond a purely intergovernmental consensus based on the lowest common denominator. The Commission's strategy would therefore be quite clearly different from that of a neutral broker.

Given the concept of dual legitimacy, the Commission can play an independent role of its own, acquiring influence partly from its knowledge and expertise, and partly from the support of other institutions, especially from the European Parliament, and relevant interest groups. The Commission would make extensive use of the institutional structure of the Community, seeking allies such as ECOSOC and the new Regional Committee in order to promote its position against the Council and the Member States. It would have a 'forward strategy' characterised by the building of alliances and strong negotiating positions.

During the evolution of the Community, this image has materialised increasingly as a result of major constitutional and political developments. With its specific competences and rights, the Commission has been accepted in the European Council and in areas of intergovernmental cooperation such as the CFSP and justice and internal affairs. This development also involves the Commission in specific roles in external relations, including participation in Western summits of the G-7 (Krenzler 1992) and in several forms of external dialogue, such as summit meetings with the President of the United States and with representatives from the countries of the Visegrad Group, where the Community has been represented by the President of the Commission as well as the President of the Council.

At the same time, the Commission's role has been reinforced by the development of the Community's institutional triangle (Dewost 1980). With the increased role of the European Parliament in budgetary policy, followed by its growing participation in the legislative process as well as in external relations, the Commission will more than ever before have to be an interlocutor for both the Council and the Parliament in order to facilitate compromises between the two institutions (a role presaged by the Vedel Report of 1972, Vedel 1972, p. 72). It will be able to play this role only by maintaining a certain independence of its own.

The behaviour of the Commission — empirical data and their interpretation

The Commission and the legislative output of the Council

A complementary and useful way of looking at these different images of the Commission is to describe basic behavioural trends in its relations with the Council. Empirical data should help to identify which images correspond best to 'reality'.

One indicator is the evolution of the legislative output of the Council, since this documents the intensity of its work and the extent of cooperation between the two bodies. Figure 5 shows a legislative output which has grown quantitatively throughout the history of the EC and also in comparison to the work of the Parliament of one of the Member States, the Federal Republic of Germany. The figures indicate that the concerted actions of both bodies are fairly productive.

Linked to this increase in the output of the Council is the Commission's role as initiator, a role which has generally become more important over the decades (see also Chapter 1). Although the numbers of occasions on which majority voting takes place in the Council is not known to the outside world, it is clear that with the possibility of majority voting, the first draft of the text, i.e., the Commission's, is of crucial importance for the final outcome. National governments and administrations have to adapt their strategies to the Commission's proposals early and flexibly. They therefore often feel pressed by the dynamics of the bargaining process, in which, of course, the Commission plays an important role.

Concern that the Commission plays too great a role in the policy process through its monopoly of the formal initiative was made clear at the Birmingham summit of 1992. Heads of State and of Government welcomed the suggestion that the Commission should undertake more extensive consultation with Member States before a draft proposal is presented (Annex 1 of the European Council Declaration, October 16, 1992). This concern harks back to the 1965 'empty chair' crisis. The resulting 'Luxembourg Compromise' blocked off the trend towards a technocracy or government image supposedly being pursued by the then President of the Commission, Walter Hallstein and his colleagues (von der Groeben 1982). In the negotiation of the 'Luxembourg Compromise' the French government stressed the point that the Commission should contact the appropriate level of government in the Member States before making any proposal. Indeed, it held that it should only publish a draft proposal after the Council had officially been apprised of the matter. As a result, ideas and ambitions for a strong Commission were blocked and the Commission was forced to review the basic assumptions of its strategy. The effect was to compel consideration of a new definition of the Commission's role.

The Commission and the Council: patterns of participation

In addition to the legislative output, we can look, too, at other patterns of participation as indicative of the Commission's role. The Commission and its services and the Council and its administrative bodies are in various, fairly

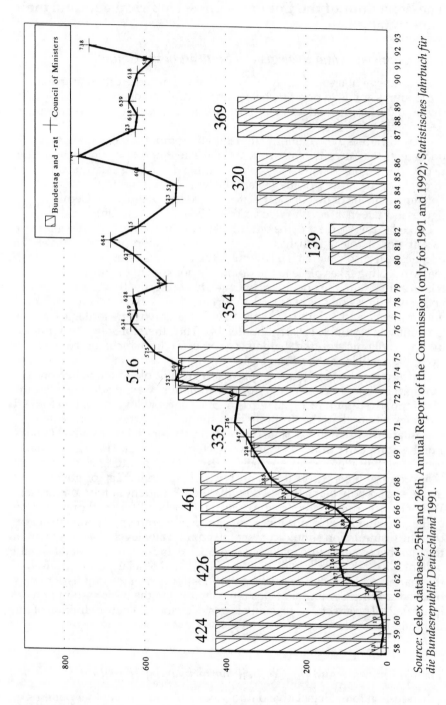

Figure 5: *Comparison of the legislative output of the Council of Ministers (per year) and the German* Bundestag *and* Bundesrat *(per legislative period)*

permanent relationships with each other. There are several different forms of policy cycles in the Community as well as additional patterns which concern intergovernmental procedures and other bodies.

(a) Expert groups established by the Commission

The first step in an ordinary policy cycle in the EC consists of deliberations within the Commission. In this phase, national civil servants and other experts participate *'à titre personnel'* in the expert groups of the Commission which have grown over the years and numbered more than 500 in 1992 (the authors' own calculations based on the Internal Communication of the Secretariat General of the Commission of March 27, 1992 — E/311/92). The Commission controls the game in this phase, but its basic strategy is one of *'engrenage'*, i.e. to include relevant national civil servants early enough in its work to get additional information and insights, and also to establish a solid network of influence (Poullet and Deprez 1977). From the point of view of national civil servants, there is an expectation that their input will be taken seriously by the Commission and that its later proposals will not include unpleasant surprises for them. Thus *'engrenage'* is a two-way process for establishing a set of mutually rewarding interactions.

(b) Working groups of the Council

A proposal launched by the Commission will inevitably go via the Council and COREPER to one of the Council's working groups. Their number varies according to the priorities and possibilities set by the Presidencies of the Council; an average number ranging between 180 and 200 per Presidency. At that level, the Commission's proposal is debated and negotiated in detail from the point of view of the Member States. In addition to the Commission's civil servants, officials from the Presidency, who chair the respective working groups, play a major role. As a general rule, around 90 per cent of the final texts of legislation or action are decided at that level. Although controversial issues are shifted upwards, to COREPER and the Council itself, we should nevertheless bear in mind that this secondary level of decision-making is of crucial importance for the output of the Community's work. In many cases, the products of this bargaining process in the working groups are passed by the Council without further deliberation, the so-called 'A' points on the Council agenda. At the working-group level, technical knowledge is at a premium, and it is there, especially, that the Commission's officials have often had the advantage of having a better overview of the positions of all the Member States than officials from any one of them. However, although most of the national civil servants may be participating in the deliberations only as a part of their normal workload, they nonetheless possess fundamental knowledge of the subject area. Moreover, they increasingly take into account the positions of other member countries and are aware of the procedures applied. They are therefore no 'walk-over' for the Commission civil servants, as might have been expected from the technocracy model. Cleavages within the working groups are not necessarily officials from the Member States pitted against the Commission. The constellation of interests is normally more complex, and various coalitions and counter-coalitions are possible in which the Commission is but one actor.

(c) Committee of Permanent Representatives (COREPER)

There are usually two separate COREPER meetings each week (in addition to the meeting of a parallel body, the Special Committee for Agriculture, the SCA). Ambassadors meet in COREPER II on Thursdays, with Deputies meeting in COREPER I the day before. In principle, COREPER I deals with matters traditionally defined as domestic, i.e. the internal market, environment, transport etc., while COREPER II deals with external relations. COREPER meetings normally last only one or two days each. The Antici Group, which is linked to COREPER II, prepares the timetable and agenda for meetings of COREPER, the Council of Ministers and the European Council. Apart from the Permanent Representatives, members of the Antici Group are normally the only national civil servants allowed into the conference rooms of the European Council to give information to, or receive instructions from their respective heads of government. The Commission's representative in the Antici Group is the head of unit dealing with the Council in the Secretariat General. The Group meets on a Tuesday in order to allow the Commission and the Member States to coordinate and finalise negotiating positions before the formal COREPER meeting, thus avoiding at least some potential blockages. The efficient functioning of the Antici Group is a key element in the efficient organisation of each Presidency.

The responsible Director General of the Commission generally participates in COREPER meetings along with the Deputy Secretary General. The diplomats and senior civil servants representing their governments in COREPER are nearly always highly experienced Community insiders who, in terms of both procedure and substance, are well-equipped to face the Commission — or at least they become so after a short period of acclimatisation. At the same time, they play a crucial role in the relationship between national administrations and their ministers taking decisions in the Council. Their sense of the political balance is thus well-developed, which as a result tends to reduce the freedom of manoeuvre on the part of the Commission representatives.

(d) Council sessions

At Council sessions, the Commission is normally represented by the Commissioner in charge of the particular policy under discussion. The Commissioner rarely has any great freedom of manoeuvre as he or she is bound by the Commission's mandate; individual ministers will vary in the degree to which they have leeway to negotiate on the basis of positions agreed in their national capitals.

The number of Council sessions and the range of sectors they cover have been considerably extended over the 30 years of the EC (see Figure 6 and Table 1). At the same time, the number of participants who are involved in the decision-making process has increased. With delegations from 12 member countries, each of which can include up to six members and sometimes even more (it has not been unknown for the German delegation to take up some of the seats reserved for the neighbouring Greek delegation) and with the representatives of the Commission and the Council Secretariat, the number of participants in the room can number more than 100. The 'tour de table' of all delegations can therefore sometimes be quite long and time-consuming.

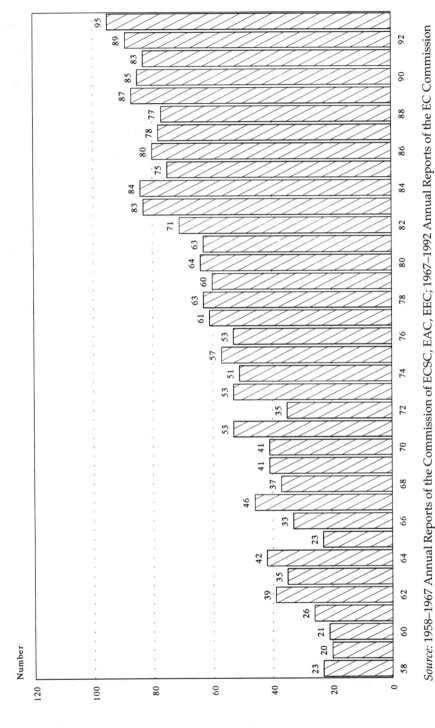

Figure 6: *Council of Ministers — number of sessions (per year)*

Source: 1958–1967 Annual Reports of the Commission of ECSC, EAC, EEC; 1967–1992 Annual Reports of the EC Commission

A major feature in the historical development of the Council has been the growing importance of the Presidency (Ó'Nuallain 1985; de Bassompierre 1988; Vornbäumen 1985). Besides its straightforward procedural role of chairing meetings, the Presidency is also supposed to be a dynamic and active consensus-broker, trying to reach as many decisions as possible during its six months in office. For this, it employs a variety of strategies ranging from the use or the threat of using the procedural possibilities of putting the issue to a vote, 'arm-twisting' in so-called 'Presidency confessionals' and various other forms of leverage on national delegations, including package deals and other trade-offs. As the Presidency of the Council usually has a political interest in achieving a successful Presidency, it sometimes has to offer something itself in difficult negotiations in order to reach a consensus.

Table 1: *Number of meetings of the Council of Ministers according to Policy Fields (1975, 1980, 1990)*

Policy Fields	1975	1980	1990
Others	2	4	–
Agriculture	15	14	16
General affairs	16	13	13
ECOFIN	8	9	10
Internal market	–	–	7
Environment	2	2	5
Research	2	–	4
Industry	–	–	4
Traffic	2	2	4
Development	3	1	4
Social affairs	2	2	3
Fishery	–	7	3
Energy	2	2	3
Education	1	1	2
Telecommunications	–	–	2
Budget	2	3	2
Consumer	–	–	2
Health	–	–	2
Culture	–	–	2
Catastrophe protection	–	–	1
Tourism	–	–	1
External trade	–	–	1
TOTAL	57	60	91

Source: 23rd, 28th and 38th Annual Report of the Council of Ministers.

The role of Commissioners in this political bargaining process often seems limited. With the exception of particularly strong personalities, such as Jacques Delors or Sir Leon Brittan — or, in the past, Vicomte Davignon — members of the Commission do not play a major role in shaping the final decision. The threat to withdraw a Commission proposal occurs very rarely. The member of the Commission present in the Council is only seldom mandated by the college to act in such a way. On the other hand, the Commission is extremely concerned during the debates in the Council to safeguard its constitutional prerogatives and its institutional role. One issue which frequently creates differences between the Council and the Commission is that of comitology, i.e. the question of which type of committee should act with the Commission in implementing the Community's decisions (Blumann 1992; see also Chapter 5). Whereas the Commission usually looks for a weak committee with only procedural rights, i.e. an advisory committee, the Council is much more interested in having a regulatory committee, since it gives national civil servants in the committee a veto power over the executive actions of the Commission (albeit through a qualified majority vote). In matters relating to the internal market especially (see Table 2), the Council has imposed its will on the Commission to the latter's detriment (Roumeliotis 1990). The Commission, as a result, regularly criticises the restrictions on its executive functions (see, for example, the *General Report of the Activities of the European Communities* for 1991 and 1992).

Table 2: *Number of Committees suggested by the Commission and decided by the Council, July 1987 to November 1990 (Internal Market only)*

Total in the field of the Internal Market	Commission	Council
Advisory Committee	36	12
Committee on Technical Norms	10	9
Management Committee		
Type II a	1	1
Type II b	1	1
Regulatory Committee		
Type III a	46	41
Type III b	7	34
'Clause de sauvegarde'		
Type IV a	1	2
Total	102	100
In the field of Article 100a		
Advisory Committee	20	9
Committee on Technical Norms	10	9
Management Committee		
Type II a	1	1
Type II b	1	1
Regulatory Committee		
Type III a	11	26
Type III b	0	0
'Clause de sauvegarde'		
Type IV a	0	0
TOTAL	43	46

Source: Communication from the Commission to the Council on the Conferment of Implementing Powers on the Commission, SEC (90) 2589, 10.1.1991.

Given the number of participants in a normal Council session, national Ministers often feel an element of control is being exercised by their national civil servants, especially when they come from other ministries. One way Ministers have sought to avoid this and enhance the possibility of agreement has been through the institutionalisation of informal meetings, either over luncheon or at weekends, frequently at a castle or country house and often within the electoral district of the President-in-Office. These informal Councils are limited to seven per Presidency, with Ministers of foreign affairs, agriculture and finance usually accounting for one each. The Presidency decides in collaboration with the Secretaries General of the Council and the Commission whether further informal meetings are necessary. In order to preserve the informal nature of the meetings, there is no officially-available agenda and no official documents and declarations are produced before or after the meeting. Members of the Commission are fully involved in these sessions and thereby have the opportunity to develop their own personal relationships with Ministers. This can be of crucial importance in establishing reliable and productive interaction. Bilateral visits serve the same function.

(e) (Implementation) committees

Committees established by the Council, often according to somewhat Byzantine formulae (see the Council Decision of July 13, 1987), supervise the execution and administration of Community policies by the Commission (see Chapter 5). The Commission, however, chairs the committees and can sometimes dominate them in terms of substance as well as procedures. In spite of the legal quarrels between the Council and Commission over the choice of the committee structure, because of the extent to which national officials can block the actions of the Commission, in practice Commission officials and those of the Member States are less interested in procedural wrangling than in substantive agreement. They tend to share responsibilities and combine forces. One indication of this is the fact that there have been practically no negative votes taken over the last few years in the extensive system of management committees for agricultural products and policies (Commission 1988 and annually to 1992). The Commission has been fairly successful in defending its position though, of course, the Commission's officials are careful to anticipate possible opposition on the part of the majority of the Member States. More than in other phases of the decision-making cycle, there has been an administrative fusion or merger of Community and national responsibilities in terms of procedural matters and even in terms of policy substance.

(f) European Council

The Commission plays a significant role in intergovernmental and other bodies at the highest political levels as well as in the various forms of administrative interaction suggested above. The European Council was created as a body outside the formal Community structure through a purely intergovernmental resolution (Wessels 1980; Bulmer and Wessels 1987; von Donat 1987; Hoscheit and Wessels 1988). Only with the Single European Act was the European Council given a legal basis. But under Maastricht, just as under the SEA, the European Council remains expressly outside the constitutional system of institutional checks and balances of the European Community. In the Maastricht Treaty, it is mentioned only in the Common Provisions of the Treaty. Most importantly, the actions and activities of the European Council are not subject to rulings by the Court of Justice of the European Communities which cannot therefore pass judgment on the constitutional conformity of actions taken by the Heads of Government.

Since Giscard d'Estaing and Helmut Schmidt, the European Council has developed an informal style of interaction between the political leaders of Western Europe. The differences in the power and authority of the Member States and their respective leaders are felt more directly than in the Council of Ministers. Revealingly in terms of his role, the President of the Commission was invited to participate in the European Council meetings from the very beginning. He is, indeed, among the 'founding members' of the European Council, enumerated in the Common Provisions among the group of Heads of Government (rather than in the list of secondary participants). However, given the power structure within the European Council and the greater procedural informality, the position of the President of the Commission depends heavily on his prestige and personality. To a large extent, it also depends on the subject area under debate.

Contrary to initial fears that the European Council would be an instrument for downgrading the Commission to a mere secretariat, it has often proved useful for the Commission's own political strategies. The Commission frequently uses the European Council's declarations and conclusions as a means of setting new goals and developing new initiatives. The Commission's President is normally quite amenable to receiving extended mandates from the Heads of Government for the Commission to develop new proposals which can then be put on the agenda of the Council with some political support. On the other hand, the European Council expects the President of the Commission to play an active role in its meetings in presenting reports etc., which then can be discussed and commented on by the Heads of Government. This seems to be especially the case on tricky issues such as unemployment and the economic recession; President Delors, for example, introduced an eight-point paper on economic renewal in Europe at the Copenhagen summit of June 22–23, 1993, which by the Brussels summit in December 1993 had become a full-blown White Paper (COM(93)700 Final).

One way in which the European Council makes an important contribution to the development of the integration process is by concluding package deals which link several Member States' 'demands' and 'offers' across several different policy fields. Only Heads of Government can take decisions which might combine economic, social, environmental, foreign, budgetary and institutional issues. Several important steps in the history of the European Community, including the SEA and the Maastricht Treaty, are the result of the European Council performing this major function (Hoscheit and Wessels *op. cit.* pp. 7–35). The Commission's President has only a limited capacity to offer anything in this bargaining process, but he can propose package deals which may move Member States to accept an upgraded common denominator. Jacques Delors has been especially successful in his extensive use of the European Council, winning agreement, for example, to two 'Delors packages' on budgetary issues, to the installation of the Delors Committee on Economic and Monetary Union, and to specific policies towards third countries such as the PHARE Programme. The Commission was also able to play a major role in the Intergovernmental Conference leading to the Single European Act, though its role in framing the Maastricht Treaty on European Union was much less significant (Laursen and Vanhoonacker 1992).

The role of the Commission in shaping such package deals is one that not only identifies major issues, but also adds a progressive integration perspective. The Commission President's role is thus best described as one of promotional brokerage.

(g) Community-related intergovernmental bodies

The extension of common activities by Member States into new policy areas has been partly achieved by using Community provisions, especially Articles 235 and 236 (see Chapter 6). But it has also come about through new intergovernmental procedures and mechanisms which — since the early 1970s — have increasingly been linked to the Community. In the area of European Political Cooperation, the Commission has slowly become fully associated with the meetings of ministers and the Political Committee, and with all the other working groups as well as the meetings of Community ambassadors in third countries (at least when a Commission delegation exists there — see Chapters 10 and 11). The Commission's delegation can sometimes play a significant role in some third country capitals, especially when major Community financial projects are involved or when trade issues are of importance.

A major chapter of the Maastricht Treaty, the Common Provisions, envisages a unitary institutional system for all three pillars of the European Union. As a result, the formal powers of the Commission are extended, providing it with a (non-exclusive) right of initiative in both the Common Foreign and Security Policy pillar and cooperation in the field of home affairs and justice. The Commission's role in intergovernmental meetings and in the various working groups was often in the guise of an 'expert guest' who could contribute to the deliberations prepared and run by the Presidency-in-Office; if, that is, the policies on the agenda came within the Community's fields of competence. Commission officials could sometimes achieve influence because of their expertise and past experience, especially, of course, when national diplomats' knowledge of the legal framework and the activities of the Community is limited.

The Commission's role in the second and third pillars of the Union depends largely on the functions attributed to it by the President-in-Office. The division of labour is often related to the personality and quality of the Commission representatives as well as to those of the Presidency and its civil servants. Smaller or less experienced Community countries rely more on the Secretariat of EPC and on the Commission than larger member countries, especially if the President is himself a long-serving Foreign Minister (such as Hans-Dietrich Genscher or Douglas Hurd).

(h) Participation in mixed bodies

The growth of the Community and its activities and the advent of the Union have also demanded a highly complex form of representation in the international system. The Commission plays an important role, for example, in 'group-to-group dialogues' with groups of third countries, especially in long-lasting conferences (Edwards and Regelsberger 1990). In the framework of negotiating the Lomé Agreements, for instance, the Commission also developed a strong role in areas not directly part of the legal competence of the European Community.

A good illustration of the Commission's role are the summit meetings with political leaders from third countries, especially with the President of the United States. Here, 'Europe' is represented by both the President of the European Council and the President of the Commission. In the Transatlantic Dialogue, President Delors has sometimes played a major role, especially in cases where the President of the European Council has come from a smaller country with no or no major experience in relevant Community business such as trade issues. Insofar as he represents continuity and extensive political experience, the President of the Commission often plays a *de facto* role which goes beyond that of the President of the European Council.

The Commission President also participates in the (Western) Summit meetings of the seven most powerful industrialised nations (Bonvicini and Wessels 1984; Krenzler 1992). At early meetings the representation of the Community (the Council and the Commission) was much contested, especially by the French, the British and the Germans. They were opposed by the smaller EC Member States, who themselves wanted to be present at G-7 meetings. Today, the presence of the Commission and the Council Presidency at such Summits is quite normal — and also necessary because of the extended competence of the Community in the fields of trade, agriculture, environment etc. (see Chapter 10). The Commission's involvement also extends to the administrative preparation of the meetings.

Conclusions

If one looks at the procedural and legal texts of the last few decades and at the behavioural trends and patterns (see above), there is one dominating trend: the Commission's role in relation to the Council has evolved to become one of a co-player. It has extended its participation and procedural rights and has acted more and more like a promotional broker. The Commission has neither developed into a body which fits the image of a dominating technocracy nor has it been reduced to an expert secretariat of secondary importance. That is not to say, however, that the Commission has not sometimes played such roles in certain policy areas and on particular political occasions. But, in general, the provisions of the Maastricht Treaty as well as the developments of the last years indicate that the role of a promotional broker is being reinforced. The Commission is thus likely to remain a unique body in a unique institutional set-up.

The uniqueness of the relationship between the Council and the Commission is based on their mutual dependence: neither institution can act without the other. Through its administrative capacity and its technical expertise, the Commission has clearly won political weight in the EC decision-making process. However, the Council and the European Council have extended their control and influence and remain the main decision-making bodies. The question of the direction of further developments remains open: the Union's enlargement could well weaken the decision-making capacity of the Council and thereby strengthen the Commission's role as 'promotional broker'; on the other hand, a Council of 16 or more members will be even more complex in terms of decision-making and the Commission may find its freedom of manoeuvre further constrained. The Commission may therefore find itself with two options in the future: it either falls back into the role of a simple secretariat to a dominant Council; or it develops its brokerage role further. The number of Member States will be important. So too, though, will the position and strength of the European Parliament with its additional rights under the Maastricht Treaty. The Commission's brokerage role may therefore become more important in the 1990s within a newly-structured institutional triangle.

References and bibliography

Aberbach, J., Putnam, R. and Rockman, B. (1981) *Bureaucrats and Politicians in Western Democracies*, Cambridge Mass: Harvard University Press.

Berlin, D. (1987) 'Organisation de la Commission', in Cassese, S. *et al. The European Administration*, Paris: Institut International des Sciences Administratives, pp. 38–39.

Blumann, Claude (1992) 'La Comitologie: L'exercice de la fonction exécutive dans la Communauté Européenne', in Engel, Christian and Wessels, Wolfgang (eds.) *From Luxembourg to Maastricht: Institutional Changes in the European Community after the Single European Act*, Bonn: Europa Union Verlag, pp. 89–108.

Bonvicini, Gianni and Wessels, Wolfgang (1984) 'The European Community and the Seven', in Merlini, Cesare (ed.) *Economic Summits and Western Decision-Making*, London/Sydney: Croom Helm, pp. 167–91.

Bulmer, Simon and Wessels, Wolfgang (1987) *The European Council: Decision-Making in European Politics*, Hong Kong: Macmillan 1987.

Commission of the European Communities (1988 and annually) *General Report on the Activities of the European Communities*, Brussels.

da Costa Pereira, Pedro Sanchez (1988) 'The Use of a Secretariat', in Pijpers, Alfred *et al.* (eds.) *European Political Cooperation in the 1980s*, Dordrecht: Martinus Nijhoff for the Trans-European Studies Association, pp. 85–103.

de Bassompierre, Guy (1988) *Changing the Guard in Brussels, An Insider's View of the EC Presidency*, New York: Praeger.

de Gaulle, Charles (1970) *Discours et Messages*, Vol. 8, Paris: Plon.

Dewost, Jean Louis (1980) 'Les relations entre le Conseil et la Commission dans le processus des décisions communautaires', *Revue du Marché Commun*, No. 238, June–July, pp. 289–94.

Edwards, Geoffrey and Regelsberger, Elfriede (eds.) (1990) *Europe's Global Links: The European Community and Inter-Regional Cooperation*, London: Pinter Publishers.

Haas, Ernst B. (1964) *Beyond the Nation State, Functionalism and International Organization*, Stanford: Stanford University Press.

Haas, Ernst B. (1968) *The Uniting of Europe*, 2nd edition, Stanford: Stanford University Press.

Hallstein, Walter (1979) *Die Europäische Gemeinschaft*, 5th edition, Düsseldorf/Wien: Econ.

Hoscheit, Jean-Marc and Wessels, Wolfgang (eds.) (1988) *The European Council 1974–1986: Evaluation and Prospects*, Maastricht: European Institute of Public Administration.

Krenzler, Horst-Günter (1992) 'Die Rolle der Europäischen Gemeinschaft beim Weltwirtschaftsgipfel', Integration 2, pp. 68–79.

Laursen, Finn and Vanhoonacker, Sophie (eds.) (1992) *The Intergovernmental Conference on Political Union*, Maastricht: European Institute of Public Administration.

Lindberg, Leon N. and Scheingold, Stuart A. (1970) *Europe's Would-Be Polity. Patterns of Change in the European Community*, Englewood Cliffs: Prentice Hall.

Lipgens, Walter (ed.)(1985) *Documents on the History of European Integration, Vol. 1: Continental Plans for European Union 1939–45*, Berlin/New York: de Gruyter.

Louis, J-V. and Waelbroek, D. (1989) *La Commission au coeur du système institutionnel des Communautés Européennes*, Brussels: Editions de l'Université de Bruxelles.

Ludlow, P. (1991) 'The European Commission', in Keohane, R. O. and Hoffmann, S. (eds.) *The New European Community: Decision-making and Institutional Change*, Boulder: Westview Press, pp. 85–132.

Mayntz, R. (1985) (ed.) *Soziologie der öffentlichen Verwaltung*, Heidelberg/Karslruhe: Westdeutscher Verlag.

Monnet, Jean (1976) *Mémoires*, Paris: Fayard.

Nuttall, Simon (1992) *European Political Cooperation*, Oxford: Clarendon Press.

O'Nuallain, Colm (ed.) (1985) *The Presidency of the European Council of Ministers*, London/New Hampshire: Croom Helm.

Ott, S.J. (1989) *The Organizational Culture Perspective*, Chicago: The Dorsey Press.

Poullet, Edouard and Deprez, Gérard (1977) 'The Place of the Commission within the Institutional System', in Sasse, Christoph *et al. Decision-Making in the European Community*, New York: Praeger, pp. 206–10.

Roumeliotis, P. (1990) Rapporteur, Institutional Committee of the European Parliament, 19 November 1990 Doc. A3-0310/90.

Spinelli, Altiero (1958) *Manifest der Europäischen Föderalisten*, Frankfurt: Europäische Verlagsanstalt.

Spinelli, Altiero (1985) 'The United States of Europe and the Various Political Trends', in Lipgens, Walter (ed.) *Documents on the History of European Integration, Vol. 1: Continental Plans for European Union 1939–45*, Berlin/New York: de Gruyter, pp. 484–9.

Stillman, R.J. (1988) *Public Administration, Concepts and Cases*, 4th ed., Boston: Houghton Mifflin Co.

Thatcher, Margaret (1988), Speech at the College of Europe, Bruges, British Documentation, British Embassy, Bonn. No. D17/88, 21.9.1988.

Timsit, Gérard (1985) 'L'administration', in Gransk, Madeleine and Leca, Jean (eds.) *Traité de science politique Vol 2. Les régimes politiques contemporains*, Paris: P.U.F. pp. 446–510.

Vedel Report (1972) (German version) *Bulletin of the EC*, No. 4, Brussels.

von der Groeben, Hans (1982) *Aufbaujahre der Europäischen Gemeinschaft. Das Ringen um den Gemeinsamen Markt und die Politische Union (1958–1966)*, Baden-Baden: Nomos.

von Donat, Marcell (1987) *Das ist der Gipfel. Die EG-Regierungschefs unter sich*, Baden-Baden: Nomos.

Vornbäumen, Axel (1985) *Dynamik in der Zwangsjacke, Die Präsidentschaft im Ministerrat der Europäischen Gemeinschaftals Führungsinstrument*, Mainzer Beiträge zur Europäischen Einigung, edited by Werner Weidenfeld, Vol. 5, Bonn: Europa Union Verlag.

Wallace, Helen (1985) 'The Presidency: Tasks and Evolution', in O'Nuallain, Colm (ed.) (*q.v.*).

Wallace, H., Wallace, W., and Webb, C. (eds.) (1983) *Policy-Making in the European Community*, Chichester: J. Wiley.

Wallace W. (1990) 'Introduction: the dynamics of European Integration', in Wallace, W. (ed.) *The Dynamics of European Integration*, London: Pinter Publishers, pp. 3–5.

Wessels, Wolfgang (1980) *Der Europäische Rat, Stabilisierung statt Integration? Geschichte, Entwicklung und Zukunft der EG-Gipfelkonferenzen*, Bonn: Europa Union Verlag.

Wessels, W. (1985) 'Community Bureaucracy in a Changing Environment: Criticism, Trends and Questions', in Jamar, J. and Wessels, W. (eds.) *Community Bureaucracy at the Crossroads*, Bruges: De Temple, pp. 8–36.

Wessels, W. (1991) 'The EC Council. The Community's Decision-Making Centre', in Keohane and Hoffmann (eds.) *q.v.*, pp. 133–55.

9.   The Commission and the Parliament

Martin Westlake

Introduction

The Commission and the Parliament form part of an evolving constitutional system, in which the Community's competences and Parliament's powers are growing in tandem. The essence of their relationship lies in a fundamental contradiction; theoretically rivals, the two are *de facto* partners. The European Parliament (EP) and the Commission, are "fully-integrated Community institutions" (Noël 1988, p. 31), but there are clear differences in the nature of the two institutions; the Commission is a collegiate organisation, its members nominated by Member State governments, whereas the Parliament is a representative, pluralistic body. Much like a government, the Commission must simultaneously reconcile collegiality and policy coherence, and respond to the pluralistic representations of the Parliament. Unlike a government, the Commission lacks the direct, suffrage-based legitimacy the Parliament has enjoyed since 1979. Thus, the Parliament has become the Commission's natural ally in the latter's search for popular legitimation of its policies, while the Parliament sees the Commission as its natural ally *vis-à-vis* the Council. Despite the apparent differences and rivalry between the two, the Commission and the Parliament are an objective partnership involving a mutual interest in the enhancement of Parliament's powers. But the partnership is not a simple one. While the Commission's rights and duties under the Treaties oblige it to take into account Parliament's views (Parliament has the right to censure and 'sack' the Commission), it must also reconcile its own policy options with the views of the Member States. This Chapter reviews Commission–Parliament relations and demonstrates the rivalry and the partnership in practice.

The Treaties' provisions governing Commission–Parliament relations fall into two broad categories. The first consists of the Commission's rights and duties with regard to its attendance, statements, replies and its general participation in Parliament's work. Article 140 EEC provides that "members of the Commission may attend all parliamentary meetings and shall, at their request, be heard". It further provides that "the Commission shall reply orally or in writing to questions put to it by the European Parliament or by its members". In addition, Article 155 EEC establishes the Commission's autonomy in Treaty-based procedure and provides that the Commission shall "have its own power of decision and participate in the shaping of measures taken by the Council and by the European Parliament".

A second category concerns the various Community decision-making procedures: consultation, cooperation, co-decision, assent, budget, budgeting discharge, and censure. The range of Treaty articles where each of these procedures applies was extended considerably as a result of the implementation of the Treaty on European Union (TEU) in 1993. The Treaties also provide for the Commission to produce and Parliament to debate an annual general report on the activities of the Communities. Although the Commission continues to produce these reports, their importance has considerably diminished. Greater attention is now focused on the annual legislative programme exercise described below.

In fact the Treaty provisions amount to the barest of skeletal frameworks. The bones have been fleshed out by a series of conventional arrangements including Treaty amendments and associated acts and regulations, joint declarations, European Council conclusions, inter-institutional agreements, political undertakings, and *ad hoc* conventions. Commission–Parliament relations owe as much to these devices as they do to the Treaties. Clearly, legislative machinery based on such *ad hoc* approaches could not function efficiently without the goodwill and understanding of a truly cooperative relationship. Yet the founding fathers foresaw a 'classic' executive–assembly relationship between the two institutions, characterised by independent scrutiny and control. As this Chapter makes clear, in practice Parliament frequently foregoes the full extent of its powers in order to realise particular policy outcomes.

Organising inter-institutional interaction inside the Commission

The College

Commissioners may be called upon to defend or speak to any dossier before Parliament although, like ministers, they prefer to speak on subjects within their own briefs. Three Commissioners have specialised roles. The President generally represents the Commission on all formal occasions, in major political and constitutional parliamentary debates, and in inter-institutional fora or negotiations. In 1973, the Commission created a specific portfolio for parliamentary relations. This Commissioner stands in for the President and represents the Commission in his own right before Parliament, taking a special interest in the maintenance and development of inter-institutional relations. He also represents the Commission in Parliament's primary management body, the Conference of Presidents (made up of the political group leaders) and reports Parliament's views back to the College. Third, Parliament's budgetary powers are considerable and its powers of oversight exercised constantly and the budget Commissioner maintains a particularly close symbiotic relationship with his parliamentary interlocutors.

Parliament's work is a separate point on the agenda of every ordinary Commission meeting. Indeed, the Commission's weekly meeting is held in Strasbourg during Parliament's plenary sessions, enabling the Commission to participate more fully in Parliament's plenary work. A member of the Commission is almost always present in the plenary, while Commission members attend committee meetings and other fora in the margins of plenary sessions.

The Commission is always present during legislative votes. This relates to Parliament's power of delay. Before the final legislative vote, Parliament may ask the Commission to accept certain amendments (and thus amend its proposal to the Council). If not satisfied, Parliament can decide to refer a proposal back to committee, and thus delay the legislative process in order to force concessions. To facilitate rapid response, Commissioners are authorised ('habilitated') in advance by the College to accept (or reject) parliamentary amendments. An accelerated procedure enables proposals subsequently to be re-drafted and sent to the Council (see Chapter 6).

Commissioners frequently attend parliamentary committee meetings and address political group meetings. They reply to written and oral parliamentary questions and letters from MEPs, and receive individual MEPs and parliamentary delegations.

Cabinets, *parliamentary attachés and the 'GAP'*

Within each Commissioner's *Cabinet*, one individual is appointed as parliamentary attaché to the Commissioner, liaising closely with the appropriate committees and political groups as well as with the Commission services. Following the June 1979 direct elections, the Commission decided to establish an internal body designed to enhance Commission–Parliament relations and reinforce collegiality. This *'Groupe des affaires parlementaires'* (GAP) is composed of all 17 parliamentary attachés and a specialised representative of the legal service. Meetings are serviced and minuted by the Secretariat General (SG) and chaired by the *Cabinet* of the Commissioner responsible for relations with the Parliament.

The GAP meets every Thursday except during the week of the parliamentary plenary. Its primary role is the administrative and political preparation for the next parliamentary session. This usually includes confirming the presence of Commissioners and their responsibilities for votes and dossiers, taking into account the many last-minute changes to Parliament's agenda. The GAP considers requests for urgent consultations, parliamentary questions, work in committee, and Commission statements. It assures collegiality by approving all draft answers to parliamentary oral questions, and prepares politically important portfolios and debates. Its minutes and decisions are transmitted to and noted by the Commission College, via the *Chefs de Cabinet*.

The Secretariat General

The Secretary General represents the Commission *vis-à-vis* his counterpart in the Parliament. Under certain circumstances, he may also represent the

College. The Secretary General receives his own extensive parliamentary correspondence and occasionally receives parliamentary delegations. The steadily-increasing range of competences and *ad hoc* duties delegated to the Commission have led the Secretary General to appear before several Parliamentary committees. Since 1973, the Deputy Secretary General has been charged with particular administrative responsibility for relations with the European Parliament. As with the Secretary General, the consequences of the changing geo-political situation have led to specific, *ad hoc* representative duties *vis-à-vis* the Parliament.

A small directorate ('Directorate E') within the Secretariat General (SG) is responsible for relations with the Parliament. It answers to the Secretary General and his Deputy and, at the political level, to the President, the responsible Commissioner, and the College. The directorate is divided into several overlapping units. One is responsible for parliamentary questions, written and oral. The small size of this unit belies its large and constantly expanding workload. The unit attributes parliamentary questions to the Commissioners, *Cabinets* and DGs concerned, chases up replies, submits draft replies to the collegial process (through the GAP), and transmits written replies to the Parliament. A small section coordinates the Commission's follow-up to Parliament's legislative and non-legislative opinions and recommendations (see below *'suites données'*).

A second, larger unit is responsible for parliamentary relations in plenary and in committee, and has specific responsibilities in relation to the Single European Act (SEA) procedures (cooperation, assent), parliamentary petitions and the new co-decision procedure resulting from the Treaty on European Union. The unit coordinates the political and administrative preparation for parliamentary plenary sessions in close liaison with the *Cabinets*, legal service, DGs and the GAP. Typically, a small team of five officials drawn from the unit resides in Strasbourg throughout the parliamentary plenary week. It keeps the College abreast of agenda changes, gives early warning of political and institutional problems, covers parliamentary committee meetings, and 'manages' Commission representation in the chamber itself. Both in the run-up to and during the plenary week the SG plays an important liaison role with the *Cabinet* of the EP President and with Parliament's session office.

Away from Strasbourg plenaries, the unit is represented in all parliamentary committee meetings, where its duties similarly concern coordination and information. The unit also acts as the conduit and archive for all Commission–Parliament communications (transmission of documents, correspondence, etc.). A small team within the unit coordinates all Commission–EP procedures. It liaises closely with individual *Cabinets* and services (particularly through the GAP and the coordinators' meeting — see below), with the SG's directorate for relations with the Council, with the SG's legislative planning unit, with the Commission legal service and, vitally, with the EP's services and committees (particularly through the 'Neunreither Group' described below).

Parliament relies heavily on the Commission for the efficient functioning of its petitions procedure. Another small team within the SG unit coordinates and manages this cooperation, forwarding notices to the relevant Commissioner, *Cabinets* and DG, ensuring collegial approval for all replies and information given, and generally managing communications.

The Directorates General (DGs)

Once the Parliament has received a legislative proposal, Commission representatives from the competent Directorate General will be expected to explain and defend it in the parliamentary committees concerned. Parliament has traditionally relied on these Commission representatives to give some indication of the trend of negotiations in Council working groups (the tradition, enhanced by the advent of the cooperation procedure, has been formalised by a Commission undertaking). Throughout parliamentary readings, the competent officials within the DGs collaborate closely with their parliamentary coordinators, the responsible Commissioners and *Cabinets*, the parliamentary relations directorate in the SG, and the secretariats of the competent parliamentary committees. The shepherding of Commission proposals through parliamentary committees frequently involves the briefing of parliamentary rapporteurs and draftsmen, sometimes extending to help in the drafting of mutually-acceptable technical amendments. Directors General and Directors are naturally involved in all strategic and tactical discussions relating to proposals emanating from their services, and regularly appear before the parliamentary committees covering their competences.

DGs draft answers to parliamentary questions (written and oral) and petitions, and prepare briefings for their Commissioner's appearances before Parliament. Those DGs (or services within them) whose competences are directly paralleled by parliamentary committees have a continuous role in informing and updating those committees. DG XIX, the Budget DG, for example, has a particularly close symbiotic relationship with Parliament's Budgets and Budgetary Control Committees, being seen both within Parliament and within the Commission as the chief interlocutor on all matters of Community finance.

After the SEA it became the norm for those DGs having frequent dealings with the Parliament to appoint officials to manage parliamentary relations, particularly in committee. An individual or a unit responsible for EP relations now exists within each DG. These parliamentary coordinators enjoy easy access vertically to their Directors and Directors General and *Cabinets* and horizontally to the various branches of the service. They liaise with the SG and with the corresponding parliamentary committees' secretariats. On the first Monday following each plenary session, the coordinators meet as a group to prepare the following fortnight's parliamentary committee meetings and the next parliamentary plenary session.

While still evolving procedurally, the annual legislative programming exercise has become a centrepiece of Commission–Parliament relations and is set to take on further importance given the Treaty on European Union's provisions on the nomination of the Commission. Early each year, the Commission President presents the Commission's Programme to Parliament for debate. The Programme is not an exhaustive document but sets out the main themes and political priorities of the Commission for the coming legislative year. Parliament attempts to gain maximum influence over the Programme, particularly by setting out its own political priorities in advance and continuing to exert influence thereafter. Parliament has logically attempted to provide an additional dimension by drawing in the work programme of the Council Presidency-in-office. The December 1992 Edinburgh Council endorsed a Commission proposal that the annual work programme be produced in October of the preceding year, providing Parliament with more time to exert policy influence.

Together with its Programme, the Commission submits to Parliament an indicative legislative timetable, setting out all major legislative proposals for the forthcoming year and including all proposals related to the political priorities in the Commission's Programme. The timetable lists those areas where it intends drafting green papers. The indicative legislative timetable is divided into quarterly rolling programmes and constantly updated. It gives concrete form to the Commission's Programme, is designed to involve the other Community institutions, and serves as the basis for coordination with them.

The Treaty on European Union significantly extended and consolidated Parliament's legislative powers, triggering off intense reflection within that institution as to how, at the procedural level, those powers could best be fully realised. Parliament now sees the Community's annual and pluri-annual legislative planning and financial programming exercises as the dual key. It therefore seeks closer coordination and consistency between its political priorities and the budgetary procedure.

It also puts increasing pressure on the Commission to include all intended acts, whether legislative or pre-legislative, in its draft legislative programme, and on the Council (both the Presidency-in-office and the Troika) to participate fully in the legislative programming exercise. In the longer term, Parliament sees significance in the decision to synchronise the mandates of the Parliament and the Commission in such a way that each new Parliament's election will precede each new Commission's nomination and confirmation. Those six months, it has been argued, will give Parliament not only the time to organise itself internally, but also to establish its political priorities and negotiate the realisation of these, via the programming exercise, with the incoming nominated President and Commission.

The Commission–Parliament interface

The 'Neunreither' Group (Inter-Institutional Coordination Group)

For Parliament, the SEA was both a disappointment and a challenge. It had called for but did not receive co-decision powers with the Council, but was aware that the key to whether future Intergovernmental Conferences (IGCs) might grant it further powers depended on its successful and responsible management of the new SEA procedures. Parliament saw the key to success, as the European Council had intended, in inter-institutional cooperation. A special coordinating group was established.

This 'Neunreither Group' (named after the parliamentary official who established it) meets in Brussels on the Thursday preceding plenary sessions. Representatives from the Commission, the Economic and Social Committee and Council General Secretariats are invited, together with a representative of the current Presidency. Representatives from Parliament's sessional services and from the *Cabinet* of its President also attend. Initially intended to deal only with SEA-related matters, the Group's scope has been extended to all matters on the plenary agenda, and to establishing priorities for future plenary agendas in accordance with the joint annual legislative programme. The Group is also responsible for the procedural implementation of the Treaty on European Union. The Commission SG participates fully in the activities of the Group.

The Conference of Presidents

Parliament's managerial functions are primarily exercised through its Conference of Presidents, consisting of the Chairmen of the political groups. It traditionally meets in Strasbourg in the margins of the plenary session to prepare the agenda of the next month's plenary session. The meeting provides a regular forum for inter-institutional communications and an opportunity for the Commission (and the Council) to request changes to the agenda. The Commission may also be invited to participate in other discussions in the Conference of Presidents, such as those related to the Annual Legislative Programme.

The censure motion

The Commission's relations with Parliament are fundamentally derived from the provisions of EEC Article 144, which grants Parliament the power to censure the Commission. Parliament's 'nuclear weapon' is carefully circumscribed, both by the Treaties and, in self-denying ordinance, by Parliament's Rules of Procedure. Parliament has never censured the Commission. Of the seven motions formally tabled (only three since 1979), five were defeated, and two withdrawn. The censure motion has been described as a "reserve power of limited practical significance in the day-to-day work of the Communities" (Jacobs and Corbett 1990, pp. 190; 203). To its critics, the censure motion is defective, non-discriminatory and ill-targeted. Others argue that the power is designed as an ever-present potential sanction. However distant the prospect, the potential exists, and the Commission remains sensitive and responsive to all expressions of parliamentary dissatisfaction.

The budget: Article 203 procedure

The budget is the policy area where Parliament's powers, particularly in relation to the Commission, are currently furthest advanced. Parliament and the Council form the Community's budgetary authority, and only Parliament's President can sign the budget into law.

The Commission plays important formal roles as the author of the preliminary draft budget, as the technical and statistical service during the procedure, and as the eventual executor of the agreed budget. At the practical and political levels the Commission is intimately involved throughout. It participates in Parliament's establishment of 'guidelines'. It has to defend its preliminary draft budget (PDB) to the Council and to the Parliament. It provides 'active assistance' to the Council–Parliament conciliation committee preceding the Council's adoption of the draft budget. It is constantly at hand in the Parliament's Budgets Committee during the latter's deliberations on the draft budget (DB), both in its role as secretariat and, more important, as chief defender of the Commission's PDB. It is again actively present in the conciliation meeting preceding the Council's second reading and during the second reading itself. The budget Commissioner is present in any 'trialogues', before or after Parliament's second reading, and is actively present in the Budget Committee's and the parliamentary plenary's second reading. The Commission is also responsible for the implementation of the budget as adopted. Similar procedures and a similar role for the Commission are involved for supplementary and rectifying budgets and, throughout the budgetary year, the Commission is obliged to seek authorisation from the budgetary authority in relation to any transfer requests.

Parliament may reject the budget and did so in December 1979 and in December 1984. (A supplementary budget was rejected in 1982.) The Commission tables 'new budgetary proposals' intended to modify and complement the Council's second reading with a view to Parliament's position. The budget is then effectively submitted to a third reading in Council and Parliament. Should a budgetary year commence before a budget has been signed into existence, the Community has to subsist on the basis of 'provisional twelfths', which the Commission has to calculate and implement.

Budgetary inter-institutional agreements

Between 1988 and 1992, the traditional 'Article 203' budgets procedure was fundamentally modified by an Inter-Institutional Agreement (IIA) between Council, Parliament and Commission, designed to establish budgetary calm to facilitate the implementation of the SEA. So successful was the IIA in realising these aims that another similar five-year IIA, to ease the provisions of the Maastricht Treaty into play, was adopted by the institutions in 1993. Prior to the 1988 IIA, the budgetary procedure was frequently stormy. Should the 1993 IIA prove as successful as its predecessor, IIAs and relative budgetary calm may well become the norm.

The IIA establishes five-year financial perspectives, effectively imposing ceilings for annual expenditure for each category within the overall budget. The Commission calculates an annual adjustment to the financial perspectives, based on a mixture of economic indicators. This introduces a new element and phase into the annual cycle, with Parliament closely examining and on occasion contesting the Commission's calculations. The previously-agreed category ceilings, together with all three institutions' prior commitment to the method involved, reduces the budgetary procedure thereafter to a zero-sum game.

The institutional consequences of the IIAs have been far-reaching. Within Parliament, the Budgets Committee has to arbitrate far more rigorously between the competing demands of the spending committees, and this has led to a change in its attitude towards the Commission's Provisional Draft

Budget (PDB). Previously, there had been a tendency to reinstate the PDB amounts to lines that had been cut in the Council's first reading, and to leave alone those lines on which Council and Commission had agreed. Under the IIA's rigour, the Budgets Committee scrutinises all lines closely, both those cut by Council and those untouched, with particular reference to the Commission's previous expenditure. The point is to see where cuts might be left or further cuts made in order to create room for manoeuvre which could then be used to satisfy Parliament's own preferred policy priorities or, at the least, to facilitate the necessary parliamentary majorities by 'buying off' insistent spending committees.

The IIA obliges the Commission to provide continuous information on the implementation of the budget, and to defend those lines where take-up seems low. The Commission's PDB, particularly projected administrative staff expenditure, is the subject of rigorous scrutiny and no longer benefits from a presumption in its favour. Council cuts are no longer automatically restored in parliamentary first readings, and the onus falls on the Commission to defend 'vulnerable' lines. On the other hand, the Budgets Committee has come to expect the Commission to back it up when making difficult choices against the competing desires of spending committees. For its part, the Commission has established new internal procedures to ensure the greatest possible coherence within the PDB and to prioritise its projected expenditure so as to pre-empt any eventual search for 'head room'-creating cuts by the Budgets Committee or other spending committees. At the same time, DG XIX's horizontal role has been enhanced, with a concomitant reduction in direct lobbying of parliamentary committees by other DGs.

Budgetary discharge

Council and Parliament, assisted by the Court of Auditors, grant the Commission *post facto* discharge for the implementation of each year's budget. The Commission is obliged to submit annually to the Council and the Parliament the accounts of the preceding financial year. Before granting discharge, Council and Parliament examine these in the light of the Court of Auditors' annual report and the Commission's comments upon it. The procedure numbers among Parliament's most important supervisory powers. The entry into force of inter-institutional agreements and the adoption of financial perspectives has given scrutiny of the Commission's implementation of the budget additional importance, since Parliament is eager to ensure that expenditure in one sector does not encroach on projected expenditure in any other sector. Responsibility for this scrutiny has chiefly devolved upon the EP's Budgetary Control committee, which works closely with the Court of Auditors and the Commission's Directorate General for the Budget (XIX).

Parliament has the power to refuse discharge. Both institutions regard refusal to grant discharge as a grave occurrence, and although the Treaties are silent on the consequences of refusal, the Commission takes its duties in regard to parliamentary control very seriously. From Parliament's point of view, the discharge procedure, like the censure motion, has flaws, but remains a potent instrument.

The new Article 206 in the Maastricht Treaty elaborates upon the old discharge procedure. Before granting discharge the Parliament may call upon the Commission to "give evidence with regard to the execution of expenditure or the operation of financial control systems". Significantly, the Commission must "take all appropriate steps to act" on Parliament's observations, whether in the discharge decision or in general relation to the execution of expenditure.

In its September 1993 rule changes, Parliament has established an explicit link between these provisions and those of EEC Article 175, whereby the Parliament may bring an action against the Commission before the Court of Justice to establish the Commission's failure to act. The Treaty has thus introduced the possibility for an intermediate form of parliamentary sanction of the Commission, between the power of delay and the power to refuse discharge.

Legislative procedures

The consultation procedure

A number of Treaty articles provide for the consultation of Parliament. Parliament's role in this procedure was considered weak (since neither the Council nor the Commission was obliged to take the Parliament's opinion into account) until an unexpected 1980 Court ruling gave it a *de facto* power of veto. In the *Isoglucose* case, the Court ruled that where the Treaties provided for the consultation of Parliament, the Council could not take a decision until it had received Parliament's opinion. Parliament subsequently re-wrote its rules so that it could delay giving its opinion (through referral back to committee) in order to force concessions. Clearly, the power is strongest where legislation is urgent. Parliament sees the Commission as the key to its effectiveness in the procedure. As sole author, the Commission may withdraw or alter a proposal as it sees fit. In 1973, following the Court's jurisprudence, the Commission and the Council agreed that Parliament should be reconsulted whenever 'significant changes' were made to the text on which Parliament had initially delivered its opinion. The Commission takes its duties to Parliament seriously, although it must also take into account its strategic judgement as to what it thinks it will be able to get through Council. The situation is more difficult where the Treaty explicitly provides for unanimity in Council (see Chapter 6).

The cooperation procedure

Introduced by the SEA, the cooperation procedure involves two stages. The first reading is almost identical to the consultation procedure, Council consulting Parliament on the basis of a Commission proposal. Acting by qualified majority, the Council then adopts a 'common position', which is returned to Parliament for a 'second reading'. Parliament has three months in which to react. Where Parliament unconditionally approves the common position, either explicitly or by default, the Commission has no further role to play, and "the Council shall definitively adopt the act in question in accordance with the common position" (Article 189c EEC). Where Parliament rejects the common position, it will fall unless, within three months and acting unanimously, Council decides otherwise. Since the Commission considers that it may withdraw its proposal at any stage in the procedure, Council could only so decide with tacit Commission approval.

Where Parliament proposes amendments, the Commission must within one month 're-examine' its original proposal, the Council's common position, and Parliament's amendments, and forward its re-examined proposal to the Council. Amendments refused by the Commission may be accepted by the Council, acting unanimously. Amendments accepted by the Commission are incorporated into its re-examined proposal, which the Council may adopt by a qualified majority. The Council can only amend the Commission's re-examined proposal by unanimity. Once it has received the re-examined proposal, the Council has three months in which to act. If it does not act within that period, the proposal falls.

The SEA in general, and the cooperation procedure in particular, represented a major constitutional innovation in the Community system. A badly-administered procedure could clearly lead to blockages and delays. The Commission considered the potential stalling or loss of legislation to be a major risk, particularly in the field of the internal market, where the SEA had also introduced the 1992 deadline. The Commission reformed its internal procedures and enthusiastically joined in a process of increased inter-institutional cooperation with the Parliament.

The cooperation procedure accords the Commission an important gate-keeping function at various stages. This frequently involves it in delicate political arbitration. Both the Commission and Parliament recognised the importance of the first reading stage. There is no majority requirement nor any deadline, and Parliament can still hope to influence Council deliberations before a majority common position has emerged. For the Commission, parliamentary emphasis on the first reading diminishes the risk of blockage at second reading and reduces the number of situations where it has to arbitrate between conflicting desires. Emphasis on the first reading has given Parliament's power of delay fresh significance.

The cooperation procedure entailed a general change in institutional attitudes. Parliament's powers in the legislative process were transformed from the weak and essentially non-constructive power of delay to a stronger and potentially constructive role in the drafting of legislation.

The co-decision procedure

A major innovation of the Treaty on European Union was the extension of Parliament's legislative powers through the establishment of a co-decision procedure. This can consist of up to three readings. Although there are significant differences, the first two readings are similar to the cooperation procedure, but rejection by Parliament at the second reading stage may lead either to the proposal falling *or* a third reading stage involving a conciliation committee. Ultimately, Parliament may veto draft legislation. Commission and Parliament have expressed misgivings about the procedure, particularly the later stages. While the Commission is expected to play an active broker's role in the conciliation committee following the second reading stage, it no longer retains a proprietorial right over its legislative proposals. Parliament feels that the balance of respective powers of Council and Parliament in the case of a third reading (i.e., where the conciliation committee has failed to reach agreement) is tipped in favour of the Council. Parliament retains only a negative right of veto, and then only if it can muster the far from negligible condition of an absolute majority. At the practical level, the procedure is far more complex and potentially time-consuming than the cooperation procedure and, although the Commission plays important gate-keeping functions throughout the first and second readings, its formal role thereafter is reduced. As with the cooperation procedure, Parliament has most hope of seeing its amendments adopted at the first reading stage.

For all of these reasons, both the Commission and the Parliament place emphasis on the first and second reading stages, with Parliament placing great emphasis on reaching agreement before, or by, the second reading conciliation procedure. In its initial reaction to the Maastricht Treaty, Parliament called upon the Commission to withdraw automatically its proposals where Council and Parliament have been unable to reach agreement in the conciliation committee. Parliament has since modified its attitude, becoming more amenable to the logic that "the third reading will rather be an instrument of dissuasion which would induce the Council and the Parliament to agree during the [conciliation committee] negotiations" (Noël 1992). Any automaticity would vitiate this dissuasive element. The Commission has indicated that it would regard a request to withdraw a proposal, or rejection of a proposal, as a very important expression of parliamentary opinion, on which the Commission would deliberate, giving all due political weight to the position of Parliament, without accepting any automaticity. The Commission would exercise its right to withdraw with the Community interest in mind.

The conciliation procedures

A 1975 joint declaration established "a conciliation procedure between the European Parliament and the Council with the active assistance of the Commission". The procedure may be followed for "Community acts of general application which have appreciable financial implications". The aim of the procedure is to negotiate agreement between the two arms of the budgetary authority, the Council and the Parliament, but the Commission has an important role to play. At the outset, it has to indicate whether it feels a proposal may be subject to the procedure and it participates fully in the work of the Conciliation Committee. The procedure itself may be initiated by either the Parliament or the Council where "the Council intends to depart from the opinion adopted by the European Parliament" (Joint Declaration 1975). Representatives of the two institutions negotiate until their differences are sufficiently small for Parliament to be able to give a new opinion. The conciliation procedure is a classic 'smoke-filled room' process, with the Commission playing an important role as honest broker.

The budget procedure involves two hybrid conciliation committees. One, just before the Council adopts its (first reading) draft budget, is more an occasion for the institutions to identify where major differences exist. A second occurs just before the Council's second reading and is a more pro-active occasion for differences to be 'ironed out'. A third conciliation committee may occur where Parliament rejects the budget (nowadays an improbable occurrence).

The Maastricht Treaty introduced two new conciliation procedures within the co-decision procedure; one where Parliament indicates its intention to reject a common position (second reading), and one where Council decides to reject Parliament's amendments to the common position. In both cases, the conciliation committee is composed of an equal number of Council and Parliament representatives, but the Commission is also actively represented in the committee. Indeed, Article 189b(4) declares that the Commission "shall take all the necessary initiatives with a view to reconciling the positions of the European Parliament and the Council". Parliament has stressed the crucial role of the Commission, reminding it that "on the basis of its confidential relationship with the Parliament, and in accordance with both the letter and the spirit of Article 189b, it should exercise the options open to it so as to facilitate agreement between Parliament and Council" (European Parliament Resolution on the Conciliation Procedure, adopted 17 December 1992).

The assent procedure

Historically, the Parliament's Treaty-based powers in the field of external economic relations have been weak and limited (see Chapter 10). EEC Article 228 provides for the Commission to negotiate agreements which "shall be concluded by the Council after consulting the Parliament", but only Article 238 EEC (Association Agreements) provides for such consultation (together with those acts which would require internal legislation involving the cooperation or co-decision procedures). Even after Maastricht, the main instrument for international agreements, EEC Article 113, still does not mention Parliament. Here, the Commission drafts negotiating mandates which are adopted by the Council. The Commission then negotiates and initials agreements which are concluded by the Council. From an early date, Parliament sought to correct what it saw as a grave institutional imbalance. Under its consistent pressure, various conventions have been agreed over the years, extending Parliament's role, and that of the Commission in relation to it.

In 1964, the Council undertook to involve Parliament in the discussions preceding the opening of negotiations for association agreements, and to keep it informed during the negotiations. As draftsman of the negotiations and as chief negotiator, it falls to the Commission (as well as the Council) to participate in the debates, and to the Commission alone to brief Parliament's committees during negotiations. In the wake of the 1972 Paris summit, it was agreed the Commission should participate in any parliamentary debate (in committee or in plenary) on the negotiation of commercial agreements, and brief Parliament's committees accordingly during negotiations (this information process became collectively known as the Luns-Westerterp procedure). The late 1970s and early 1980s saw a growth in the negotiation of cooperation agreements which, not being specifically provided for under the Treaty, required the use of Article 235, and hence the consultation of Parliament. In this context, the Commission's role, and Parliament's powers, are much the same as they would be under any 'classic' consultation. Under the 1983 Stuttgart 'Solemn Declaration on European Union', it was agreed that Parliament should be formally consulted on all 'significant' international agreements and on accession Treaties, and the Luns-Westerterp procedures were extended to cover all important agreements.

The jewel in the crown of the Parliament's external relations powers is the assent procedure introduced by the 1986 SEA, which has been of far greater and more immediate scope than its draftsmen apparently intended. Parliament's assent is required for the conclusion of all association agreements and any protocols. (Assent by an absolute majority is required for the accession of new Member States.) The procedure has given the Parliament an important foreign policy lever, particularly in relation to human rights, but this influence is exercised chiefly through the Community's chief negotiator, the Commission. Indeed, the Commission is constantly involved with the Parliament throughout the procedure. The Maastricht Treaty arguably weakened Parliament's assent powers by relaxing what had previously been an absolute majority requirement.

The Parliament has so far wielded its assent powers sparingly. Of the 50-odd acts Parliament has considered under the procedure to date, just two have been rejected and a further five failed to gain an absolute majority. All seven were later passed. In all cases, Parliament's concern was human rights. In overall terms, Parliament's steady accrual of rights to information and consultation has led to an increasingly intimate relationship with the Commission's external relations DGs, which are now constantly engaged in updating and informing Parliament and its competent committees on negotiating mandates, on the state of the negotiations themselves, and on the contents of agreements.

The Treaty on European Union has altered and extended the assent procedure in three significant ways. First, in the 'traditional' field of external relations, the procedure is extended beyond association agreements and accession of new Member States to "other agreements establishing a specific institutional framework by organising cooperation procedures, agreements having important budgetary implications for the Community and agreements entailing amendment of an act adopted under the (co-decision) procedure". Secondly, the procedure has been extended beyond the traditional field of external relations into specific legislative areas (see below). Thirdly, the previous condition of an absolute majority has been relaxed to a simple majority in most cases (the exceptions being the procedure for European elections, and the accession of new Member States).

Where the procedure applies in the traditional external relations field, Parliament will almost certainly call for consultation on negotiation mandates. By default, this duty will probably continue to fall principally to the Commission, though the information it gives will necessarily remain oral and confidential.

For legislative proposals, Parliament has unilaterally introduced provision for the possibility of a conciliation procedure with the Council. The provision may be of considerable significance for the Commission. Unlike the classic consultation procedure, the assent procedure grants Parliament an infinite power of delay and an absolute power of rejection. In order to gain a more discriminating legislative power, Parliament's rules provide for the possibility of "an interim report . . . with a draft resolution containing recommendations for modification or implementation of the proposal". If at least one of those recommendations is approved with the same majority as would be required for the final assent, then Parliament's President would automatically request the opening of a conciliation procedure; with the responsible committee making its final recommendation "in the light of the outcome of the conciliation with the Council". Although the Commission is nowhere mentioned, one implication is clear; Parliament would strongly expect the Commission to modify its proposal in line with its recommendations, either before or during the conciliation procedure, or risk seeing it refused assent.

The Commission's accountability to Parliament

Commission statements

Article 140 EEC provides that "Members of the Commission may . . . be heard on behalf of the Commission". Parliament's Rules similarly provide that the Commission may "at any time" ask the President "for permission to make a statement". In practice, this facultative provision has been turned on its head, with the Commission's right to be heard practically transformed into an obligation to make statements should Parliament so require. The reason for this transformation is a combination of the relative availability and cooperativeness of the Commission, and Parliament's internal rules relating to the holding of debates. If Parliament manages to persuade the Commission to make a statement (the Commission usually finds it very difficult to refuse), then Parliament can hold a debate and adopt a resolution. In a Parliament of 567, it is easy to find the required 23 signatories, and MEPs have increasingly resorted to Commission statements as a way to stage debates on topical issues.

Urgencies

The Commission is sometimes obliged to make an urgent proposal at short notice. Such proposals frequently have to be enacted within a few weeks and thus fall outside the usual four-week rhythm of committee, group, and plenary meetings. Under these circumstances, Parliament's rules allow the Commission or the Council to request urgency. Parliament votes on whether to consider such proposals under an accelerated procedure at the beginning of its plenary sessions. Urgencies involve the organisation of meetings of the competent committees in the margins of the Strasbourg plenary session, a practice frowned upon because of pressure on plenary time and parliamentary resources. The procedure puts a double onus on the

Commission to prove its case: first, by convincing the plenary that the proposal is sufficiently urgent to merit consideration under the urgency procedure; and second, by arguing the merits of its case in committee and, ultimately, in the plenary again.

Topical and urgent debates

Parliament usually sets aside the Thursday morning of its plenary week for debates on topical and urgent matters. Subjects for debate are proposed by the political groups. The President draws up a short-list of these topics, from which five are selected by the plenary itself. Two almost invariably come under the umbrella headings of 'catastrophes and natural disasters', and 'human rights'. The other three usually concern matters of major political importance. The Commission attends and participates in these debates; it answers questions, provides information, gives its opinion, promises action where appropriate, and takes note of the views expressed.

Questions

The Treaties provide simply that the Commission "shall reply orally or in writing to questions put to it by the European Parliament or its members". Parliament has derived three procedures from this — written questions, oral questions, and question time. Two different general functions are involved and frequently overlap; information and scrutiny. Because of its many different institutional roles, its access to a large administrative apparatus, and its relations with national administrations, the Commission is increasingly seen by parliamentarians as a cooperative information source.

Written questions are forwarded to the competent Commissioners and DGs by the parliamentary unit in the SG. Replies are drafted by the services and forwarded up through the competent *Cabinet* to the College for approval (by written procedure), before transmission back to Parliament by the SG.

In practice, only oral questions tabled by political groups and committees are put on the agenda. Clearly, where questions are directed to it, the Commission will be required to answer them, but it is generally expected to follow Parliament's deliberations and participate in set-piece debates. To this end, the practice has grown of tabling questions on the same topic to both the Commission and the Council and combining them with a debate on a related topic.

Question Time occupies a regular 'slot' on Wednesday nights at each plenary session, though not many MEPs often attend. A Commissioner replies to each question, and parliamentarians in attendance may then ask a limited number of supplementary questions. Questions not taken receive written answers. This obliges the Commission to follow a procedure almost identical to that elaborated for normal written questions, the sole difference being that the written answers to questions taken orally are rendered otiose. The procedure is much criticised (it is not rare to see more Commissioners than parliamentarians in the chamber) but has stubbornly survived.

'Suites données'

A monthly document is forwarded to Parliament listing all legislative undertakings given and the Commission's follow-up. The document, which also includes updated figures on emergency aid disbursed in the preceding period, is published as a session document, and a short period of plenary time is set aside for Parliament to question the Commission. In addition to the monthly communication, the SG compiles a bi-annual document of the Commission's follow-up to all non-legislative recommendations. Once approved by the College, this document is forwarded to Parliament and distributed to all members. It can be the subject of questions and debate, though plenary time is not automatically set aside.

Petitions

Petitions to Parliament frequently concern implementation at local or national level of European legislation. In a majority of cases, Parliament decides that it either requires further information or the Commission's opinion. In both cases the matter is referred to the special SG unit. Petitions are forwarded to the competent Commissioners and DGs for further action, with the SG playing an internal and external coordinating role, including the setting of an internal timetable. In recent years, petitions to the Parliament and subsequent referrals to the Commission have increased significantly. Indeed, the parliamentary petitions procedure, now enshrined by Maastricht, can only effectively function with the collaboration of the Commission's services.

The Commission and the Parliament: between custom and law

The conventional context

Commission–Parliament relations depend heavily on a large number of conventions of indeterminate constitutional status. Four particularly important conventions are facultative consultations, Green and White papers, inter-institutional agreements and 'parallelism'.

In 1960, the Council gave a general undertaking to consult Parliament on all important problems, whether or not consultation was specifically required by the Treaties. This practice, known as 'facultative' consultation, has since been extended to virtually all legislative (1964) and non-legislative (1968) texts. The large majority of such legislative and non-legislative texts emanate from the Commission, which must explain and defend them, in parliamentary committee and in plenary, just as it would in the case of formal consultations.

The Commission has increasingly resorted to the convention of indicating its legislative intentions through the publication of Westminster-style 'Green Papers' which set out intended legislation in tentative form. Green Papers amount to pre-legislative consultations of Council and Parliament. At the

1992 Edinburgh Council, the Commission undertook to broaden the consultation process through much greater use of Green Papers, signalling its resolve by annexing a list of intended Green Papers to its 1993 Legislative Programme. Consequent legislation would in any case always figure in the legislative programme. More rarely, the Commission publishes White Papers.

Treaty-based inter-institutional relations have been fleshed out by a large number of agreements. Despite unclear legal and constitutional status, most have resulted in generally-respected conventions, and many have proved important to the working of the Community's legislative procedures, particularly in the budgetary field and in facilitating the implementation of the SEA. Such agreements fall into three broad categories: those concluded by all three institutions and which transfer new responsibilities to Parliament in the legislative process; those of a bilateral or trilateral nature intended to improve procedure, whether legislative or not; and common declarations made by, and exchanged of letters between, the Presidents of the three institutions. A good example of such a convention is the 1990 'code of conduct' agreed between the Commission and the Parliament to facilitate SEA procedures.

Under a 1990 bilateral inter-institutional agreement, implemented in 1991, the Commission undertook to ensure strict 'parallelism' in the transmission of all documentation to the Council and the Parliament, both in content and in timing. Parliament sees such measures as part of a broader thrust towards the more equal constitutional status with the Council it feels is appropriate to its ultimate aim of co-decision in a bicameral system. In the same context, in 1986 the Commission decided that, as a general rule, its representation in parliamentary committees should be at a comparable level to its representation in Council bodies.

The legal context

As Usher stresses in Chapter 6, the legal basis the Commission chooses for any particular proposition will determine the nature and extent of Parliament's role in the legislative process. The potential for confusion over the 'correct' legal base has traditionally arisen out of the procedures and provisions instituted by the SEA, with Parliament pressing its case where its legal advisors believe there is scope for interpretation. In general, the transition to the SEA 'regime' went remarkably smoothly.

Parliament scrutinises the legal bases of new proposals on a case-by-case basis. Committees can consult the Legal Affairs Committee and may take questions over legal bases back to plenary. On the assent procedure, Parliament has been involved more than had been foreseen, and its fears that the Commission would be sparing in its use of Article 238 have proved unfounded.

A further area of contention is 'comitology', which is also discussed elsewhere (see especially Chapter 5). Ideally, Parliament would like to see the Commission exercising full and untrammelled executive powers, with direct responsibility and clear accountability to the Parliament. The SEA provided for the Commission to rationalise the previously confused situation by making a proposal on conferred powers. This it duly did, but the Council's subsequent July 13, 1987 decision (discussed in Chapter 5) did not entirely follow the Commission proposal. Neither the Commission nor the Parliament was happy with the decision which, while rationalising committee structures, effectively increased the blocking powers of Member States. While undertaking never to propose certain types of committee, the Commission argued pragmatically that the Community would have to make do with the imperfect tools the Council had given it.

For its part, Parliament's committee chairmen and Bureau adopted a series of guidelines, the gist of which was systematically to propose amendments seeking to increase the Commission's autonomy and decrease the Council's blocking powers. Despite the intensity of the doctrinal debate, Parliament has been prepared to compromise when necessary. In a 1988 exchange of letters between President Delors and the then President Plumb, the Commission agreed to keep Parliament fully informed of all proposals it submits to 'comitology' committees. Parliament has introduced an internal procedure for vetting these proposals and for flagging those considered important for consideration in committee. However, a cultural divide in Parliament, together with the sheer bulk of Parliament's legislative load, has led to the benign neglect of these provisions, though they could be re-activated at any stage. Parliament's constitutional purists, with a future bicameral arrangement in mind, bemoan the continued interference by the future upper chamber (the Council) in the Commission's executive responsibilities.

Implementation of the Maastricht Treaty has involved wholesale changes in legal bases, creating a delicate role for the Commission, great sensitivity on the part of the Parliament, and greater probability of disagreement between the three institutions principally involved. Both Parliament and the Council now look to the Commission for what each considers correct choices of legal bases, although, if implementation of the SEA is any guide, a broad consensus is likely to evolve, at least between the institutions' legal advisors.

A problematic process has been those proposals involving a change in procedure where Parliament has already given an opinion (i.e. a former classic consultation or first reading under the cooperation procedure). In the longer term, the wider range of procedures and the greater envisaged participation of Parliament will result in continued, closer scrutiny of the Commission's initial choice of legal base, with new considerations, such as application of the principle of subsidiarity and respect for the fundamental rights of citizens, entering calculations.

Parliament's tactics and use of rules in an evolving institutional context

Parliament's aim to maximise its formal and informal powers can involve imaginative use of rules to extend or elaborate upon existing Treaty provisions. Although the Commission may sympathise with these aims, it has a duty of constitutional propriety (derived, above all, from its role as guardian of the Treaties), and has been wary of becoming an unwitting 'accomplice'. In particular if, by not objecting, the Commission was seen as implicitly acquiescing in such tactics, Parliament might claim the Commission as an explicit ally.

Parliament's political agenda

Parliament's consistent espousal of its own political concerns has had a knock-on effect on the attitudes of the other institutions. Apart from the cause of European integration itself and the related subject of the internal market (particularly small- and medium-sized enterprises, SMEs), major items on the EP's agenda include: development matters and hunger in the world; human rights; racism and xenophobia; the drugs problem and the drugs trade; women's rights; the environment; and combating fraud and organised crime. Where possible, Parliament uses its budgetary powers to redirect resources in favour of its preferred activities. The assent procedure has given Parliament a powerful, if occasional, economic lever (through the Commission) on human rights in third countries. Inviting Commissioners and Commission officials as witnesses at parliamentary committees of inquiry is another favoured method of tying the Commission into Parliament's agenda.

The Parliament and the Commission in the context of Intergovernmental Conferences (IGCs)

Parliament remains excluded from the negotiations within IGCs. In the case of the 1985 IGC, Parliament was obliged to rely heavily on the Commission, not only to state its case and fight for its views, but also to report back on the state of progress in negotiations. Parliament was frustrated by its lack of direct influence, by its spectator's role, by the fact that the Commission was directly involved, and by its suspicion that the Commission did not always defend the Parliament's case as much as Parliament would have liked. In the case of the 1990–1991 IGCs on Economic and Monetary Union and on Political Union, Parliament exploited further avenues of influence, but was again excluded from the negotiations themselves. However, the conference process was more open, and Parliament was in a better position to compare its position with that of the Commission. There were actually many minor differences, and other more substantial differences surfaced during the negotiations, although the two institutions were agreed on the general constitutional thrust. There was one fundamental difference: Parliament called for a 'limited', but nevertheless automatic, right of initiative. The Commission could not accept such an inroad, however circumscribed, believing its sole right of initiative to be a constitutional prerogative vital to the good functioning of the Community's institutional balance and its legislative machinery. Parliament seemed unsettled by this concrete recognition of a substantive constitutional difference between it and its natural ally. Parliament would probably uncomplainingly accept the Commission's right to its own views on constitutional reform, were it to enjoy the same participatory role in IGCs, a development which the Commission has always vociferously supported. Until this occurs, future IGCs are likely to find the Commission in the same uneasy and split role, as it attempts simultaneously to defend Parliament's potentially divergent views and its own constitutional prerogatives.

As individual sections of this Chapter have outlined, the Treaty on European Union created a plethora of procedures, with a variety of permutations concerning the voting requirements in Council and Parliament. Five basic legislative procedures now exist, together with four variants on the conciliation procedure. And Parliament has also been granted significant new competences and powers over the Commission in other fields. Three areas are of particular relevance: Parliament's right to approve the Commission President and the College; its right to request initiatives; and the practical results of the principle of subsidiarity.

A major advance has been Parliament's right of approval of the Commission and its President. The nomination of Jacques Santer in July 1994 illustrates well the potential of the new procedure. Maastricht amended the process for the nomination of the Commission and its President in four important ways. First, from January 1995, the term of office of the Commission will be extended from four to five years, and will thus be synchronised with the five-year term of office of the Parliament. Secondly, although the Member State governments will continue (by unanimity) to nominate the President of the Commission, they must first consult the Parliament. Thirdly, governments will no longer nominate the other members of the Commission by unanimity but, rather, in consultation with the nominee for President. Lastly, the President and the other members thus nominated will be subject as a body to a vote of approval by the Parliament, and only then appointed, by unanimity, by the Member State governments. Such changes had long been sought by both Commission and Parliament, and should be seen in the context both of Parliament's retention of its power to censure the College and the increasing importance of the annual legislative planning exercise. As the former Commission Secretary General put it:

"These measures will lead to the accentuation of the political character of the Commission. Very soon the preliminary approval of its membership by the Parliament will be the decisive factor; the final appointment by the governments will retain only a formal character." (Noël 1992)

The Treaty on European Union provides that Parliament "may, acting by a majority of its members, request the Commission to submit any appropriate proposal on matters on which it considers that a Community act is required for the purpose of implementing (the) Treaty". The provision puts Parliament on an equal footing with the Council (EEC Article 152). However, Parliament recognises that resort to the right must be sparing and realistic. To this end, it has introduced a series of filtering mechanisms. By restricting itself in this way, Parliament hopes to exert maximum pressure on the Commission to accede to its requests. For its part, the Commission will respond as it does in the case of Council requests; i.e. a request would receive serious consideration, but a formal proposal would not follow automatically.

Article 3b of the Treaty enshrines the principle of subsidiarity. The December 1992 Edinburgh Council spelled out the manner in which the principle would be implemented. A detailed annex set out a number of 'procedures and practices', three of which are of particular relevance to this analysis of the Commission's role in relation to Parliament. First, the Commission undertook to broaden the pre-legislative consultation process through a more systematic use of consultation documents and, in particular, Green Papers. Second, each Commission proposal contains a recital justifying the relevance of the initiative with regard to the principle of subsidiarity and, additionally, the accompanying explanatory memorandum may give further details. Even before the implementation of Maastricht, Parliament's legislative committees were scrutinising Commission proposals for compatibility with the principle of subsidiarity, and this practice has been consolidated now that the Treaty has been implemented. The Commission notified the Edinburgh Council that, "notably following debates in Parliament" it intended to revise a number of its pending proposals so as to reduce "excessive detail". However, it also indicated that it would be "tougher about rejecting amendments proposed by the Council and Parliament". Thirdly, the Commission is obliged to submit an annual report to the European Council and the Parliament on the application of the subsidiarity principle, a provision that will further intensify Parliament's scrutiny of the Commission and its proposals.

Conclusions: constitutional pragmatism

With the Treaty on European Union, inter-institutional agreements have come of age and a new symbiosis is emerging between the Commission and the Parliament. Article 138c of the Treaty provides that "the detailed provisions governing the exercise of [Parliament's] right of inquiry shall be determined by common accord of the European Parliament, the Council and the Commission". An annex to the conclusions of the Edinburgh Council stated that "an agreement on the balanced implementation of Article 3b [on subsidiarity] shall be sought . . . between the European Parliament, the Council and the Commission". Another annex, on future financing, called upon the Council "to reach agreement with the Commission and the European Parliament on a revised Inter-institutional Agreement". In all these areas, inter-institutional agreements have either been agreed or are being negotiated. In addition, inter-institutional agreements have been reached on the implementation of the new conciliation procedure and on the parliamentary Ombudsman, and an inter-institutional declaration on democracy, transparency and subsidiarity was signed in October 1993. Parliament has also called for inter-institutional agreements on Economic and Monetary Union, the Common Foreign and Security Policy, and cooperation in the fields of justice and home affairs. Thus, the detailed implementation of the Maastricht Treaty has so far involved at least four, and may possibly involve several more, IIAs. In each case, the Commission's precise role depends very much on its stance in the IIA negotiations, which is necessarily cooperative and generally positive.

The Treaty on European Union thus establishes new procedures, extends the scope of old procedures, and institutes mixtures of both. It extends the Community's competences, and hence those of the Commission and the Parliament. It provides for strict procedural deadlines. Commission and Parliament now have vested, mutual interests in the closer cooperation evidently necessary to make the new procedures work. Should they fail, or work only imperfectly, the Commission's legislative proposals and hence the Parliament's legislative powers may be lost. Thus, the importance of inter-institutional fora, such as the 'Neunreither Group', of internal coordination mechanisms, such as the GAP and the SEA unit within the Commission's SG, and of key institutional players, particularly the Commissioner responsible for relations with the Parliament, will be significantly increased.

A number of general observations and conclusions flow from the analysis in this Chapter. First, relations between the Commission and the Parliament are largely managed within a framework of rules and conventions lying outside and beyond the Treaties, with a resultant premium on mutual understanding and goodwill. Second, through a broad range of competences and contexts, Parliament is functionally dependent upon the Commission and its resources. As a result of this functional dependence and cooperative symbiosis, Parliament's theoretical constitutional independence is heavily compromised, Parliament frequently preferring to sacrifice the weight of its institutional prerogatives in favour of shorter-term policy aims. Third, it is instructive that the two institutions do manage to cooperate amicably over the range of procedures and competences; in other words, plurality and collegiality can co-exist. The SEA negotiators' faith in the institutions' capacity to cooperate was justified. Last, in the context of the two institutions' shared federal vocation, Parliament is obliged to recognise that the Commission must be retained as an ally even at the cost of shorter-term objectives.

In the 'teeth-cutting' period immediately following the SEA's implementation, the then Commissioner responsible for relations with the EP, Peter Sutherland, gave a description of the Commission's position which is just as valid after the implementation of the Maastricht Treaty. He declared that:

> "The Commission's general approach consists of seeking to improve the decision-making process, of improving the balance of powers in the inter-institutional triangle, while preserving the Commission's autonomy and independence." (Sutherland 1988)

He further pointed out that:

> "We see no contradiction between this process of integrating Parliament into the decision-making process in a responsible and constructive way and longer-term institutional changes. We do not know where the institutional debate may be going. We should guard against a *priori* views or stereotypes. It is quite possible that the new model European Parliament, which will in any event be different from the sum of the national parliamentary traditions in our Member States, will take a *sui generis* form. Perhaps it will even owe more to the American model of an autonomous parliamentary institution, independent from the executive. Who knows? We should not close our minds." (*ibid.*)

References and bibliography

Arp, H. (1992) 'The European Parliament in European Community Environmental Policy', EUI Working Paper, 92/13. Florence: European University Institute.

Bardi, L. (1984) 'Members of the European Parliament: Experiences, Attitudes and Perceptions', in Reif, K. (ed.) *q.v.*

Bieber, R. (1992) *Das Verfahrensrecht von Verfassungsorganen. Ein Beitrag zur Theorie des inner-und interorgangemeinschaftlichen Rechtsetzung in der Europäischen Gemeinschaft, im Staatsrecht und Völkereicht*, Baden-Baden: Nomos.

Boumans, E. and Norbart, M. (1989) 'The European Parliament and Human Rights', *Netherlands Quarterly of Human Rights*.

Bradley, St C. K. (1992) 'Comitology and the law; through a glass darkly', *Common Market Law Review*, 29.

Commission (1989) *Les finances publiques de la Communauté*, Luxembourg: Official Publications of the EC.

Commission (1991) 'Conférences inter-gouvernementales; contributions de la Commission', *Bulletin des Communautés européennes*, Supplement 2/91.

Corbett, R. (1986) 'Testing the New Procedures: the European Parliament's First Experiences with its New 'Single Act' Powers', *Journal of Common Market Studies*, XXVII (4), pp. 359–72.

Corbett, R. (1992) "The Intergovernmental Conference on Political Union', *Journal of Common Market Studies*, XXX (3), pp. 271–98.

Earnshaw, D. and Judge, D. (1993) 'The European Parliament and the Sweetners Directive; from Footnote to Inter-institutional Conflict', *Journal of Common Market Studies*, 31 (1), pp. 103–16.

European Parliament (1993) *Rules of Procedure*, 8th (provisional) edition.

Fitzmaurice, J. (1988) "An Analysis of the European Community's Cooperation Procedure', *Journal of Common Market Studies*, XXVI (4), pp. 389–400.

Harris, G. (1990) *The Dark Side of Europe*, Edinburgh: Edinburgh University Press.

Jacobs, F. and Corbett, R. (1990) *The European Parliament*, Harlow: Longman.

Jenkins, R. (1989) *European Diary*, London: Collins.

Jenkins, R. (1992) *A Life at the Centre*, London: Pan.

Keohane, R. and Hoffman, S. (eds.) (1991) *The New European Community*, Boulder: Westview.

Louis, J. V. (1989) *Le parlement Européen dans l'évolution institutionelle*, Brussels: Editions de l'université de Bruxelles.

Nicoll, W. (1986) 'La procédure de concertation', *Revue du Marché Commun*, No. 293.

Nicoll, W. (1986) 'Les procédures Luns/Westerterp', *Revue du Marché Commun*, No. 300.

Nicoll, W. (1987) 'Qu'est-ce que la comitologie?', *Revue du Marché Commun*, No. 306.

Nicoll, W. (1988) 'L'accord inter-institutionel', *Revue du Marché Commun*, No. 319.

Noël, E. (1988) *Working Together: the Institutions of the European Community*, Luxembourg: European Communities.

Noël, E. (1992) 'Reflections on the Maastricht Treaty', *Government and Opposition*, 27 (2).

Pryce, R. (ed.) (1987) *The Dynamics of European Union*, London: Routledge.

Reif, K. (ed.) (1984) *European Elections: 1979/81 and 1984*, Berlin: Quorum.

Spence, D. (1991) "Enlargement Without Accession: the EC's Response to German Unification', RIIA Discussion Paper 36, London: RIIA.

Sutherland, Peter (1988) 'Commission–Parliament relations in the legislative procedure', speech delivered to a symposium at the Université Libre de Bruxelles, 10.12.88.

Tugendhat, C. (1987) *Making Sense of Europe*, London: Pelican.

Vallance, E. and Davies, E. (1986) *Women of Europe, Women MEPs and Equality Policy*, Cambridge: CUP.

Westlake, M. (1990) 'The Origin and Development of the Question Time Procedure in the European Parliament', EUI Working Paper 90/4, Florence: EUI.

Westlake, M. (1991) 'The Community Express Service: the Rapid Passage of Emergency Legislation on German Unification', *Common Market Law Review*, 28.

Westlake, M. (1994) *Britain's Emerging Euro-Elite? The British in the European Parliament, 1979–1992*, Aldershot: Dartmouth.

Westlake, M. (1994) *The Parliament and the Commission: Partners and Rivals in the European Policy-Making Process*, London: Butterworths.

10. The Commission and external relations

Michael Smith

Introduction

The European Community was from its inception an international phenomenon, and the development of a complex set of external relations has been an integral part of its evolution. Many authors have attributed a major role in the establishment of the Community both to general international conditions such as the Cold War and the Bretton Woods system, and to specific international forces; American foreign policy being the prime example (Milward 1984; Smith 1994). Since its foundation, the Community in its various guises has assumed an ever-growing weight in the world economy, and has become a participant in a wide range of international economic institutions. Indeed, the very existence of the Community has become a central element in the policy concerns of most countries in the international arena. There is a great deal of *prima facie* evidence, therefore, that external relations are an inevitable and growing part of the Community's existence. It has even been argued that they played a central role in the generation of pressures for the 1992 programme (Smith 1992, 1994; Fielding 1991; Nicoll and Salmon 1990; Cameron 1992).

From this initial observation flows a number of more specific issues and problems, many of them directly linked to the role of the Commission as a source of and channel for policy. Although the Treaty of Paris setting up the ECSC contained no explicit Community role in the external field, reserving that domain for the Member States (Kaptein and van Themat 1990), the Treaty of Rome not only has such provision but also gives the Commission a pivotal function. Successive policy developments and treaties, culminating in the agreements reached at Maastricht in 1991, have confirmed the role of the Commission, but have also raised a number of enduring questions about its relationship both to other Community institutions and to the outside world (Devuyst 1992; Fielding 1991).

Many of the problems faced by the Commission in the pursuit of external relations are effectively 'boundary problems'. The development of complex linkages in the world economy has made it quite difficult for even the most monolithic of states to say where 'domestic' policy ends and 'external' policy begins. A related problem is that of the boundary between 'economic' issues and 'political' or 'security' issues. In the post-Cold War era, it is no longer clear (if indeed it ever was) how this line can be drawn and maintained. As a result, external relations issues increasingly cut across sectors and raise unexpected problems of coordination or action (Smith and Woolcock 1993). This is as true for the European Union as it is for the Member States, but in addition to these broad problems of international life in the1990s, the Commission and the Community have a number of other boundary issues with which to contend. The first is the question of competence. Where does the writ of the Commission run, and how are disputes or tensions between the Commission and Member States handled? Closely related to this question is that of institutions. How are the potentially competing interests of the Commission, the Council, Parliament and the Court of Justice to be reconciled in the cause of coherent Community external action? And even within the Commission itself, any clear allocation of policy areas, with DG I holding the key responsibilities for all external economic relations matters, has been challenged by the linkages between sectors and interests. Indeed, DG I's position has been further complicated by the creation of DG IA, the Directorate General responsible for external *political* relations, including responsibility for the external delegations. The changing nature of the international arena has drawn the Commission inexorably into more 'political' areas, where the tensions between Union and Member State policies are closer to the surface.

This Chapter explores the ways in which these developments have modified both the role of the Commission and its relations with other EU institutions and the Member States. It begins by exploring the foundations for external policy laid down in the Treaty of Rome and its successors and the resulting administrative structures in the Commission. Secondly, it identifies the key elements in policy formation and the ways in which the Commission carries out its responsibilities alongside other EU bodies.Thirdly, it looks at the substance of policy and Commission involvement in a number of issue areas and institutional contexts. Fourthly, it examines the changes in external relations, and in the agenda for Union action, which have produced new challenges for the 1990s, including enlargement. Finally, it assesses the ways in which the structure and roles of the Commission have been or might be adapted to face the changing context and the demands of the new agenda.

The foundations of Commission responsibility for external relations

The Treaty of Rome and its successors gave a central role in external relations to the Commission. The Treaties confer express powers in the area of Common Commercial Policy (CCP) in Articles 113–114 EEC in conjunction with Article 228 (Devuyst 1992, Fielding 1991). Here, the Commission, in principle, has exclusive competence for an area of policy which arises directly from the creation of a customs union and the operation of the Common External Tariff, though it is increasingly unclear how the boundaries around the Common Commercial Policy can be drawn or maintained. Although the European Coal and Steel Community (1951) had a number of international implications, particularly in terms of the trade in steel, there was no explicit treatment of policy-making for external relations at Community level in the Treaty of Paris. Over the history of the Community as a whole, this 'gap' in the Treaty of Paris has caused a number of uncertainties, not least because of the sensitive nature of industrial policy and competition policy and their growing international ramifications (Mény and Wright 1987). Thus, it was with the Treaty of Rome that the elaboration of a framework for external policy was undertaken in a conscious and systematic fashion. The core of the Treaty as it affects external relations is to be found in Articles 110–116, which set out the principles of the CCP and some of the mechanisms through which it is to be conducted (Devuyst 1992, Nicoll and Salmon 1990). Though the Treaty on European Union (TEU) makes some amendments, the core principles remain the same (see Annex A for texts).

As Devuyst says, "The Common Commercial Policy is the logical corollary of the customs union set up by the EEC Treaty"(1992, p. 68). The establishment of a common external tariff, and thus of a boundary between the internal free trade area and the external world, necessitates common approaches among the members to the issue of international trade, and the development of instruments with which to pursue and defend Community interests. In the case of the EEC, the establishment of the Common Commercial Policy was accompanied by another logical but not self-evident step: the allocation of competence to the European Commission, and the understanding that in matters affecting the CCP this competence was to be exclusive. From the outset, therefore, the Commission was given the power to conduct a common policy, but, while the assumption was that of exclusive competence, there were other aspects of the Treaty which were bound to make this a source of tension and potential conflict (Devuyst 1992, Fielding 1991).

Articles 110–116 of the EEC Treaty set out both the broad goals of the CCP and a number of specific provisions. It is important to note that the aims set out in Article 110 were cast at least partly in terms not of Community interests, but of those of the international economy as a whole. Thus the Community set out not only to express the external needs of its members, but also:

"to contribute, in the common interest, to the harmonious development of world trade, the progressive abolition of restrictions on international trade and the lowering of customs barriers."

In pursuit of these aims, it was clear that the Community's 'internal' policies could come into conflict with its actual or potential international obligations. As a result, balancing the internal needs of the Community and the demands of the external world has always been a central task facing the Commission in external relations (see below). It has thus been argued that the very foundations of the EEC contained a fault line which was to create considerable difficulty for the Commission (Taylor 1983).

A number of articles in the Treaty of Rome, such as Article 111, dealt with the actions to be taken during the transitional period before the establishment of the full customs union, and they have withered away as time has passed. The Treaty on European Union formally eliminated a number of them. Central to the whole edifice of the CCP, though, was Article 113. This committed the signatories to the elaboration of common principles for trade policy and included a (non-exhaustive) list of actions and issues covered by the CCP. It was in this Article also that the competence of the Commission was firmly established, alongside provisions for qualified majority voting in the Council in the CCP area and the arrangements enabling the Commission to take on a major international negotiating role, for example in the GATT (along with Article 229). The strength of the grant of competence, allied to a certain vagueness about the range of commercial policy areas in which it was to be exercised, has proven a major boon to the Commission as an international actor. But it has also led to tensions with the Council of Ministers and with individual Member States.

While Article 113 was thus the centrepiece of the external relations pursued by the Community, it was supplemented (some would say, qualified) by Article 115, which provided for action to be taken where economic difficulties arose for one or more Member State. Initially, during the transitional period, it also allowed Member governments within the Community to take action to protect themselves in cases of emergency. (This was amended under the TEU whereby governments are to seek authorisation from the Commission to take such action — see Annex A.) Article 116 further committed the parties to common action in the framework of international economic institutions as they affected the common market and the customs union. (This was repealed by the TEU.) But it was Article 113 which mattered, and on which the Commission erected a complex web of international commercial diplomacy.

A number of other articles in the Treaty of Rome bore on the conduct of external relations under what is known as "implied powers" where internal competence serves as a basis for external competence. Thus, Article 228 gave the Community the general competence to conclude international agreements, including commercial agreements. Other articles, such as those on the common transport policy (Articles 74–84 EEC), appeared to confer the capacity to negotiate internationally, and to arrive at regulatory agreements on the basis of Community action. There was some uncertainty in these cases, though, about the precise extent of Commission competence. It was not clear whether the essentially internal concerns of the common market could give rise to external competencies comparable to those explicitly conferred by Article 113. This question of 'implied competence' has not been eliminated. Indeed, the development of ever more intense linkages between 'internal' and 'external' issues relating to the Community has given rise to further uncertainties in areas such as competition law or transport policy (Close 1990; Kaptein and van Themat 1990).

The principle of external competence arising from internal competence is based on a ruling of the European Court of Justice in Case 22/70, *Commission v. Council* (1971) ECR 263 on the European Road Transport Agreement. Here, the Court held that treaty-making powers were not confined to the issues covered by Articles 113 and 228. It held that there were implied powers to conclude treaties with third countries, which "may flow from other provisions of the Treaty and from steps taken, within the framework of these provisions, by the Community institutions". Thus, where common rules affecting internal policies were laid down, the Member States no longer had the right to conclude treaties with non-Member States.

The judgment has given rise to some tension between the Commission and some Member States who wished to restrict the definition of "common rules" to areas where binding Community legislation exists, as opposed to the non-binding instruments of Council declarations, resolutions and recommendations often used in such fields as health, culture and education. The Commission traditionally had a more relaxed view of the potential scope of implied powers and it was a moot point whether the Court would uphold the Commission's or, say, the UK's or France's view on the matter. The problem has been that the Community clearly has competence if there is an indisputable set of internal rules in an area which becomes subject to a Community treaty with a third party. But there are preliminary forms of agreement, for example, in negotiating mandates (discussed below), where the law is unclear as to how binding an agreed policy line becomes in terms of its limitation of an individual state's ability to diverge from an agreed Community position before negotiations with third parties are actually concluded. The apparent breaking of ranks by the French government in the final stage of negotiations in the GATT in 1993 is a case in point. It is, of course, different if there is no agreed Community line; when, for example, the Council has not yet taken a decision on a Commission proposal for a negotiating mandate, there is arguably no binding obligation on the Member States to depart from their own national position. If, however, Member States conduct negotiations or enter into agreements properly within the competence of the Community and which could inhibit or prejudice future Community action in a given field, there may be a case for recourse to the Court for a ruling under Article 228 or, at the very least, grounds for a Commission proposal for a Community negotiating mandate in that area. The room for debate about the Commission's rights and obligations in this area is thus considerable.

An important area of 'express powers' in which external relations formed part of the Treaty of Rome was that of associations between the Community and third states or with international organisations. Article 238 has been used as the basis for the development of a wide-ranging network of treaties and cooperative ventures. Among these, the most salient are those concerning the African, Caribbean and Pacific countries in the context of the Lomé Conventions, the EFTA countries (now largely translated into the provisions for the European Economic Area), a number of Mediterranean countries, and the countries of Eastern and Central Europe, particularly since the break-up of the Soviet bloc after 1989. In a broad sense also, the Community provisions for enlargement and the admission of new members can be seen as a form of external relations power. But it must be noted that in neither of these areas (association and enlargement) is the Commission given exclusive competence. While its 'opinion' is the start of the legislative process for enlargement and it can propose action and provide opinions and information in these areas, the essential powers lie with the Member States acting in the Council of Ministers. Action in respect of external associations has also given rise to a wide range of 'mixed agreements', in which the negotiation and the implementation of international accords are subject to both Commission and Member State participation (Kaptein and van Themat 1990; Neuwahl 1990).

'Mixed agreements' occur where the subject matter of an international agreement falls partly within Member State and partly within Community competence. Here, both the Community and the Member States are signatories to agreements. The Commission's view has been that such mixed agreements do not adequately assert the Community's identity, but the European Court has not always supported the Commission. Its Ruling 1/78(IAEA Physical Protection Convention (1978) ECR 2151) and its Opinion 1/78 (Rubber Agreement (1979) ECR 2871) have confirmed the validity of mixed agreements, particularly where individual states provide finance in the framework of such agreements. The Commission and the Member States therefore agreed to suspend judgment on competence on commodity agreements within the UNCTAD Integrated Programme of Commodities and for Community representations with regard to customs arrangements and negotiations within the OECD on accounting standards. Both the Community and the Member States are signatories.

The important point here is not so much the apparent ambiguity in areas of mixed competence as the revealing nature of potential sources of tension over boundary disputes between the Commission and the Member States. Community competence is not a static concept. As the European Union gains competence in new areas, such as health, culture and education under the TEU, so the scope for Commission responsibility is expanded; its role in external relations as representative of the Community interest and as negotiator in international treaties is extended and enhanced.

In order to put flesh on the bones of Article 113 and other grants of competence, the Community acquired as it grew a complex set of trade policy instruments. The most notable among these are anti-dumping measures, rules of origin, including such provisions as those on 'local content', and instruments designed to counteract unfair trading practices (Fielding 1991). Clearly, the growth and integration of the Community market, and the stakes attached to access to that market, have necessitated defensive measures. At times, these have led to accusations of 'fortress Europe' policies, particularly from the USA and Japan, but it is not clear that EC policies were any more or less restrictive than those of other major industrial trading areas. From the point of view of this chapter, the key factor is that these regulatory and other instruments emanate from the essential grant of trade policy competence to the Commission, and thus are administered by it.

In order to back up its actions and to sustain its capacity to exercise the competence granted to it, the Commission has developed a substantial bureaucratic and diplomatic machinery. In Brussels itself, the key focus is DG I (External Economic Relations) of the Commission which has the lead responsibility for economic relations with non-EU countries. Internally, DG I is structured in accordance with the main concerns of the CCP, although in 1993, there were significant structural changes following the bifurcation of economic and political responsibilities in external relations and the increase from one to three Commissioners concerned (see Annex B and also Chapter 11). As is the case in many a national foreign office, there are both geographical and functional sub-divisions to DG I, with particular sections established to handle major international negotiations.

Despite the neatness of the formal structure, the interpenetration of 'external' and 'internal' policy concerns has meant that almost every part of the Commission has an interest in external policy of some kind. In addition, action taken for what appear to be purely 'internal' purposes can have important external policy ramifications. In recent years, the development of the world economy and the European internal market has magnified this tendency. The role of DG I in internal coordination and the achievement of coherent external policy has therefore grown apace. The Single European Act of 1986 explicitly provided, as did the TEU, for the maintenance of 'consistency' between different areas of EU activity. External relations is the area *par excellence* in which this is a central need. But guaranteeing consistency is not easy. In some areas the status of DG I is rather like that of the US Trade Representative (USTR) in Washington, trying to coordinate and moderate the needs and interests of powerful internal baronies without possessing a great deal of coercive power (Destler 1992).

Outside the Community, DG I developed an extensive mechanism of international representation and reporting, responsibility for which has now been transferred to DG IA. While some of this relates to specific negotiations and has a temporary air — even when they extend over a period of some years — there is now an elaborate permanent network reminiscent of many a country's diplomatic service. Indeed, some of the 119 missions in overseas capitals have the formal status of embassies headed by ambassadors, as in Washington and Tokyo. Other missions are attached to international institutions such as the OECD, the GATT or the UN, where they play an important continuous negotiation role as well as that of representation. Equally important are the many diplomatic missions accredited to the Community (effectively the Commission) itself. By 1994, there were 105 of these, and their presence produced a diplomatic network supplementary to, and often replacing the traditional interstate network. No clearer indication of the latter trend could be found than the displacement in mid-1993 of the British Ambassador to Belgium from his official elegant residence in central Brussels by the UK Permanent Representative (Ambassador) to the EC.

The foundations of Commission action and mechanisms in the realm of external relations are thus not merely those which are found in the treaties, extensive as they are. These 'constitutional' powers are supplemented by the growth of a bureaucratic and diplomatic network and by the perceived status of the Commission as a focus of attention for outsiders, both at governmental and non-governmental levels. The Community has established a major presence in the international arena, and the Commission is central to this presence.

Policy formation and implementation

As with policy foundations, discussing the Commission's role in external policy formation requires some key distinctions. Perhaps the most important general distinction is that between the formal role of the Commission as set out in the treaties and administrative procedures, and the informal and often highly political process by which the Commission enters the policy arena. Another important area of distinction is that between policy formation and implementation. In each case, there are several stages and contexts to be considered. Here, as in the earlier discussion, the focus will largely be on the development of policy and policy-making before the radical changes of the1990s, with the aim of establishing a framework for later consideration of those changes and their implications.

Articles 110–116 of the Treaty of Rome set out not simply the competencies of the Commission, but also key aspects of the procedures to be followed. As in other areas of policy, the intermingling of Commission, Council and Member State roles is typical of the external relations domain. Under Article 113, the Commission makes recommendations to the Council concerning the negotiation of trade agreements and the Council then adopts a 'directive' by qualified majority. This sets the mandate and the general framework for the negotiations. When the negotiations are concluded, the Commission as negotiator has the power to initial the agreement, but the Council formally 'concludes' the agreement, acting by qualified majority. Thus the multilateral negotiations undertaken during the Uruguay Round of the GATT saw the Commission as the sole formal negotiator for the Community, with the Member States as close supervisors both in the context of the GATT itself and in the Council.

The 'watchdog' role of Member States is expressed particularly through the '113 Committee', which constitutes a standing check on the negotiators and is in a sense the guardian of the negotiating mandate. This situation is not unlike the position in the USA, where Congress produces legislation to empower the Executive to negotiate, but has the right to be kept informed of the negotiations and also the ultimate power to approve or reject any deals made. It could also be argued that the result in policy formation terms is rather like that in the USA, with the constant possibility of rigidity and the difficulty of changing the mandate once it is agreed. Clearly, this is particularly a factor in the case of long-term and large-scale negotiations, where circumstances (even Member State governments) and the mandate may change, and where there are complex linkages between the various items on the agenda (see below).

In addition to the negotiating roles set out in and developed under Article 113, the Commission plays a central role in the monitoring of external policy, and in coping with commercial disputes. The two activities are often closely linked. For example, the Commission's monitoring of trade practices by other countries can lead to anti-dumping findings, to the application of measures under the rules of origin, or to claims of unfair trading practices against a variety of outsiders. Here, the role of the Commission is a regulatory and at times coercive rather than a negotiating one, and it is not surprising that its activities have sometimes drawn a certain amount of criticism, not only from outsiders but also from some Community members. Rather than a general negotiating directive, the instruments of policy can be punitive duties or restrictions, imposed by the Commission though subject to approval by the Council. Perhaps the most obviously punitive or coercive measures in Community external policy are those entailed in commercial sanctions against a range of countries, often for explicitly political purposes. Here, Article 113 can again be used as the basis, although the treaties also provide a number of other routes with less exclusive Commission competence (such as Article 224).

Moving outside the CCP, there is a range of other policy areas in which the Commission has more or less exclusive competence, and which have external relations effects. Many areas of common policy have inescapable external dimensions. The most dramatic, perhaps, has been the Common Agricultural Policy (CAP), which is built at least in part on the exercise of Community Preference, and thus on variable levies on imports in what is an increasingly global world food market. From the outset, the CAP meshed uneasily with the CCP, adding a major set of constraints to the external trade policies of the Community. Particularly in relations with the USA, there has been a constant thread of conflict, which has spread to influence the multilateral trading system more generally. The Commission is deeply implicated as the guardian both of the CAP and of the CCP, but the balance has at times been very difficult to strike. Although less dramatic, the development of common policies in fisheries and air transport has also led to the need for Commission diplomacy and at times to intense conflict with other countries and organisations.

Outside the common policy arena, the external relations of the Community are less securely within the control of the Commission, and the mixed nature of policy and negotiation becomes apparent. From the early days of the Community, it has been possible for member countries to conclude their own treaties of economic cooperation, reflecting the fact that though the Community may act (for example under Article 228), it has no exclusive competence. In the autumn of 1993, it was reported that the Commission was anxious to extend its competence, given the persistence of bilateral cooperation agreements which could be used by Member States to circumvent Community measures. The stimulus for this pressure was the attempted evasion by Germany of sanctions imposed by the Community in a dispute with the USA over public procurement regimes (Barber and Gardner 1993b). Article 228, used as the basis for a wide range of economic cooperation and assistance agreements, requires the Commission and the Council to receive an opinion from the European Parliament. More specific are the provisions under Article 238 for association agreements. Here, the Commission and the Member States are entangled in mixed agreements, and the Parliament has the right to give its assent by a majority vote of all its members.

It is clear from this review that the role of the Commission is determined not merely by the formal treaty provisions but also by the nature of the issues at stake and the attitudes of other EU institutions. Even in areas of common policy, it is possible for the Council and for individual Council members to act as a brake on progress. In other domains, it is clear that there is negotiation within the Community as well as between the Community and other entities. The issues are often essentially domestic or parochial interests in one or more Member States, producing what can be seen as a multilevel 'game' with complex stakes and rules. The Commission is by no means disadvantaged in this game, but its expanding area of concern has placed a severe strain on its administrative and political resources (Ludlow 1992).

The process of policy formation and implementation in external relations is thus a political as well as a technical or administrative one. This is not a new insight, but it does contrast sharply with a view based largely or solely on the treaties, on competence in the legal sense and on the assumption that implementation follows logically from the agreement of measures. Indeed, in this respect, it intersects with one of the central themes about the Commission: the perception that the Commission is not a good implementer, and that it is hamstrung both by its lack of human resources and by constraints exercised by the Council. Moreover, the political/administrative mix highlights problems of the establishment of boundaries around policy domains. It has often been unclear outside the core of the CCP what the competence of the

Commission is or ought to be, and the Commission itself has had to try and redefine the scope of commercial policy as a means of establishing a presence in developing areas such as air transport.

As to coordination between the Commission and the Member States, where Community competence is clear there are few problems. Tensions arise when decisions have to be taken about whether the Commission, the Presidency or individual Member States have policy responsibility. Sometimes, the Community is represented by a bicephalous delegation. Here, the Presidency and the Commission speak on behalf of the Community. Alternatively, a single delegation composed of Commission and Member State officials may exist, though usually the Commission delegate is the spokesman. In a third variant, the Commission heads up a delegation supported by representatives from the Member States. The Commission's strategy in this area is to seek to extend its own competence where possible. It does this by building precedents, for example, where preambles to its own texts reflect previous Council declarations in non-related areas, or by using implied competence in one area as a precedent for acquiring competence in a new area.

The political nature of the Commission's role, and of the context within which it operates, is further underlined by the range of influences to which the Commission is subjected or with which it interacts in the area of external relations. It has already been noted that national governments retain a strong watching brief on commercial policy, and that in the context of organisations such as the GATT and Organisation for Economic Cooperation and Development (OECD), they are present alongside the Commission negotiators — a situation which can lead to confusion about who is really representing the Community (Devuyst 1992). In addition, the Commission is the centre of attraction for a large range of non-member governments and other external lobbies, some of them with a great deal of expertise and clout. In EC/US relations, for example, the Commission finds itself dealing with the US Mission to the Community, with the US government itself in a number of different contexts, with trade associations, with state governments, with multinational firms and with individuals with particular interests or grievances. This makes the generation and implementation of policy a matter of the greatest complexity, but also a matter quintessentially of politics rather than administration.

Quite apart from the range of influences on Community policy and Commission policy-making in external relations, there is an elaborate set of legal and institutional contexts for the conduct of negotiations and the pursuit of commercial disputes. Some of these are set up by the Community in the context, for example, of the Lomé Conventions or other association arrangements. Others are bilateral, as with the working groups set up under the Transatlantic Declaration and other agreements with industrial countries. Still others are multilateral, ranging from international commodity agreements of many kinds through other regional arrangements and up to the global organisations, chief among them the GATT. The Commission can often find itself negotiating on a wide range of fronts at any given time, thereby increasing the strain on its limited resources and diffusing its attention with potentially damaging results.

Given the intense dependence of the EU on international trade of all kinds, it is clear that policy-making and implementation in external relations are the highest of high politics, while at the same time being complex and technical in nature. As Nuttall points out in Chapter 11, there is also an intimate linkage between external relations, 'foreign policy' and 'security policy' in the changing conditions of the 1990s. Here, it is important to register the intermeshing of different policy styles in the Commission's external relations activity. As pointed out by Peters (1992) and Mazey and Richardson in Chapter 7, the Commission finds itself at the intersection of several types of policy network, and has generated its own distinctive brand of 'bureaucratic politics' as a result. External relations is subject to this trend as are other areas of policy, but one crucial difference is the intersection of external relations with almost every other area of Commission concern. This is reflected in the substantive agenda of Commission activity in the external policy domain.

The evolving policy agenda

The discussion so far has concentrated on the background to policy-making and the policy process itself. But the substance of policy needs to be explored before we turn to the radical changes since 1989 in the role of the Commission. In examining the policy agenda, two issues are of immediate concern: first, the ways in which Community, and particularly Commission, activity is constrained by external forces; and second, the ways in which institutional frameworks operate to focus and channel these forces. The Commission's position at the intersection of a range of economic, political and institutional networks gives rise to a range of specific problems in handling the evolving agenda of policy.

The central thrust of Community external relations towards trade and commercial diplomacy and the key role of the Commission makes it natural that much of the activity occurs in the context of the GATT and, to a lesser extent, the OECD. Here, the Commission functions to a large extent in the same way as any of the other members (or Contracting Parties). In fact, it is not the same as the others, since the Community Member States maintain individual membership even while the Commission speaks and negotiates for them. The issue of 'voice' is thus ambiguous, and there have been a number of episodes in which the Community voice has not made itself heard in a united and effective way. On the whole, though, the pursuit of the CCP has been a matter for the Commission acting in GATT, while at the same time keeping an eye on its 'domestic' constituency among the Member States (Devuyst 1992). Indeed, Sir Leslie Fielding, former Director General in DG I, in his work on the Community's external relations, has concluded that the Community (and thus the Commission) has played a vital role in the continuing existence and growth of the GATT (Fielding 1991).

Given the fundamental importance of the GATT to the Community and to the Commission, it is important to distinguish between two types of 'agenda items' arising from it. On the one hand, the GATT is a central mechanism for dealing with specific disputes and crises within the world trading system. Thus, the Commission has found itself over the years engaged in a very wide range of negotiations arising from frictions, either generated by the development of the Community itself or by the policies of its major trading partners. Some of the most notable have arisen in relations with the USA, and particularly in agriculture, from the so-called 'chicken war' of the 1960s to the cheese, citrus, grain and pasta 'wars' of the 1970s and 1980s. Alongside these have been disputes over industrial products in declining sectors such as steel or in high-technology developments such as that centring on the European Airbus (Fielding 1991). This is the type of conflict in which no-one is without sin, particularly the USA and the Community, and it has increasingly extended to include Japan as the competitive interdependence of the world's three greatest industrial powers has intensified. The Commission, as the guardian of Community instruments in anti-dumping, rules of origin and fair trade, has incurred its share of odium, not only for the policies adopted, but also for its inability to demonstrate what to others is the necessary flexibility in their implementation. This reflects to a certain extent the structure of policy-making in the Community as a whole, and it is a problem not unknown in other trade policy machines. Indeed, it may even prove useful for Member State governments to be able to credit (or blame) the Commission for current EU policy.

The GATT also functions at a second, more fundamental level. It shapes the framework for the development of world trade and engages in the necessary reforms to respond to changes in the global arena. The negotiating rounds, starting on a large scale in the early 1960s and lasting into the 1990s, cover virtually the same period as the history of the EEC, then the EC and now the EU, and this is no mere coincidence. For many commentators, it was only with the emergence of the Community as a unified interlocutor with the Americans in the 1960s that the development of a truly multilateral world trading system became possible. It also became somewhat difficult, as the development of intense global interdependence tested the capacity both of the Community and of the USA to find appropriate reforms to meet rapidly changing problems (Preeg 1970; Diebold 1972).

As a result, the competence of the Commission to act for the Community in the GATT negotiating sphere has been exercised in a very challenging context indeed. As with the more specific dispute settlement procedures, the Community Member States retain a voice in the process, and the presence of the Article 113 Committee provides a constant check on the Commission's activities. As the GATT has extended its attention with successive negotiating rounds from tariffs to non-tariff barriers, and from trade in industrial goods to agriculture and services, it is also not surprising that the diversity of views among the Member States has become more pronounced, and the result has been a more turbulent and taxing political context for the Commission's activities. Perhaps the high (or low) point of this came with the attempt to steer a course between competing national positions on agriculture during the Uruguay Round of negotiations. This did not only involve frictions between EU members but was also an issue which cut across several Directorates General in the Commission and which generated intense conflicts between competing groups in the Community. It is thus important to note the differing ways in which the GATT can form a context for the conduct of EU external relations and action by the Commission.

The OECD has a powerful but less well-focused impact on the Community and on the Commission. Here, the aim is largely the exchange of information and discussion of macro-economic strategies, along with specialist study of such issues as export credit finance. In many of these areas the Commission has only conditional competence at best, but it does have the status of active participant in the Organisation. Thus, the OECD is an organisation in which the EU can at times speak with 13 voices, with only one of them belonging to the Commission and supposedly representing the Union. But the close links between the Commission and the OECD Secretariat make for effective information exchange and the building of the vital consensus of the Organisation's work (Fielding 1991, pp. 33–34). In a somewhat similar way, the Commission has a role in a number of UN bodies such as UNCTAD, where there is a Community observer delegation consisting of representatives both of the Commission and of the Council Presidency, as well as national delegations from some of the Member States. Since a number of these bodies spend a good deal of their time on trade or trade-related issues, the ambiguous status of the Commission is not always helpful, though it can also be a way of diffusing conflict or embarrassment.

Intersecting a number of the Community's involvements with international organisations are contacts at the bilateral or limited-multilateral level, particularly with other industrialised partners. The Community has a large number of regular consultations with its industrial partners, in which the Commission plays an active role as well as providing a range of facilitating resources. In some cases, such as the Group of Seven industrial countries (G-7) and the annual Western Economic Summits associated with them, the Commission has gradually established itself as a key participant. But there are large areas of policy, particularly those touching on monetary and macroeconomic problems, where the Commission has very little formal standing, and from which it can be effectively excluded. It remains to be seen whether changes either in the EU or in the world economy will alter this situation. As is to be expected, the Commission is certainly central to the trade-related policy issues discussed in the G-7 context, and during the early 1990s the development of the so-called 'quadrilateral group' became a key feature of the G-7 approach to GATT negotiations. Grouping as it did the EC, the USA, Canada and Japan, it began to remind some observers of the growth of a 'world of regional blocs', but it must be stressed that its impact was relatively limited and specifically restricted to trade.

Among the industrial partners of the Community, the USA and Japan hold pride of place, given their dominance in external trade and direct investment. It is therefore not surprising that there have been moves to institutionalise the links between the Community and both of these economic 'superpowers'. During 1990 and 1991, joint declarations were adopted first by Canada and then the USA and the Community, and later by Japan. These established regular processes of consultation, with specific working groups focusing on matters of industrial, scientific and regulatory policy. Although the Commission was heavily involved in both the negotiation and the implementation of these arrangements, the processes were those of a mixed agreement, with the Member States and particularly the Council Presidency holding a central position. Nonetheless, the continuation of the growing 'infrastructure' of specialist policy consultation was both a direct reflection of the changing nature of external relations and a confirmation of the role played by the Commission in facilitating and supporting policies (Fielding 1991; Schwok 1992; Alting von Geusau 1993).

Although the main focus of EU external relations has historically been the industrialised countries, there has also grown up a sophisticated infrastructure of institutions and contacts dealing with the Third World. In particular, the Lomé Conventions (so far there have been four, with the first taking effect in 1975 and the fourth in 1990) have produced a range of preferential trading agreements and technical assistance agreements unique among the links between industrialised and developing countries. The administration of these agreements, and of broader Community policy towards developing countries, is entrusted to the Commission, although it is not an area of exclusive Commission competence except insofar as it deals with specifically trade or CCP related issues. The Lomé Conventions themselves are concluded under Article 238 of the Treaty of Rome, and administered not through DG I but through DG VIII (Development) of the Commission. Significantly, they rely on national allocations of aid and assistance, which have to be negotiated with the Commission on a regular basis (Hewitt 1989; Hine 1985; Lister 1988). A particular aspect of policy towards the Third World has been the growth of the Commission as a coordinating body for crisis and humanitarian assistance as well as longer-term technical assistance. The legitimacy built up in this area has had major implications for Commission activism in the crises of the 1990s, both in the Third World and closer to home.

The Commission also has a central role in the initiation and the monitoring of association and cooperation agreements, which fall into a number of categories. In the first place, there are those agreements which are explicitly designed to pave the way for membership by the associated country (as was the case with Greece, for example, before its membership). Secondly, there are agreements which are designed to create free exchange and a close economic relationship but without the presumption of eventual membership, such as those with a number of Mediterranean countries. The European Economic Area Agreement (EEA) signed with the EFTA countries began without the presumption of membership but was later seen as a staging post to full membership for Sweden, Norway, Finland and Austria. Finally, there are the cooperation agreements, for example, with China. In these cases, the Commission's role may be 'arm's length' while in the closer forms of association there is a constant demand on Commission attention and expertise as the detailed arrangements are monitored. By extension, the investigation of applicants for Community membership and the provision of formal 'opinions' on their credentials, is a key Commission responsibility, although, as in other areas, the power of decision lies with the Council of Ministers and, by virtue of the assent procedure (see Chapter 9), to some extent the Parliament.

A final area of Commission involvement in external relations is in inter-regional arrangements. The Community has developed a series of links with other regional organisations, particularly those of an economic nature, in Latin America and Asia particularly (Edwards and Regelsberger 1990). The conclusion of these agreements, and the oversight of the often complex technical activities to which they give rise, is a Commission responsibility, often cutting across a number of Directorates General. In a number of cases, the arrangements envisaged and developed a political dimension. This was the case, for example, of the Community's links with ASEAN and with

Central and Latin American organisations. Perhaps the most explicit example, and one raising the issue of the boundary between economic and political activities, was the Euro-Arab Dialogue of the 1970s. Given the atmosphere surrounding the Arab-Israeli conflict both then and later, the Dialogue was an issue in which the political sensitivities not only of EC Member States but also of powerful outsiders such as the USA were bound to be aroused. The result was a series of 'border incidents' which did little to advance the cause of the Commission in that the Dialogue was organised within EPC, though the bulk of the discussions focused on economic development with which the Commission was closely concerned (Allen 1978). During the later 1980s, the often rather distant relations between the Community and the countries of Eastern and Central Europe, either individually or in the framework of the Council for Mutual Economic Assistance, also underwent considerable development which raised again the economic/political 'boundary' issue (Pinder 1991).

This question of the 'boundary' between economic and political affairs was also raised during the 1980s by a number of episodes in which economic sanctions were either contemplated or used by the Community. At one level, it is clear that the growing economic weight of the EU gives it the potential to mobilise that weight against those of whom it disapproves. But given the complexities of both the legal and the political framework of the Union, it is equally clear that the move to economic sanctions poses delicate problems of competence and legitimacy. Not only this, but the increasingly interpenetrated nature of the world economy gives rise to important operational issues of control and effectiveness attached to any use of the economic weapon. During the 1980s, the Community several times faced the demand for sanctions, either from within its membership or from powerful outsiders such as the USA. Iran, the USSR, Argentina, South Africa, Iraq, former Yugoslavia were all potential targets, and the record both of coordinated action and effectiveness is patchy to say the least (Holland 1993). The Commission role in most if not all of the cases was a dual one: first, to provide information and estimates of the impact of sanctions, and to coordinate this with national authorities; second, in those cases where Article 113 was the basis of action, to impose, maintain and monitor the effects of the sanctions. As Nuttall points out, though, the political determination (or lack of it) in all of these cases depended not on the Commission but on the national governments of the Member States; though the Community and the Commission could provide the instruments if the governments were minded to give them the authority (see Chapter 11).

The picture presented here is one of a growing and elaborate network of contacts between the EU and the outside world, in which the Commission plays a central but sometimes ambiguous role. Its status as repository of expertise and information is widely acknowledged. It often takes a key role in representing the Community, either solely or in conjunction with the Council Presidency; and it is in many respects the guardian of the framework within which the EC's external relations grew until the late 1980s. Despite the fact that it has exclusive competence only in a limited number of sectors, it has been able to establish an effective presence and to operate as an interlocutor at varying levels of authority. It also has the custodianship of a vast infrastructure of working groups and day-to-day relationships which have greatly increased the confidence of partners in both the Community in general and the Commission in particular. But questions are raised precisely by the extent of this commitment. Can the Commission continue to muster the expertise, the human resources and the attention to play its full effective role? Such issues were around in the 1980s, but have been given particular relevance by the radical changes of the 1990s.

From development to transformation

It has been argued in many contexts that the affairs of Europe during the 1990s have gone beyond mere developmental change to a state of radical transformation (Smith and Woolcock 1993; Allen and Smith 1991/2; Alting von Geusau 1993; Story 1993). The focus of this Chapter so far has been on developments in Community external relations up to the end of the 1980s, but clearly it is of key importance to explore the impact of the political and economic changes of the 1990s. These have been such as to throw into sharp relief both the benefits and the limitations of action through the Community, and thus also to throw into question the role of the Commission itself.

In essence, the changes, although not all rooted in the 1990s alone, have reshaped both the context and the agenda of the EC's external relations. The most dramatic has been the disappearance of the division of Europe, carrying with it the need to recreate relationships with a wide range of countries, often in trying economic and political circumstances. Alongside this has gone the already-noted trend towards extensive economic interpenetration between industrial societies and the accompanying need to reform the international economic institutions, including the GATT. A major role has been played in addition by the EC's 'internal' efforts to remake itself, particularly through the Single European Market programme (SEM).

The combination of change in the European political and economic order, with change at the level of the world economy, and with the pervasive impact of the SEM, has meant a radical transformation of EU external relations in an increasingly turbulent world. This in its turn has both highlighted some long-standing problems, and created some new ones, for the role of the Commission. Three questions emerge: first, can the Commission maintain its role as provider of information, representation and negotiating expertise in an increasingly demanding world? Second, is the Commission capable of managing and coordinating a transformed policy agenda for external relations? Finally, can the Commission respond effectively to changing political conditions which are bound to affect the conduct and content of external relations in the 1990s? Before coming to a judgement on these issues, an examination of some key policy problems may prove helpful.

The first such problem is the SEM itself. Although this might be seen as an 'internal' policy programme, it was clear from the outset that it had international aims and ramifications. One of its major motivations was to enhance EC competitiveness against the USA and Japan, and many of the measures it contained had implications for international trade policy as well as for the activities of international corporations within the Community (Calingaert 1988; Smith 1992). For the Commission, this had the makings of a major problem in the management of policy, given that within the EC the SEM cut across almost all significant areas of activity. The international perception of the SEM, whether as the basis of a possible 'fortress Europe' or as an opportunity for the exploitation of new markets, was also a central feature of the policy context.

The Commission's initial handling of this problem was not surefooted. Almost the first public recognition of the external implications of the SEM was in a speech made by Willy de Clercq, the External Relations Commissioner, in July 1988, in which he appeared to be arguing that the SEM was too precious to be negotiated away, and that any concessions on market access to (say) the USA and Japan would only be granted if those countries gave equivalent concessions (Montagnon 1988). This aroused predictable fury, particularly in Washington, and although the Commission was quick to rectify the situation, the memory lingered. 'Fury' was also raised in some Member States against the Commission when defending the 'European' interest in the SEM conflicted with national concerns. Such issues as Japanese car and video imports smouldered on well into the 1990s. Other aspects of the SEM were less public, but no less potentially the sources of friction: the regulation of financial services, public procurement, technical standards and certification, telecommunications and transportation, all held the seeds of conflict with outsiders. The other feature common to all was that they were not the preserve of DG I, a fact which raised problems of policy coordination at the highest level.

Further complications were added to the policy mix by the fact that the SEM programme ran alongside the Uruguay Round of the GATT. Was the SEM to be the basis for a new EC policy on world trade more generally, or the basis for further constructive contributions to the liberalisation of world trade? For the Commission, negotiating in Geneva, a key problem was that the negotiating stance on world trade issues depended heavily on the progress made in the SEM. In fact, this problem was handled with considerable efficiency as the Round progressed, and there were no dramatic confrontations at the multilateral level. The same could not be said for the bilateral relationship with the USA. In the early part of 1993, the Community faced direct threats of retaliation against the effects of newly-implemented directives on public procurement, which the Americans saw as damaging their interests. Not only this, but the suspicions of the USA about the effects of EC policies on standards and certification had not been allayed. This had particular impact on sectors such as telecommunications, which were also central to the public procurement dispute (US Congress 1992).

The Commission has thus been faced with a variety of new challenges in policy coordination which bridge the theoretical gap between external and internal policy. Nor are these confined to the 'new agenda' created by the SEM. The Uruguay Round also threw up coordination issues in 'traditional' areas of trade, and particularly agricultural trade. Efforts to achieve internal reform of the CAP through the McSharry proposals of 1992 were rendered much more problematic by the fact that they coincided with the most delicate stage of GATT negotiations, and that they engaged the deepest perceptions of national and local interest in Community countries. Thus, the Commission has found itself in a double if not a triple bind, between the demands of the GATT (and particularly the Americans), the agreed internal reform programme, and the perceived vital interests of EU members, particularly the

French. In November 1992, the so-called Blair House Agreement, reached in Washington between the Community (represented both by the External Relations and the Agriculture Commissioners), appeared to have resolved the issues. But as time passed, the French made increasing efforts to argue for a renegotiation based on the agreement's incompatibility with the CAP reforms. Significantly, their arguments were also based on the fact that the agreement had been initialled by the Commission and the US government, but not 'concluded' by the Council of Ministers; a telling demonstration of the mixed nature of EC decision-making in this area (*Economist* 1993b).

By 1994, then, the scene in EU external relations was complex to say the least, with a host of unresolved issues even on the well-established agenda of trade and the SEM. But the early 1990s also saw a quantum leap in the number of other major external policy areas in which the Commission has a role. The reality is not merely an increase in numbers, but also an increase in the scale, complexity and political sensitivity of what is being attempted. Four such areas of policy can be identified and briefly reviewed: first, the problems of dealing with new countries in Eastern and Central Europe; second, the attempt to deal with the EFTA members through the establishment of the European Economic Area leading to full-blown enlargement negotiations; third, new dimensions in the use of economic sanctions and economic and humanitarian assistance; and finally, a new range of 'global issues' arising from the intensification of global interdependence and the need for regulation. In each of these domains, the Commission has been led more or less willingly into new and often uncertain enterprises.

East and Central Europe

When the Soviet-backed regimes of Eastern and Central Europe progressively collapsed during 1989 and 1990, one of the most pressing needs was for economic and technical assistance. Although there was a massive expansion of bilateral aid efforts, there was a clear need for coordination and the linking of aid to the political reform process. Significantly, the USA was disinclined (some have argued, financially incapable) to undertake the lead role in what some saw as a second Marshall Plan. They actively promoted the Community as the channel for coordination, and the Commission as the lead agency in what became the Group of 24 aid donors (G-24). By 1993, the Community had contributed 60 per cent of the total funds expended through the G-24. The Commission had become the recognised centre of expertise and the home of coordinated programmes such as PHARE in East and Central Europe and TACIS, directed at the former Soviet Union itself. To be sure, there were frictions not only with the Americans but also between EC policies and extensive national aid efforts, particularly those of the Germans, but the legitimacy of the Commission was firmly established. A linked enterprise, the setting up of the European Bank for Reconstruction and Development, was less fully subject to Commission control, and less clearly successful.

Alongside the innovative Commission role in G-24 went an attempt to establish new trading relationships with countries previously constrained by the bloc politics and economics of the Cold War. One of the first demands of the Central and East European states was for new association agreements with the Community, and for the promise of eventual membership. At one level, this was a technical question, but it was also inescapably political, bearing on the future shape of the Community in an undivided Europe and on the future stability of the 'new states'. The result was a series of so-called 'Europe Agreements', which granted asymmetrical trade and market access concessions to the East Europeans, and foresaw eventual EU membership. But they also reflected the fundamental tensions in the Community position. A number of Member States found it difficult to contemplate early membership for new states, particularly in the light of their own domestic economic and social problems. There were also specific areas of tension such as agriculture and steel, where the prospect of free entry for goods from the new states was unattractive to many EC producers and their governments. The Commission was caught in the centre of these tensions, with the capacity to monitor, to provide information and to shape negotiations, but without the competence to determine the shape of any outcome.

From the European Economic Area to enlargement of the Union

At the same time as dealing with the effects of the changes in Eastern and Central Europe, in the 1990s the Commission became deeply implicated in the negotiations for closer relations between the Community and the EFTA countries. These have been a curious hybrid in several ways. The European Economic Area Agreement of December 1992 implied that the EFTA members would accept a very large part of the Community *acquis* without acquiring the benefits of full Community membership. The Agreement reflected a formidable negotiating effort both by the Commission and by the EFTA members. But it also provoked important tensions which revealed the underlying problems of EC policy-making in this area. The first came to light almost as the Agreement was signed, with the European Court of Justice refusing to grant legitimacy to the arrangements for judicial review and dispute settlement under the agreement. This was resolved, but was followed by the Swiss referendum decision in December 1992 to reject the Agreement (and by implication to suspend the start of full entry negotiations). The EEA thus proved distinctly fragile even before its implementation on January 1, 1994. In addition, a number of EFTA members decided to apply directly for entry to the Community, thereby creating a major new commitment for the Commission in the process. In many respects, the Commission, at the political level, could only observe this process, while continuing to build the necessary infrastructure for management of whatever relationship finally emerged.

Building such an infrastructure was not always straightforward. When the Edinburgh European Council of December 1992 decided enlargement negotiations were to begin in early 1993, the administrative ramifications of creating a 50-strong Task Force for Enlargement produced distinct tensions within the Commission. The Task Force was independent of DG I and of DG IA, though the responsible Commissioner, Hans van den Broek, was also directly responsible for the new DG IA. Most of the negotiating substance concerned the policies of the 'internal' DGs and DG I, and it was from these sources that the officials of the Task Force were drawn. The enlargement negotiations involved the Commission in extensive 'pre-negotiations' or 'exploratory talks' with the candidates with the aim of assessing how much of the *acquis communautaire* could be implemented without negotiations over derogations or transitional arrangements. In the latter two cases, the Commission then made proposals and negotiated with Member States in an attempt to form a common position to be subsequently defended by the Presidency on behalf of the Union in direct talks with the applicant states.

The politics of humanitarian aid and economic sanctions

Economic and humanitarian aid was always a part of the Commission remit, but the 1990s have greatly expanded it and brought it into an ever closer relationship with political and security issues. The intersection of political turmoil in Eastern and Central Europe with a number of existing conflicts and crises created new demands on the Commission as the channel for economic and humanitarian measures in the 1990s. At one level, there has been a large-scale increase in the application of economic sanctions, most dramatically since the Gulf Crisis of 1990–91 and the break-up of the former Yugoslavia from 1990 onwards. The diplomatic and security aspects of these issues is dealt with further in Chapter 11, but it is important here to note the ways in which the Balkan conflict especially has increased the load on the Commission as the regulator of the 'economic weapon'. In the case of Bosnia between 1992 and 1994, the addition of large-scale humanitarian assistance needs to the already existing economic sanctions meant that the Commission was effectively taking on the non-military aspects of a major war, with all of the administrative (not to mention political) demands that came with it. Moreover, in the summer of 1993 it was even suggested that the Commission should take on the administration of certain cities in the event of an agreed peace plan for Bosnia. Each of these expectations and demands added to the burden on the Commission in quite new areas, and it must be remembered that they went alongside the extensive old and new agendas already described (Ludlow 1991; Alting von Geusau 1993)

Global interdependence and the need for regulation

A final piece in the rapidly developing jigsaw of EU (and by extension Commission) concerns in external relations is the impact of a series of global and transnational issues. Some have been given formal recognition in the TEU provisions. Three examples suffice to highlight issues raised for the role of the Commission by developments in this area. First, there is the problem of international environmental regulation and policy-making. At the global level, this is entangled with other issues such as trade policies in the context of the GATT, or technical assistance activities in the UN framework and elsewhere. On a bilateral level, it enters into relations with the USA and other major industrial partners. At a more immediately European level, it engages with the wide range of issues attaching to changes in Eastern and Central

Europe. In all of these contexts, the Community is a natural channel for the concerns of West European countries, and the Commission is the natural spokesman for the Community in the broader institutional context.

A second item on the 'new agenda' is the increasing need to regulate transnational networks in the areas of traditional Community concern. A challenging example is that of air transport, where regulatory issues at the national or the Community level have an inevitable spill-over into the global arena. As noted earlier in this Chapter, here the Commission has competence, but not of an unchallenged or unchallengeable nature. The question is whether the Commission can or should arrogate competence to itself (for example under the CCP) or whether the solution lies in new forms of cooperative action between the national, the Community and the corporate levels.

A third example of global interdependence and the need for regulation is furnished by the increasingly transnational nature of policy-making in high technology sectors, which in its turn reflects the global integration of production and R and D activities. One of the key aims of the Community from the outset has been the maintenance of competitive high technology industries in Western Europe, but increasingly this has appeared to be an aim not attainable at the European level alone. It also involves the need to coordinate EU policies across several areas of the Commission, with rather different priorities and modes of operation. At a number of points it also intersects with issues of national and international security, and thus entails the need for the Community and the Commission to interact with organisations in that area.

Each of these short examples demonstrates how Commission involvement in new patterns of policy-making is evolving and also where the rules of the game either remain to be worked out or are almost non-existent. When they are taken together with the expanding agenda already described in this Chapter, major questions arise about the competence of the Commission in formal terms, but also about the ability of the Commission and its members to shape the process of policy-making both at the Community and at the broader international level.

Conclusions: the Commission in a new world

Although there is a lot of evidence that the external relations of the Community are entering a new era of change and challenge, the structure and functioning of the Commission machinery and the Commission itself were not a central preoccupation of the Intergovernmental Conferences during 1990 and 1991. As Devuyst has noted (1992, p. 72), very little time was spent on the CCP itself, and as a result there were few major changes. The Commission was prepared to argue for an extension of exclusive competence to cover a number of trade-related economic and regulatory issues, but this idea got fairly short shrift in the broader preoccupation with EMU and Political Union. At the procedural level, there was no move to establish a 'fast track' negotiating authority for the Commission, despite the problems which had become apparent during the Uruguay Round. Although the European

Parliament's right of assent to international agreements was to some extent enlarged, this was not seen as applicable to agreements reached under Article 113 or the CCP in general. The impact of the growing range of association arrangements described above is still to be evaluated in this context. The discussions and the agreement on economic and monetary union paid little attention to the linkages between external monetary management and the role of the Commission, except to require that the Commission should be 'fully associated' with positions taken in international fora relating to economic and monetary policy.

While the IGCs really contained very little in the way of concrete change to the structure of external economic policy-making, less formal factors have been operating to produce change in the Commission's role and status. But not all the changes are to the Commission's advantage. The increasing role of the Commission on issues affecting Central and Eastern Europe and the growth of new agenda issues in which national governments have limited competence or interest have clearly made the Commission the target of rising expectations. The intersection of, say, the CCP with highly-charged political issues, or the interaction of the CAP with external trade policy, can create severe jurisdictional problems.

Perhaps the most important example of the Commission's response to changing realities is the creation in 1993 of a 'bicephalous' approach to external relations and the arrival of the new DG IA. For some time, it had been apparent that external relations could not be managed on the assumption that they were all economic in character. The sheer volume and diversity of work in the area made it necessary to think of institutional innovation. The TEU only added to this tendency by strengthening the relationship between external relations and common foreign and security policy. Thus, the new Commission appointed for the two-year term 1993/94 made provision for two Commissioners in the external relations area. Sir Leon Brittan was to deal with the explicitly economic issues on what might be called the traditional agenda, while Hans van den Broek, the former Dutch Foreign Minister, was to take responsibility for external political relations. Such an innovation can clearly be related to the changes and challenges dealt with above, and as such it represents a positive attempt on the part of the Delors Commission to adapt to the new context.

The difficulty, as soon became apparent in 1993, is that having two external DGs creates problems of coordination and what in Washington are called 'turf battles'. When this is added to the existing issues of coordination between external relations and development policy, or competition policy (a link of which Sir Leon Brittan was well aware as the negotiator of competition policy agreements with the USA), it can be seen that there is the potential for new divisions and disputes. In the early part of 1993, these duly appeared, for example in respect of the EEA and former Yugoslavia (*Economist* 1993a). Even if coordination can effectively be achieved, would it have any external impact on the role and status of the Commission in a period when the 're-nationalisation' of EU policies and the resurgence of intergovernmentalism is widely noted? The interaction of the Commission not only with national governments but also with the Council Secretariat is likely to be a key determinant here. In a situation where van den Broek faced scepticism not only from EC Member States and the Council but also from within the

Commission and his DG I partners, the assertion of a new competence and role is likely to be a hard row to hoe for the foreseeable future (Barber and Gardner 1993a).

At the beginning of this Chapter, it was suggested that one way of looking at the Commission's role in external relations was as a set of 'boundary problems', in which the Commission found itself up against the demands posed by the interlinking and competition of many issues and policy arenas. It is clear from the evidence examined here that this is indeed the case, and in a number of ways. The Commission faces issues of formal competence, of informal status and standing, and of the need to combine several distinct and often competing roles. It also faces the problems created by a rapidly changing external relations agenda, in which the essentially evolutionary processes of its first 30 years have been replaced by processes of radical and even revolutionary change.

Not unnaturally, the responses both of the Commission and of EU Member States have been hesitant in the face of the new demands faced during the 1990s. It remains to be seen whether the attempt to bridge 'classical' external relations and the new political and regulatory concerns explored here will be a success. What is clear is that the Commission has over the years developed a powerful set of management procedures for its core external relations business, and that the boundaries of its activity had expanded considerably even before the transformations of the 1990s. A number of long-established problems remain, and should not be obscured by the impact of the new agenda. Indeed, they suffuse the new agenda and give evidence of a solid if sometimes debated core of status and competence for the Commission. One thing is certain, that the nature, definition and management of the external relations of the European Union will be central to the development of the Union itself, the wider Europe and the world political economy. The Commission will remain at the heart of this process, but as always the centrality and boundaries of its role will be contested both from within and from without.

References

Allen, D. (1978) 'The Euro-Arab Dialogue', *Journal of Common Market Studies*, Vol. XVI (4).

Allen, D. and Smith, M. (1991–92) 'The European Community in the New Europe: Bearing the Burden of Change', *International Journal*, Vol. XLVII (1), Winter, pp. 1–28.

Alting von Geusau, F.A.M. (1993) *Beyond Containment and Division: Western Cooperation from a Post-Totalitarian Perspective*, Dordrecht: Nijhoff.

Barber, L. and Gardner, D. (1993a) 'A brief to build bridges', *Financial Times*, 8 March 1993.

Barber, L. and Gardner, D. (1993b) 'Brussels wants US Treaties modified', *Financial Times*, 15 July 1993.

Calingaert, M. (1988) *The 1992 Challenge from Europe: Development of the European Community's Internal Market*, Washington DC: National Planning Council.

Cameron, D.R. (1992) 'The 1992 Initiative: Causes and Consequences', in Sbragia, A. (ed.) *Europolitics: Institutions and Policy-Making in the 'New' European Community*, Washington, DC: Brookings, pp. 23–74.

Close, G. (1990) 'External Relations in the Air Transport Sector: Air Transport Policy or the Common Commercial Policy?', *Common Market Law Review*, Vol. 27(1), Spring, pp. 107–27.

Destler, I.M. (1992) *American Trade Politics'*, Washington DC: Institute for International Economics/Twentieth Century Fund.

Devuyst, Y. (1992) 'The EC's Common Commercial Policy and the Treaty on European Union — An Overview of the Negotiations', *World Competition*, Vol. 16(2), December, pp. 67–80.

Diebold, W., Jr (1972) *The United States and the Industrial World: American Foreign Economic Policy in the 1970s*, New York: Praeger, for the Council on Foreign Relations.

Economist (1993a) 'Kitchen Capers', 6 March, p. 44.

Economist (1993b) 'France and the Gatt: Draw, Pardner', 25 September, pp. 50–51.

Edwards, G. and Regelsberger, E. (eds.) (1990) *Europe's Global Links: The European Community and Inter-Regional Cooperation*, London: Pinter.

Fielding, Sir L. (1991) *Europe as a Global Partner*, London: University Association for Contemporary European Studies, Occasional Paper No. 7.

Hewitt, A. (1989) 'ACP and the Developing World', in Lodge, J. (ed.) *The European Community and the Challenge of the Future*, London: Pinter.

Hine, R. (1985) *The Political Economy of European Trade*, Brighton: Harvester-Wheatsheaf.

Holland, M. (1993) *European Community Integration*, London: Pinter.

Hufbauer, G.C. (ed.) (1990) *Europe 1992: An American Perspective*, Washington, DC: Brookings.

Kaptein, P.J.G. and Van Themat, P.V. (1990) *Introduction to the Law of the European Communities*, Deventer: Kluwer, London: Graham and Trotman.

Lister, M. (1988) *The European Community and the Developing World: the Role of the Lomé Conventions*, Aldershot: Gower.

Ludlow, P. (1991) 'The European Commission', in Keohane, R.O. and Hoffmann, S. (eds.) *The New European: Decision-making and Institutional Change*, Boulder, Co: Westview.

Mény, Y. and Wright, V. (eds.) (1987) *The Politics of Steel: Western Europe and the Steel Industry in the Crisis Years (1974–84)*, Berlin: Walter de Gruyter.

Milward, A.S. (1984) *The Reconstruction of Western Europe, 1945–1951*, London: Methuen.

Montagnon, P. (1988) 'De Clerq offers glimpse of Community Trade Policy', *Financial Times*, 14 July.

Neuwahl, N.A. (1990), 'Joint Participation in International Treaties and the Exercise of Power by the EEC and its Member States', *Common Market Law Review*, Vol. 28(4), pp. 717–40.

Nicoll, W. and Salmon, T. (1990) *Understanding the European Communities*, London: Philip Allan.

Peters, B.G. (1992) 'Bureaucratic Politics and the Institutions of the European Community', in Sbriaga, A. (ed.) *Europolitics: Institutions and Policy-Making in the 'New' European Community*, Washington, DC: Brookings.

Pinder, J. (1991) *The European Community and Eastern Europe*, London: Pinter, for the Royal Institute of International Affairs.

Preeg, E.H. (1970) *Traders and Diplomats: An Analysis of the Kennedy Round of Negotiations under the General Agreement on Tariffs and Trade*, Washington, DC: Brookings.

Riley, A.J. (1992) 'Nailing the Jellyfish: the Illegality of the EC/US Government Competition Agreement', *European Competition Law Review*, Vol. 13 (3), May–June, pp. 101–19.

Schwok, René (1992) 'The European Free Trade Association: Revival or Collapse?', in Redmond, John (ed.) *The External Relations of the European Community*, New York: St Martins Press.

Smith, M. (1992) '"The Devil You Know": the United States and a Changing European Community', *International Affairs*, Vol. 68(1), January, pp. 103–120.

Smith, M. (1994) 'The United States and Western Europe: Empire, Alliance and Interdependence', in McGrew, A. (ed.) *The United States in the Twentieth Century*, Milton Keynes: Open University.

Smith, M. and Woolcock, S. (1993) *The United States and the European Community in a Transformed World*, London: Pinter, for the Royal Institute of International Affairs.
Story, Jonathan (ed.) (1993) *The New Europe*, Oxford: Blackwell.
Taylor, P. (1983) *The Limits of Integration*, London: Croom Helm.
US Congress (1992) *Europe and the United States; Competition and Cooperation in the 1990s*, Study Papers submitted to the Subcommittee on International Economic Policy and Trade and the Subcommittee on Europe and the Middle East of the Committee on Foreign Affairs, US House of Representatives. Washington, DC: US Government Printing Office.

ANNEX A

Treaty establishing the European Economic Community	Treaty on European Union
Article 28	*Article 28*

Any autonomous alteration or suspension of duties in the Common Customs Tariff shall be decided by the Council acting by a qualified majority on a proposal from the Commission.*

* *Article as replaced by Article 16(1) of the SEA*

Any autonomous alteration or suspension of duties in the Common Customs Tariff shall be decided by the Council acting by a qualified majority on a proposal from the Commission.

Article 110

By establishing a customs union between themselves Member States aim to contribute, in the common interest, to the harmonious development of world trade, the progressive abolition of restrictions on international trade and the lowering of customs barriers.

The common commercial policy shall take into account the favourable effect which the abolition of customs duties between Member States may have on the increase in the competitive strength of undertakings in those States.

Article 110

By establishing a customs union between themselves Member States aim to contribute, in the common interest, to the harmonious development of world trade, the progressive abolition of restrictions on international trade and the lowering of customs barriers.

The common commercial policy shall take into account the favourable effect which the abolition of customs duties between Member States may have on the increase in the competitive strength of undertakings in those States.

Article 111

The following provisions shall, without prejudice to Articles 115 and 116, apply during the transitional period:

1. Member States shall coordinate their trade relations with third countries so as to bring about, by the end of the transitional period, the conditions needed for implementing a common policy in the field of external trade.

   The Commission shall submit to the Council proposals regarding the procedure for common action to be followed during the transitional period and regarding the achievement of uniformity in their commercial policies.

Article 111

(Repealed)

2. The Commission shall submit to the Council recommendations for tariff negotiations with third countries in respect of the common customs tariff.

   The Council shall authorise the Commission to open such negotiations.

   The Commission shall conduct these negotiations in consultation with a special committee appointed by the Council to assist the Commission in this task and within the framework of such directives as the Council may issue to it.

3. In exercising the powers conferred upon it by this Article, the Council shall act unanimously during the first two stages and by a qualified majority thereafter.

4. Member States shall, in consultation with the Commission, take all necessary measures, particularly those designed to bring about an adjustment of tariff agreements in force with third countries, in order that the entry into force of the common customs tariff shall not be delayed.

5. Member States shall aim at securing as high a level of uniformity as possible between themselves as regards their liberalisation lists in relation to third countries or groups of third countries. To this end, the Commission shall make all appropriate recommendations to Member States.

   If Member States abolish or reduce quantitative restrictions in relation to third countries, they shall inform the Commission beforehand and shall accord the same treatment to other Member States.

Article 112

1. Without prejudice to obligations undertaken by them within the

Article 112

1. Without prejudice to obligations undertaken by them within the

framework of other international organisations, Member States shall, before the end of the transitional period, progressively harmonise the systems whereby they grant aid for exports to third countries, to the extent necessary to ensure that competition between undertakings of the Community is not distorted.

On a proposal from the Commission, the Council shall, acting unanimously until the end of the second stage and by a qualified majority thereafter, issue any directives needed for this purpose.

2. The preceding provisions shall not apply to such a drawback of customs duties or charges having equivalent effect nor to such repayment of indirect taxation including turnover taxes, excise duties and other indirect taxes as is allowed when goods are exported from a Member State to a third country, in so far as such drawback or repayment does not exceed the amount imposed, directly or indirectly, on the products exported.

Article 113

1. After the transitional period has ended, the common commercial policy shall be based on uniform principles, particularly in regard to changes in tariff rates, the conclusion of tariff and trade agreements, the achievement of uniformity in measures of liberalisation, export policy and measures to protect trade such as those to be taken in case of dumping or subsidies.

2. The Commission shall submit proposals to the Council for implementing the common commercial policy.

3. Where agreements with third countries need to be negotiated, the Commission shall make

framework of other international organisations, Member States shall, before the end of the transitional period, progressively harmonise the systems whereby they grant aid for exports to third countries, to the extent necessary to ensure that competition between undertakings of the Community is not distorted.

On a proposal from the Commission, the Council shall, acting unanimously until the end of the second stage and by a qualified majority thereafter, issue any directives needed for this purpose.

2. The preceding provisions shall not apply to such a drawback of customs duties or charges having equivalent effect nor to such a repayment of indirect taxation including turnover taxes, excise duties and other indirect taxes as is allowed when goods are exported from a Member State to a third country, in so far as such a drawback or repayment does not exceed the amount imposed, directly or indirectly, on the products exported.

Article 113

As amended by Article G(28) TEU

1. The common commercial policy shall be based on uniform principles, particularly in regard to changes in tariff rates, the conclusion of tariff and trade agreements, the achievement of uniformity in measures of liberalisation, export policy and measures to protect trade such as those to be taken in the event of dumping or subsidies.

2. The Commission shall submit proposals to the Council for implementing the common commercial policy.

3. Where agreements with one or more States or international organisations need to be negotiated, the

recommendations to the Council, which shall authorise the Commission to open the necessary negotiations.

The Commission shall conduct these negotiations in consultation with a special committee appointed by the Council to assist the Commission in this task and within the framework of such directives as the Council may issue to it.

4. In exercising the powers conferred upon it by this Article, the Council shall act by a qualified majority.

Article 114

The agreement referred to in Article 111 (2) and in Article 113 shall be concluded by the Council on behalf of the Community, acting unanimously during the first two stages and by a qualified majority thereafter.

Article 115

In order to ensure that the execution of measures of commercial policy taken in accordance with this treaty by any Member State is not obstructed by deflection of trade, or where differences between such measures lead to economic difficulties in one or more Member States, the Commission shall recommend the methods for the requisite cooperation between Member States. Failing this, the Commission may authorise Member States to take the necessary protective measures, the conditions and details of which it shall determine.

In case of urgency during the transitional period, Member States may themselves take the necessary measures and shall notify them to the other Member States and to the Commission,

---

Commission shall make recommendations to the Council, which shall authorise the Commission to open the necessary negotiations.

The Commission shall conduct these negotiations in consultation with a special committee appointed by the Council to assist the Commission in this task and within the framework of such directives as the Council may issue to it.

The relevant provisions of Article 228 shall apply.

4. In exercising the powers conferred upon it by this Article, the Council shall act by a qualified majority.

Article 114

(Repealed)

Article 115

As amended by Article G(30) TEU

In order to ensure that the execution of measures of commercial policy taken in accordance with this treaty by any Member State is not obstructed by deflection of trade, or where differences between such measures lead to economic difficulties in one or more Member States, the Commission shall recommend the methods for the requisite cooperation between Member States. Failing this, the Commission may authorise Member States to take the necessary protective measures, the conditions and details of which it shall determine.

In case of urgency, Member States shall request authorisation to take the necessary measures themselves from the Commission, which shall take a decision as soon as possible; the Member States

which may decide that the States concerned shall amend or abolish such measures.

concerned shall then notify the measures to the other Member States. The Commission may decide at any time that the Member States concerned shall amend or abolish the measures in question.

In the selection of such measures, priority shall be given to those which cause the least disturbance of the functioning of the common market and which take into account the need to expedite, as far as possible, the introduction of the common customs tariff.

In the selection of such measures, priority shall be given to those which cause the least disturbance of the functioning of the common market.

Article 116

From the end of the transitional period onwards, Member States shall, in respect of all matters of particular interest to the common market, proceed within the framework of international organisations of an economic character only by common action. To this end, the Commission shall submit to the Council, which shall act by a qualfied majority, proposals concerning the scope and implementation of such common action.

During the transitional period, Member States shall consult each other for the purpose of concerting the action they take and adopting as far as possible a uniform attitude.

Article 116

(Repealed)

Article 228

1. Where this Treaty provides for the conclusion of agreements between the Community and one or more States or an international organisation, such agreements shall be negotiated by the Commission. Subject to the powers vested in the Commission in this field, such agreements shall be concluded by the Council, after consulting the European Parliament where required by this Treaty.

    The Council, the Commission or a Member State may obtain

Article 228

As amended by Article G(80) TEU

1. Where this Treaty provides for the conclusion of agreements between the Community and one or more States or international organisations, the Commission shall make recommendations to the Council, which shall authorise the Commission to open the necessary negotiations. The Commission shall conduct these negotiations in consultation with special committees appointed by the Council to assist it in this task and within the framework of such directives as the Council may issue to it.

beforehand the opinion of the Court of Justice as to whether an agreement envisaged is compatible with the provisions of this Treaty. Where the opinion of the Court of Justice is adverse, the agreement may enter into force only in accordance with Article 236.

2. Agreements concluded under these conditions shall be binding on the institutions of the Community and on Member States.

In exercising the powers conferred upon it by this paragraph, the Council shall act by a qualified majority, except in the cases provided for in the second sentence of paragraph 2, for which it shall act unanimously.

2. Subject to the powers vested in the Commission in this field, the agreements shall be concluded by the Council, acting by a qualified majority on a proposal from the Commission. The Council shall act unanimously when the agreement covers a field for which unanimity is required for the adoption of internal rules, and for the agreements referred to in Article 238.

3. The Council shall conclude agreements after consulting the European Parliament, except for the agreements referred to in Article 113(3), including cases where the agreement covers a field for which the procedure referred to in Article 189b or that referred to in Article 189c is required for the adoption of internal rules. The European Parliament shall deliver its opinion within a time-limit which the Council may lay down according to the urgency of the matter. In the absence of an opinion within that time-limit, the Council may act.

By way of derogation from the previous subparagraph, agreements referred to in Article 238, other agreements establishing a specific institutional framework by organising cooperation procedures, agreements having important budgetary implications for the Community and agreements entailing amendment of an act adopted under the procedure referred to in Article 189b shall be concluded after the assent of the European Parliament has been obtained.

The Council and the European Parliament may, in an urgent situation, agree upon a time-limit for the assent.

4. When concluding an agreement, the Council may, by way of derogation from paragraph 2, authorise the Commission to approve modifications on behalf of the Community where the agreement provides for them to be adopted by a simplified procedure or by a body set up by the agreement; it may attach specific conditions to such authorisation.

5. When the Council envisages concluding an agreement which calls for amendments to this Treaty, the amendments must first be adopted in accordance with the procedure laid down in Article N of the Treaty on European Union.

6. The Council, the Commission or a Member State may obtain the opinion of the Court of Justice as to whether an agreement envisaged is compatible with the provisions of this Treaty. When the opinion of the Court of Justice is adverse, the agreement may enter into force only in accordance with Article N of the Treaty on European Union.

7. Agreements concluded under the conditions set out in this Article shall be binding on the institutions of the Community and on Member States.

Article 228a

As inserted by Article G(81) TEU

Where it is provided, in a common position or in a joint action adopted according to the provisions of the Treaty on European Union relating to the common foreign and security policy, for the action by the Community to interrupt or to reduce, in part or completely, economic relations with one or more third countries, the Council shall take the necessary urgent measures. The Council shall act by a qualified majority on a proposal from the Commission.

Article 229

It shall be for the Commission to ensure the maintenance of all appropriate relations with the organs of the United Nations, of its specialised agencies and of the General Agreement on Tariffs and Trade.

The Commission shall also maintain such relations as are appropriate with all international organisations.

Article 230

The Community shall establish all appropriate forms of cooperation with the Council of Europe.

Article 231

The Community shall establish close cooperation with the Organisation for European Economic Cooperation, the details to be determined by common accord.

Article 232

1. The provisions of this Treaty shall not affect the provisions of the Treaty establishing the European Coal and Steel Community, in particular as regards the rights and obligations of Member States, the powers of the institutions of that Community and the rules laid down by that Treaty for the functioning of the common market in coal and steel.

2. The provisions of this Treaty shall not derogate from those of the Treaty establishing the European Atomic Energy Community.

Article 233

The provisions of this Treaty shall not preclude the existence or completion of regional unions between Belgium and Luxembourg, or between Belgium, Luxembourg and the Netherlands, to the extent that the objectives of these

---

Article 229

It shall be for the Commission to ensure the maintenance of all appropriate relations with the organs of the United Nations, of its specialised agencies and of the General Agreement on Tariffs and Trade.

The Commission shall also maintain such relations as are appropriate with all international organisations.

Article 230

The Community shall establish all appropriate forms of cooperation with the Council of Europe.

Article 231

As amended by Article G(82) TEU

The Community shall establish close cooperation with the Organisation for Economic Cooperation and Development, the details of which shall be determined by common accord.

Article 232

1. The provisions of this Treaty shall not affect the provisions of the Treaty establishing the European Coal and Steel Community, in particular as regards the rights and obligations of Member States, the powers of the institutions of that Community and the rules laid down by that Treaty for the functioning of the common market in coal and steel.

2. The provisions of this Treaty shall not derogate from those of the Treaty establishing the European Atomic Energy Community.

Article 233

The provisions of this Treaty shall not preclude the existence or completion of regional unions between Belgium and Luxembourg and the Netherlands, to the extent that the objectives of these regional unions are not attained by

regional unions are not attained by application of this Treaty.

application of this Treaty.

Article 234

The rights and obligations arising from agreements concluded before the entry into force of this Treaty between one or more Member States on the one hand, and one or more third countries on the other, shall not be affected by the provisions of this Treaty.

To the extent that such agreements are not compatible with this Treaty, the Member State or States concerned shall take all appropriate steps to eliminate the incompatibilities established. Member States shall, where necessary, assist each other to this end and shall, where appropriate, adopt a common attitude.

In applying the agreements referred to in the first paragraph, Member States shall take into account the fact that the advantages accorded under this Treaty by each Member State form an integral part of the establishment of the Community and are thereby inseparably linked with the creation of common institutions, the conferring of powers upon them and the granting of the same advantages by all the other Member States.

Article 235

If action by the Community should prove necessary to attain, in the course of the operation of the common market, one of the objectives of the Community and this Treaty has not provided the necessary powers, the Council shall, acting unanimously on a proposal from the Commission and after consulting the European Parliament, take the appropriate measures.

Article 236

The Government of any Member State or the Commission may submit to the Council proposals for the amendment of this Treaty.

Article 234

The rights and obligations arising from agreements concluded before the entry into force of this Treaty between one or more Member States on the one hand, and one or more third countries on the other, shall not be affected by the provisions of this Treaty.

To the extent that such agreements are not compatible with this Treaty, the Member State or States concerned shall take all appropriate steps to eliminate the incompatibilities established. Member States shall, where necessary, assist each other to this end and shall, where appropriate, adopt a common attitude.

In applying the agreements referred to in the first paragraph, Member States shall take into account the fact that the advantages accorded under this Treaty by each Member State form an integral part of the establishment of the Community and are thereby inseparably linked with the creation of common institutions, the conferring of powers upon them and the granting of the same advantages by all the other Member States.

Article 235

If action by the Community should prove necessary to attain, in the course of the operation of the common market, one of the objectives of the Community and this Treaty has not provided the necessary powers, the Council shall, acting unanimously on a proposal from the Commission and after consulting the European Parliament, take the appropriate measures.

Article 236

(Repealed)

If the Council, after consulting the European Parliament and, where appropriate, the Commission, delivers an opinion in favour of calling a conference of representatives of the Governments of the Member States, the conference shall be convened by the President of the Council for the purpose of determining by common accord the amendments to be made to this Treaty.

The amendments shall enter into force after being ratified by all the Member States in accordance with their respective constitutional requirements.

Article 237

Any European State may apply to become a member of the Community. It shall address its application to the Council, which shall act unanimously after consulting the Commission and after receiving the assent of the European Parliament which shall act by an absolute majority of its component members.

The conditions of admission and the adjustments to this Treaty necessitated thereby shall be the subject of an agreement between the Member States and the applicant State. This agreement shall be submitted for ratification by all the Contracting States in accordance with their respective consitutional requirements.

Article 238

The Community may conclude with a third State, a union of States or an international organisations agreement establishing an association involving reciprocal rights and obligations, common action and special procedure.

First paragraph as replaced by Article 8 of the SEA

Article 237

(Repealed)

Article 238

As amended by Article G(84) TEU

The Community may conclude with one or more States or international organisations agreements establishing an association involving reciprocal rights and obligations, common action and special procedure.

ANNEX B
Directorate General I — External Economic Relations

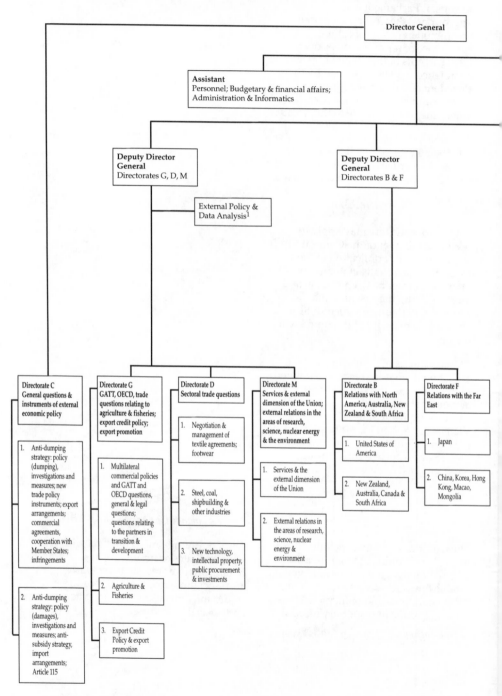

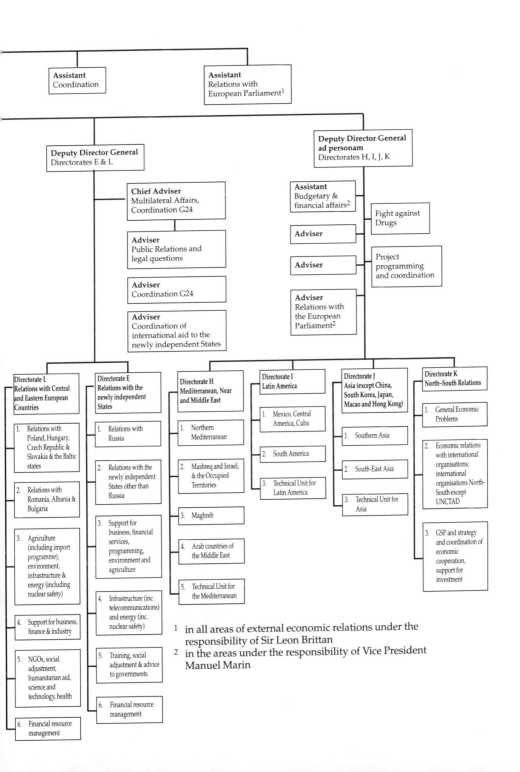

Assistant
Coordination

Assistant
Relations with
European Parliament[1]

Deputy Director General
Directorates E & L

**Deputy Director General
ad personam**
Directorates H, I, J, K

Chief Adviser
Multilateral Affairs,
Coordination G24

Assistant
Budgetary &
financial affairs[2]

Fight against
Drugs

Adviser
Public Relations and
legal questions

Adviser

Project
programming
and coordination

Adviser
Coordination G24

Adviser

Adviser
Coordination of
international aid to the
newly independent States

Adviser
Relations with
the European
Parliament[2]

**Directorate L
Relations with Central
and Eastern European
Countries**

1. Relations with
   Poland, Hungary,
   Czech Republic &
   Slovakia & the Baltic
   states

2. Relations with
   Romania, Albania &
   Bulgaria

3. Agriculture
   (including import
   programme),
   environment,
   infrastructure &
   energy (including
   nuclear safety)

4. Support for business,
   finance & industry

5. NGOs, social
   adjustment,
   humanitarian aid,
   science and
   technology, health

6. Financial resource
   management

**Directorate E
Relations with the
newly independent
States**

1. Relations with
   Russia

2. Relations with the
   newly independent
   States other than
   Russia

3. Support for
   business, financial
   services,
   programming,
   environment and
   agriculture

4. Infrastructure (inc.
   telecommunications)
   and energy (inc.
   nuclear safety)

5. Training, social
   adjustment & advice
   to governments

6. Financial resource
   management

**Directorate H
Mediterranean, Near
and Middle East**

1. Northern
   Mediterranean

2. Mashreq and Israel,
   & the Occupied
   Territories

3. Maghreb

4. Arab countries of
   the Middle East

5. Technical Unit for
   the Mediterranean

**Directorate I
Latin America**

1. Mexico, Central
   America, Cuba

2. South America

3. Technical Unit for
   Latin America

**Directorate J
Asia (except China,
South Korea, Japan,
Macao and Hong Kong)**

1. Southern Asia

2. South-East Asia

3. Technical Unit for
   Asia

**Directorate K
North–South Relations**

1. General Economic
   Problems

2. Economic relations
   with international
   organisations;
   international
   organisations North-
   South except
   UNCTAD

3. GSP and strategy
   and coordination of
   economic
   cooperation,
   support for
   investment

1 in all areas of external economic relations under the
   responsibility of Sir Leon Brittan
2 in the areas under the responsibility of Vice President
   Manuel Marin

ANNEX C

Directorate General IA — External Political Relations

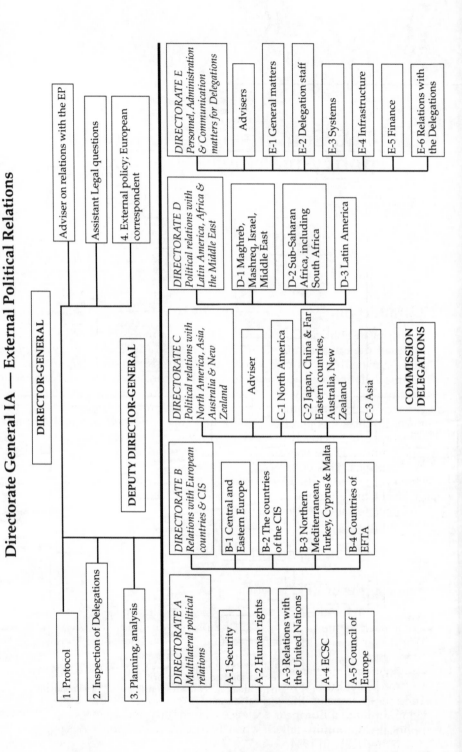

DIRECTOR-GENERAL

1. Protocol
2. Inspection of Delegations
3. Planning, analysis

Adviser on relations with the EP

Assistant Legal questions

4. External policy; European correspondent

DEPUTY DIRECTOR-GENERAL

DIRECTORATE A
Multilateral political relations

- A-1 Security
- A-2 Human rights
- A-3 Relations with the United Nations
- A-4 ECSC
- A-5 Council of Europe

DIRECTORATE B
Relations with European countries & CIS

- B-1 Central and Eastern Europe
- B-2 The countries of the CIS
- B-3 Northern Mediterranean, Turkey, Cyprus & Malta
- B-4 Countries of EFTA

DIRECTORATE C
Political relations with North America, Asia, Australia & New Zealand

- Adviser
- C-1 North America
- C-2 Japan, China & Far Eastern countries, Australia, New Zealand
- C-3 Asia

COMMISSION DELEGATIONS

DIRECTORATE D
Political relations with Latin America, Africa & the Middle East

- D-1 Maghreb, Mashreq, Israel, Middle East
- D-2 Sub-Saharan Africa, including South Africa
- D-3 Latin America

DIRECTORATE E
Personnel, Administration & Communication matters for Delegations

- Advisers
- E-1 General matters
- E-2 Delegation staff
- E-3 Systems
- E-4 Infrastructure
- E-5 Finance
- E-6 Relations with the Delegations

11. The Commission and foreign policy-making

Simon Nuttall

Introduction

European Political Cooperation (EPC), the process by which the Member States of the European Community have sought to coordinate their foreign policies, was from its beginnings in 1970 based on an intergovernmental approach. It operated according to the rule of consensus, and the Community institutions, especially the Commission, were excluded as far as was practicable. However, this doctrine could not forever be defended in its pure form. Political Cooperation soon found that it needed to operate in areas which impinged closely on matters which were the legal responsibility of the Community. There was no choice but to admit the Commission to EPC's deliberations. This occurred on an increasingly less restrictive basis as the years progressed. The Commission is now fully accepted as the thirteenth guest at table, although even after Maastricht's boost to its status discussed in this Chapter, it is still not allowed to play the same role as it does in the Community.

The origins of EPC

The origins of EPC and the Commission's exclusion from it must be sought as far back as the beginnings of the process of European integration after World War II. The first flush of federalist enthusiasm soon gave way to the hard grey light of government-to-government negotiation, in which supranational mechanisms were rejected for fear of loss of sovereignty. Thus, the Council of Europe was set up on intergovernmental lines, and the French attempt to transfer the supranational procedures of the Coal and Steel Community to a European Defence Community and an incipient European Political Community failed, when France's own National Assembly voted down the Treaty in 1954.

It was significant that the stumbling block was France, even before General de Gaulle returned to power. René Pleven's bold initiative for a defence community came to nothing, not least because the French government was by then dependent on Gaullist support. One of their most senior representatives, Michel Debré, had made plain the Gaullists' repugnance to federal systems, particularly in foreign policy. In their view, attempts could and should be made to harmonise national positions, but if these attempts failed, the discussions had to stop there.

This was the line taken by General de Gaulle when he returned to power in 1958. A text approved by him in August 1958 stated that:

> "La coopération européenne doit s'affirmer aussi en dehors de l'Europe, a l'égard des grands problèmes mondiaux . . . des consultations régulières auront lieu entre les gouvernements intéressés. Ce mécanisme de consultations pourra prendre un caractère en quelque sorte organique au fur et à mesure qu'il se développera." (Nuttall 1992, pp. 37–38)

The desire for a European foreign policy, independent of the United States, was combined with a wish to provide an intergovernmental straitjacket for the Community's supranational institutions. This thinking governed the attitude taken by the General throughout the negotiations which he launched in 1960 (the so-called Fouchet Plan, named after the French Ambassador in Copenhagen, who chaired the negotiations) but which had to be abandoned in April 1962. Their ultimate failure sprang in part from the requirement of the Benelux countries to have either supranational institutions, or else the United Kingdom in the Community, in both cases as a guarantee that the small Member States would not be subject to a Franco-German directorate. The rift between de Gaulle and the Belgian and Dutch Foreign Ministers, Paul-Henri Spaak and Joseph Luns, over this issue prefigured a long wrangle with the European Commission over its own pretension to power, with de Gaulle insisting at a press conference on January 31, 1964 that "le pouvoir et le devoir executifs n'appartiennent qu'aux gouvernements" (Grosser 1984, p. 191).

When the subject was taken up again at the Hague Conference in 1969, President Pompidou adhered to the Gaullist line on foreign policy. But, as part of a package that also involved enlargement to include the UK and the stabilisation of the EC budget, he obtained agreement that the renewed movement towards political unification should, in the first instance, concentrate on foreign policy questions and should follow the lines traditionally defended by France. European Political Cooperation as it emerged from the 1970 Luxembourg Report was therefore purely intergovernmental. The machinery which was set up — Ministerial Meetings and a Political Committee — was largely inspired by the experience of political cooperation which had briefly flourished at the time of the Fouchet negotiations. France was anxious to ensure that the Community Institutions, and especially the Commission, had no part to play in the new system. Yet the French knew that to insist on a replay of the Fouchet debate was to invite a stalemate. Some concessions were therefore made. The Commission was not to be regularly associated, but "should the work of the Ministers affect the activities of the European Communities, the Commission will be invited to make known its views" (Luxembourg Report Part II(V) 1970).

The implementation of this principle proved tortuous and distressing. The Commission had to fight for every invitation, sometimes with the support of other Member States but always against the fierce opposition of France. The battle began at the first Ministerial Meeting at Munich in November 1970. The Commission was excluded from the first part of the meeting dealing with the Middle East and from the discussion which followed on the Conference on Security and Cooperation in Europe (CSCE), and was ushered in only for the last hour when discussions on the CSCE turned to the Community aspects of the question. Commission President Malfatti called for the participation of the Community as such in the CSCE, and was supported by the German and Dutch Foreign Ministers, Walter Scheel and Joseph Luns. However, the French Foreign Minister, Maurice Schumann, was more restrictive, pointing out that the Conference would be dealing mainly with security questions, not economic ones, and would be between States, not blocs. Nevertheless, the economic aspects of the CSCE process could not in the end be denied. The Commission was in fact consulted by France itself, which then held the Presidency, on a paper on CSCE economic cooperation, prepared by the Political Committee. It was invited to the next Ministerial Meeting in Paris for the discussion on the CSCE and even to dinner the night before. However, it was not invited to the discussion on the Middle East at that meeting, nor at all to the meeting in Rome the following November.

As discussions on the CSCE proceeded, it became increasingly obvious that the Commissions's presence and indeed assistance on the economic side was indispensable. Initially the Commission provided input to the CSCE Subcommittee set up by the Political Committee, though without being allowed to attend its meetings because of objections raised by France. It did, however, participate in an *ad hoc* Group set up to deal with the economic aspects of the Conference. The Group was in EPC but not of it, designed especially to provide a forum which the Commission might join. The Commission's status was finally fixed in the formula approved at the beginning of the second phase of the CSCE in Geneva, whereby "in order to give expression to Community views in those areas mentioned in the statement by the [Danish] Foreign Minister, representatives of the Commission of the European Community appear on the list of the Danish delegation" (Nuttall 1992, p. 111).

The Commission thus made slow but steady progress in inserting itself into EPC mechanisms. It made itself acceptable by the modesty of its behaviour and indispensable by its technical expertise, especially on trade policy questions. From a practical point of view, and setting aside theoretical considerations, this was something the Member States could not do without.

A similar development followed a few years later with regard to the Middle East. This was another particularly sensitive area for the French, who, at the beginning of EPC, strictly denied the Commission access to the discussions. Between 1970 and 1973, the Commission was only associated in discussions on the question of increased financial assistance for the Palestinian refugees. The situation changed with the establishment of the Euro-Arab Dialogue, launched by France in 1973 in the confused situation after the October War. The original intention had been for the Dialogue to be primarily political and hence the exclusive responsibility of the Member States. In the event, because of pressure from the United States, it turned out to be largely economic. The

Commission's contribution thus became essential and its presence unavoidable.

Commission representatives therefore took part in the work of the Coordinating Group, especially set up to report to both the Political Committee and COREPER, depending on the substance of its discussions. They joined with colleagues from the Presidency in conducting preparatory discussions with the Arabs and they chaired some of the Working Groups dealing with technical economic questions. By the time the Dialogue was finally launched in 1976, the Commission had successfully embedded itself in EPC mechanisms and procedures. As in the case of the CSCE, this had been done by providing an indispensable input of technical expertise.

The successful association of the Commission with work on the CSCE and the Euro-Arab Dialogue did something to allay mistrust and thus facilitate participation in work in other areas. The hardline position still adopted by France nevertheless acted as a brake on many occasions. Commission contributions to studies on developments in Eastern Europe were rejected. Its representatives were excluded from the Mediterranean Working Group dealing with the question of Cyprus. Indeed as late as 1978, the author of this Chapter, representing the Commission at a meeting of that Group, had his presence questioned by the representative of France on the grounds that Cyprus was of no concern to the Community. The Commission representative remained in the room but abstracted himself from the proceedings by ostentatiously reading the newspaper; honour was satisfied.

By the end of the 1970s, the Commission's position in EPC was recognised, but uncertain. It was represented at Ministerial Meetings and the meetings of the Political Committee, but not the meetings of European Correspondents, the body which coordinated the work of EPC and advised on practice and procedure. The Commission representative was invited to the Political Directors' luncheon, but not to their dinner. The Commission was not linked to the Coreu network — the confidential telex network linking the Foreign Ministries — but received copies of some telegrams courtesy of the Belgian Foreign Ministry. Even then a whole category of telegrams was denied it. The Commission had to be specially invited to attend any Working Group meeting, and was not always warned when meetings were taking place. The then European Correspondent of the Commission spent much of his time conducting a private intelligence service to find out when items of interest to the Commission were likely to be discussed, and then trying to secure an invitation to attend. This was done through the good offices of Member States who found the exclusion of the Commission absurd, but were not in a position to persuade Member States who were reticent, especially France, to change their views.

The opportunity had arisen on a number of occasions to improve the position of the Commission, but had not been taken. The Copenhagen Report of 1973 limited itself to noting in its Annex the participation of the Commission in discussions on the economic aspects of the CSCE and the future role of the Council of Europe. Neither the Paris Summit of 1974 nor the Tindemans Report on European Union of 1975 produced any advance on this position. By 1981, although discussions were under way to produce a new

Report to follow up the Luxembourg and Copenhagen Reports, there was still no change in the positions of Member States regarding the participation of the Commission.

The London Report

This situation changed suddenly with the coming to power of the socialist government in France in May 1981. The new French Foreign Minister, Claude Cheysson, a former Commissioner, had suffered from its patchy association with EPC and lost no time in changing the traditional French position on the point. The London Report, adopted in October of that year, finally admitted the Commission to full association with EPC. The relevant passage read: "Within the framework of the established procedures the Ten attach importance to the Commission of the European Communities being fully associated with Political Cooperation at all levels" (London Report Part II(12) 1981). This tortuous drafting reflected Denmark's concern to ensure that the Commission did not as a result acquire the sort of powers in EPC that it had in the Community. The Danish Minister was rather embarrassed at the position he was obliged to take, and underwent some gentle teasing at the Ministerial meeting at the hands of Lord Carrington, who was in the chair. But whatever the formulation, the way was now clear for the full association of the Commission with EPC.

What this meant in practical terms still had to be worked out. Although the discussions on implementation were marked by a rearguard action on the part of Gaullist elements in the Quai d 'Orsay, it was nevertheless established within a few months that the Commission representatives would take part in all EPC activities without exception, including all meals, and would take part in Groups from which they had previously been excluded, like the Correspondents' Group, the Middle East Group, the UN-Disarmament Group and the Group of Heads of Communications. The arrangements also included association with Political Cooperation in third countries and a direct link to the Coreu network so that it could receive all Coreus and in turn be able to send them. In return the Commission gave written undertakings mainly concerned with security.

The full association of the Commission was timely. Within the next few years came a proliferation of events requiring close interaction between EPC and the Community in which the Commission was called on to play its Community role in the forwarding of EPC policies. The series began in February 1982, with the imposition on the Soviet Union of Community sanctions by Council Regulation following the declaration of martial law in Poland. This was the first time that sanctions had been imposed by the Community as such. The prospect had been mooted in Political Cooperation, but the decision was taken by the Council, which adopted its Regulation on the basis of a proposal from the Commission. This served as a good precedent when two months later Argentina invaded the Falkland Islands. The imposition of Community sanctions once again required the Commission to make a proposal to the Council, following deliberations in EPC. The fact that the Commission was represented by the same officials in both fora (while the

Member States were not) made the process easier and enhanced the role of the Commission. The same procedure was followed some years later for the imposition of "restrictive measures" against South Africa. On that occasion the legal situation was more complicated because of the diversity of the measures taken, which led to disputes about the legal base of any action. The Commission nevertheless played an essential role both in the technical preparation of the texts and in their official tabling as part of the Community institutional procedure.

The budgetary dimension

The Commission's role was not confined to the imposition of sanctions. It also had an important part to play when EPC needed to have recourse to the Community's financial instruments for the furthering of its policies. The preliminary draft Community budget is prepared by the Commission, which must see to it that the necessary appropriations are included for this purpose. The Commission is also solely responsible for the execution of the Budget. This has on occasion given rise to tensions with Member States, especially over the selection of projects in politically sensitive areas.

In the early 1980s the Ten were anxious to conduct an active policy with regard to Central America, an area in which they saw themselves as a neutral point of reference for countries torn between loyalties to the United States and the Soviet Union. The central point of their analysis was that the tensions and conflicts ravaging Central America frequently stemmed from grave economic problems and social inequalities (Roy 1992, p. 78). It was therefore logical that part of the Ten's programme in the region should depend on economic assistance. But Political Cooperation had no budget; for this they had to turn to the Community. It suited the Commission to have this political support for its own efforts to secure extra Community funding from the budgetary authority (Council and Parliament). It exploited the situation to secure approval of a special action programme for Central America in 1982 which the Council would not have agreed otherwise. Moreover, the additional funds made available in the 1985 budget would probably not have been found without the stimulus provided by the conclusion that year, for political reasons, of the EC–Central America Agreement.

A similar situation arose in the case of South Africa. The Member States were anxious that their restrictive measures should be accompanied by a programme of positive measures to assist the victims of apartheid. This programme was financed by the Community budget and administered by the Commission. The secrecy with which the Commission carried out its duties, and which it saw as being essential to protect the beneficiaries from reprisals by the South African authorities, was resented by Member States, who therefore demanded a greater share in the decisions on individual projects. An *ad hoc* arrangement was made to give the Member States an advisory role, but this was centred on the Community framework.

Similar difficulties arose, and similar arrangements had to be made, in the case of the Community's programme of aid to the Occupied Territories. The Consuls General of the Member States in Jerusalem claimed to know better than Commission officials in Brussels how the Community's money could best be spent. Likewise in the case of Afghanistan, the provision of aid from the Community budget following the withdrawal of Soviet troops was conditioned by the political framework adopted in EPC. This time, however, the *ad hoc* Group which oversaw the 'political aspects' of the selection of projects was based on the EPC, rather than the Community framework. The tendency has been for Member States in both the EPC and the Community framework to demand closer control over the selection of projects, and for the Commission to attempt to preserve its prerogative as sole executor of the Community budget.

The Single European Act

The Single European Act (SEA), implemented in 1987, did not introduce any substantial change in the status of the Commission. Its importance lay largely in placing EPC on a legal basis. Title III of the SEA for the most part took up the existing practices and procedures of EPC, confirming the full association of the Commission with the proceedings of political cooperation (Title III Article 30 (3b)). It conferred no new responsibility on the Commission except for one important one, shared with the Presidency of the Council, of ensuring that consistency between the external policies of the European Community and the policies agreed in EPC was sought and maintained (Article 30(5)). Even so, it was stipulated that the Presidency and the Commission should act "each within its sphere of competence". This proviso was introduced at the request of Denmark to make it clear that the Commission did not thereby acquire any new powers in EPC. But, as one Belgian official put it:

> "Toutefois, on peut se demander si le paragraphe 5 de l'article 30 de l'Acte Unique, qui exprime l'obligation de cohérence, ne donne pas à la Commission un droit de s'opposer à des decisions qui ne sont pas cohérentes avec la politique commerciale commune ou avec des conventions auxquelles la Communauté est partie." (de Ruyt 1987)

The SEA thus had the additional, and unexpected, effect of recalling the Commission's rights and duties under the Community Treaties.

While conferring no new powers, the SEA confirmed the practice which had grown up since the London Report whereby the Member States and the Commission intensified cooperation between their representatives in third countries and international organisations. This was to be largely through mutual assistance and information. A parallel decision adopted by Foreign Ministers on February 28, 1986, on the occasion of the signing of the SEA, set out a long list of relevant areas for cooperation, ranging from the exchange of political and economic information and pooling of information on administrative and practical problems to communications, consular matters, cultural affairs and development aid. The heads of missions and Commission representatives were encouraged to meet regularly to coordinate views and prepare joint reports either at the request of the Political Committee or on their own initiative.

The New European Order

The Commission's role in Political Cooperation took on a new dimension in 1989. This was less the result of the entry into force of the Single European Act than of the cataclysmic changes taking place in Central and Eastern Europe. The fall of one Communist regime after another changed the face of politics in Europe and in the Western world as a whole. The situation required an immediate response from the Community and that response was an economic one. Throughout the spring of 1989, negotiations were in preparation or under way for economic agreements of different sorts with Czechoslovakia, Poland, Hungary, Bulgaria and the Soviet Union. The Commission had been playing its normal Community role in the preparation and conduct of these negotiations.

Although on two occasions the Member States called for consistency between EPC and Community policies, in the sense of combining the potential of the two frameworks to produce an effective Community policy, in fact, EPC gave the impression of following events, with leadership devolving to the Community side and in particular to the Commission. This leadership was given international recognition when the Western Economic Summit meeting at the Arche in Paris in July 1989 decided to entrust the Commission with the task of coordinating international assistance efforts to Poland and Hungary. By valiant efforts of impromptu organisation, during the summer holidays, the Commission succeeded in launching the coordination operation which became known as G24. This brought together 24 donor countries, all members of the OECD. The Community's own aid operation, known as PHARE, was financed by the Community budget and run by the Commission, with the Member States acting in a consultative capacity.

Likewise, the negotiation of second-generation agreements with the countries of Central and Eastern Europe, as well as agreements with the Soviet Union and later with its successor States, was primarily the responsibility of the Commission. The Commission proposed negotiating directives to the Council, played a crucial part in their adoption and subsequently carried them out. Even the discussions with the Community's partners on the tricky political issue of conditionality — that is, the link between the relationship with the Community and the acceptance of democratic principles and the transition to a market economy — were conducted by the Commission.

The policy of the Community towards its Eastern neighbours in Europe at a time of such uncertainty and change may well have been the most important that Political Cooperation had to formulate. And yet it was the Commission which held the levers of power, whether through its control of the implementation of the Community budget, its coordination of the international aid effort on behalf of the countries of East and Central Europe or its mastery of the process of negotiating agreements on behalf of the Community. Small wonder if the Commission seemed to loom large in the counsels of Political Cooperation and to occupy a position which would have raised eyebrows at the time the Single European Act was passed. It would have been deemed rank heresy a decade before that.

It was therefore not surprising that the Intergovernmental Conference which negotiated the political union part of the Treaty on European Union paid some attention, within the chapter on foreign and security policy, to the role and powers of the Commission. The outcome marked some advances over the Single European Act, but it did not go as far as the Commission had hoped and as its increasing stature might have been thought to justify.

The Treaty of Union

The Single Act had given a faithful picture of the state of Political Cooperation at that time. It could therefore have been expected that the Treaty on European Union would at least do the same for its time, including on the status of the Commission. The ambition was, however, much greater than that. Several Member States, and the Commission, wished to take the opportunity of bringing EPC to a much greater extent within the Community framework. This would have meant merging the EPC and EC machinery within the Council, at least at Ministerial level. It would also have meant introducing a degree of majority voting for foreign policy questions and providing the Commission with a role resembling the one it performed in the Community institutional order.

Moves in this direction may be seen in various papers circulated in the preparatory stage preceding the Conference proper. The Belgian memorandum of March 19, 1990 identified the developments in Eastern Europe as a challenge illustrating clearly the limitations of the existing machinery of EPC. The paper proposed an approach which was pragmatic and prudent but nevertheless designed to be operational. Ministers should meet regularly in a dual Council–EPC framework, "so that the General Affairs Council should once again become the Community's political decision-making centre". COREPER and the Political Directors should together prepare decisions regarding Central and Eastern Europe, "and the role of the Commission should be better defined, so as to secure the desired consistency". A specialised task force would be set up, bringing together national diplomats and Commission officials specialising in Eastern European countries, to "serve as a centre of analysis, study and coordination on Eastern Europe to the benefit of both the Council and the Commission" (Laursen and Vanhoonacker 1992, p. 269).

This inventive approach had the merit of suggesting practical ways for Member States and the Commission to work together in an area in which there was demonstrable need, and where the Commission had already shown that it had much to give and conversely had no need to fear a takeover by Member States. Had the Belgian approach been followed up, it might have produced procedures and practices with potentially wider application. From the point of view of the integrationists, it was a pity it was not. It was overtaken by the call, launched by President Mitterrand and Chancellor Kohl in their letter of April 19, 1990, for an intergovernmental conference to "define and implement a common foreign and security policy" (ibid., p. 276).

Subsequently, the European Parliament's Resolution of July 11, 1990 (ibid., p. 282) called for matters currently dealt with under EPC to be dealt with in the Community framework with appropriate procedures, thereby abolishing the distinction between EPC and the Community's external economic relations. It also urged that the Commission should have a right of initiative in proposing policies and a role in representing the Community externally.

Denmark, on the other hand, took a more reserved position. While accepting in its memorandum of October 4, 1990 that a decision-taking structure could be set up in which the General Affairs Council could be a united forum for both EC and EPC questions, with coordinated prior preparation of dossiers, it was not prepared to say more about the Commission than that its "current position as an equal partner in European Political Cooperation should be confirmed in the text of the Treaty" (ibid., p. 293). Portugal's memorandum of November 30, 1990, took the same view on the unitary role of the General Affairs Council, and proposed that the Commission "should be formally accorded a non-exclusive right of initiative in foreign policy matters" (ibid., p. 304). The United Kingdom was against bringing EPC into the Community framework and opposed a greater role for the Commission in EPC (ibid., p. 423).

The Commission itself had gone along with what might be called the advanced mainstream in its approach to a common foreign and security policy for the Community. In the official opinion it was called upon to produce in preparation for the Intergovernmental Conference, and which was published on October 21, 1990, it suggested a gradual transfer of topics from EPC to the scope of a common policy, but also majority voting on matters other than those directly affecting security. As regards its own position, it proposed that, together with the Presidency and the other Member States, it should be given the right of initiative in the field of the common foreign and security policy (Bulletin Supplement 2/91 1991, 75–82).

The European Council in Rome on December 14–15, 1990, which launched the Intergovernmental Conferences, adopted a measured approach which took into account the different positions that had been expressed. The Council should form a single decision-making centre, and the Commission should have a reinforced role through a non-exclusive right of initiative. On the decision-making process, consensus should remain the rule in defining guidelines, though agreed policies might be implemented through majority voting.

Discussions in the Conference throughout 1991 and the drafting of the Treaty agreed by the European Council at Maastricht in December of that year, did not, on these questions at least, depart greatly from the indications given by the European Council at Rome. At one stage during the conference proceedings (March 1991), the Commission tabled a draft for the Common Foreign and Security Policy (CFSP) section of the Treaty, with the object of considerably enhancing its own role and making it an equal partner with the Presidency in the   conception and management of policy. While not technically going much beyond what was finally agreed, the Commission succeeded in presenting itself in such a lurid light that the Member States took fright, and its contribution did not become a basis for discussion.

Instead, the Conference concluded on what had previously emerged as the broad consensus. The Council was given a unitary role, the previous ministerial meetings of EPC now officially disappearing; the EPC Secretariat was merged with the Council Secretariat, the old bogey of an autonomous political secretariat detached from the Community institutions and operating out of Paris finally being laid to rest; and the Commission was given a non-exclusive right of initiative. It can be argued that this last existed already in that the Commission, at least since the SEA, had not felt inhibited from informally tabling suggestions on matters in which the Community was directly concerned. It is also the case that a non-exclusive right will not allow the Commission to shape the agenda and policy (subject to the final decision of the Member States) or to carry out the medium- and long-term planning function in Political Cooperation that it does within the Community. However, in formalising the right of initiative, the Maastricht Treaty provides the Commission with the opportunity to act in a more structured and consistent way and to make an important contribution to the formation of foreign policy. Provided the Commission made an intelligent and sensitive use of its new right, it might lead to a *de facto* exclusive right of initiative without raising institutional hackles, as the formalisation of such a right surely would.

But while these three measures mark a coming together of the Political Cooperation and Community frameworks, thereby marking an advance on the SEA, they reflect or are foreshadowed by existing practice. One of the most important innovations was the concept of majority voting for the implementation of 'joint actions' under Article J3. The decision to decide by majority has to be taken unanimously and progress in defining the areas open to joint action, within which majority voting would be possible, has been halting. Indeed, the provisions for majority voting are so hedged about with conditions, mainly to satisfy the United Kingdom, that it seems unlikely that a vote would ever be taken.

The measures introduced under Maastricht would appear therefore to remain firmly in the intergovernmental mode within their separate 'pillar' of the Union. They fall considerably short of what was sought by those who wanted foreign and security policy questions to be decided essentially by Community procedures.

The Commission and the operation of EPC and CFSP

Despite this disappointment of the Commission's hopes for greater convergence between Political Cooperation and Community activities, it nevertheless gained responsibilities under the Maastricht Treaty. It therefore had to give urgent thought to how it would carry out these functions, bearing in mind that, at the time of signature of the Treaty in February 1992 and until the Danish referendum in June, the general expectation was that the Treaty would come into force on January 1, 1993, to coincide with the appointment of a new Commission.

The Commission's machinery for dealing with its relationship with Political Cooperation had grown haphazardly over the years and remained limited in scope. Responsibility for such participation in EPC as was admitted by Member States, and for the coordination of Commission positions, rested from the beginning with the Secretariat General. This was because the Secretariat General had overall responsibility for coordination among the Commission services, and because it was the President of the Commission, rather than the Member responsible for external relations, who took part in EPC meetings, especially in the early days. The only department at the direct disposal of the President, apart from the Legal Service, is the Secretariat General.

It was therefore natural, on both these counts, that the Secretariat General should be given overall responsibility for the Commission's relations with EPC. Within the Secretariat General, operational responsibility was given to the Deputy Secretary General, who at the time was Klaus Meyer, a senior official originally from the German Foreign Service. It was Meyer, rather than his counterparts in external relations, who represented the Commission in the difficult days when the Commission was trying to secure a toehold in this new intergovernmental exercise in which it was very definitely not welcome. Although in the CSCE exercise the input, which was of a highly technical nature, came mainly from DG 1 (the Directorate General for External Relations), the Secretariat General played a strong coordinating role. When it came to the Euro-Arab Dialogue, the Secretariat General was responsible for the entire exercise within the Commission, with Meyer devoting personally a great deal of time to the issue.

This administrative arrangement persisted even after the Commission's position in EPC had eased and it no longer had to fight so hard for invitations to meetings. When Meyer left the Secretariat General to become Director General for Development, he took the Euro-Arab Dialogue with him, but overall responsibility for EPC coordination and the position of the Commission representative in the Political Committee remained with his successor as Deputy Secretary General. There was some discussion as to whether the job would not be better done by the Director General or Deputy Director General for External Relations. It remained with the Deputy Secretary General for two reasons. First, increasingly, the Commission's input into Political Cooperation was coming from several departments (the Directorates General for External Relations and for Development, and occasionally others) and only the Secretariat General, under the authority of the President in the Commission's collegiate system, was in a position to exercise overall control. Second, the Deputy Secretary General was also the Commission's representative in COREPER. He was thus able to exploit his dual presence in COREPER and the Political Committee, an advantage enjoyed by no Ambassador or Political Director of a Member State. This maximised the Commission's role as a bridge between the EPC and Community frameworks.

A small unit took shape under the Deputy Secretary General to look after day-to-day contacts with EPC and in-house coordination. In 1981, this consisted of two Category A officials, the 'European Correspondent' of the Commission (who was not allowed to attend the meetings of the European Correspondents) and his colleague. Between them, these two officials attended all EPC meetings to which the Commission was invited, often but not always accompanied by a colleague from the sectoral department concerned. Their duties were to make whatever contribution to the debate was possible and admitted, to make a record of the discussions and circulate it to those concerned within the Commission and to act as a general channel of communication between EPC and the Commission.

The full association of the Commission with Political Cooperation after the London Report of 1981 increased the volume, but did not change the nature of the work. By 1987, when the Single European Act came into force, the unit had grown in size, but still to only four category A officials instead of two. It had also acquired the Commission Cypher Office, as much by chance as by design. The author of this Chapter, then working in the Office of the Clerk of the Commission, had been responsible for the Cypher Office since it had been set up in 1975, partly to provide cypher communications between the Commission and its Delegations abroad, but also against the day when the Commission would be admitted to the Coreu network. When he was appointed European Correspondent, the author took with him responsibility for the Cypher Office. This proved to be a convenient move, since six months later, the Commission did indeed join the Coreu network. The episode is an example of the way in which the Commission, with inadequate financial and staff means, had to improvise arrangements for its association with what was still seen as something out of the mainstream of Community activities.

The steady increase in EPC work, which coincided with the Single European Act and which came to a head with the events in Central and Eastern Europe, meant that these improved arrangements were no longer adequate. Already in 1987, the Commission had appointed a full-time Political Director (of grade A2 standing) in the Secretariat General. He replaced the Deputy Secretary General as Commission representative in the Political Committee. The advantage of the same person being present in both the Political Committee and COREPER was lost, but the change had become inevitable because of the increased pressure of work. Much more travelling was involved than previously, given the surge in EPC contacts with third countries.

This upsurge particularly affected the Commission because of its regular association with all activities that took place according to the 'Troika' formula. This was a device whereby Political Cooperation conducted contacts with third countries through a team comprising the current, preceding and succeeding Presidencies. It had been used originally for discussions with the Arab League in the Euro-Arab Dialogue, when the Commission had been associated, but its use had been generalised from 1978 on and the Commission had then been excluded. The Troika was put on a regular basis by the London Report of 1981, but the Commission still did not become a member of it as part of the arrangements which were then made for its full association with EPC. One of the difficulties which Member States saw, when the possibility was later discussed, was that the Commission would thereby secure a significant advantage over Member States. Each Member State would be in the Troika for only 18 months every six years (in a Community of 12), while the Commission would be permanently present. It was therefore all the more significant that the then President of the Commission, Gaston Thorn, secured in April 1983 agreement on the Commission's presence in the Troika as a general rule.

The appointment of a Director with no responsibilities other than for Political Cooperation (and related duties, such as participation in the political aspects of the Western Economic Summit process) entailed the establishment in the Secretariat General of a Directorate bringing together various activities relevant to the Commission's association with EPC. The Directorate was made up of three divisions. The first was under the European Correspondent. This division looked after day-to-day and organisational matters. The second division comprised a small planning staff, also responsible for organising seminars on the Community for national diplomats, a function which had been performed with some success for several years. The third was concerned with human rights. By redeployment of staff and a modicum of barrel-scraping, these units were sufficiently manned to give the Commission an embryo of policy-making capacity in the foreign-policy field, separate from the desks in the Directorates General, whose main interests were external economic relations.

At the same time, the Delegations of the Commission outside the Community were increasingly involved in EPC activities. From a handful in the early 1970s, these had risen to over 100 by the time the Maastricht Treaty was signed. This figure includes the Delegations in the ACP countries, which at first had taken an exclusively developmental view of their functions and had had a special administrative status at one remove from the established Commission civil service. They were gradually brought within the normal Community regime. The external Delegations were associated with Political Cooperation in stages in parallel with the Commission in Brussels. They were included in the arrangements made for the association of the Commission following the London Report of 1981. (This was by no means a foregone conclusion at the time, even though the practice had existed sporadically before then.) They were further covered by the Directives for cooperation in third countries issued by the Political Committee in 1984 and confirmed in the Decision of February 28, 1986 (see above). The Delegations send to Brussels political as well as economic reports which provide the Commission with the raw material for foreign policy-making, thus putting it on an equal footing with all but the largest Member States. The Commission benefits from the fact that it has a diplomatic presence in more third countries than do most Member States (see also Chapter 10).

The prospect of the entry into force of the Maastricht Treaty on European Union obliged the Commission to reflect anew on its administrative arrangements for relations with what would no longer be EPC but the CFSP. To be in a position to use its new if non-exclusive right of initiative effectively, the Commission needed a more extensive apparatus than it currently had, even with the benefits of the relatively recently-established Directorate in the Secretariat General. The new Commission, due to take office on January 6, 1993, decided at an informal meeting at the Palais d'Egmont in Brussels the previous month, that the responsibility for political and economic external relations would be split. Hans van den Broek, previously Foreign Minister of the Netherlands, was made responsible for external political relations and the CFSP, while Sir Leon Brittan and Manuel Marin were made responsible for external economic relations with developed and developing countries respectively. At the same time, it was agreed that a new Directorate General would be set up for external political relations. These arrangements were confirmed at the Commission's first meeting on January 6.

The structure of the new Directorate General was agreed by the Commission in March 1993. Directorate General 1A (the old DG 1's responsibilities now being limited to external economic relations) was to have a Director General (the former director in the Secretariat General), two Deputy Directors General, and five Directorates. Directorate A is responsible for multilateral political relations, including the United Nations, CSCE and the Council of Europe. It also houses the European Correspondent's unit, although the Correspondent, like in Member States' Foreign Ministries, will be working directly to the Director General/Political Director. Directorate B is responsible for Europe and the CIS (ex-Soviet Union), Directorate C for North America, Asia, Australia and New Zealand, Directorate D for Latin America, Africa and the Middle East. Directorate E is responsible for the management of the Delegations outside the Community, a unit transferred from the Directorate General for Personnel and Administration (DG IX). Protocol, the Inspectorate of Delegations, and the planning staff previously part of the EPC Directorate in the Secretariat General, all come under the direct authority of the Director General.

Conclusion

Just as the Community is at a turning-point in the development of its foreign-policy capability, so the Commission is at a turning-point in the role it may be called upon to play. Both depend not on the text of the Treaty on European Union, but on the spirit in which it is implemented. The dynamism which the absorption of EPC into the Community would have given to the foreign-policy process has been eschewed. To the extent that public opinion is not yet ready to accept the implications of such a transfer of sovereignty, the decision of Member States was no doubt correct. It will be the responsibility of the Commission in the coming years, by tactful use of its new powers, not only to bring greater substance to foreign policy, but also to bring about a climate of opinion in which the transfer of sovereignty appears less intimidating than it does today. Given the still modest institutional role the Commission plays in the CFSP, and the unease with which it is regarded by many Member States, which, ironically, has increased as the Commission has consolidated its position in EPC, this will not be an easy task.

References and bibliography

Allen, D. (1978) 'The Euro-Arab Dialogue', *Journal of Common Market Studies*, 16, pp. 323–42).
de Ruyt, Jean (1987) *L'Acte Unique Européen*, Brussels: Université de Bruxelles.
de Schoutheete, P. (1992) 'The Treaty of Maastricht and its significance for third countries', *Österreichische Zeitschrift für Politikwissenschaft*, 92/3, pp. 247–60.
Edwards, G. (1984) 'Europe and the Falklands Crisis', *Journal of Common Market Studies* 22/4, pp. 295–313.
Grosser, A. (1984) *Affaires Extérieures: la politique de la France 1944–1984*, Paris, Flammarion.
Holland, M. (1988) *The European Community and South Africa*, London: Macmillan.
Kramer, H. (1993) 'The EC's response to the "New Eastern Europe"', *Journal of Common Market Studies*, 31. 2.
Laursen, F. and Vanhoonacker, S. (eds.) (1992) *The Intergovernmental Conference on Political Union*, Maastricht: IEAP/EIPA.
Nuttall, S. (1988) 'Where the European Commission comes in', in Pijpers, A. *et al.* (eds.) (1990) *European Political Cooperation in the 1980s*, Dordrecht: Martinus Nijhoff, pp. 104–117.

Nuttall, S. (1992) *European Political Cooperation*, Oxford: Clarendon Press.
Roy, J. (ed.) (1992) *The Reconstruction of Central America; the role of the European Community*, Miami: ISI/ECRI.

ANNEX

The CFSP pillar of the European Union (Title V, Art. J) and its links with the EC and WEU

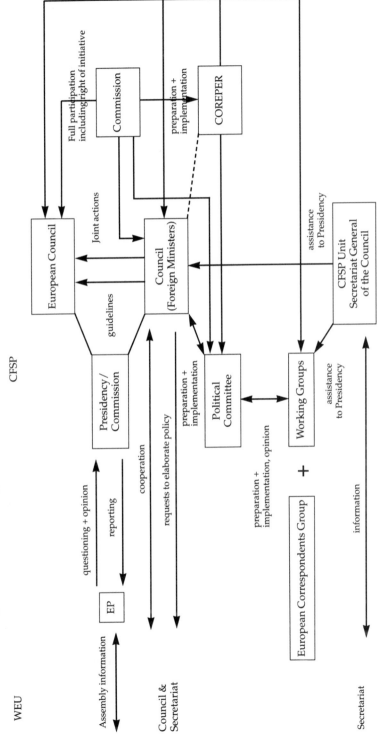

INDEX